European Agencies and Risk Governance in EU Financial Market Law

The phenomenon of 'agencification' describes the EU legislator's increasing establishment of European agencies to fulfil tasks in a variety of EU policies. The creation of these decentralised administrative entities raises a number of questions; for example, on the limits to such delegation of powers, on the agencies' institutional development and possible classification, and on the role of comitology committees as an institutional alternative.

This book examines the EU's 'agencification' with regard to these questions, on the basis of and with reference to which the focus is laid on the European agencies operating in the field of financial market risk governance. This analysis not only encompasses the three European Financial Market Supervisory Authorities (the ESAs), but also takes into account the institutional change brought about by the Banking Union, more specifically the Single Supervisory Mechanism (SSM) and the Single Resolution Mechanism (SRM). While the SRM sets in place a new European agency, the Single Resolution Board (SRB), the SSM establishes and empowers a new body within the organisation of the European Central Bank (ECB), the Supervisory Board.

By exploring the organisation, the tasks and the powers of these actors in financial market regulation and supervision, the book points at the current peak of the institutional development of European agencies and assesses organisation and unprecedented powers with a view to their compliance with EU law, in particular the Treaties and the respective case law of the European courts.

As an evaluation of various aspects of the progressing centralisation of regulatory power on the EU level, which is exercised by an increasingly decentralised administrative apparatus, this book will be of great interest and use to students and scholars of EU law, financial law and regulation, and European politics.

Paul Weismann is a researcher at the University of Salzburg.

T0414060

Routledge Research in EU Law

For a full list of titles in this series, please visit www.routledge.com.

European Agencies and Risk Governance in EU Financial Market Law

Paul Weismann

LONDON AND NEW YORK

First published 2016 by Routledge

2 Park Square, Milton Park, Abingdon, Oxfordshire OX14 4RN
711 Third Avenue, New York, NY 10017

Routledge is an imprint of the Taylor & Francis Group, an informa business

First issued in paperback 2018

British Library Cataloguing in Publication Data
A catalogue record for this book is available from the British Library

Library of Congress Cataloging in Publication Data
Names: Weismann, Paul, author.Title: European agencies and risk governance in EU financial market law / Paul Weismann.Description: Abingdon, Oxon ; New York, NY : Routledge, 2016. | Series: Routledge research in EU law | Includes bibliographical references and index.Identifiers: LCCN 2015050859| ISBN 9781138899995 (hbk) | ISBN 9781315707549 (ebk)Subjects: LCSH: Financial institutions--Law and legislation--European Union countries. | Risk management--Law and legislation--European Union countries.Classification: LCC KJE2188 .W453 2016 | DDC 346.24/082--dc23LC record available at http://lccn.loc.gov/2015050859

ISBN: 978-1-138-89999-5 (hbk)
ISBN: 978-1-138-61415-4 (pbk)

Typeset in Galliard
by Fish Books Ltd.

Contents

Preface

European integration has gone through a number of crises: the political crisis in the years 1965/66 ('Empty Chair Crisis'), the political and economic depression in the 1970s ('Eurosclerosis') and the corruption affairs in the late 1990s, which led to the resignation of the *Santer* Commission – to name just the best known. The recent economic and financial turmoil certainly is the most momentous in that it has substantially and sustainably changed the institutional landscape of the EU.

This study deals with the phenomenon of European agencies, its historical development, its legal and institutional framework and the expression it finds in case of the agencies operating in financial market risk governance (EBA, EIOPA, ESMA, SRB). While the earliest European agencies date back to the 1970s, the agencies focused on here are all anti-crisis measures, which is to say measures intended to remedy drawbacks in risk governance that the recent financial crisis has revealed.

This work is largely based on my thesis entitled *The 'Agencification' of the EU's Institutional Scenery in the Field of Risk Governance: The New Financial Market Supervisory Authorities*, which was approved as a dissertation at the University of Salzburg in June 2013. In this context I would like to once again express my gratitude to my supervisors Professor Dr *Stefan Griller* and Professor Dr *Nicolas Raschauer*, and to Professor Dr *Stefan Storr* who – along with Professor *Griller* – reviewed the thesis. The legal developments that have occurred and the literature that has been published since then up until October 2015 have been incorporated, where relevant. The structure of the text has been subject to minor amendments, some parts have been shortened, some extended.

I would like to thank all those who – in whichever way – supported me when working on this book, in particular my parents.

For reasons of legibility, only the masculine forms of personal pronouns and nouns are used in this work when referring to an undetermined person or group of people. They shall be understood as including female actors as well, as appropriate.

Paul Weismann
Salzburg, December 2015

Abbreviations

ACER	Agency for the Cooperation of Energy Regulators
AG	Advocate General
arg	*argumentum* (Latin): (legal) argument
BEREC	Body of European Regulators for Electronic Communications
BoA	Board of Appeal
BRRD	Bank Recovery and Resolution Directive
BSC	Banking Supervision Committee
BSE	Bovine spongiform encephalopathy
CAP	Common Agricultural Policy
CCP	Common Commercial Policy
CdT	Translation Centre for Bodies of the European Union
CEBS	Committee of European Banking Supervisors
Cedefop	European Centre for the Development of Vocational Training
CEIOPS	Committee of European Insurance and Occupational Pensions Supervisors
CEP	Centrum für Europäische Politik
CEPOL	European Police College
CESR	Committee of European Securities Regulators
cf	*confer* (Latin): compare
CFCA	Community Fisheries Control Agency
CFR	Charter of Fundamental Rights of the European Union
CFSP	Common Foreign and Security Policy
CHAFEA	Consumers, Health, Agriculture and Food Executive Agency
CHMP	Committee for Medicinal Products for Human Use
CJEU	Court of Justice of the European Union
COMP	Committee for Orphan Medicinal Products
CPVO	Community Plant Variety Office
CRA	Credit Rating Agencies
CVMP	Committee for Medicinal Products for Veterinary Use
DG	Directorate-General

EACEA	Education, Audiovisual and Culture Executive Agency
EAR	European Agency for Reconstruction
EASA	European Aviation Safety Agency
EASME	Executive Agency for Small and Medium-sized Enterprises
EASO	European Asylum Support Office
EBA	European Banking Authority
EBC	European Banking Committee
EC	European Community (Communities)
ECB	European Central Bank
ECDC	European Centre for Disease Prevention and Control
ECHA	European Chemicals Agency
ECJ	(European) Court of Justice (as appropriate)
ECOFIN	Economic and Financial Affairs
ECR	European Court Reports
ECSC	European Coal and Steel Community
ECSCT	Treaty establishing the European Coal and Steel Community
ed(s)	editor(s)
EDA	European Defence Agency
edn	edition
EEA	European Economic Area
EEA	European Environmental Agency
EEC	European Economic Community
EFC	Economic and Financial Committee
EFCA	European Fisheries Control Agency
EFSA	European Food Safety Authority
EFSF	European Financial Stability Facility
EFSM	European Financial Stability Mechanism
EFTA	European Free Trade Association
eg	*exempli gratia* (Latin): for example
EIGE	European Institute for Gender Equality
EIOPA	European Insurance and Occupational Pensions Authority
EIOPC	European Insurance and Occupational Pensions Committee
EIT	European Institute of Innovation and Technology
EMA	European Medicines Agency
EMCDDA	European Monitoring Centre for Drugs and Drug Addiction
EMCF	European Monetary Cooperation Fund
EMEA	European Agency for the Evaluation of Medicinal Products
EMSA	European Maritime Safety Agency
EMU	Economic and Monetary Union

ENISA	European Network and Information Security Agency
EP	European Parliament
ERA	European Railway Agency
ERC	European Research Council
ERCEA	European Research Council Executive Agency
ERN	European regulatory network
ESA(s)	European Financial Market Supervisory Authority/-ies
ESC	European Securities Committee
ESCB	European System of Central Banks
ESFS	European System of Financial Supervisors
ESM	European Stability Mechanism
ESMA	European Securities and Markets Authority
ESRB	European Systemic Risk Board
ESRC	EU Securities Regulators Committee
ESRC	European Systemic Risk Council
et al.	*et alii* (Latin): and (the) others
etc.	*et cetera* (Latin): and the remaining things
ETF	European Training Foundation
EU	European Union
EUI	European University Institute
EUISS	European Union Institute for Security Studies
EUMC	European Monitoring Centre for Racism and Xenophobia in the European Union
EU-OSHA	EU Agency for Safety and Health at Work
Euratom	European Atomic Energy Community
EUROFOUND	European Foundation for the Improvement of Living and Working Conditions
Eurojust	European Union's Judicial Cooperation Unit
Europol	European Police Office
EUSC	European Satellite Centre
f (ff)	and the following page(s) or paragraph(s)
FESCO	Forum of European Securities Commissions
FI	financial institution(s)
FMP	financial market participant(s)
FRA	European Union Agency for Fundamental Rights
FRONTEX	European Agency for the Management of Operational Cooperation at the External Borders
FSB	Financial Stability Board
GNSS	Global Navigation Satellite System
GSA	European GNSS Agency
ibid.	*ibidem* (Latin): at the same place
ie	*id est* (Latin): that is
IIMG	Inter-institutional monitory group
IIWG	Inter-institutional working group
IMF	International Monetary Fund

INEA	Innovation and Networks Executive Agency
ITA	European Agency for the operational management of large-scale IT systems in the area of freedom, security and justice
ITS	Implementing Technical Standards
JHA	Justice and Home Affairs
leg cit	*legis citatae* (Latin): of the cited norm
lit	*littera (e)* (Latin): letter(s)
MS	Member State(s)
MoU	Memorandum of Understanding
NGO	Non-Governmental Organisation
no	number
nyp	not yet published in the European Court Reports
OHIM	Office for Harmonisation in the Internal Market
OJ	Official Journal of the European Communities/Union
para(s)	paragraph(s)
PJCC	Police and Judicial Co-operation in Criminal Matters
pMS	participating Member State
REA	Research Executive Agency
REACH	registration, evaluation, authorisation and restriction of chemicals
RoP	Rules of Procedure
RTS	Regulatory Technical Standards
SEA	Single European Act
SME	small- and medium-sized enterprise(s)
Spec Ed	Special Edition
SSM	Single Supervisory Mechanism
SRB	Single Resolution Board
SRF	Single Resolution Fund
SRM	Single Resolution Mechanism
subpara	subparagraph
TEC	Treaty establishing the European Community
TEEC	Treaty establishing the European Economic Community
TEU	Treaty on European Union
TFEU	Treaty on the Functioning of the European Union
UCITS	undertakings for collective investment in transferable securities
UK	United Kingdom of Great Britain and Northern Ireland
US	United States of America
WHO	World Health Organisation

Tables

Cases

Introduction

The 'agencification' of the administrative space of the EU and its predecessors has been ongoing since the 1970s. The move from the low-key information-gathering agencies in the mid-70s to the establishment of the – in comparison – enormously powerful Single Resolution Board (SRB) in 2014/15 has been a long process. This work deals with the phenomenon of European agencies from a legal perspective, thereby focusing on those agencies operating in financial market risk governance. More particularly, the following factors shall be addressed:

1. the limits of the EU's agencification as laid down, in particular, in the so-called *Meroni* doctrine; the historical development, the common characteristics and possible classifications of European agencies; the relationship between comitology and European agencies as the two main (institutional) regimes in E(E)C/EU risk governance; the (potential) role of European agencies in the near future; and against this background:
2. the historical development of the European System of Financial Supervisors (ESFS) and, in particular, the legal foundation, the tasks and powers, the organisation, the network and the financing of the three European Financial Market Supervisory Authorities (ESAs) within this system;
3. the institutional change brought about by the Banking Union, in particular by the establishment of the Single Supervisory Mechanism (SSM) and the Single Resolution Mechanism (SRM) and its meaning for the ESFS, specifically in the field of banking regulation/supervision.

The work shall be structured as follows: After an introduction to the essential terms, concepts and approaches in Chapter 1, the issues listed under item 1. above shall be addressed in Chapter 2. This chapter begins with a presentation and an analysis of the *Meroni* judgement and its follow-up case law with a view to the existing limits to the delegation of powers (I.). Subsequently, the system of comitology shall be approached with a view to its historical development, the relevant procedures under current law, the dichotomy of delegated and implementing acts, as introduced by the Treaty of Lisbon, and the momentum of comitology today (II.). Thereafter, the phenomenon of European agencies shall be addressed from an institutional perspective: historically, with a view to common as well as distinctive features, and with a view to classifying the inhomogeneous group of over 40 European agencies. Then an assessment of the (prospective) meaning of European agencies shall be provided (III.). In a next step, comitology committees and European agencies shall be compared in terms of their legal foundation, their rationale and their independence. An excursus on the legal status of expert opinions, which is relevant for both systems, shall conclude this sub-chapter (IV.). Eventually, three of the most prominent of recent EU anti-crisis measures shall be analysed with regard to whether or not, and for what reasons, the political decision-makers have availed themselves of the 'agency option' (V.).

Chapter 3 deals with the matters listed under item 2. above. At first an account of the historical development of the current system of EU financial market regulation and supervision over the past 15 years shall be given, thereby focusing on the implementation of the *Lamfalussy* procedure and its two different categories of committees. A short presentation of the *de Larosière* Report shall lead to the current regulatory and supervisory system as enshrined in the ESFS (I.). Subsequently, the ESRB and the three ESAs as the EU bodies within the ESFS shall be studied in particular with a view to their competences and their organisation. The role of the ESAs in adopting regulatory and implementing technical standards, their decision-making power as laid down in the ESA-Regulations and their power to adopt guidelines and recommendations, including the respective means of legal protection, shall be explicated at some length. Then, the composition and the functioning of the ESAs' organs shall be dissected and, finally, the ESAs' cooperation with other EU and national bodies, and their financial resources respectively, shall be addressed (II.). The findings of Chapter 2 provide a better understanding of the issues dealt with in Chapter 3, in particular in terms of the limits to a delegation of powers set out in *Meroni* and as regards the rule-making set out in the *Lamfalussy* procedure on the one hand, and the rule-making laid down in the ESA-Regulations on the other hand, thereby drastically deviating from delegated and implementing rule-making as applied in other fields of EU administration. Above all, against this background the ousting of comitology committees in the adoption of implementing technical standards can be understood better.

In Chapter 4 (see item 3. above) the institutional changes brought about by the Banking Union – namely the conferral of supervisory tasks on the Supervisory Board as a new organ of the ECB, and the conferral of resolution tasks and powers on a new European agency, the SRB – shall be investigated (I.–III.), thereby elaborating on the ramifications this entails for the other actors in the field of EU financial market risk governance, in particular the ESFS and, within it, the European Banking Authority (EBA) (IV.).

Methodologically, I shall apply the generally accepted methods of legal interpretation (which are also applied in EU law), that is to say, in particular, the verbal/grammatical interpretation, the systematic interpretation, the historical interpretation and the teleological interpretation. Also, complementary approaches towards legal interpretation as applied by the Court, for example the *effet utile*, shall be considered to the extent necessary.[1] Where justified, a legal development beyond the interpretation of norms (in particular by means of legal analogy) shall be contemplated.

As regards the comparison between the two systems – comitology and European agencies – undertaken in Chapter 2, it ought to be stressed that this comparison does not primarily entail the legal comparison of norms, but the legal comparison of systems with a view to selected questions. In particular with the categories of comparison 'rationale' and 'independence' also political considerations (as documented in the literature or in other sources) shall be considered.

Apart from the relevant primary and secondary law, and its interpretation by what is now called the Court of Justice of the European Union (CJEU), and apart from the relevant literature that – in the case of European agencies – has immensely expanded in recent years, I shall draw legal conclusions from a variety of non-binding output, in particular from the European Commission and from the ESAs.

---

1   On the varying importance of the traditional methods of interpretation in EU primary law see Pechstein and Drechsler 132–138. On the meaning of the *effet utile* in the ECJ's jurisdiction see Griller, Verfassungsinterpretation.

1   Preliminaries

I.   THE TERM 'AGENCY' IN GENERAL AND IN THE CONTEXT OF EU LAW IN PARTICULAR

1.   Introduction

European agencies have arguably been among the most intensively discussed phenomena of EU institutional law in the past 15 years, having been debated *inter alia* with respect to their purpose, democratic legitimacy, accountability and – more generally – their merit, by both lawyers and political scientists. Nevertheless, it is still not 'crystal clear' what it is that positively characterises European agencies, on the one hand, and what conceptually separates them from other bodies, or even the institutions of the EU, on the other. The range of tasks and competences European agencies are entrusted with is wide and so is the spectrum of practical influence each of them has in the EU administration, the latter ranging from 'supportive assistant' to 'pivotal player' in the respective policy field.

The characterisation offered by the European Commission in 2008 that '[i]n a nutshell, they [the agencies] are typified by their diversity' might be amusing for its lack of precision, but it is – for the same reason – certainly not satisfactory.[1] On the contrary, in spite of the apparent 'piecemeal logic'[2] the EU has applied for a long time when it came to setting up agencies, it is imperative to search for similarities, among other things in terms of organisational structure, of competences vested in European agencies, of their practical functioning and their degree of independence in order to get an idea of what the term 'agency' encompasses in the context of EU administration.[3] In order to get this idea, however, it shall first be discussed in which different under-

---

1   Commission, MEMO 08/159, 1; see Bodiroga-Vukobrat and Martinović 68. In its Communication COM (2008) 135 final – which is related to the MEMO – the Commission concedes that a sound institutional characterisation of European agencies is still outstanding (no 'overall vision'), and attempts a first systematisation; on the follow-up of this Communication see Comte 65; see also EU working group, No 1, 1. For a more exhaustive account see Griller and Orator, Everything 7 with further references.
2   D Curtin, Power 147.
3   Cf Kreher 227.

standings the term 'agency' has been used in legal and political science scholarship – also beyond the realm of Union law. Against the background of these views, the shape of *European* agencies shall become more distinct.

The following paragraphs are intended as a short *tour d'horizon* through various definitions of the term 'agency' – in a general context and in the context of EU administration. A classification of European agencies shall be attempted later in this work.

2. Different meanings of the term 'agency'

2.1. *In a general context*

In legal and political theory one can encounter different approaches towards defining the term 'agency'. Most of these approaches do not specifically refer to agencies within a certain entity (eg a state), but apply a more general, if not universal, understanding. *Levi-Faur*, for instance, has defined a (regulatory) agency as a 'non-departmental public organization mainly involved with rule making, which may also be responsible for fact-finding, monitoring, adjudication, and enforcement'.[4] This quotation gives an idea of what all the *terminus technicus* '(regulatory) agency' can comprise – *can* being the operative word. Another definition is provided by *Everson* stating that agencies 'habitually perform both legislative and executive tasks, as well as often undertaking a judicial role'.[5] In short, they 'facilitate decision-making'.[6] According to *Thatcher*, agencies regulate the operation of markets (eg competition authorities) or are 'responsible for promoting "public interest" goals other than competition'.[7] These three examples of verbal approximations towards the term 'agency' are functional. They reflect the variety of tasks an agency may perform.

On the institutional level – on which the structural placement of an agency within a certain organisation is at issue – the characteristics one can possibly list are very limited. Agencies are organisationally separated from other administrative institutions – *Busuioc* calls it the 'organisational divorce'.[8] They do not belong to the institutional core of administration (eg the government). In that sense they are institutionally decentralised, which is said to be one *conditio sine qua non* for their political independence. The political independence is more difficult to measure and hence has to be handled with care, when applied as one of the characteristics of agencies. *Thatcher* argues that for an entity to be called an 'independent regulatory agency' it is required that it 'has its own powers and responsibilities under public law; it is organisationally separated from ministries; it is neither directly elected nor managed by elected officials'.[9]

---

4   Levi-Faur 15.
5   Everson, Independent Agencies 181.
6   Ibid., 185.
7   Thatcher, Delegation 127.
8   Busuioc, Accountability 601.
9   Thatcher, Delegation 127.

On the whole, agencies have been established in order to disburden what above was called the institutional core of administration. Tasks of a certain kind (regularly 'technical' or 'regulatory' tasks) are transferred from the governmental bureaucracy to decentralised agencies. The *terminus technicus* for this transferral of powers is 'delegation'. The delegator (or 'principal') 'gives away' some of its competences by vesting the delegate (or 'agent') therewith.[10] Delegation is a paradigm of division of labour within an organisation (eg a state).[11] *Gilardi* draws the line of delegation from the citizens to their representatives in parliament, from the parliament to the government, from the government as a collegiate body to the single ministers, from the government to the bureaucracy and – as the '"ultimate" step of delegation' – from the government to independent agencies.[12] Ideally, the rationale for such a delegation of powers regularly is a reduction of costs via a pooling of resources and expertise and thereby facilitating faster and better decision-making. Another 'logic of delegation', which might be pursued either as an end in itself or as a collateral effect of cost efficiency, is enhanced credibility of the political performance.[13]

2.2. *In the context of EU administration*

In the context of EU administration the term 'agency' today is used to name two different kinds of entities: executive agencies and regulatory agencies. Executive agencies are (for the time being: six) EU bodies with legal personality set up by the Commission,[14] which are in charge of executing certain EU policies. Their main tasks are connected to the management of funding programmes in different policy fields, namely research (ERCEA, REA), SMEs (EASME), education, audiovisual and culture (EACEA), consumers, health, agriculture and food (CHAFEA) and innovation and networks (INEA). They work in close cooperation with the competent DG in the Commission – their respective 'parent-DGs' – and follow their instructions. It is fair to say that the executive agencies are conceptualised and operate as the extended arm of the Commission.[15] They are not intended to be

---

10   This principal–agent relationship, although rooting in contractual law, and the law of representation, respectively, has been subject to an abundant literature in the field-of political science and economics: eg Kassim and Menon 121; Laffont and Martimort; Kleine.

11   On the general merits and drawbacks of delegation of powers in a political system see Tallberg, Delegation 25f.

12   Gilardi 3; see also D Curtin, Actors 524ff.

13   Majone, Logics; Görisch 371 for the differentiation between 'true' delegation and other forms of delegation; see also Shapiro, US.

14   See Article 3 of Council Regulation 58/2003.

15   It ought to be mentioned here that the ERCEA has a somewhat exceptional status – at least on a factual level. Due to its organisational proximity to the ERC, which again is governed by the Scientific Council, a body composed of renowned scientists and scholars, the ERCEA is less strongly exposed to Commission intervention.

independent from their delegator, the Commission. It is in stark contrast to the executive agencies that the 'European agencies' – also referred to as 'regulatory' or 'traditional' agencies[16] – have to be perceived. They constitute the core interest of this work. When reference is made to 'agencies' here, it is – in case of doubt – the regulatory agencies that are meant to be addressed.

With regard to the EU's institutional architecture, the Commission has correctly pointed out that '[t]he establishment of agencies case by case ... has not been accompanied by an overall vision of the place of agencies in the Union'.[17] Nevertheless, common characteristics of European agencies can be identified both in functional and institutional terms. As concerns purely functional definitions of European agencies, suffice it to say for now that they are entrusted with a range of – more or less 'technical' – tasks ranging from the observation of certain sectors of the internal market, or cross-sectional matters (such as the environment) throughout the internal market, to the implementation of legal frameworks or the coordination of executive practices in the Member States (MS). In a somewhat tentative (functional) but nevertheless illustrative approach, the Commission states that 'some [agencies] can adopt individual decisions with direct effect, applying agreed EU standards; some provide additional technical expertise on which the Commission can then base a decision and some focus more on networking between national authorities'.[18]

In their comparative analysis *Geradin* and *Petit* have listed seven (either functional or institutional) 'common features' of European agencies. First, European agencies regularly have a limited mandate of primarily technical, scientific and management tasks. Second, on the whole, they have very limited powers – above all, many of them do not have the power to render binding decisions. Third, they dispose of an executive director who works as a 'general manager' of the everyday workload of the agency.[19] Fourth, in European agencies MS are represented[20] in an administrative or management board that shall supervise the agency's director.[21] Fifth, committees play an important role in the performance of the agencies' tasks. Sixth, European agencies are decentralised. This regards not only the tasks – they are 'withdrawn from the centralized responsibility of the Commission' – but also the geographical location of the agencies. Seventh, (in 2004) a majority of the European agencies were legally based on the flexibility clause (now: Article 352 TFEU).[22]

---

16   This naming goes back to the Commission, COM (2008) 135 final, 2.

17   Commission, COM (2008) 135 final, 2; see also Koenig et al. 228.

18   Commission, COM (2008) 135 final, 5.

19   With respect to the agencies' monitoring of their activities see Court of Auditors 30.

20   On MS' pushing for representation in agencies see Kelemen and Tarrant 929; cf Michel, Gleichgewicht 109.

21   See Commission Roadmap on follow-up to Common Approach 1.

22   Geradin and Petit 41ff; on the role of the flexibility clause as a legal basis for the foundation of agencies see also Remmert 137ff; see also Chapter 2 IV.1. below.

II.   *RISK GOVERNANCE* AS A GENERIC TERM OF A CERTAIN SET OF POLICIES

1.   Terminology

European agencies are largely operating in what could be called the field of risk governance. Hence it is required to introduce the term itself as well as the most important concepts of risk governance.

To start with a definition: Risk governance obviously is the governance of risks. So what is a risk? One definition states that 'the term "risk" denotes the possibility that an undesirable state of reality (adverse effects) may occur as a result of natural events or human activities'.[23] The famous economist *Frank Knight* clearly differentiates between risk and uncertainty. For him risk is a calculable parameter, a function of probability based on the multiplication *risk = probability x effect*. He perceives risk as the product of two factors, something that can be calculated in full. Uncertainty, on the contrary, encompasses hazards that are hardly calculable or even incalculable.[24]

Today's scholarship largely does not follow *Knight's* calculation theory. The full calculability of risks has been questioned and *Knight's* antagonism was eventually given up in favour of an 'uncertain risks' conceptualisation. This was not least because of the practice of European risk assessors as well as risk managers to treat *Knightian* 'risks' and uncertain hazards alike.[25] Even the term 'unknown risk' is in use, which appears to be the ultimate step in the gradual extension of the meaning of the *terminus technicus* 'risk' – from risk as a calculable parameter to 'uncertain risks' – an assumption that is based on some evidence, at least – to completely 'unknown risks'.

The definition of risk given above – the 'possibility that an undesirable state of reality (adverse effects) may occur as a result of natural events or human activities' – is open both for *Knight's* narrow and for the wider understanding of 'risk' applied today.

Now for the second element of our composite term: 'Governance' is a term that has been subject to a multitude of different concepts, hence 'notoriously slippery'[26] and, according to *Dawson*, even 'intentionally vague'.[27] Etymologically the word stems from the fourteenth-century French noun *gouvernance*, which again has roots in the Latin verb *gubernare* (steering [originally: the rudder], guiding, directing). Since the term has been differentiated and specified in so many ways, these translations may serve as synonyms only for certain understandings of governance. As *Pierre* and *Peters* have summarised,

---

23   Renn 1 with reference to Robert W Kates et al., *Perilous Progress: Managing the Hazards of Technology* (Westview Press 1985) 21.
24   See van Asselt et al. 361.
25   See ibid.
26   Pierre and Peters 7.
27   Dawson 210.

in practical terms governance has been understood either as a structure (hierarchies, markets, networks, communities) or as a process ('steering and coordinating'). It has also been understood in theoretical terms, which is to say, as a concept. Compared with traditional political science approaches, the concept of governance shifts the focus from political institutions and political power to other factors, such as entrepreneurialism and political skill.[28] That way, it is less centristic and more open to perceive 'different actors as well as non-hierarchical modes of interaction'.[29] In the given context, governance shall be conceived in broad terms, so as to encompass structures and processes alike. It is not only the Who, but also the How, which is of interest here.

Following the above approximations, we can describe risk governance as the structures and the processes in place – and actually in use – for the purpose of dealing with adverse effects that may occur as a result of natural events or human activities. More specifically, risk governance includes the tripartite regime of risk analysis (risk assessment, risk management and risk communication).[30] The possible fields of risk governance could not be more diverse. They may range from ensuring food safety to facilitating environmental protection, or from financial market supervision to the licensing of medicines.

In today's political practice (as reflected in the literature) we can observe a turning away from traditional, hierarchical forms of risk governance. Legitimate steering in a certain field requires the involvement of the actors concerned – the stakeholders. Hence the degree of stakeholder participation both in the relevant steering bodies and in the decision-making process is a crucial factor in the assessment of governance – ie answering the question whether or not it is actually 'good governance'.[31] One new approach proposed in this context is called 'deliberative governance', which is characterised by enhanced 'public participation', including as broad a range of stakeholders as possible ('inclusive risk governance'). This horizontal dialogue, it is argued, should take place on a level above the level of the nation states. The reform proposals, and the debate in general, are based on the perspicuous finding that the adverse effects of risks do not 'respect physical boundaries, disciplinary bonds, territorial statehood or political spheres of influence'.[32]

In the wake of the White Paper 'Completing the Internal Market' (1985),[33] which sketched the main political agenda of President of the Commission *Jacques Delors*, myriad new legislation was put on track. This was backed up by the extension of Community competences brought about by the Single European Act (SEA) (1987) and the Treaty of Maastricht (1993). These developments have gradually led to a new level of European (risk) governance

28   Pierre and Peters 14–24.
29   Risse 366.
30   Cf Article 3 para 10 of Regulation 178/2002.
31   This term is used here as a popular political buzzword. For the original concept and its roots see Kohler-Koch and Rittberger 29.
32   Klinke 399.
33   Commission, COM (85) 310 final.

with ramifications also for the institutional landscape of the E(E)C/EU. Although the White Paper does not mention institutional changes, the establishment of numerous European agencies in the early 1990s, eg the European Medicines Agency (EMA), the Office for Harmonisation in the Internal Market (OHIM) or the Community Plant Variety Office (CPVO), certainly has to be seen as part of the implementation of the political aim of 'completion of the internal market'.[34] While these developments have root in a substantial policy – the completion of the internal market – the 'new governance' discussion,[35] which started in the late 1990s, has equally facilitated the establishment of agencies, though with a genuinely (not: collaterally) institutional direction of impact.[36] The European agency has been seen as a body relatively fit to facilitate this new understanding of (multilevel) risk governance:[37] 'the interdependence of actors operating at different territorial levels – local, regional, national, supranational' and 'the growing importance of nonhierarchical forms of policy-making such as dynamic networks which involve public authorities as well as private actors'.[38] Against this background the gradual 'agencification' of the EC/EU has to be perceived.

2. Excursus: *objective* science and *subjective* politics – a fallacy?

2.1. *The theory of the interplay between science and politics*

European agencies are, as 'central nodes of networks'[39] and among other things, in charge of gathering the information necessary for a rational policy-making. Against this backdrop, the relation between science (as the generation of information) and politics appears to be particularly important. European agencies[40] are expected to deliver the informational substance required for drawing reasonable political conclusions, they are the preliminary think tanks, as it were, of EU politics. They gather and – to varying degrees – assess the 'objective' information necessary for the political decision-makers to make their 'subjective' decision.[41] In the terminology of risk governance, the first, 'objective', part is called risk assessment (taking place in 'knowledge-based

---

34 The White Paper sets 1992 as a deadline for the completion of the internal market. But even after that the EC/EU has continuously been working on the further development of the internal market. Some question the completion by 1992 in the first place; see Pelkmans 66f.

35 Cf Commission, COM (2001) 428; for a critical analysis of this White Paper see Scharpf.

36 See Dawson 213.

37 See Kohler-Koch and Rittberger 41 with further references.

38 Ibid., 34 with further references.

39 Majone, Delegation 336.

40 The focus on agencies should not hide the fact that there are also other sources of scientific information, also within the Commission (eg the Joint Research Centre).

41 For a critical analysis of the ideal of 'objective science' see Kuhn; Nickles.

arenas'), whereas the political decision-makers are in charge of risk management (taking place in 'power-based arenas').[42]

In theory, risk assessment is envisaged as something unequivocal, a process in which thorough ('objective') scientific or technical research is undertaken and at whose end there is one, by all participants of the process unanimously confirmed, report. In the second, 'subjective', phase of the decision-making process the 'objective' findings are dealt with in light of ethical, social and economic values. These issues, and therefore also the forum in which they are discussed, are – as opposed to the factors in the risk assessment phase – open to different opinions. This is the political battlefield where ideological and moral views, however much they might differ from each other, are stated and fervently both attacked and defended.

Here also the various and often contradictory claims of interest groups or stakeholders – NGOs, international organisations such as the WHO, trade unions, etc. – come into play. Whereas the first phase is generally coined by agreement, the second phase is emphatically signified by disagreement. At the end of this exchange of different views, the participants with the better arguments, or with the greater political influence, might have managed to convince their counterparts. However, practically speaking it turns out to be a *do ut des*, a trade-off of opposing claims, in short – to call a spade a spade – a compromise, most of the time.

All participants of the second phase are risk managers, who discuss values.[43] It is important to stress that the discussion in the risk management phase can only take place on the basis of the results of the risk assessment. The values are not discussed as a topic as such but with respect and, more than that, directed to the facts presented by the risk assessors. Phases one and two are strictly separated from each other, both concerning the goals as well as the participants of each phase. Also, the requirements for being qualified to participate in one of the phases are different. In order to work in phase one a certain expertise in the respective area is needed; working in phase two requires political legitimacy.[44] There is no such thing as an expert in matters of values or morals, since these questions are highly personal and do not require special knowledge. Any individual would be capable of arguing in moral affairs equally well. Since it is not possible to consider each and everybody's opinion, the entirety of people is represented by a comparatively small group of politicians. Hence the only entry requirement for phase two is political legitimation. This is how things work theoretically.

---

42   The word 'arenas' is taken from Maggetti and Gilardi 833.
43   See Alemanno, EU 43.
44   This is clearly expressed eg in *Pfizer*, para 201.

2.2. *Five assumptions on the practice of science and politics*

In practice, however, the scene looks different: The 'scientification of politics' occurs as much as the 'politicisation of science'.[45] This is because '[t]he line between information and politics is very thin'.[46] The inadequacies of the above model can essentially be addressed in five arguments, which will be introduced now and should be kept in mind in the further course of this work.

1. It can already be deduced from the word risk *assessment* that the concept of a completely 'objective' science is a fallacy. The image does not hold water with respect to both personal and material issues.

    On a personal front, it cannot be denied that in the field of science personal convictions, values and standpoints also play an important role. Science starts where we enter the realm of the unknown. Interpretation is also a substantial part of empirical research. This is what is innate in the word 'assessment'. Science is not only describing the facts but also interpreting them. The outcome of this interpretation is, at the very least subconsciously, coined by personal expectations, convictions and hopes. We might even say that political (ie moral in a broad sense), 'subjective' attitudes of each and every scientist intrude into their 'objective' research and shape its results to a varying extent (intrinsic motivation).

    A more collective prong of the overlapping of science and politics is the so-called 'science-policies'. Science-policies are guidelines set by (competent) political decision-makers which scientists have to follow in case of certain itemised (scientific) uncertainties. If there is a number of 'plausible accounts' towards a scientific question and it cannot be proved scientifically which account is the correct one, the guidelines predetermine which account the scientists have to suggest as a basis for further research.[47] By setting such science-policies, the policy-maker is integrating a political decision in the scientific process. A decision that would have to be made by the political decision-maker is predetermined and the actual 'execution' of the decision is delegated to the scientist.

    Hence the main rationale of science-policies is that the scientist can take the (predetermined) decision on his own without having to delay the course of the research by consulting the relevant political body. Risk assessors, functionally speaking, act as risk managers. This influence coming from outside the personal sphere of the scientist can be called extrinsic motivation. An analysis of science-policies discloses a grey area where it is difficult, if not impossible, to determine whether the question

---

45   Everson and Vos 1.
46   Schout, Environment 110.
47   See Walker 214.

remains scientific or is already a political one.[48] In this context, *Alemanno* has pointed out that as soon as scientific or technical findings are dealt with on a political level, 'scientific expertise and political decisions become so intertwined as to become impossible to separate. In fact, the elaboration of these policies and assumptions boil [sic] down to a risk management activity'.[49]

2. We have just discussed the influence of political decision-makers on scientists. Now we shall have a look at whether and, if so, how influencing works *vice versa*. Since political decision-making is based on the findings of the risk assessment phase, it can hardly be denied that the 'objective' findings influence the 'subjective' moral (political) discussion. From the order of phases it is already clear that such an influence of the research results on the political decision-makers is not only condoned but also intended. What would politicians discuss if they had no substance to direct their value arguments to? This influence turns out to work as a limitation of political discourse. What scientists have found out to be impossible evidently cannot be demanded by politicians. What scientists have found out to be a very expensive (in terms of money, danger for the environment or human health, etc.) solution will require particularly sound and convincing arguments in favour, if politicians still want to make this scientific solution a political will (ie a decision). The scientific findings, in other words, narrow down the issue and present it in a way that sketches the scope of *reasonable* political decision-making. That is not to say that – in effect – the scientists are taking the political decision, but they certainly predetermine it to a varying, on average considerable, degree.

3. From arguments 1. and 2. we may draw a first, basic conclusion. Science and political decision-making at some point in time regularly become – to some degree at least – intermingled. The *prima facie* convincing distinction between 'objective' science and 'subjective' political decision-making has turned out not to be apodictic. A more thorough analysis reveals signs of mutual penetration of both fields which are too strong to be ignored. Whether the mutually exerted influence is stronger in one or the other direction can only be assessed on a case by case basis. As regards food policies, for example, *Vos* and *Wendler* have described the relationship between the Commission, one of the risk managers, and the European Food Safety Authority (EFSA), the main risk assessor, 'as being one of a blind driver, the Commission, and a directions-giving passenger, EFSA'.[50]

---

48 See National Research Council 3. The paper uses a slightly different terminology distinguishing between 'risk assessment policy' (science-policy) and 'risk management policy'. In the paper it is argued against an institutional separation of risk assessment and risk management due to the close link between the two of them.
49 Alemanno, EU 47, with reference to Walker 263 [sic].
50 Vos and Wendler 122.

These conclusions now raise the question of which procedural setting may provide for *acceptable* outcomes. What is clear is that political legitimacy and political accountability are not only valid standards in the risk management phase, but also – for reasons of the perceived subjectivation – in the risk assessment phase.

4.   In assumption 1. above it was argued that scientists are likely to be exposed to both intrinsic and extrinsic motivation, which – as a result – can lead to distorted scientific advice. The motivation might either be to come to *one* definite result without dissenting material or to substantially come to a *certain* result. Influence of the latter kind can be exerted not only by politicians, but also by private parties: 'representatives of non-governmental organisations, local communities, interest groups and grassroots movements, as well as individual lay people in their capacity as citizens and/or consumers'.[51] Here it becomes apparent that the participation of private parties in the information-gathering process of a risk assessor can be a double-edged sword. On the one hand, their input can be a worthwhile stakeholder contribution. On the other hand, too liberal (unregulated) a participation scheme might lead to powerful actors dominating it and thereby unproportionally influencing the whole process.

5.   With regard to agencies we can say: What is in accordance with the principles of openness and participation may be contrary to the call for agencies' independence. Participation can make 'European agencies excessively permeable to private parties'.[52]

Another problem that needs to be considered is the fact that 'objective' research – as opposed to what policy-makers sometimes seem to suggest – does not always lead to consensual outcomes. Some questions might be left unanswered since the respective results cannot currently – for lack of empirical data or lack of technical possibilities – be reached. The scientists can be aware of their lack of knowledge in the sense that they know that they are – for whichever reason – unable to cater for satisfactory results on a specific subject ('known unknowns'). In this case they are informed about the fact that their research is not complete and can report to the policy-makers accordingly. 'Known unknowns' are unmeasurable uncertainties in the *Knightian* sense: '[A] *measurable* uncertainty, or "risk" proper … is so far different from an *unmeasurable* one that is not in effect an uncertainty at all' (emphasis in original).[53] Having said this, it is also possible for scientists not to be aware at all of where a certain measure entails a certain risk ('unknown unknowns'). This is certainly the less advantageous case, because here the

51   Joss 290.
52   Chiti, Part 1401.
53   Knight 20.

scientists cannot even draw the policy-maker's attention to a certain (incalculable) risk. On the contrary, they believe that the research they have undertaken is complete and – as far as the 'unknown unknowns' are concerned – that there is no risk involved.

As a side note: In practice, policy-makers often prefer one 'single "definitive" interpretation' of scientific results.[54] Not only is it then easier for them to communicate the findings to the public (risk communication), it also facilitates the political decision-making. Given this preference, scientists might be inclined to present their conclusions in a more one-sided way than the outcome allows, thereby neglecting dissenting results and/or opinions.[55] This is just another instance of 'subjective' motivations interfering with demands of 'objective' science.[56]

The main direction of impact of *this* argument is, however, the existence of, and the distinction between, known and unknown uncertainty. It goes without saying that there is need for research being undertaken before a political conclusion is drawn. But at the same time there is already a requirement for sufficient transparency in the risk assessment phase. Dissenting results and/or opinions on a scientific level must be communicated openly in order to initiate or, where there is discussion already, encourage a public debate on the matter. Admitting that science cannot give definitive answers to all questions posed at all times does not undermine its authority. It rather protects science from unsatisfiable expectations and thereby removes the pressure imposed upon it – the pressure that inclines scientists to present uncertainty, if acknowledged at all, 'in ways that reduce unknowns to measurable "risk"'.[57] A basic awareness that '*definitive* science-based decisions are … a fundamental contradiction in terms' (emphasis added) needs to be created not only among policy-makers and the public. It also needs to be stressed within the scientific community that there is nothing wrong with delivering scientific advice that, at times, offers 'a variety of alternative reasonable interpretations'.[58]

III. ADMINISTRATIVE OUTPUT AND ITS LEGAL QUALITY

1. Introduction

A thorough analysis of certain agency output in both an *ex ante* as well as an *ex post* perspective, that is to say with respect to genesis and effects, shall be part of this work (see Chapter 3 II.3.4. below). In order to pave the way for

---

54 Stirling 1029.
55 See Stirling 1029.
56 See argument 1. above.
57 Stirling 1029.
58 Ibid., 1030.

these discussions, two of the core issues of administrative output (which are again strongly connected with each other) shall be introduced at this stage. These are the most relevant type of administrative output – the 'decision' – on the one hand, and the different shades of legal quality as epitomised in the topical discussion about 'hard law' and 'soft law', on the other hand.

As regards the decision as the main form of administrative output, we may in the first place consider a general definition. The Oxford Dictionary (English) defines a decision as '[a] conclusion or resolution reached after consideration'.[59] Decisions – be they taken by ourselves or by others – are *the* determinants of our lives. They coin the most trivial details of our everyday life as well as events of historical importance to mankind, and therefore range, as it were, from the mundane sudden resolve of the worker to take a shortcut on his way home to the momentous and far-reaching declaration of war by the president of state A to the president of state B, on behalf of their respective countries.

In the given context, our attention shall focus on administrative decisions only, which means a limitation of the subject – not only quantitatively but also qualitatively. The latter is because the above definition is not sufficiently accurate to depict administrative decisions, which have a legally binding effect and are regularly subject to further criteria, such as appearance in a written form or indication of reasons. Hence even decisions (within the meaning defined above) taken in the preparation of an administrative decision are regularly not administrative decisions themselves. This also becomes relevant from a practical point of view when, for example, the administrative decision is essentially based on the expertise or the advice given by a person or entity different from the person or entity rendering the administrative decision. In this case only the administrative decision can be reviewed in the course of a redress procedure, whereas the expertise or advice as such often cannot be directly combatted.

As regards the legal quality of administrative output, we shall leave aside the question of legal validity or legal invalidity here and focus on the output's degree of bindingness. The bindingness of an administrative output can be perceived *de iure* and *de facto*. Administrative output, eg the decision of authority A ordering the operators of a factory to reduce its emissions, may have binding effect *de iure*, but – in case the operators repeatedly neglect the order – not *de facto*. Conversely, administrative output that is not binding *de iure*, eg the recommendation of the Foreign Ministry of state A addressed to its citizens not to travel to state B because of the considerable health hazard a stay in B would entail, may be followed by the citizens and hence have *de facto* binding force. In this context, *Georg Jellinek*'s famous statement of the 'normative force of the factual' [*normative Kraft des Faktischen*] comes to mind. The quotation also serves as a warning for lawyers not to be ignorant of events beyond the letter of the law when legally assessing a situation.

---

59   <www.oxforddictionaries.com/definition/english/decision>.

The relevance of this distinction between binding and non-binding administrative output – which has been addressed under the headings 'hard law' and 'soft law'[60] – becomes apparent when considering the means of redress. Legally binding administrative output can regularly be reviewed by another authority or a court upon request, whereas administrative output that is not legally binding normally cannot be challenged.

As a matter of fact, the two issues addressed – the administrative decision and the hard–soft dichotomy of law – are strongly interlinked.[61] An administrative decision is to be considered binding, whereas the expertise or the advice it is based on may not have a legally binding effect. Nevertheless, expertise or advice may *de facto* have binding effect, if the authority rendering the administrative decisions regularly follows it. Administrative output other than a decision may appear – as a 'recommendation' or a 'standard' – in a soft form. No general remark can be made on whether the expertise or the advice actually plays only a subordinate role in the decision-making process or whether it is largely predetermining the administrative decision: transitions are smooth here, and evidence is difficult to provide.

2.   The output of European agencies in the light of EU primary law

The output of European agencies moves along the lines of the above discussion. Some of the agencies (eg OHIM or EASA) have the power to issue legally binding acts. Otherwise they are limited to produce soft law output[62] or output completely lacking normative quality (eg activity reports). In EU primary law the different kinds of legal output are listed in Article 288 para 1 TFEU that stipulates: 'To exercise the Union's competences, the *institutions* shall adopt regulations, directives, decisions, recommendations and opinions' (emphasis added). It is contested whether this provision encompasses European agencies, as it mentions only 'the institutions'. The predecessor of Article 288 TFEU – Article 249 para 1 TEC – reads as follows: 'In order to carry out their task and in accordance with the provisions of this Treaty, the European Parliament acting jointly with the Council, the Council and the Commission shall make regulations and issue directives, take decisions, make recommendations or deliver opinions'. Here the institutional scope is even narrower, encompassing only the Parliament acting jointly with the Council, the Council on its own and the Commission. As regards the TEC, *Vogt* applies a strict, literal interpretation. He argues that in view of the 'exclusionary effect' [*Sperrwirkung*] of Article 249 para 1 TEC, neither other bodies mentioned elsewhere in the Treaty nor bodies not mentioned in the Treaty at all (under the Nice Treaty, agencies still were bodies of the latter kind) can be subsumed

---

60   For the malleability of the term 'soft law' see eg Abbott and Snidal 422f.
61   See eg Michel, Gleichgewicht 144f.
62   See Chiti, Agencies 102f.

under this provision.[63] *Hofmann* and others, against *Vogt*, argue that even bodies not mentioned in the Treaty may be able to issue legally binding acts according to Article 249 TEC.[64] Although the wording has been changed – and the scope of the provision explicitly extended to all institutions – in the Treaty of Lisbon, the doubts about the coverage of European agencies remain the same. The list of 'institutions' given in Article 13 TEU (EP, European Council, Council, Commission, CJEU, ECB, Court of Auditors) clearly is exhaustive. Agencies are now explicitly mentioned in (the English version of) the Treaties (eg in Article 15 TFEU), it is true, but they have certainly not been elevated to institutions according to Article 13 TEU. In that sense, a wide interpretation of Article 288 TFEU so as to include European agencies would go against the undubitable wording of the provision and hence would be *contra legem*. An application *per analogiam* would, in my view, not be justified because an unintentional normative gap cannot be assumed. When negotiating the new wording of what is now Article 288 TFEU, the masters of the Treaties must have been aware of the fact that there were European agencies in place back then, vested with the power to render legally binding acts according to secondary law.[65] In spite of this knowledge, they did not decide – for whichever reason[66] – to incorporate in Article 288 TFEU a legal basis for this fact. Conversely, we could argue that the MS were aware of the ECJ's case law in which it has many times implicitly accepted agencies' decision-making power.[67] Since they did not want to change the law in this respect, they saw no reason to explicitly include agencies in what is now Article 288 TFEU.

Either way, with Article 263 TFEU there is a provision in the TFEU that clearly indicates that there are 'bodies, offices or agencies of the Union' that adopt acts 'intended to produce legal effects *vis-à-vis* third parties'.[68] Article 277 TFEU even mentions 'act[s] of *general* application adopted by [a] … body, office or agency of the Union' (emphasis added). From this provision it can be deduced – *a maiore ad minus* – that these entities may be entitled to render decisions with an individual scope. Whether it also includes a rule-making power is much less clear, and will be discussed in Chapter 2 I.7. below. It is important to note that these provisions are not legal bases *stricto sensu*, but they only suggest that there is a legal basis for such competences in primary law. They do not say where, it is true, but they put the fact that there are agencies rendering legally binding acts on a firm footing. Nevertheless, the fact that this firm footing is not reflected in Article 288 TFEU is a legistic blemish.

---

63   Vogt 24f.
64   See Hofmann, Normenhierarchien 222f; Fischer-Appelt 119ff.
65   See Chiti, Agencies 95f.
66   The focus of the reform of the provision at issue lay on simplifying the typology of legal acts, not on extending the group of their creators. For the genesis of Article 288 TFEU see Nettesheim, Art. 288, paras 5–11.
67   See, as one of many examples, *Apollo Group* with references to preceding case-law.
68   Article 263 para 1 TFEU; cf also para 5 *leg cit*.

With regard to the adoption of soft law acts[69] the starting point in primary law is again Article 288 TFEU. It states that recommendations and opinions 'shall have no binding force'. Again, according to a literal reading of this provision, agencies are excluded from adopting such acts. Still the ECJ has, for a long time, accepted that bodies not mentioned in the Treaties may adopt such soft law acts.[70] Therefore, the above considerations on the possible intentions of the masters of the Treaties can *mutatis mutandis* be applied here, as well. This means that arguments for both interpretations of Article 288 TFEU – in favour of and against agencies' principal power to adopt soft law acts – can be found, which leaves the question unanswered. Article 263 TFEU mentions acts of agencies 'intended to produce legal effects *vis-à-vis* third parties'. *A maiore ad minus* it can be deduced that they may also adopt acts not intended to produce legal effects,[71] eg soft law acts. It goes without saying that even then the conferral of such a power must be justified by the legislator in each and every case with respect to the specific Treaty base of the empowering act of secondary law.

69   Soft law is used as an umbrella term for acts not having 'legally binding force as such, but
      nevertheless [having] certain (indirect) legal effects'; Senden 112.
70   See eg *Romano*.
71   There exist non-binding acts, which regularly do not qualify as soft law, eg annual reports,
      press releases, etc.

2 Core questions of the 'agencification' of risk governance

I. DELEGATION OF POWERS AND THE *MERONI* JUDGEMENT

1. The background of the case

In order to establish and, once established, maintain a common market for coal, iron ore, scrap and steel, the ECSCT vested the High Authority with a variety of tasks.[1] Among other things, the High Authority had to guarantee that all undertakings within the scope of the ECSCT could operate under – more or less – the same economic conditions.

In this context the High Authority entrusted the ferrous scrap equalisation bodies (hereinafter referred to as the 'Brussels agencies')[2] – bodies of originally 22 respectable steel companies[3] – with the making of the financial arrangements of the ferrous scrap equalisation system by 1 April 1954 – 'under the responsibility of the High Authority'.[4] The system was set in place to guarantee that the scrap consumers (mostly steel companies) of the common market could purchase imported scrap at a price similar to the price demanded *within* the common market by means of equalisation payments. These payments were made from a fund that was fed by contributions from ECSC-seated companies dealing with ferrous scrap.[5]

It was the Brussels agencies, companies established as *sociétés coopératives* under Belgian private law, which requested the Italian steel company *Meroni* to pay its contributions to the so-called Imported Ferrous Scrap Equalisation

---

1   The common market for coal, iron ore and scrap was opened on 10 February 1953, the common market for steel on 1 May 1953, <http://europa.eu/legislation_summaries/institutional_affairs/treaties/treaties_ecsc_en.htm>.
2   These bodies are the Joint Bureau of Ferrous Scrap Consumers and the Imported Ferrous Scrap Equalisation Fund.
3   The original number of companies is taken from Griller and Orator, Meroni. The number of members of the Bureau and the Fund rose up to 213 in 1954, and gradually dropped down to 136 in 1955 and 123 in 1957, respectively. See *Meroni* 116f.
4   Article 1 para 2 of High Authority Decisions 22/54 and 14/55. Both decisions were based on Article 53 para 1(a) ECSCT.
5   Opinion of AG *Roemer* in *Meroni*, 120. For an overview of this system see Priebe 31–34.

Fund. The calculation of the contributions was based on a lump sum assessment of the Brussels agencies in this case because *Meroni* had failed to deliver the respective figures about the tonnage of scrap it had purchased. As they could not reach an agreement with *Meroni* they turned to the High Authority, which subsequently issued two enforceable decisions requiring *Meroni* to pay a contribution of nearly 78 million (55 and 23 million, respectively) Italian lira to the fund. The High Authority essentially based its decisions on the calculations of the Brussels agencies, though with some deviations.[6] These two decisions were then challenged by *Meroni* before the ECJ.[7]

2.   The parties' submissions and the Opinion of AG *Roemer*

2.1.   *The parties' submissions*

Meroni essentially argues, first, that the High Authority in its decision failed to give reasons and thereby has violated its duties laid down in the Treaty and, second, that it has misused its powers. This latter claim is *inter alia* based on the argument that the delegation of powers to the Brussels agencies by the High Authority was unlawful.[8] In this context, *Meroni* asserts that the High Authority has delegated too much power to the Brussels agencies, since the figures provided by them were 'almost sacrosanct' and 'certainly of greater weight and authority than … decisions proper'.[9]

The High Authority confirms that it has based its decision on the numbers delivered by the Brussels agencies and argues that 'clearly no indication of reasons is required for that'.[10] It adds that it 'adopts the data furnished by the Brussels agencies without being able to add anything thereto'. The addition of further explanations or reasons by themselves would constitute an 'unauthorised interference in another body's powers for the purpose of explaining the factors involved in the elaboration of its decisions'.[11] The High Authority claims to merely make enforceable an obligation that is – substantially – determined by the Brussels agencies. It is, in that sense, not to be called a decision of the High Authority.[12]

2.2.   *The Opinion of the Advocate General*

On *Meroni*'s first point AG *Roemer* agrees that the reasoning given by the High Authority is insufficient. He states that the duty to give reasons applies

---

6   *Meroni* 142.
7   9/56 and 10/56 *Meroni*. In both procedures similar questions were at issue. The two judgements largely correspond to each other.
8   *Meroni* 145.
9   Ibid., 146.
10   Ibid., 142.
11   Ibid., 148.
12   Ibid.

to all forms of legal output of the High Authority, as laid down in Article 14 ECSCT.[13]

As regards the issue of delegation, *Roemer* lists two conditions required under national law for a lawful transferral of state competences to private bodies. First, the delegation must have a sufficiently determined legal basis. Second, the delegate must be adequately controlled by the state and there must be full legal protection against the decisions of the delegate. These requirements for lawful delegation to private actors are, according to *Roemer*, for lack of an explicit rule in the Treaty also applicable on the Community level. The legal protection according to the Treaty includes the duty to give reasons for a decision as well as the possibility to challenge a decision before the ECJ. Hence there are two possibilities to lawfully delegate tasks to private bodies on the Community level. Either decisions of the delegates are equated with decisions of the High Authority or the competence of the delegate is limited to merely preparatory tasks, the formal decisions being rendered by the High Authority itself.[14]

In *Roemer*'s view, the alleged duty of the steel companies to report the amount of imported scrap to the Brussels agencies does not have a legal basis, let alone the Brussels agencies' 'right' to make an estimate.[15] The determination of the contributions to be paid by the steel companies should be made under consideration of the current situation of the scrap and steel market in order to promote the proper functioning and the competitiveness of this market. Therefore the determination of the contributions – within an obligatory system – is an 'important instrument of economic policy' [*wichtiges Instrument der Wirtschaftspolitik*].[16] The discretion the Brussels agencies have in making their decision is reinforced by the fact that the High Authority has not adopted any provision regulating the determination of the contribution, its publication and its reasoning.[17]

3.   The decision of the Court

On the first ground, the ECJ holds the reasoning of the contested decision to be insufficient, since it 'lacks the supporting reasons indispensable for the exercise of judicial review'. This is in violation of Article 15 ECSCT that requires decisions of the High Authority to 'state the reasons on which they are based'.[18]

Only an 'exact and detailed statement of all the individual items comprised in the claim, payment of which was made enforceable by the decision' would meet the threshold of sufficient reasoning, since only then would it be possible for the Court to review the decision.

13   Opinion of AG *Roemer* in *Meroni* 108.
14   Ibid., 115.
15   Ibid., 116ff.
16   Ibid., 120.
17   Ibid., 122.
18   *Meroni* 142.

As regards the delegation of powers, the ECJ examines whether it is a 'true delegation' of powers of the High Authority according to the Treaty (variant one), or whether the competences transferred are limited to the drawing up of resolutions, leaving their application to the High Authority (variant two).[19] Having considered the statements of both parties, in particular those of the High Authority, the ECJ comes to the conclusion that 'Decision No 14/55 brings about a true delegation of powers, and [that] the question whether such delegation accords with the requirements of the Treaty must be examined'.

In order to establish the duties the Brussels agencies actually have, the ECJ applies the following hypothesis. Had the High Authority itself exercised the powers conferred on the Brussels agencies in Decision 14/55, it would have been subject to the following duties: the duty to state reasons for its decisions (Article 15 ECSCT), the duty to publish annually a general report on its activities and its administrative expenses (Article 17), the duty to publish data that could be useful to governments or to any other party concerned (Article 47).[20] With Decision 14/55, the High Authority delegated to the Brussels agencies some of its powers without at the same time delegating these duties accordingly. By conferring powers bare of the related duties, the High Authority has – in essence – delegated 'more extensive powers' than it has.[21]

With regard to the assessments of the contributions to the fund, the ECJ holds that there is 'no legal basis for the Brussels agencies' assessment on their own authority'. That is not to say that a delegation of powers is precluded *in general* under the ECSCT. Even though the ECSCT does not contain any provision on this issue, 'the possibility of entrusting to bodies established under private law, having a distinct legal personality and possessing powers of their own, the task of putting into effect certain "financial arrangements common to several undertakings" ... cannot be excluded'. However, the Court stresses, a delegation cannot be presumed: '[E]ven when empowered to delegate its powers the delegating authority must take an express decision transferring them'.[22]

Another issue is the margin of discretion granted to the agencies. In this context the ECJ remarks:

> The consequences resulting from a delegation of powers are very different depending on whether it involves clearly defined executive powers the exercise of which can, therefore, be subject to strict review in the light of objective criteria determined by the delegating authority, or whether it involves a discretionary power, implying a wide margin of discretion

---

19   Ibid., 147.
20   Ibid., 149.
21   Ibid., 150.
22   Ibid., 151; see also *FMC Chemical* [2007], para 66.

which may, according to the use which is made of it, make possible the execution of actual economic policy.[23]

Since no 'objective criteria' that essentially determine the delegate's output are laid down, the agencies 'must exercise a wide margin of discretion'.[24] This runs counter to the Treaty.[25]

Finally, the question arises whether the power of the permanent representative of the High Authority in the Brussels agencies to make a decision subject to the High Authority's approval (Article 9 of Decision 14/55) remedies the *prima facie* defective delegation. According to the ECJ, the power of the High Authority to refuse a decision of the Brussels agencies does not suffice. This is because not only is this power limited to cases in which the Brussels agencies do not make their decisions unanimously, but also the High Authority cannot effectively control the correctness of the data provided by the Brussels agencies. The High Authority – as it has itself submitted – 'adopts the data furnished by the Brussels agencies without being able to add anything thereto'.[26]

In its concluding paragraph, the Court held that '[i]n those circumstances the delegation [in question] … gives those agencies a degree of latitude which implies a wide margin of discretion and cannot be considered as compatible with the requirements of the Treaty'.[27] A delegation of discretionary powers to bodies not established by the Treaty and without due supervision 'would render less effective the guarantee resulting from the balance of powers established by Article 3'.[28]

4.   Some remarks on the judgement

As a preliminary remark it ought to be mentioned that what is referred to as the Brussels agencies in the *Meroni* case is not to be confounded with what we call European agencies today. The Brussels agencies and European agencies

---

23   *Meroni* 152; see Hilf 83f, who claims that the Court was above all concerned about the fact that the High Authority could not properly examine and, if required, correct the Brussels agencies' decisions.

24   *Meroni* 154.

25   Ibid., 151.

26   Ibid., 154.

27   Ibid.

28   Ibid., summary para 10. In more recent case law and scholarship the term 'institutional balance' is used. See eg *Parliament v Council* [1990], paras 21ff; see Michel, Gleichgewicht 74 with regard to the terminological change in the ECJ's case law. In the context of the *Meroni* doctrine, see Everson, Governance 148; Smismans 89. For a more flexible approach see Yataganas, Treaty.

are two different animals altogether.[29] The main differences to current
European agencies can be addressed in four points – one concerning the legal
sphere, one the organisation, one the delegator and one supervision.

First, the Brussels agencies were established under (Belgian) private law,
and not by virtue of a legal act of the EC legislator. The Court does not
exclude a delegation of powers to a (new) Community body, though.[30]
Second, compared with European agencies the Brussels agencies were
organised differently. Established as *sociétés coopératives* under Belgian law,
obviously they did not provide for MS participation in their administration.
Third, the Brussels agencies were delegates of the High Authority, whereas
European agencies exercise powers conferred upon them by the legislator. To
that extent, *Meroni* is rather the leading case for executive agencies, entrusted
by the Commission, than of European agencies.[31] However, with respect to
the issue 'delegation of powers' in general – and the limits thereto – *Meroni*
is relevant also in the context of European agencies. Fourth, for the Brussels
agencies – unlike for European agencies today – neither an internal nor an
external system of effective supervision was set in place.

In today's perspective – knowing about the hot spots of delegation, as it
were – it seems more adequate to create a body tailored to meet the requirements set by means of a regulation than to limit one's choice to what the
numeri clausi of bodies established under the private laws of the MS allow
for. In the early days of the Communities, however, a delegation to private
bodies was obviously deemed more opportune – not least because the Brussels
agencies have already been set in place. With no case law at hand and no
sophisticated general awareness for the problem of delegation, it is not
surprising that the High Authority quite ingenuously – not ingeniously –
approached the delegation at issue. This legal naivety is also reflected in its
inconsistent submissions. On the one hand, the High Authority stresses the
pivotal influence the Brussels agencies have on its decisions. It uses the
Brussels agencies as a 'shield' in its defence, as the ECJ aptly pointed out.[32] On
the other hand, it obviously attempts to protect the Brussels agencies' output
from being scrutinised by the ECJ. In order to achieve this protection it

29   See Griller and Orator, Everything 19; see also Bartodziej 302; Fischer-Appelt 107, who
      claims the *Meroni* cases to be only of limited value in the context of European agencies.
      Fischer-Appelt argues that the Brussels agencies – being private bodies situated beyond the
      scope of the Treaties – cannot be institutionally compared with current agencies, which are
      interwoven in the EU's institutional structure. Critically also Yataganas, Delegation 27:
      '[T]he transposition of this judgement *in toto* to the context of agencies is mistaken and
      misleading.'

30   See Hilf 82. When it comes to the transfer of powers from the Community level to an
      international organisation, however, the Court – generally speaking – has been cautious;
      see opinions *Fund for waterway vessels, EEA, ECHR I, ECHR II.*

31   See Griller and Orator, Everything 19. See also early follow-up cases of *Meroni*: *Barge,
      Macchiorlati Dalmas.*

32   *Meroni* 142.

demands that the applicant must 'demonstrate that in the contested decision the High Authority *took over as its own* the deliberations of the Brussels agencies...' (emphasis added).[33] This is a very bold and risky line of argumentation, as it emphasises the importance of the Brussels agencies' work while at the same time trying to protect their output from legal scrutiny or even substantial supervision.

As regards the quality of delegated powers, the ECJ differentiates 'clearly defined executive powers', which are subject to strict review by the delegator, and 'discretionary power implying a wide margin of discretion which may ... make possible the execution of actual economic policy'.[34] It is to be noted here that with regard to the *terminus technicus* discretion the French legal understanding ought to be applied. In the French version of the *Meroni* judgement the Court uses the word 'marge d'appréciation' (page 46). This margin of appreciation is more malleable than the term discretion understood *stricto sensu*, as applied above all in German scholarship.[35] In its wider understanding it simply describes a certain latitude when applying a legal act. This latitude can be granted due to the necessity to interpret broad terms used in a provision (eg the 'orderly supply to the common market'[36]) as well as by allowing the decision-maker to weigh certain interests. Both spheres are overlapping, though, and the differentiation *in praxi* is not always as clear as theory suggests.[37] A certain interpretative leeway can hardly ever be excluded, also with 'clearly defined executive powers'.[38] In the *Meroni* case, the ECJ has made clear, the discretion – or margin of appreciation – delegated to the Brussels agencies was too wide and actually encompassed 'political'[39] choices. However, the Court did not approach the question of what kind, and what degree respectively, of discretion *may* be delegated and hence it did not supply elaborate guidance for future delegations.[40] Leaving this question unanswered, the Court has considerably reduced the High Authority's/Commission's motivation to delegate further powers (see 6. below).

---

33   Ibid., 148.

34   Ibid., 152.

35   See eg Bernhard Müller 21; B Raschauer, Leitlinien 36. Strictly understood, the term discretion ('Verwaltungsermessen') encompasses the discretion to act or not to act (*Handlungsermessen*) and the discretion to choose between two different actions (*Auswahlermessen*); see Priebe 110f; on the interpretation of legal terms under the ECSCT see Soell 346.

36   Article 3 lit a ECSCT.

37   See Fischer-Appelt 109 and 111 f.

38   Cf Hart 607f. *Hart's* famous core-penumbra model distinguishes between the 'core' and the 'penumbra' of a norm. Parts of the norm whose content is not clear at first glance ('penumbra') will only be assigned to the 'core' of the norm, once they have been interpreted and are thus 'made clear'.

39   On the meaning of the term 'political' in this context, see Fischer-Appelt 109.

40   In view of the vagueness of the *Meroni* judgement in this respect, some deem exaggerated the restrictive interpretation that has long been applied by the institutions in its aftermath; see Geradin 222.

5.   Post-*Meroni* case law on delegation

After *Meroni*, the ferrous scrap equalisation system had repeatedly been challenged before the ECJ,[41] the main argument of the claimants focusing on the 'necessary checks'[42] made by private companies in order for the High Authority to get the information required to establish the amount of imported ferrous scrap. In the *Barge* case, for instance, it was the *SA Fiduciaire Suisse* that, based on the Decisions 13/58 and 16/58 of the High Authority, made these checks for the High Authority. Here the Court held that the High Authority did not actually delegate its powers, it merely exercised its powers according to the Treaty, which in its Article 47 para 1 *expressis verbis* allows it to '*have* made' (emphasis added) necessary checks. That 'clearly shows that the High Authority ... may instruct for this purpose any person whom it thinks fit to carry out the work'.[43] In another case based on similar facts – *Macchiorlati Dalmas* – the Court held that 'the checks carried out by the High Authority ... through private auditing companies are not a delegation by it of its powers but the exercise by it of its own powers by making use of information which it has obtained on its own responsibility'.[44] In these cases the Court found that the private companies were only providing the information on which the High Authority then based – on its own responsibility – its decisions. In that sense, the collection of information is to be understood as a merely preparatory work, which the High Authority is allowed to instruct others – eg private companies – to do.

More than 20 years after *Meroni*, in the early 80s, the ECJ in the case *Romano* had to deal with an instance of delegation not by the Commission, but by the Council. The *Tribunal du travail de Bruxelles* – the Brussels labour court – made a reference to the ECJ for a preliminary ruling concerning the Administrative Commission on Social Security for Migrant Workers and its powers.[45] This body was established pursuant to Article 80 of Council Regulation 1408/71 of 14 June 1971 and had to deal, among other things, with 'all administrative questions and questions of interpretation arising from this Regulation'.[46] The question at issue was whether the Administrative

---

41   See, for example, *Barge, Merlini, Macchiorlati Dalmas*. Surprisingly, only in *Merlini* (11) is reference made to *Meroni*; cf Koenig et al. 230f.

42   Article 47 para 1 ECSCT.

43   *Barge* 259.

44   *Macchiorlati Dalmas* 54.

45   The composition of the Administrative Commission – which, under the new name Administrative Commission for the Coordination of Social Security Systems, still exists today – was quite similar to today's regulatory agencies: one representative per MS, assisted, where necessary, by expert advisors. One representative of the Commission in an advisory capacity was allowed to attend the meetings; see Article 80 para 1 of Council Regulation 1408/71. The Administrative Commission, however, was (is) neither organisationally nor functionally independent from the Commission (Article 80 para 4 *leg cit*) and can therefore not be added to the group of European agencies.

46   Article 81 lit a of Council Regulation 1408/71.

Commission could adopt certain interpretations of (then) Community law, which were binding for social security institutions responsible for applying Community law in this field. The Administrative Commission itself, and arguably also the MS, considered its interpretations to be binding.[47] The Court held that a body such as the Administrative Commission 'may not be empowered by the Council to adopt acts having the force of law'.[48] Since the case at issue deals with output having a general scope, we can conclude that the Court wanted to preclude a delegation of 'rule-making' powers. The Court did not address the conferral of individual decision-making power, nor did it say anything about the threshold regarding delegated discretion.[49]

The bodies at issue in *Meroni* and the following cases set within the ECSCT scrap equalisation system are private bodies[50] empowered by the High Authority, whereas European agencies are, first, bodies established under Community/Union law and, second, empowered by the legislator.[51] *Romano* is about a Community body on which the legislator has conferred powers and therefore appears to be more pivotal in some respects.[52] That *Meroni* is applicable also to relations between Community bodies was made clear in the more recent case *Alliance for Natural Health*, in which the Court referred to *Meroni* in the context of implementing powers delegated to the Commission. On the substance of the doctrine, however, the Court merely reiterated that the delegator (in this case: the legislator) must ensure 'that that power [the Commission's power to adopt implementing acts] is clearly defined and that the exercise of the power is subject to strict review in the light of objective criteria'.[53] Also in the *Tralli* case – where the delegation of powers within the organisation of the ECB was at issue – the Court referred to *Meroni*, stating that if it is possible (within limits) that a Community body delegates powers to private entities, *a fortiori* this must be true for in-house delegations within a Community body. The Court added that only 'clearly defined executive powers' could be delegated by an 'express decision', and requirements such as stating the reasons of and publishing a decision in a certain way could not be waived.[54] Although the Court has made reference to *Meroni* only in a few cases, a review of this jurisprudence shows that: first, the preclusion of a delegation of wide discretionary powers has – as a principle – never been

---

47 See Priebe 40 with further references.
48 *Romano*, para 20. It is surprising that also in this case the ECJ did not make reference to *Meroni*, nor did it use the term 'delegation' or 'delegate'.
49 See also Chamon 1064.
50 On the delegation of powers to private bodies by the Commission see also *International Film*, paras 52f.
51 Cf Pawlik 158–160 with further references.
52 See Griller and Orator, Everything 3, who claim *Meroni* to be a landmark decision also and especially for executive agencies.
53 *Alliance for Natural Health*, para 90.
54 *Tralli*, paras 42f.

questioned by the Court;[55] second, this principle has been applied to very different examples of delegations of powers, thereby extending the scope of the doctrine.

6.   The *Meroni* doctrine and the rise of European agencies

In the years after *Meroni* the Commission as well as the Council were very cautious of delegating powers[56] to bodies not established under Community law as well as to Community bodies.[57] The refusal of delegations of wide powers was also backed by the then prevailing view in legal literature.[58]

In the early 1970s, however, this 'climate of non-delegation' slowly gave way to more institutional openness.[59] This openness finds its expression in various legislative proposals by the Commission that envisage a delegation of preparatory and implementing powers by the Council to other bodies, including bodies not established under Community law.[60] Nevertheless, the political actors were eager not to strain *Meroni*.[61] The two agencies founded in the 1970s – Cedefop and EUROFOUND – were not vested with strong competences and intended only to have a 'soft policy-making impetus'.[62] In the aftermath of the Commission White Paper 'Completing the Internal Market'[63] launched in 1985, at the beginning of the presidency of *Jacques Delors*, a plethora of new legislation was adopted.[64] The completion of the internal market was planned for 1992, but also after the entry into force of the Treaty of Maastricht in 1993 internal market legislation was launched – not least due to new competences of the EC. For the implementation of all this new legislation a number of agencies were established in the 1990s and the years 2000 – partly with far-reaching competences. *Meroni* was – at least

---

55   Cf Priebe 114, who, at the end of the 1970s, anticipated otherwise, namely that the ECJ will not maintain its strict case law as regards delegation.

56   See ibid. 34f with further references. According to *Ehlermann*, some members of the Commission's bureaucracy even deemed such delegation to be 'heresy' [*Ketzerei*]; Ehlermann, Errichtung 198. For a more recent analysis of the institutions' attitude towards *Meroni* see Kühling 129.

57   For the Council's wariness in the context of the establishment of comitology committees in the 1960s see Morand 212. For the blunt approach proposed by the French government see Bradley, Comitology 706.

58   See Ehlermann, Probleme 259 with further references; Chiti, Part 1421f.

59   See Kreher 228.

60   See Ehlermann, Errichtung 199f with examples; see also Priebe 42ff. The Administrative Commission at issue in *Romano* (established in 1971) serves as an early example of a conferral of powers to a (new) Community body.

61   Cf Bradley, Comitology 698.

62   Everson and Majone 76.

63   Commission, COM (85) 310 final.

64   About 300 legislative acts had been launched in the frame of *Delors'* internal market programme; see Tallberg, Paths 629.

implicitly – referred to by the Commission,[65] but not applied as strictly as it used to be.[66] The MS followed more or less willingly.[67]

But it was not only the internal market programme of the *Delors* Commission that lead to a more liberal interpretation of *Meroni* by the Commission, the Council and – with its legislative powers increasing since the entry into force of the SEA 1987 – the EP, and consequently to the E(E)C's/EU's gradual agencification. Later supposedly it was the 'continuous loss of prestige and influence'[68] of the Commission – the peak of which constituted the resignation of the *Santer* Commission in 1999 – and the confidence crisis of comitology in the second half of the 1990s that politically facilitated the delegation of powers to European agencies.[69] As will be elaborated later in this work, at that time European agencies had been conceptualised as an alternative, if not counterpart, to what was often referred to as the 'jungle of committees' within comitology.[70] While earlier comitology was perceived as an apt means of MS control of the Commission exercising implementing powers,[71] it has lost credibility due to the seemingly unfettered growth of committees[72] and above all due to the role it played in the BSE affair.[73] It is the fervent claims for more openness, transparency and visibility – evidently overlapping terms[74] – uttered as a result of the perceived lack of institutional legitimacy in the EC/EU of the late 1990s that had their share in facilitating the further agencification and in influencing the current appearance of European agencies.[75]

Today the relevant decision-makers are divided in a 'pro-delegation faction' and an 'anti-delegation faction' (traditionally the MS and the Commission's

---

65   See eg Commission, COM (2001) 428, 24; COM (2008) 135 final, 5.

66   See Majone, Dilemmas 92f; *Pawlik*, on the contrary, claims that the Commission has stuck to *Meroni* consistently; see Pawlik 152.

67   MS tended to perceive agencies as competitors of their respective national authorities; see Fleischer 222. However, there was 'no declared opposition' to the setting up of agencies; Curtin and Dehousse 194.

68   Majone, Dilemmas 92.

69   See Dawson 209–210; Joerges 27f; Yataganas, Delegation 34–36; critically, Harlow 67.

70   Craig, EU (#2) 178; Majone, Delegation 330. Critical as to whether the assumed move away from the Commission towards European agencies will be successful: Shapiro, Problems 291.

71   For the judicial approval in the 1970s and the development of comitology from the mid-1980s see Craig, EU (#2) 114–119.

72   See Savino 3.

73   See Everson, Agencies 128.

74   Cf Alemanno, Principle.

75   For the paradigm shift in public governance see eg Commission, COM (2001) 428, for the five principles of 'good governance' – openness, participation, effectiveness, accountability, coherence – see ibid. 10; on the background of 'new governance' in the EU since the late 1990s see Dawson 209–211.

Legal Service[76]), the former apparently being on the rise.[77] *Pro* or *anti* delegation is not only a legal question, a matter of different interpretations of the ECJ's case law. These positions are also taken in a struggle for power: while parts[78] of the Commission staff principally are against delegation for fear of loss of power,[79] MS by trend want to protect their national bureaucracies' influence.[80]

Meroni is the first decision of the ECJ that deals in some detail with the topic 'transferral of powers'.[81] It does, beyond doubt, deal with the key factor of agencification, ie the outer limits of delegation, and the required supervision of the delegate by the delegator.[82] But neither does it provide guidance on how a presumptive delegate should be organised (internal structure) nor does it sufficiently address the issue of accountability to the delegator. Also with regard to the limits of delegation, *Meroni* is rather vague.

7.   The *Meroni* doctrine revisited: the *ESMA* case

The development of the *Meroni* doctrine has reached a new stage with the ECJ's decision in the so-called *ESMA* case. In this case, the Court had to decide on the conformity with EU law of Article 28 of Regulation 236/2012. This provision allows the ESMA 'in exceptional circumstances' a) to impose duties of notification or disclosure on persons who have net short positions in relation to certain financial instruments and b) to prohibit, or impose conditions on, the entry by a person into a short sale or transaction that creates, or relates to, a [certain] financial instrument' (Article 28 para 1 lit b). The ESMA may only take such a decision if it 'address[es] a threat to the orderly functioning and integrity of financial markets or to the stability of the whole or part of the financial system' in the EU and if there are cross-border implications. Such a decision is only allowed if – cumulatively – 'no competent authority has taken measures to address the threat' or only measures have been taken that 'do not adequately address the threat' (para 2 lit a and b). In addition to that, the ESMA has to take into account that the decision 'significantly addresses the threat' or 'significantly improves' the ability of the competent authorities to monitor the threat (para 3 lit a), that it 'does not create a risk of regulatory arbitrage' (lit b) and that it 'does not have a detrimental effect on the efficiency of financial markets ... that is disproportionate

---

76   Majone, Delegation 330 and 334; Yataganas, Delegation 25 with reference to a memorandum of the Commission's Legal Service.

77   A number of scholars have argued in favour of a relativisation of the (old) *Meroni* doctrine; see references in Pawlik 156 (footnote 776).

78   For the parts in favour of delegating powers to European agencies see Majone, Dilemmas 92.

79   See Pawlik 152f.

80   See Fleischer 222.

81   Cf Chiti, Part 1421f; cf Commission, COM (2001) 428, 24.

82   Critical with regard to the applicability of *Meroni* in its entirety to the case of European agencies: Yataganas, Delegation 27; Majone, Dilemmas 89.

to the benefits of the [decision]' (lit c). The paragraphs 4–11 stipulate procedural requirements (consultation, notification, publication, review and effect of the decision), which shall not be discussed here.

The UK antagonised this 'loaded gun'[83] of the ESMA, basing its action on different legal arguments. In this context, the discussion shall be limited to the argument that Article 28 infringes the ECJ's case law as expressed in *Meroni* and *Romano*. This is, the UK argues, because para 2 'entails "a very large measure of discretion"'[84] and because paragraph 1 grants the ESMA 'a wide range of choices as to which measure or measures to impose', which may have 'very significant economic and financial policy implications'.[85] It adds that ESMA decisions according to this provision 'will require an analysis of the significant economic policy implications ... which, in turn, have long-term consequences as to general overall confidence in the markets. These are "unquantifiable ... judgements" and cannot be categorised as decisions made on the basis of set criteria amenable to objective review'.[86]

First of all, the Court in its judgement confirms (again[87]) that *Meroni* is applicable also in case of a conferral of powers from the legislator to an EU body.[88] Furthermore it declares that the ESMA's competences according to Article 28 are 'precisely delineated and amenable to judicial review'[89] and that the legislator has delegated no discretion conflicting with *Meroni*.[90] *Ad Romano* it held that the Treaty of Lisbon, and in particular Article 263 para 1 and Article 277 TFEU, has created a new 'institutional framework' that 'expressly permits Union bodies, offices and agencies to adopt acts of general application'.[91]

It is not the purpose of this sub-chapter to critically discuss the judgement in detail.[92] It shall be examined only with regard to its ramifications for the ECJ's case law on the conferral of powers, in particular the *Meroni* doctrine – or should it be called 'ESMA doctrine'[93] now? According to the Court, the Lisbon Treaty has newly weighed the institutional balance of the EU. Article

---

83   Adamski 825.
84   *ESMA*, para 28. This is, as the inverted commas in the judgement make clear, the wording of the applicant, the UK. In para 54 of the judgement the Court quotes these words again; see, on the contrary, *Bergström*, who claims these to be the Court's own words: System 240.
85   *ESMA*, para 30. With regard to the lacking involvement of MS authorities or the Commission in the procedures laid down in Article 28 *leg cit* see Adamski 825.
86   *ESMA*, para 31.
87   *Alliance for Natural Health*.
88   *ESMA*, paras 43 and 66.
89   Ibid., para 53.
90   Ibid., para 54.
91   Ibid., para 65.
92   Such a critical analysis can be found elsewhere. See eg Adamski; Babis, Power; Marjosola, Gap; Weismann, Neues; on the Opinion of AG *Jääskinen* see Marjosola, Case; Orator, Zulässigkeit.
93   Adamski 812.

277 TFEU – the re-drafted successor of Article 241 TEC – seems to refer to the possibility of bodies, offices or agencies of the EU to adopt acts of a general application. However, the Court does not answer the question where in EU primary law such a competence is based. Article 277 does acknowledge, but does not establish it. The Court also refers to Article 263 TFEU[94] in this context, which in its para 1 only states that bodies, offices or agencies of the EU may adopt acts 'intended to produce legal effects *vis-à-vis* third parties'. From the wording of this provision it is unclear whether it refers to individual decisions only or whether it also includes acts of a general scope.[95] Hence the only provision hinting at the possibility to delegate to bodies, offices or agencies of the EU the power to adopt decisions of a general scope is Article 277.[96] In that sense, the Court has made 'painfully clear' that a solid legal basis for an agency's rule-making power is missing.[97] As regards the latitude granted to the ESMA in its decision-making, the Court states that the exercise of the powers under Article 28 'is circumscribed by various conditions and criteria which limit ESMA's discretion'.[98] From the facts a) that the ESMA has to 'examine a significant number of factors' set out in Article 28 paras 2 and 3, b) that the powers at issue are laid down in principle already in Article 9 para 5 of the ESMA-Regulation[99] and c) that ESMA has to meet consultation and notification requirements and that the decisions are of a 'temporary nature' only,[100] the Court deduces that the powers 'comply with the requirements laid down in *Meroni v High Authority*'.[101] Hence the Court, while stressing the continuity of its case law, deviates considerably from the old *Meroni* decision: judicial activism camouflaged as *stare decisis*, as it were.

As a concluding remark we can state the following: the cautiousness of the Commission and the legislator to delegate powers has turned out to be unnecessary essentially in two ways. First, the Court appears not to apply *Meroni's* prohibition of delegating wide discretionary powers too strictly – or put more bluntly: '[i]t turns the *Meroni* doctrine upside down'.[102] A Regulation allowing a European agency to weigh different (economic) interests, which are listed in the respective legal basis, seems to be lawful for

---

94   *ESMA*, paras 65 and 80.
95   Even after Lisbon, however, it was deemed unlawful in the literature to delegate rule-making powers to European agencies; cf Craig, EU (#2) 150f on (only) quasi-regulatory agencies.
96   Critically, Weismann, Neues 125.
97   van Gestel 195; see Michel, Gleichgewicht 114-116, who argues that Articles 290f TFEU cannot serve as legal bases for the conferral of external decision-making powers on European agencies, but that these provisions do not exclude such a conferral, either.
98   *ESMA*, para 45.
99   In a different context the Commission seems to argue that Article 9 para 5 does not (yet) constitute a 'self-standing empowerment'; Commission, COM (2014) 509 final, 9; in the same vein: Parliament, Review 105f.
100   *ESMA*, para 48–50.
101   Ibid., para 53.
102   Adamski 827.

the Court.[103] This 're-confirms the view that the Court will be very reluctant to strike down mechanisms put in place to safeguard financial stability'.[104] Second, the Court in principle permits a conferral of rule-making powers to European agencies.[105] This, the Court claims, is due to the entry into force of the Treaty of Lisbon on 1 December 2009, which lets the institutional framework of the EU appear in a modified shape.

II. COMITOLOGY – A FORESHADOWING OF AGENCIFICATION?

1. The development of comitology over time

Comitology[106] describes a system of committees mainly composed of MS representatives[107] set up to control the Commission when exercising its implementing powers. These powers are conferred on the Commission by the legislator when it comes to establishing the more 'technical' details of a piece of legislation[108] – a task which the Council (later: together with the EP), a group of politicians rather than experts, in the course of the long-winded legislative procedures seems unfit to perform.[109] Starting in the early 1960s in

---

103 See already *de Alquitranes* [2013], paras 76 and 115, in which the General Court acknowledges the ECHA's 'broad discretion in a sphere which entails political, economic and social choices on its part, and in which it is called upon to undertake complex assessments'. On the ECHA's powers with regard to the assessment of substances see Pawlik 93f.

104 Babis, Power 269 with reference to the ECJ's *Pringle* judgement.

105 See case *de Alquitranes* [2013], para 58, which deals with 'a regulatory act within the meaning of the fourth paragraph of Article 263 TFEU' rendered by the ECHA. It ought to be noted that the REACH system was introduced in 2007, that is to say prior to the entry into force of the Lisbon Treaty.

106 There have been myriad committees established by the Council, the Council and the Parliament, or the Commission, in the history of the ECs and the EU. In this chapter, however, I shall concentrate on those committees that are set up by a legal act adopted by the legislator and need to be consulted compulsorily by the Commission (comitology committees); see Vos, Rise 212; Ilgner 109f. On different categories of committees in the EU see Harcourt 10; Weiß 50. On the ECJ's adoption of the term 'comitology' in the late 80s see Ilgner, 109f (footnote 479).

107 The MS may compose their respective delegations of representatives of different interest groups (*Länder*, industry, employees, etc.). For the example of Germany see Töller 271f. For the composition of committees consulting the comitology committees see Hustedt et al. 123 with further references.

108 Nevertheless, implementing acts of the Commission can have quite a real-life impact. On impact assessments undertaken (also) with regard to Commission implementing acts see Alemanno and Meuwese; for the actual impact assessment reports see <http://ec.europa.eu/smart-regulation/impact/ia_carried_out/cia_2015_en.htm>; see also Daiber.

109 Critical with regard to this functionalist explanation Blom-Hansen, Origins 208f. However, it ought to be noted that under Article 291 TFEU (still) also the Council may be vested with implementing powers (without being controlled by committees, though).

the field of CAP,[110] the scope of comitology has gradually been extended to all policy fields in which – on the level of the details – 'technical' regulation and/or ongoing adaptation of rules in the respective market segments was required. The comitology system – soon a pivotal tool in the implementation of policies – has become a 'standard feature attached to the delegation of power to the Commission'.[111] It has allowed for political controversies between the Commission and the Council and, later, the EP, but also between single MS,[112] to be solved more swiftly in the course of 'proxy wars' between experts from the national bureaucracies in the committees (referred to by some as 'small Councils'[113]), and has served the purpose of limiting the Commission's influence on the implementation of policies.[114]

The legality of the management committee procedure, the original procedure[115] used in the field of CAP in the 60s and 70s, was confirmed by the ECJ in a number of cases, the first of them being the *Chemiefarma* case,[116] followed by the better-known *Köster* case.[117] The central Treaty provision in this context was Article 155 TEEC that – '[i]n order to ensure the proper functioning and development of the common market' – required the Commission to 'exercise the powers conferred on it by the Council for the implementation of the rules laid down by the latter'. The ECJ stated that the Council, when conferring powers on the Commission according to Article 155 TEEC, has to provide 'detailed rules to which the Commission is subject in exercising the power conferred on it'. The management committee procedure, according to the Court, met this threshold laid down in Article 155 TEEC. With respect to the powers of the management committee, it held that:

> [t]he function of the management committee is to ensure permanent consultation in order to guide the Commission in the exercise of the powers conferred on it by the Council and to enable the latter to substitute its own action for that of the Commission. The management committee does not therefore have the power to take a decision in place of the Commission or the Council. Consequently, without distorting the Community structure and the institutional balance, the management

---

110 For an overview of the development and the role of comitology in the CAP see Blom-Hansen, Origins 213-218; Hustedt et al. 131–134.

111 Craig, EU (#2) 113.

112 See ibid.

113 Eg by Falke 331; see also references in Blom-Hansen, EU 612.

114 See eg Craig, Institutions 64; Harlow 67; cf Ehlermann, Errichtung 198.

115 For the variety of different proposals made and the power struggles between Council, Commission and MS in the late 50s and early 60s see Bergström, Comitology 46ff; for the two variants of the management procedure see Ilgner 117.

116 *Chemiefarma*, in particular paras 61f.

117 *Köster* (see also summary and analysis of this case by Scheunig), followed by *Rey Soda* and *Tedeschi*; cf Bergström, Comitology 139.

committee machinery enables the Council to delegate to the Commission an implementing power of appreciable scope, subject to its power to take the decision itself if necessary.[118]

In 1968 in the field of the emerging CCP the regulatory committee procedure was introduced.[119] The new committee procedure, which was initially referred to as the 'legislative committee procedure' by the Commission, was applied in the context of more general and permanent implementing rules.[120] Contrary to the management procedure in which 'no negative opinion' sufficed, in the regulatory procedure a positive opinion of the committee was required for the Commission to adopt the implementing measure. If the opinion was negative or if no opinion was adopted, the Commission had to turn to the Council, which decided with a qualified majority.[121] Now it could happen that the Council – in intricate and/or politically sensitive matters – did not manage to take a decision on the committee proposal in due time. In this case the Commission was originally allowed to adopt the measure as proposed (*filet*; safety net). Soon another safety net – this time for the Council – was introduced. In the case, for example, of the Standing Veterinary Committee the procedure provided for the Council to prevent the Commission from proceeding as proposed according to the *filet*. It could do so by a simple majority of its votes (*contre-filet*).[122] In terms of numbers, the regulatory committee procedure can certainly be called a success story. From only six in 1970 the number of committees rose to 41 within a decade.[123]

As a result of this constant struggle between the Council (as representative of the MS) and the Commission, comitology had become an intricate system with various procedures, rules and exceptions – the famous 'jungle of comitology' or – more polemically – 'a nightmare for European studies students'.[124] The Comitology Decision[125] of 1987 was a first attempt to systematise and to simplify the rules by limiting the myriad committee

---

118　*Köster*, para 9.
119　See eg Council Regulation 802/68/EEC; Bergström, Comitology 83; Craig, EU (#2) 113f.
120　Bergström, Comitology 85.
121　See eg Article 14 para 3 of Council Regulation 802/1968/EEC.
122　For an account of the *filet* and the *contre-filet* in comitology see, for instance, Bergström, Comitology 87f; Craig, EU (#2) 113f; Vos, EU 25; Commission, SEC (90) 2589 final, 7; House of Lords, Delegation, para 34.
123　See Bergström, Comitology 141 with further references. For the purpose of comparison see Commission, COM (2007) 842 final, 6, according to which the number of committees rose from 250 in 2005 to 277 in 2006.
124　EU Presidency.
125　Council Decision 87/373/EEC. Article 145 TEEC as amended by the SEA – third indent – now served as the prime legal basis for comitology. It strengthened the Commission's position by emphasising that the Council *should* entrust the Commission with implementing powers; see *Commission v Council*, para 10; cf Article 291 para 3 TFEU. See Bergström, Comitology 189ff; Bradley, Comitology 720; Steunenberg et al. 37ff.

procedures to four: the advisory, the management, the regulatory and the safeguard committee procedure.

The EP, which in the late 80s and early 90s – cooperation 1987, co-decision 1993 – generally appeared to be on the rise against the background of the emerging 'democratic deficit' discussion,[126] had been neglected in the comitology system. Its struggle to gain influence in this important decision-making regime took place on many different levels, even on the Court level.[127] While the Parliament's endeavour to outlaw the then current practice of comitology was in vain, the *Modus Vivendi* of 1994 clearly appears as a stage win for the Parliament. This political agreement between the Parliament, the Council, and the Commission provides that – where the basic act was adopted by co-decision – the 'appropriate committee of the European Parliament shall be sent, at the same time and under the same conditions as the [respective comitology] committee ..., any draft general implementing act submitted by the Commission and the timetable for it'.[128] It also provides that '[t]he Council shall adopt a draft general implementing act which has been referred to it in accordance with an implementing procedure' only after it has informed and asked the EP for its opinion within a certain deadline, and, 'in the event of an unfavourable opinion, taking due account of the European Parliament's point of view without delay, in order to seek a solution in the appropriate framework'.[129] The three institutions furthermore agreed that comitology shall be re-considered in the course of the next Treaty revision, which was then planned for 1996.[130] This 'next Treaty revision' is known as the Treaty of Amsterdam, which surprisingly left untouched the wording of the legal basis of comitology, ie Article 145 (renumbered Article 202) TEC. The creation of a new comitology system was now up to the legislator. The Commission elaborated a proposal for a new Comitology Decision and submitted it to the Council and the EP for discussion. At the end of a long-winded and wearing political skirmish the details of which can be neglected here,[131] there was a new Comitology Decision.[132] *Comitology II* simplified the most important procedures,[133] which is to say the management and the regulatory committee procedure, mainly by abolishing its variants, and strengthened the EP's position in the latter.[134] The EP could not, however, push through a complete

126   For an account of the democratic deficit discussion in the EU see, for example, Dehousse, Reform 121ff; Weiler et al., 32f;

127   See, for example, *European Parliament v Council* [1997]; see also Craig, EU (#2) 117f; Hustedt et al. 107f. For a brief summary of the EP's struggle to gain influence in comitology from the mid-1980s onwards see House of Lords, Delegation, paras 38ff.

128   Modus Vivendi, para 4; see Ilgner 123–125.

129   Modus Vivendi, para 5.

130   Ibid., para 3.

131   For the EP's arguments see *Aglietta* Report; for a thorough account of the political debate preceding *Comitology II* see Bergström, Comitology 247ff.

132   *Comitology II*. See Vos, EU 23ff.

133   On the 'strictness' of the single procedures see Blom-Hansen, EU 610.

134   Article 5 para 5 of *Comitology II* .

elimination of the much disliked regulatory procedure.[135] In another attempt to pacify the EP's longing for influence, *Comitology II* was amended in 2006.[136] The main novelty of this amendment was the introduction of the 'regulatory procedure with scrutiny',[137] which allowed for enhanced control by the EP – though not on an equal footing with the Council[138] – of acts implementing legislation which was adopted by co-decision. This amendment fulfilled one of the main demands of the EP[139] and therefore did a good job in pouring oil on troubled water.[140]

With the Treaty of Lisbon, the implementation (in a wider sense) of Union law by the Council was re-structured profoundly. The Lisbon Treaty differentiates between delegated acts and implementing acts. By means of delegated acts the Commission 'supplement[s] or amend[s] certain non-essential elements of [a] legislative act' (Article 290 para 1 TFEU) under the direct control of the Council and the EP. Implementing acts, on the contrary, serve the purpose of creating 'uniform conditions for implementing legally binding Union acts' (Article 291 para 2 TFEU). The power to adopt implementing acts may be conferred on the Commission or – exceptionally – the Council. Here the Commission is not controlled by the legislator, but by the pertinent comitology committee. Prior to Lisbon, the Commission was subject to comitology control also when adopting acts supplementing or amending non-essential parts of legislative acts. By introducing a new category of 'delegated acts', in the adoption of which the Commission is controlled (only) by the Council and the EP, the masters of the Treaty have considerably reduced the scope of comitology.[141]

As regards the comitology procedures, the legislator decided to reconsider and simplify them once again. With Regulation 182/2011, adopted under Article 291 para 3 TFEU, the legislator – for the first time Council and EP together – has adopted a new comitology regime. *Comitology III* limits the number of procedures to two: the advisory procedure (Article 4) and the examination procedure (Article 5). Furthermore it establishes an appeal committee to which the Commission may refer in case the committee has delivered a negative opinion.[142] The referral to the appeal committee[143] replaces the referral to the Council which in return – and next to the EP – gets

---

135   See House of Lords, Delegation, paras 85f.
136   Council Decision 2006/512/EC; see Bradley, House 837; Schusterschitz and Kotz.
137   This procedure is described in some detail in Kaeding and Hardacre 384–386.
138   See Ilgner 138.
139   See Commission, COM (2007) 842 final 2.
140   See Roller; Wolfram; critically, N Raschauer, Strukturprobleme 317; von Danwitz 634, who claims there to be a democratic deficit through a lack of parliamentary legitimation.
141   See Hustedt et al. 109f with further references.
142   Article 5 para 4 of *Comitology III*. The appeal committee was not envisaged in the original Commission proposal, but was suggested and incorporated by the Parliament in the course of the legislative procedure leading to the adoption of *Comitology III*.
143   See, as an illustrative example in this context, *Laboratoires CTRS*, in which both the committee and the appeal committee issued a negative opinion on the Commission's draft implementing act. The Commission re-drafted the act and sent it to the committee again.

a right to scrutiny:[144] In case a draft implementing act exceeds the Commission's implementing powers provided for in the basic act, the Council and/or the Parliament may indicate this to the Commission. The Commission 'shall review the draft implementing act, taking account of the positions expressed'.[145] If it maintains the act, however, the only remedy for the Council and the EP is an action according to Article 263 TFEU.[146]

2.   The procedures

As was sketched above, there have been a considerable number of different procedures in the history of comitology.[147] Suffice it here to present the two main procedures[148] provided for under the current regime, *Comitology III*.

2.1   *Advisory procedure*

As its name suggests, in this procedure – which was in use already prior to *Comitology III*[149] – the Commission is not obliged to follow the committee's opinion on the draft implementing measure, it merely has to take 'the utmost account of the conclusions drawn from the discussions within the committee and of the opinion'.[150] Only a simple majority (one vote per MS) is required in the committee for there to be an opinion.[151] Since the influence of the MS is – due to the non-bindingness of the committee opinion – limited, this procedure has been used for issues with little political relevance, for example the awarding of small funds or grants.[152] That it shall apply 'as a general rule' for implementing acts not falling within the ambit of the examination procedure[153] does not increase its importance. This is because the ambit of the examination procedure laid down in Article 2 para 2 of *Comitology III* is worded widely and more than that is not exhaustive (arg 'in particular'). And although there is room for extension of its scope in 'duly justified cases'[154] to

---

144   See Berrisch et al.
145   Article 11 of *Comitology III*.
146   See Ilgner 243 with further references.
147   For some of the procedures applied earlier see Ballmann et al. 557–560.
148   Critical with regard to the alleged simplification brought about by *Comitology III*: Christiansen and Dobbels 47f.
149   See Ilgner 126.
150   Article 4 para 2 of *Comitology III*.
151   In general and regardless of the procedure applied, committees strive for consensus – which they usually reach. It is only in exceptional (politically contested) cases that a consensus cannot be reached; see Hustedt et al. 112. With regard to the advisory procedure this striving for consensus is also reflected in the wording of Article 4 para 1 of *Comitology III*: '[T]he committee shall deliver its opinion, *if necessary by taking a vote*' (emphasis added). A differentiated view on the reasons for and the frequency of consensual decisions in comitology committees is taken by Dehousse et al. 849–851.
152   See Hardacre and Kaeding 8.
153   Article 2 para 3 of *Comitology III*.
154   The malleability of the term 'duly justified' can only be hinted at here. For a critical account of this provision see Craig, Acts 678.

fields in which normally the examination procedure would apply,[155] the meaning of the advisory procedure remains very limited.[156]

2.2   *Examination procedure*

In this procedure, the scope of which is set out in Article 2 para 2 of *Comitology III*,[157] the committee may deliver an opinion on a draft implementing act with a qualified majority as applied in the Council.[158] If it is a positive opinion, the Commission shall adopt the measure.[159] If it is negative the Commission shall not adopt the draft measure, but may submit an amended version thereof to the same committee within two months or submit the original draft to the appeal committee within one month. The appeal committee adopts its opinions by qualified majority, as well.[160] Any of its members can suggest amendments to the draft measure until an opinion is delivered.[161] The composition of the appeal committee is not specified in the Comitology Regulation. According to the Commission's website, however, they are composed like comitology committees[162] – ie of representatives of the national bureaucracies and chaired by a Commission representative – but 'at a higher level of representation', which means of higher professional rank.[163]

In case the committee fails to render an opinion, the Commission may adopt the measure, unless a) the measure concerns taxation, financial services, the protection of the health or safety of humans, animals or plants or definitive multilateral safeguard measures; b) the basic act does not so provide; or c) a simple majority of the component members of the committee opposes it.[164] In these cases, the Commission may proceed as with a negative opinion, ie amend the draft or approach the appeal committee.[165]

---

155   Article 2 para 3 of *Comitology III*.
156   This statement can be underpinned quantitatively: out of 302 comitology committees in 2013 only 25 were advisory committees; see Commission, COM (2014) 572 final 6.
157   For the possibility of the advisory procedure to be applied also within the ambit of the examination procedure see above.
158   *Comitology III* in its Article 5 para 1 refers to Article 16 paras 4f TEU (and Article 238 para 3 TFEU). For the new voting mode applying since 1 November 2014 and the transitional rules in place until 31 March 2017 see Article 3 of the Protocol on Transitional Provisions (Protocol No 36).
159   See *Laboratoires CTRS*, paras 2–8, according to which the Commission did not act in accordance with the opinions of the committee, and the appeal committee, respectively.
160   Article 6 para 1 of *Comitology III*.
161   Article 6 para 2 of *Comitology III*.
162   See also Ilgner 241.
163   <http://ec.europa.eu/dgs/health_food-safety/dgs_consultations/regulatory_com mittees_en.htm>.
164   Article 5 para 4 lit a–c of *Comitology III*. For the derogating procedure in the case of adoption of draft definitive anti-dumping or countervailing measures see Article 5 para 5 *leg cit*; for the consequences of this threshold see Daiber 245f.
165   Article 5 para 4 subpara 3 of *Comitology III*.

As mentioned above: Where the basic act was adopted by co-decision, the EP or the Council may at any time indicate to the Commission that a certain draft implementing act exceeds the implementing powers provided for in the basic act. The Commission then has to review the act considering the viewpoints of the EP and/or the Council, and inform them whether it intends to maintain, amend or withdraw the act at issue.[166]

According to Article 7 of *Comitology III* the adoption of implementing measures in 'exceptional cases' allows for the Commission to adopt a draft implementing act (where the functioning of the agricultural market or the financial interests of the EU within the meaning of Article 325 TFEU[167] are at risk) without prior assessment by a committee. In such cases the Commission shall submit the – already adopted – measure to the appeal committee. Only if the appeal committee delivers a negative opinion, the measure has to be repealed by the Commission. Otherwise it remains in force.

Another 'emergency procedure' is laid down in Article 8. If the legislator so provides in the basic act – the Article 7-procedure requires no such permission[168] – 'on duly justified imperative grounds of urgency' the Commission's implementing act shall enter into force immediately. This provision is envisaged for measures in force only for up to six months, but the basic act may provide otherwise.[169] The measure shall be submitted to the committee at the latest 14 days after its adoption. If its opinion in the examination procedure is negative, the Commission shall repeal the measure immediately,[170] otherwise it remains in force.[171]

3.   Delegated and implementing acts – the new regime

With the entry into force of the Treaty of Lisbon a new classification of what earlier (according to the TEC) could be accommodated under the heading 'implementing powers'[172] was introduced. The TFEU now differentiates between 'delegated acts' (Article 290) and 'implementing acts' (Article 291). From a theoretical point of view the difference between delegated and implementing acts seems coherent. It seeks to clearly separate the competences of the Union on the one hand (delegated acts), and of the MS on the other hand (implementing acts).[173] The previous comitology regimes encompassed

---

166   Article 11 of *Comitology III*.
167   Article 325 TFEU refers to measures to be taken in order to 'counter fraud and any other illegal activities affecting the financial interests of the Union' (para 1).
168   See Daiber 248.
169   Article 8 para 2 of *Comitology III*.
170   Article 8 para 4 of *Comitology III*.
171   For the special rules in case of provisional anti-dumping or countervailing measures (implementing acts) see Article 8 para 5 of *Comitology III*.
172   See Ilgner 21 with further references.
173   See Wolfram 17.

measures of the character of both what is now delegated *and* implementing acts.[174]

Article 290 TFEU provides that 'legislative acts may delegate to the Commission the power to adopt non-legislative acts of general application to supplement or amend certain non-essential elements of the legislative act'.[175] *Supplementation* and *amendment* are overlapping terms, *amendment* being the wider one. The *supplementation* of a legal act always entails an *amendment* thereof.[176] However, supplementations of non-essential elements of a piece of legislation are generally less problematic, since they are less likely to intrude into the will of the legislator – unlike other amendments.[177]

When exercising its delegated powers the Council and the EP control the Commission.[178] While Article 290 has its roots in the old regulatory procedure with scrutiny (*Comitology II*), it does away with comitology within its scope of application.[179]

Comitology lives on in Article 291, which allows the rule-maker to confer implementing powers on the Commission (and in exceptional[180] cases: the Council) by all secondary law, including delegated acts.[181] Principally, it is the MS that are responsible for the implementation of legally binding Union acts. Only where uniform conditions of implementation are needed,[182] the

---

174   Structurally, the new regime with its 'partial abolishment of comitology' [*partielle[]* *Abschaffung der Komitologie*] in the first place serves the Commission at the cost of the MS; see Hustedt et al. 123f with further references; similar with regard to *Comitology III*: Ilgner 238.

175   The ECJ held that these characteristics are the only elements on which the legislator's choice to confer a delegated power on the Commission depends; *Commission v Parliament/Council* [2015], para 32. On the criterion 'essential'/'non-essential' see already *Germany v Commission*, paras 36f.

176   See Kröll 201.

177   Cf Ruffert, Art. 290, para 6. The supplementation can turn out to have a critical effect, nevertheless. This is, for example, the case when a term used in the delegating legislation is defined more closely in a delegated act. If then the delegated act provides a different definition from what was intended by the legislator, it might not be an amendment strictly according to the letter of the law, but works as an amendment, nevertheless. See Craig, Acts 672f; for similar terminological problems in the comitology system see N Raschauer, Strukturprobleme 338f.

178   In the preparation of draft legislative acts in the field of financial services the Commission furthermore continues to consult experts appointed by the MS 'in accordance with its established practice' (cf Declaration No 39). On the exhaustiveness of the legislator's means of control see Kröll 203f.

179   For a comparison of the regulatory procedure with scrutiny and Article 290 see Kaeding and Hardacre 385; Szapiro 109.

180   On the rule-exception (Commission–Council) relationship contained in the first explicit Treaty base of implementing powers, introduced by the SEA, see Ilgner 36f; see also Blom-Hansen, EU 608f.

181   See Nettesheim, Art. 288, para 25f; in the affirmative with regard to recommendations: Ruffert, Art. 291, para 11.

182   On this need of uniform conditions see Kröll 204f.

Commission ought to be entrusted – with comitology set in place as a means of MS' control.[183]

A clear formal differentiation between delegated and implementing acts is hardly possible,[184] not least because the terms 'delegation' and 'implementation' do not entail an opposition. In both cases the power to 'implement' (in a broader sense)[185] legislation is conferred on another body.[186] Nevertheless, the two regimes are meant to be mutually exclusive.[187] Delegated acts amend (as mentioned above, this includes: supplement) non-essential elements of a legislative act, whereas implementing acts do merely concretise[188] the basic act; the line between mere concretisation on the one hand and in particular supplementation on the other hand in certain cases is very difficult to draw.[189] The amount of discretion to be granted to the Commission does not as such speak in favour of either of the two regimes.[190] Delegated acts – in spite of their 'non-legislative' character – are conceptualised in Article 290 as acts of general application,[191] implementing acts, on the contrary, can be adopted in all the legally binding forms laid down in Article 288 TFEU, according to *Nettesheim* also in the form of recommendations and opinions.[192] Also as regards the body entrusted there are differences. With delegated acts this can only be the Commission; as concerns implementing acts this regularly is the Commission, but in certain cases may also be the Council.[193] The Commission is controlled by the legislator when adopting delegated acts (the Council and the EP), when adopting implementing acts the Commission is – by means of comitology – controlled by the MS.

---

183   The Lisbon regime largely has done away with instances of Council control; see Christiansen and Dobbels 44.

184   See Weiß 59 with further references. For the difference and the connection between the *termini technici* 'delegation' and 'implementation' already prior to Lisbon see C Möllers 492ff.

185   For the wide understanding of the term 'implementation' under the TEC see Ilgner 27–30; see also *Commission v Parliament/Council* [2014], paras 35ff.

186   On the change of character of implementing acts (in a wider sense) in the course of decades in a factual perspective see Kaeding and Hardacre 383.

187   See Scharf 21; confirmed by the ECJ in *Commission v Parliament/Council* [2014], para 23.

188   See Ilgner 216.

189   See eg *Parliament v Commission*, para 67; *Commission v Parliament/Council* [2015], paras 20–22.

190   See *Commission v Parliament/Council* [2015], para 32.

191   *Craig*, in spite of the wording of Article 290 TFEU, describes delegated acts as '"legislative" or "quasi-legislative" in nature'; Acts 672.

192   See Nettesheim, Art. 288, para 27.

193   A conferral of implementing powers to European agencies is not provided for in Article 291 TFEU; Kröll 207 with further references; on the contrary, AG *Jääskinen* in his Opinion in *ESMA* (para 86) confirms the possibility of conferring implementing powers on European agencies.

The splitting up of executive acts into delegated and implementing acts – against the backdrop of the *status quo ante* Lisbon – appears artificial and creates, in *Craig*'s view, a 'conundrum'.[194] The predecessor of the Article 290-procedure clearly is the regulatory procedure with scrutiny.[195] The main novelties are the absence of a committee, and the unlimited[196] right of the Council and the EP to oppose a draft measure, the details of which are laid down in a *Common Understanding* on delegated acts.[197]

In legal scholarship the predominant opinion seems to be that the distinction between delegated and implementing acts according to the TFEU is not 'crystal clear', to say the least.[198] In the *Biocides* case[199] the Court had to deal with this distinction, but added little to clarify things. The Commission claimed that while Article 291-measures were 'purely implementing in nature, [the Commission] has quasi-legislative powers under Article 290 TFEU'.[200] The Court requires for Article 290 TFEU to be applied that 'the objectives, content, scope and duration of the delegation of power must be explicitly defined'[201] in the basic act, whereas on the basis of Article 291 TFEU 'the Commission is called on to provide further detail in relation to the content of a legislative act, in order to ensure that it is implemented under uniform conditions in all Member States'.[202] Since these characteristics are merely repeating the wording of Article 290, and Article 291, respectively, they do not seem apt to bring light into the dark. By stating (confirming[203]) that the legislator has discretion whether to confer delegated or implementing power on the Commission under a certain basic act, and that therefore 'judicial review is limited to manifest errors of assessment',[204] the Court avoids a more in-depth analysis of the Lisbon regime.[205] In that sense, the Court 'clarified' little more than that the separation of the two concepts – delegated and implementing acts – in practice is very difficult.

---

194   Craig, Acts 673.
195   See Hardacre and Kaeding 12.
196   Under *Comitology II* as amended in 2006 the Council's and the EP's scrutiny was limited to three reasons: excess of implementing powers; lack of compatibility of the draft measure with the aim or content of the basic act; lack of respect for the principle of subsidiarity or the principle of proportionality.
197   Common Understanding.
198   See eg Craig, Acts 672ff; Dobbels 44; Ilgner 253; Kröll 201f; Scharf 21.
199   *Commission v Parliament/Council* [2014].
200   Ibid., para 22. See also Craig, Acts 672, who – somewhat at odds with the Treaties ('non-legislative acts'), but content-wise certainly more accurate – uses this terminology, as well.
201   Ibid., para 38. On the widespread view that Article 290 TFEU is appropriate when a margin of discretion is left to the Commission (which the Court omitted to deal with) see references in Ritleng 251f.
202   *Commission v Parliament/Council* [2014], para 39.
203   See eg Auswärtiges Amt 126; Craig, Acts 677ff.
204   *Commission v Parliament/Council* [2014], para 40; see also *Commission v Parliament/ Council* [2015], para 28.
205   Critically, Ritleng 252.

4. Comitology today

Whereas comitology has been simplified to some extent by *Comitology III* and reduced considerably by the introduction of the new category of 'delegated acts', Commission implementing powers – the realm of comitology –, far from being 'endangered',[206] remain a respectable part of the EU's regulatory activity. The respective figures circumstantiate this assumption. In 2014 there was a total of 287 comitology committees operating in the EU in policy fields as diverse as Agriculture and Rural Development, Enlargement and Justice, which amounts to a slight decrease compared with 2013 (302).[207] Altogether they have held a total of 733 meetings,[208] which means that on average each committee had 2.69 meetings in 2014. The Commission has adopted 1,563 implementing acts.[209] In 2009 – prior to Lisbon – there were only 266 committees – with 1,839 adopted implementing measures.[210] Measured in terms of numbers, the introduction of the Lisbon regime has not reduced the momentum of comitology. But also apart from that a demise of comitology is not to be expected. The need for uniform conditions for the implementation of legally binding Union acts will continue to exist. The Commission – due to its combination of sufficient resources and legitimacy – will continue to be the best-suited institution to exercise such implementing powers. Under the assumption that the implementation of Union law is first and foremost the MS' task, and that when exercising this task the Commission should be controlled by the MS, comitology – in principle – seems to be without a (viable) alternative.[211] Comitology does not only serve as a means of MS control, but also as a well of information and expertise for the Commission.[212] It is true that European agencies represent a competing regime; they have been vested with the competence to implement Union law by individual decisions and non-binding acts of a general scope already for more than 20 years. Agencies' competences to implement by adopting legal acts of a general scope, however, are very limited so far.[213]

The opaqueness of comitology has long been one of the strongest arguments against this regime. As regards the transparency of the *actual* course of the procedures – not: the procedural rules laid down in the relevant provisions – things have improved in the recent past. In that sense, comitology is not any more the 'jungle' it used to be. With the establishment of the comitology register[214] (online since 2005[215]), any interested person can access

---

206   Szapiro 114.
207   Commission, COM (2015) 418 final, 4.
208   Ibid., 6.
209   Ibid., 7. For further figures and comparisons, see Blom-Hansen, EU 610f and Kaeding and Hardacre.
210   Commission, COM (2014) 572 final, 5 and 7f.
211   See also Ilgner 145.
212   See Gundel, Kompetenzen 32.
213   *de Alquitranes* [2013], para 58; *ESMA*, para 65.
214   Now pursuant to Article 10 para 5 of *Comitology III*.
215   See Harcourt 11.

inter alia a list of committees, the agendas of committee meetings and the voting results, and can thereby, in the words of the Commission, 'trace the different stages of an implementing measure throughout its entire lifecycle'.[216] The documents of the register still can only be accessed by the Council and the Parliament.[217] Some DGs, on a voluntary basis, even publish the minutes of the committee meetings, which previously were supposed to be secret.[218]

By means of this register one cannot track each and every thought of each and every member of a committee, and the names of the participants and their respective voting behaviour is still not required to be disclosed (eg to national parliaments), but it is fair to say that comitology is no longer (if it ever was at all) 'the least transparent policy-making process in the democratic world', as *Shapiro* has pointedly put it.[219]

III.   THE EU'S 'AGENCIFICATION' – INSTITUTIONALISATION, CLASSIFICATION AND CONTINUATION

1.   'Four waves' of the EU's agencification?

On the EU level – it was said – agencies have emerged in waves.[220] There is something to be said for that metaphor, but for the more recent agency foundations it is not adequate any more. Especially in the years after 2000 agencies have rather been established in constant drops than in waves.[221] Let it suffice to quote *Shapiro* who in 2011 said that there has been a 'continuing, indeed increasing, enthusiasm for independent agencies among the shapers of Union institutions'.[222] In the following, a brief chronological summary of the development of agencies shall be provided.[223]

---

216   <http://ec.europa.eu/transparency/regcomitology/index.cfm?CLX=en>. On the development of transparency measures in comitology before Lisbon see Szapiro 92–94.
217   Article 10 para 4 of *Comitology III*; critically Ilgner 246.
218   See Hustedt et al. 125 with reference to the important *Rothmans* case, in particular para 61, which declares the refusal to access the minutes of comitology committees illegal.
219   Shapiro, Problems 291.
220   See Craig, EU (#2) 147; Majone, Europeanization 191; cf Hummer 98ff describing four phases in which 'three generations' of European agencies have emerged.
221   In the years 2001 to 2010 each year at least one agency was established (the years 2003 and 2007/108 being the exception). For the 'European megatrend' [*europäischer Megatrend*] 'agencification' also in the MS see Ruffert, Verwaltungseinheiten 431ff. For a graphic representation of the number of agencies in the EU from 1975 to 2008 see D Curtin, Power 147.
222   Shapiro, Agencies 119.
223   For a non-chronological list of European agencies see Ruffert, Art. 298, para 7. A list of all European agencies currently in place containing data related to seat, tasks and relevant figures is contained in the document 'EU Agencies working for you' (2014) which is accessible online.

The Cedefop,[224] operational in the field of 'vocational training', which was founded in 1975 – at a time when the term 'European agency' was not yet coined by politics and social sciences scholarship[225] – is said to be the first European agency.[226] In the same year another agency was established with the aim of improving living and working conditions: EUROFOUND.[227] Despite the considerable development European agencies have experienced in the ensuing decades, particularly in terms of competences – Cedefop and EUROFOUND must be perceived as merely 'operational or promotional, rather than regulatory, bodies'[228] –, the legislative objectives of these two agencies are paradigmatic for the Community's and now EU's agencification as a whole: the approximation of MS' (soft and hard) rules[229] and the provision of a sound scientific basis for political action,[230] thereby allowing for an adequate stakeholder participation.[231]

After this first wave (or rather: ripple) for the rest of the 70s and throughout the 80s no further agency was established.[232] The so-called second wave[233] was initiated in 1989 by the *Delors* Commission proposing the establishment of the EEA,[234] based on the newly introduced Articles 130r and 130s TEEC (SEA).[235] The core task of this agency, which has been operational since 1993

---

224   Council Regulation 337/75.
225   See Majone, Europeanization 191.
226   In most of the literature Cedefop is referred to as the first agency; see Craig, EU (#2) 145; Kelemen, 115 (footnote 37); see also Commission, COM (2008) 135 final, 4. Another agency-type body of the EC was established already two years earlier: the European Monetary Cooperation Fund. The EMCF was founded in 1973 as a step towards an EMU in the wake of the demise of the *Bretton Woods System*. With its Board of Governors composed of the Governors of the central banks of the MS and no Director or Executive Manager in place it does not perfectly fit within the agency scheme. With the start of the second stage of the EMU by 1 January 1994, the EMCF was liquidated and its tasks were transferred to the newly established European Monetary Institute, which again was succeeded by the ECB on 1 June 1998; see Council Regulation 907/73; see also Ehlermann, Errichtung 193; Gleske 17f; Kenen 5ff.
227   Council Regulation 1365/75.
228   Majone, Europeanization 191.
229   See Recital 3 of Council Regulation 337/75.
230   See Recital 1 of Council Regulation 1365/75.
231   See Recital 4 of Council Regulation 337/75 and Recital 1 of Council Regulation 1365/75.
232   The European Agency of Cooperation, established by Council Regulation 3245/81, which ended its activities in November 1998, can be neglected here since it lacked the agency-typical element of MS representation. Its administrative board was merely composed of Commission staff.
233   The second wave has to be seen in the context of the Commission's aim to have completed the internal market by 1992; for more details see Kelemen and Tarrant 929 with further references; for a different wave scheme see Groenleer 97ff.
234   Council Regulation 1210/90; see now Regulation 401/2009.
235   Cf Sander 16.

only,[236] is to collect and coordinate environmental information.[237] The EEA-Regulation of 1990 in the same year was followed by the ETF, a body whose task it is now 'to contribute, in the context of EU external relations policies, to improving human capital development' in 29 partner countries in Northern Africa and Western and Central Asia.[238] In 1993, the EMCDDA,[239] the EMA (originally named: EMEA)[240] and the OHIM[241] were established. The EMCDDA essentially collects information on drugs and drug abuse at the European level and provides it for the MS. It furthermore offers information of best practice in the MS and facilitates an exchange thereof.[242] Among the EMA's most important tasks is the provision of scientific evaluation in the European marketing authorisation procedure for human and veterinary medicines before the Commission, to monitor the safety of medicines and to facilitate pharmaceutical research.[243] The OHIM manages the Community Trade Mark and Community Design registration system. It is responsible for examination, registration, opposition and cancellation procedures. It was the first European agency with a comprehensive[244] power to render binding decisions *vis-à-vis* third parties.

The year 1994 saw the establishment of three more agencies, namely the EU-OSHA,[245] the CPVO[246] and the CdT.[247] The EU-OSHA, in cooperation with governments, employers and employees, collects information, analyses pertinent scientific research, gives advice and facilitates best practice in order to improve working life in the EU.[248] The CPVO is competent to grant intellectual property rights for plant varieties, which are valid throughout the EU.[249] The establishment of the CdT was an instance of the EU's preparation for the 1995 enlargement. It is competent to do translation work for other Union bodies.

---

236 See Schlögl 177f.
237 For a history of the EEC's environmental policy prior to the establishment of the EEA see G Curtin; on the relative 'modesty' of the EEA see Everson and Joerges 530.
238 Article 1 of Regulation 1339/2008; ETF's webpage <www.etf.europa.eu/web.nsf/pages/Where_we_work>.
239 Regulation 1920/2006.
240 Regulation 726/2004.
241 Council Regulation 207/2009.
242 EMCDDA's webpage <www.emcdda.europa.eu/about/mission>.
243 EMA's webpage <www.ema.europa.eu/ema/index.jsp?curl=pages/about_us/general/general_content_000091.jsp&murl=menus/about_us/about_us.jsp&mid=WC0b01ac058 0028a42>. Critically with regard to the EMA's original organisation, which still rooted in its predecessor comitology committee: Joerges 28. On the EMA's quasi rule-making powers see Dehousse, Politics 20.
244 On the (exceptional) decision-making power of the EM(E)A see Riesz 152; see *Schering-Plough*, paras 22f.
245 Council Regulation 2062/94.
246 Council Regulation 2100/94.
247 Council Regulation 2965/94.
248 EU-OSHA's webpage <http://osha.europa.eu/en/about>.
249 CPVO's webpage <www.cpvo.europa.eu/main/en/home/about-the-cpvo/its-mission>.

In 1997 the EUMC[250] was established, which was succeeded by the FRA by March 2007.[251] The FRA, which was given a wider scope than its predecessor, shall essentially support EU bodies, and MS when implementing Union law, in fundamental rights issues. In 1998 Europol[252] was founded in the field of the then third pillar JHA (later PJCC).[253] It coordinates law enforcement activities of the MS, especially in the fields of illicit drug trafficking, illicit immigration, terrorism, forgery of money, trafficking in human beings and money laundering.[254] The last European agency established in the 90s was the EAR[255] the task of which was to manage the main assistance programmes in the Republic of Serbia, Kosovo, Montenegro and the former Yugoslav Republic of Macedonia.[256] It does not exist any more, since its mandate ended late in 2008.[257]

From 2000 onwards the legislative trend of establishing new agencies has continued and even intensified under the political watchword 'externalisation'.[258] The start was made with the then second pillar agencies EUISS[259] and the EUSC in 2001.[260] While the EUISS is a think tank responsible for research on security issues related to the EU,[261] the EUSC provides products related to an analysis of satellite imagery and collateral data.[262] One year later the legislator founded Eurojust.[263] Eurojust facilitates the coordination of investigations and prosecutions of the competent authorities in the MS and strengthens the cooperation between them and hence is another former third pillar agency.[264]

Thereafter the EFSA was established,[265] whose tasks include the searching, collecting, collating, analysing and summarising of scientific and technical data related to food and feed. In the very same year – 2002 – two more relatively powerful agencies were created: the EMSA[266] whose mission it is '[t]o ensure

250   Council Regulation 1035/97.
251   Article 32 of Council Regulation 168/2007.
252   Council Decision 2009/371/JHA. See now also Article 88 TFEU.
253   On the particularities of former third pillar agencies in a historical perspective see Groenleer 99f.
254   Europol's webpage <www.europol.europa.eu/content/page/mandate-119>.
255   Council Regulation 2454/1999.
256   EAR's webpage <http://ec.europa.eu/enlargement/archives/ear/agency/agency.htm>.
257   Article 1 of Council Regulation 1756/2006.
258   Commission, COM (2000) 788 final; cf Hummer 113ff with further references. This trend has been inspired by the paradigm of New Public Management; see Fleischer 212f; see also Shirvani.
259   Council Decision 2014/75/CFSP. The EUISS is the successor institution of the Western European Union Institute for Security Studies.
260   Council Decision 2014/401/CFSP. The EUSC is the successor institution of the Western European Union Satellite Centre.
261   EUISS's webpage <www.iss.europa.eu/about-us>.
262   EUSC's webpage <www.satcen.europa.eu>.
263   Council Decision 2002/187/JHA.
264   Eurojust's webpage <www.eurojust.europa.eu/Pages/home.aspx>.
265   Regulation 178/2002.
266   Regulation 1406/2002.

a high, uniform and effective level of maritime safety, maritime security, prevention of, and response to, pollution caused by ships as well as response to marine pollution caused by oil and gas installations'[267] and the foundation of which is to be understood as the political reply to the oil spill caused by the average of the oil-tanker *Erika* close to the French shore,[268] and the EASA.[269] The EASA provides scientific advice to the legislator, implements safety rules (including inspections in the MS) and issues certifications of aircraft and components.[270]

In 2004 the ENISA,[271] the ECDC[272] and the ERA[273] followed. The ENISA endeavours to enhance the capability of the EU, its MS, and the business community to 'prevent, address and respond to network and information security problems'.[274] The ECDC's task is to identify, assess and communicate current and emerging threats to human health posed by infectious diseases.[275] The tasks of the ERA encompass, among other things, the facilitation of the cooperation between MS as regards national regulation of railways, the provision of economic evaluations and the promotion of enhanced safety of railways in general.[276]

Another agency established in 2004 is the GSA.[277] The GSA is responsible for security accreditation for European GNSS systems, for the preparation of the commercialisation of the satellite navigation systems and other tasks it is entrusted with according to Article 16 of Regulation 683/2008. In the chronological line of agencies, the GSA is followed by FRONTEX,[278] which has to coordinate and assist in the MS' management of the external borders.[279] Under the former second pillar of the EU the EDA was established.[280]

In 2005 the EFCA (originally CFCA)[281] was founded. It coordinates, supports and supervises control and inspection by the MS in the field of fishing activities.[282] Later this year, in September 2005, CEPOL was established *as a European agency* (in the field of PJCC). It brings together senior police

---

267   EMSA's webpage <www.emsa.europa.eu/about/what-we-do-main/mission-statements. html>.
268   See Hustedt 150.
269   Regulation 216/2008.
270   EASA's webpage <http://easa.europa.eu/the-agency/easa-explained>.
271   Regulation 526/2013.
272   Regulation 851/2004.
273   Regulation 881/2004.
274   ENISA's webpage <www.enisa.europa.eu/about-enisa/activities>.
275   Article 3 of Regulation 851/2004.
276   ERA's webpage <www.era.europa.eu/Core-Activities/Pages/home.aspx>.
277   Regulation 912/2010.
278   Council Regulation 2007/2004.
279   Article 2 *leg cit.*
280   Council Decision 2011/411/CFSP.
281   Council Regulation 768/2005.
282   Article 3 *leg cit.*

officers from all over the EU with a view to fostering cooperation between them.[283]

The year 2006 saw the establishment of two more agencies, namely the ECHA[284] and the EIGE.[285] Whereas the ECHA's task essentially is the evaluation and registration of certain chemicals from all over the EU, the EIGE has to collect, analyse and compare data regarding gender equality and to find ways to support the integration of gender equality into all Union policies.[286]

The ACER,[287] established in July 2009, contributes to the maintenance and monitoring of the internal market in electricity and in natural gas by adopting opinions and recommendations, by facilitating cooperation between national authorities and by adopting individual decisions. The Office, also established in 2009, is tasked with the collection of information, the dissemination of best practices and the support for the BEREC in the field of electronic communications.[288]

In 2010 the EASO[289] was established. Its main tasks are to help to improve the implementation of the Common European Asylum System, and to strengthen the cooperation in asylum affairs between MS.[290] Also in 2010, taking effect on 1 January 2011, three financial market supervisory authorities were established: the EBA,[291] the EIOPA[292] and the ESMA,[293] the organisation and the tasks of which shall be dealt with extensively below.

Finally, the ITA[294] and the SRB[295] are to be mentioned. The ITA's main task is to ensure that various IT systems of the EU operate smoothly – 24 hours a day.[296] The ITA began operations on 1 December 2012. The SRB currently is the youngest of the European agencies. Within the SRM essentially it prepares resolution plans and carries out the resolution of failing banks or banks that are likely to fail (see Chapter 4 III. below).[297] It shall be fully operational from January 2016.

---

283   Council Decision 2005/681/JHA.
284   Regulation 1907/2006.
285   Regulation 1922/2006.
286   Article 3 *leg cit.*
287   Regulation 713/2009.
288   Regulation 1211/2009. The BEREC, on the contrary, is expressly not a European agency (Recital 6 of the founding regulation).
289   Regulation 439/2010.
290   Article 1 *leg cit.*
291   EBA-Regulation.
292   EIOPA-Regulation.
293   ESMA-Regulation.
294   Regulation 1077/2011.
295   SRM-Regulation.
296   <http://ec.europa.eu/dgs/home-affairs/what-we-do/policies/borders-and-visas/agency/index_en.htm>.
297   <http://srb.europa.eu> (mission).

With the EIT,[298] a research institute focusing on topics such as climate change mitigation, sustainable energy and information communication technology,[299] it is questionable whether it is an agency at all. This is due to the fact that its Governing Board is not composed of MS representatives,[300] but of distinguished scientists.[301] This view is supported by the Commission, which opines that the EIT is not an agency but a 'partnership body'.[302]

2.   Common characteristics of European agencies

In the early days of European agencies, that is to say at a time when there were still only a few of them in place in the then Community administrative space, there was no need to classify them. *Connaisseurs* of EU administrative law knew about existence, organisation and tasks of these bodies, and due to their limited number the risk of confusion was low. However, in view of a literal mushrooming of such bodies from the early 1990s onwards, the calls for a taxonomy of European agencies became more and more audible.[303] The umbrella term 'agency' serves as a very rough heading,[304] but does not do justice to the considerable and complex differences regarding organisation and competences between some of these bodies.[305] It was said that 'there is no overarching rationale cutting across agencies'.[306] While the political reasons for founding a European agency may vary, they do, however, share some characteristics, and, as we will see, even certain categories of agencies can be built.

In an attempt to systematise the 'agency cluster', 'common features' of European agencies shall now be listed – thereby supplementing and updating *Geradin* and *Petit*.[307]

Already in the founding regulation of the first European agency – Cedefop, established in 1975 – the substantial independence from 'the departments of the Commission' is addressed.[308] While we shall refer to the issue of political influence being exerted by representatives of the Commission in agencies' management boards – and the difficulties in assessing this influence – below, conceptually speaking, agencies have been established as depoliticised bodies. Second, they have legal personality, and are not otherwise institutionally

---

298   Regulation 294/2008.
299   EIT's webpage <http://eit.europa.eu/eit-community/eit-glance/mission>.
300   Arguably most of them are citizens of one of the MS, too, but they are not sitting in the Government Board as representatives of their respective home countries, but as scientists only. See Kirste 268.
301   Article 4 para 1 lit a of Regulation 294/2008.
302   Commission, COM (2008) 135 final, 3, listing further partnership bodies.
303   For an early classification see Everson, Independent Agencies.
304   See Curtin and Dehousse 193, emphasising the 'huge differences' between the single agencies.
305   See Bodiroga-Vukobrat and Martinović 68; Chiti, Modèle 49; Weiß 87.
306   Rambøll Management-Euréval-Matrix I.
307   Geradin and Petit 41ff; see Chapter 1 I.2.2. above.
308   Recital 5 of Regulation 337/75.

embedded in the sphere of the Commission or any other institution. Third, they are generally[309] set up to have a long standing – as opposed to executive agencies (see 3. below). Fourth, European agencies are spread all over the territory of the EU.[310] This decentralisation can, besides the legal personality and the long standing agencies have, be considered another prong of their independence (formal independence). The quest for (substantial and, connected therewith, formal) independence also finds its expression in the fifth characteristic, which is the agencies' essential purpose: the provision of information- and knowledge-based output. The form this output takes – opinion, decision, best practice, etc. – varies, but ideal-typically is based on technical ('objective') and not on political ('subjective') considerations (see Chapter 1 II.2. above). In that sense, agencies are conceptualised as the epitome of technocracy.[311] Sixth, as regards their legal foundations, European agencies have in common their lack of an explicit Treaty base. The foundation of a certain agency has not been and currently is not explicitly envisaged in the Treaty. Seventh, they have all been established by the EU legislator, ie the Council or the Council and the EP. Eighth, European agencies are governed by a college, a group of people the majority of whom regularly[312] are MS' representatives[313] – when including the non-voting members the boards are even more 'plethoric'.[314]

3.   Distinguishing European agencies – different approaches

Having identified common characteristics of European agencies, models of differentiation shall now be proposed, compared and discussed. In other words, the attempt to characterise European agencies via association shall be followed by an attempt to systematise them via separation.[315]

A relatively simple (but nevertheless valid) distinction can be drawn between executive and regulatory ('traditional') agencies.[316] Executive agencies are established each by an implementing decision[317] of the Commission[318] in the framework of a 2002 Council Regulation.[319] Their purpose is to support the Commission in managing Union programmes. Usually set up

---

309   The EAR whose mandate in terms of time was limited from the outset is an exception.
310   See Geradin and Petit 41ff.
311   Cf Commission, COM (2008) 135 final, 5. Also *Groenleer* describes the agencies' independence ('autonomy') as their 'key concept'; Groenleer 39.
312   For the exceptions see IV.3. below.
313   See EU working group, No 5, 1; a qualitative assessment of the actual work in administrative boards is provided by Busuioc, Agencies, in particular 725f; critically: EU working group, No 6, 5.
314   Busuioc, Agencies, in particular 727.
315   In the literature, a number of classifications can be found: see references in Weiß 90f.
316   Commission, COM (2008) 135 final, 2.
317   Eg Commission Implementing Decision 2013/778/EU.
318   Article 3 of Council Regulation 58/2003.
319   Council Regulation 58/2003.

for a limited period of time, executive agencies are governed by a Steering Committee and a Director. The Commission appoints both the five members representing the Steering Committee and the Director.[320] Their being housed in Brussels or Luxembourg is another 'obvious symbol' of the fact that they constitute, as it were, the extended arm of the Commission.[321] Whether 'the EU's appetite for creating new agencies seems limitless'[322] also with regard to executive agencies remains to be seen. For the time being, there are six executive agencies (some of them already replacing earlier established agencies). Note that the Commission earlier has used the term 'executive agencies' to describe the less powerful among the European agencies.[323]

Another line of differentiation is the (former) pillar structure of the EU. It is possible to assign each agency to one of the former pillars of the EU (ECs, CFSP, PJCC). On the official website of the EU this structure was – as regards the classification of agencies – upheld until 2012. Accordingly, the webpage listed EDA, EUISS and EUSC as agencies of the former second pillar (CFSP), whereas CEPOL, Europol and Eurojust were subsumed under the former third pillar (PJCC).[324] As long as the pillar structure of the EU had been in place, the idea to make use of it in order to classify European agencies suggested itself. Once the Lisbon Treaty has done away with it in favour of a more integrated concept and understanding of the EU, the approach taken by the Commission appeared anachronistic. Using the institution(s) on whose initiative an agency was founded – the Council, or the Council and the EP – as a differentiator, is, though indirectly, also based on the outdated pillar structure.[325]

On a functional level, various authors have approached agencies via a qualitative assessment and stratification of their output. In one of the early works on agencies, *Everson* – with a view not only to European but also to agencies on the national level – distinguishes between regulatory agencies, independent information-collecting aides, adjudicational agencies and agencies charged with the pursuit of distinct 'constitutional-type' normative goals (such as the ECB).[326] *Kreher* groups European agencies in 'information function agencies' (which he again separates in different sub-categories) and

---

320   Articles 8 para 1, and 10 para 1 respectively, *leg cit.*

321   Commission, COM (2008) 135 final, 3.

322   Geradin and Petit 4.

323   Commission, COM (2002) 718 final, eg 3; critically with regard to this: Weiß 88f. While it is true that at that time 'executive agencies' (understood as managing entities strongly connected to the Commission) did not exist, their creation has been considered for quite a while (and only eight days later the executive agencies' statute [Council Regulation 58/2003] was adopted); cf Commission, COM (2000) 788 final.

324   Official website of the EU <http://europa.eu/agencies/regulatory_agencies_bodies/index_en.htm>.

325   Cf Craig, EU 151; D Curtin, Delegation 94ff.

326   Everson, Independent Agencies 186ff.

'executive agencies'.[327] *Griller* and *Orator* draw the line between ordinary regulatory agencies, pre-decision-making regulatory agencies, decision-making regulatory agencies (*vis-à-vis* individual physical or legal persons or *vis-à-vis* MS) and rule-making regulatory agencies.[328] *Craig* classifies agencies into four groups: regulatory agencies (which, according to him, do not currently exist in the EU), decision-making agencies, quasi-regulatory agencies and information and coordination agencies.[329] Note that *Griller* and *Orator* use the term 'regulatory agency' in the Commission's understanding, whereas *Everson* and *Craig* apply a more narrow definition, which is applicable also in other administrative cultures; it describes bodies with a decision- or rule-making power, which entails a certain latitude.[330]

Typologies are by definition simplifications. A tasks-/powers-based typology of European agencies also requires a concentration on only some of them,[331] since obviously each agency has a set of different tasks and powers. The above classifications all focus on the formal powers of agencies. In the following a different – though complementary – approach shall be taken, focusing more on agencies' (substantive) tasks.

Table 2.1 A classification of European agencies

Tasks	Agencies
1 Facilitating cross-sectional policies	EEA, CdT, FRA (until 2007: EUMC), ENISA, EIGE
2 Foreign policy project management	ETF, EAR (until 2008)
3 Mainly research tasks	EUISS, EUSC
4 Security management[332]	Europol, Eurojust, CEPOL, EDA, FRONTEX, ITA
5 Weak sector-specific governance	Cedefop, EUROFOUND, EMCDDA, EU-OSHA, ECDC, ERA, GSA, Office, EASO
6 Strong sector-specific governance	EMA, OHIM, CPVO, EFSA, EMSA, EASA, EFCA, ECHA, ACER, EBA, EIOPA, ESMA, SRB

327　Kreher 236–238.
328　Griller and Orator, Everything 32ff.
329　Craig, EU (#2) 149ff; on the merits of the term 'quasi' in the given context see Orator, Möglichkeiten 143 with further references.
330　Cf Craig, EU (#2) 149f. Other approaches towards classifying European agencies are provided by Hummer 111f; critically with regard to the word 'regulatory agencies' in the EU context: Weiß 89.
331　As regards the difficulties of classifying European agencies cf Weiß 90f.
332　The European Public Prosecutor's Office, according to the Commission proposal COM (2013) 534 final, shall – due to its judicial function, but also due to its composition – not fall within the group of European agencies; see ibid., 7.

This categorisation distinguishes six groups of agencies. The first one encompasses agencies set up to follow cross-sectional policies, such as non-discrimination on grounds of gender or on grounds of ethnic origin. The focus of their tasks lies with the coordination of policies and the development and exchange of best practices, which are relevant in all policy fields (further examples: environmental protection, human rights), and hence have a horizontal scope. Second, there is one agency (historically two) entrusted with the management of projects in foreign countries – the Balkan countries (EAR and ETF), the 'European Neighbourhood'[333] in a wider sense and Central Asia (ETF). Third, there are two agencies – EUISS, EUSC – which are *predominantly* doing research and providing scientific information for the EU policy-makers. Fourth, the EU's institutional development saw the establishment of various bodies entrusted with security management tasks – inside and at the borders of the EU. In this context not only the well-known European Police Office (Europol) was founded, but also Eurojust, CEPOL (with a mainly educational mission), EDA, FRONTEX and – lastly – ITA. The vast majority of European agencies, however, can be subsumed under the heading (weak or strong) sector-specific governance. These are, admittedly, very broad categories, but – given the variety of tasks agencies are entrusted with – the introduction of further (sub)categories would undermine the aim of creating a typology.[334] The differentiation between 'weak' and 'strong' shall address the *de facto* power of the agencies. Agencies such as EUROFOUND or ECDC are examples of the 'weak' variant of sector-specific agencies. Their tasks are limited to the collection and provision of information and the coordination of actions of different actors on a national and on the EU level in the respective policy field. The 'strong' sector-specific agencies can render binding decisions/rules and/or have – *de facto* – a pivotal influence on decision-, rule- and/or legislation-making in the respective policy fields.[335] Here the EMA and the EASA can be named as examples. While the EMA does not have comprehensive decision-making powers,[336] in particular its scientific opinions are of pivotal importance in the authorisation procedure for medicinal products.[337] The EASA exercises individual decision-making powers on a regular basis. In addition to that, it is strongly involved in the creation of

---

333 Official website of the EU <http://europa.eu/about-eu/agencies/regulatory_agencies_bodies/policy_agencies/etf/index_en.htm>.

334 There are some agencies that could be grouped in a sub-category, though (eg Cedefop, EUROFOUND, EU-OSHA, which are all active in the improvement of the working environment of employees, or the agencies active in the financial market sector: EBA, EIOPA, ESMA and the SRB).

335 See Chiti, Agencies 96–98, who calls agencies mainly involved in rule-making 'agencies with instrumental powers'.

336 See 1. above.

337 For an overview of the EMA's tasks and powers see Friese, paras 59–62.

legislation.[338] The EASA can also render a variety of non-binding rules, among them so-called certification specifications. In a *de facto* perspective, these specifications determine future decisions of the EASA and the competent national authorities to a large extent.[339]

4.   Has the European agency exceeded its zenith? An assessment

With currently around 40 agencies operating in the EU, the EU's agencification quantitatively has reached a remarkable dimension. Qualitatively, that is to say with respect to their tasks and powers, the past ten years have seen a strong increase in the establishment of true decision-making agencies: the EFCA founded in 2005, the ECHA founded in 2006, the ACER founded in 2009, the three ESAs founded in 2011 and, most recently, the SRB operational since 2015/16. In addition to that, the Court in the case of two agencies – the ECHA and the ESMA – has confirmed a rule-making power.[340] Considering the powers these – and other – agencies dispose of with regard to binding legal acts, but also with regard to their often pivotal *de facto* influence on law-making, we may ask ourselves 1) whether the number of agencies will increase and 2) whether the agencies' set of powers will be further enriched in the future or whether the peak of agencification has already been reached.[341]

In June 2012 the EP, the Council and the Commission have rendered a Joint Statement on decentralised agencies, which was accompanied by a Common Approach.[342] This Common Approach – essentially worked out by the IIWG on European agencies[343] –, addresses a whole set of questions respecting European agencies in general. It attempts to unify the organisational and functional approach towards European agencies with regard eg to the establishment and ending of agencies – the latter being a politically delicate and hardly used option[344] –, to the size of and voting in the management board, to the role of the Director and other internal organs of European agencies. It also deals with the possibility of merging smaller agencies and the issue of sharing administrative services (that is a secretariat) between agencies in order to increase efficiency, in particular cost efficiency: While the agencies'

---

338   The intensity of this involvement is well-revealed in the draft recommendation of the European Ombudsman in the case 726/2012/(RA)FOR.

339   See Riedel, Gemeinschaftszulassung 125–128.

340   *de Alquitranes* [2013], para 58 (see also the order launched in the appeal proceedings; *de Alquitranes* [2014], para 19); *ESMA*, para 65.

341   See Gundel, Rechtsschutz 385, who assumes that European agencies are already beyond their heyday.

342   Parliament/Council/Commission, Joint Statement (with an annexed Common Approach). For an overview of the measures proposed therein see Scholten.

343   See EU Agencies Network 1.

344   Rambøll Management-Euréval-Matrix 33f.

total staff is now, for the first time, decreasing, the total EU contributions to agencies are still on the rise.[345] Also questions of representation are at issue in the Common Approach. The Commission, for example, shall be represented by two of its officials in each management board,[346] which shall – as is already the case with the vast majority of agencies – be composed of one representative per MS. The Common Approach shall be taken into account by the institutions of the EU 'in the context of all their future decisions concerning EU decentralised agencies'.[347]

The implementation of the measures proposed in the Common Approach is under way.[348] The Commission has collected information from European agencies, set out a roadmap for measures to be taken[349] and in a number of cases has proposed a revision of agencies' founding regulations (eg of the OHIM[350]) along the lines of the Common Approach.[351] Mention should be made of the alert/warning system that allows the Commission to warn the Council and the EP in case the agency's management board 'is about to take decisions which may not comply with the mandate of the agency, may violate EU law or be in manifest contradiction with EU policy objectives'.[352]

The Common Approach, the objective of which can be summarised with the words 'unifying, simplifying, rationalising', seems to have kicked off a soft reform process.[353] This softness applies both with regard to the measures taken – guidelines, communications,[354] reports, coordination, etc.[355] (although, as we have seen, also some legislative acts are being proposed/adopted) – and to the effects.[356] In this respect, a gentle development involving the agencies concerned, not an abrupt harmonisation 'from above' (the Commission) seems to be intended.

While the Common Approach and the actions (to be) taken in its aftermath envisage a medium-term reform, the ECJ's judgement in the *ESMA* case constitutes a more revolutionary change of the legal framework of European agencies. With its confirmation of a provision of secondary law vesting an agency with rule-making powers that entail a relatively wide discretion, the Court has done away with the main legal barrier for true regulatory

---

345   See Commission, COM (2013) 519 final, 11.
346   On the Commission's frustration with its 'minority role' in agencies' management boards see Craig, EU (#2) 31.
347   Council, Note 11450/12, 3.
348   For details see EU Agencies Network 3ff.
349   See Commission, Roadmap on follow-up to Common Approach.
350   Commission, COM (2013) 161 final.
351   See Commission, COM (2015) 179 final, 6f.
352   See Commission, Roadmap on follow-up to Common Approach 8.
353   Pessimistic as regards the expected consequences of such a coordinated Commission approach towards European agencies: See reference in Egeberg et al. 12.
354   See Annexes II–VI to Commission progress report.
355   EU Agencies Network 3ff.
356   See Roadmap in Annex I to Commission progress report.

agencies[357]: the old '*Meroni* devil'.[358] Furthermore, it has established Article 114 TFEU as a competence clause, which in principle allows for the foundation of agencies with individual decision- and rule-making power. That the ECJ tries hard to present its judgement as the consistent implication of its past case law and the latest Treaty revision is a different matter (see I.7. above).

The currently youngest agency, the SRB, was established in July 2014, after the Common Approach was adopted and also after the ECJ handed down its *ESMA* judgement. A full assessment of the SRB's (non-)compliance with the Common Approach cannot be given here. Instead, the situation of the SRB shall be spotlighted cursorily with regard to the three main objectives of the Common Approach – 'balanced governance, improved efficiency and accountability and greater coherence'[359] – and with regard to the ECJ's updated 'delegation of powers' doctrine.

Ad 'governance': The SRB is composed of a Chair (Vice Chair), four full-time members and one member appointed by each MS, representing the national resolution authorities. In addition to that, the Commission and the ECB each send one representative as observers.[360] Whether this composition is good, efficient and practicable or not: It is clearly not in accordance with the Common Approach (which is also not explicitly referred to in the SRB's founding regulation) and the related roadmap of the Commission, which envisages one representative per MS and two Commission representatives (possibly complemented by one EP representative and a limited number of stakeholder representatives).[361]

Ad 'efficiency and accountability': The appointment of four independent full-time members functioning as micro-managers of the Board, preparing the decisions to be taken in the plenary session and implementing the SRB-Regulation[362] is a new approach that – *prima facie* – seems to contribute to enhanced efficiency. The rules on accountability are collectively laid down in Article 45, followed by the requesting rights of national parliaments (Article 46) and the guarantees of independence (Article 47). If we compare this for example to the ESA-Regulations,[363] the SRB-Regulation is definitely more explicit in this respect.

---

357   For this term see Craig, EU (#2) 149f.
358   Chamon 1057.
359   See Commission, Roadmap on follow-up to Common Approach 1.
360   Article 43 of Regulation 806/2014.
361   See Commission, Roadmap on follow-up to Common Approach 1; on the role of the Commission representative and calling for its clarification and harmonisation: EU working group, No 31, 5.
362   Article 54 para 1 of Regulation 806/2014; in contrast to setting up a Management Board (as in the case of the ESAs), which again is composed of national representatives sitting in the Board of Supervisors (see Chapter 3 II.3.5.3. below).
363   See Articles 3 (on accountability) and 42 (independence) of the ESA-Regulations.

Ad 'greater coherence': Here the relationship with the host-MS may serve as an example. The Commission provides for standard provisions for headquarter agreements between the agencies and the respective seat country. So far, the SRB has not concluded a headquarter agreement with the Belgian authorities – neither have several other agencies.[364]

The SRB's founding regulation is based on Article 114 TFEU. While the legislator has provided only for 'light' rule-making powers (general instructions, guidelines; see Chapter 4 III.1. below), and has made certain SRB-decisions subject to prior endorsement by the Commission, the SRB also has true decision-making powers (eg fines against financial institutions). In that sense, the legislator has not conferred powers on the SRB to the full extent of what the Court allows according to its new *Meroni* doctrine. But it has certainly created an enormously powerful European agency performing strong sector-specific governance (see 3. above).

As an overall appraisal and outlook on the future development of agencies, let me conclude with the following remarks. The Commission and the legislator, that is the Council and the EP, seem to be keen on systematising the web of European agencies in terms of organisation, use of resources and means of controlling their performance – this is the main purpose of the reform process initiated by the Common Approach.[365] They did utter the idea of exercising self-restraint when it comes to the foundation of new agencies.[366] A good argument for such self-restraint would be that the execution of Union law by the MS appears to be, according to the Treaties, the rule, and the direct execution by EU organs the exception.[367] The constant creation of new EU bodies with new tasks could – in the long run – challenge this rule.[368] But in spite of their announcement, the Commission and the legislator appear to be happy to continue with what, for the Commission and the EP, originally only was the '"second-best" design choice'[369]: the agencification of the EU. The recent establishment of the SRB supports this assumption. The fact that the official political reasons for the establishment of agencies will – in all policy fields – continue to be relevant does as well: independence from the Commission, the implementation of inter-governmental tasks, the need for an intense dialogue with stakeholders and the development of a specific expertise or capacity.[370] Also with regard to the unofficial political reasons for the establishment of European agencies –

---

364   EU Agencies Network 3.
365   On the 'multiplicity of principals in the Union' as the main reason for the attempted harmonisation of agencification see Dehousse, Politics 16–21.
366   Parliament/Council/Commission, Joint Statement (with an annexed Common Approach) 3.
367   See Article 197 paras 1f and Article 291 para 1 TFEU.
368   See Wittinger 612–614.
369   Kelemen and Tarrant 929.
370   Rambøll Management-Euréval-Matrix 17.

in particular the MS' distrust in the Commission,[371] the MS' longing for representation[372] and for EU bodies being placed in their respective territory[373] – there is no indication that they have ceased or will cease to exist in the near future.

IV. COMITOLOGY AND AGENCIES – A BRIEF COMPARISON

In the preceding sections we have looked into the evolution, the essential characteristics and legal issues of both comitology and European agencies. In order to complete the juxtaposition of these two systems somehow situated between EU and national administration,[374] which both have evolved as support tools in the field of technical and/or scientific decision-making in a broader sense, a comparison with regard to selected issues shall be drawn. The first point of comparison is the (legal) foundation, that is to say not only the relevant legal provisions in the Treaties, but also the secondary legal acts based upon them, and policy papers such as communications, where applicable. Second, the political purpose – the rationale – of the two systems shall be addressed with a view to shedding light on conceptual differences and similarities. Third, the topic of independence shall be raised, thereby pointing at both the guarantees and the risks for the independence of these two regimes.

While a fully fledged comparison of the two systems cannot be offered here, raising three of the main issues shall at least illustrate both differences and similarities of the two approaches – alternatives actually[375] – towards balancing technical/scientific expertise and MS influence.[376]

1. Legal foundation

Already in the Treaty of Rome we can find the idea of powers being conferred by the Council to the Commission.[377] This provision is elaborated further in the SEA 1987. Not only does Article 145 TEEC (SEA) emphasise that the exercise of implementing powers by the Commission shall be the rule, implementing powers of the Council the exception,[378] it also provides that:

---

371 Cf Dehousse, Regulation 253; more recently again: Dehousse, Politics 18.
372 With regard to the MS' distrust of the Commission and their insisting on adequate representation see Kelemen 99f.
373 See Fleischer 223f; Wittinger 611. On the intransparent seating conditions leading to inefficiencies see Rambøll Management-Euréval-Matrix 40 and 44.
374 Cf Weiß 61.
375 Cf Ballmann et al. 572.
376 Cf Joerges 39.
377 Article 155 first indent TEEC (Rome); from the mid-1960s onwards gradually the conviction had gained ground that the fourth indent was the relevant provision; see Ilgner 31.
378 See Ilgner 36f with further references.

[t]he Council may impose certain requirements in respect of the exercise of these powers ... The procedures ... must be consonant with principles and rules to be laid down in advance by the Council, acting unanimously on a proposal from the Commission and after obtaining the Opinion of the European Parliament.

This clearly is a request to the legislator to systematise the measures of controlling the Commission when exercising implementing powers. As has been mentioned above (II.1.), in 1987 the EEC already disposed of an intricate system of comitology, encompassing various different procedures, exceptions and counter-exceptions, and mechanisms of mutual control. The reason for the comitology's complexity at that time was the lack of framework rules establishing a *numerus clausus* of comitology procedures. With the SEA the political goal to simplify the mess of comitology was integrated in the Treaty.

Pursuant to Article 145 TEEC (SEA) the first Comitology Decision was adopted in 1987. While Article 145 TEEC was renumbered Article 202 by the Treaty of Amsterdam, and finally renumbered Article 291 by the Treaty of Lisbon, the first Comitology Decision was followed by a second one in 1999, amended in 2006, which was eventually repealed by the new Regulation 182/2011 (*Comitology III*).

Whereas the respective Treaty provisions are the primary law bases of comitology, the 'Comitology Decisions' – the framework rules – more closely define the procedures to be applied. On a third level, the acts of legislation have to be placed that are actually conferring implementing powers to the Commission in a certain policy field, thereby referring to a particular comitology procedure.[379]

Agencies have undergone a development quite different from that of comitology committees. In terms of the legal foundation it ought to be stressed that prior to Lisbon, agencies were not even explicitly referred to in the Treaties.[380] Nevertheless, the legislator had to base its founding regulations of agencies on the Treaty.[381] The establishment of the first few agencies was therefore based on the flexibility clause, then Article 235 TE(E)C, which allowed, under certain circumstances and given a unanimous Council decision, for Community action where the Treaty did not provide the necessary powers.[382] Later on, especially from the mid-1990s onwards,[383]

---

379 See Blom-Hansen, EU 612ff, who introduces four institutional levels of comitology, the fourth one being 'the daily workings of the individual committees' (614); for a slightly different taxonomy see Töller 52.

380 See now Article 15 paras 1 and 3, Article 16 para 2, Article 24, Article 71 etc. TFEU; see Chamon 1056. However, for example in the German version of the Treaties the more encompassing term *Einrichtungen* (rather than *Agenturen*) was chosen.

381 For an overview of the various Treaty bases used in the past see Koenig et al. 228f.

382 The Article was renumbered 308 TEC in the Treaty of Amsterdam. It is now Article 352 TFEU.

383 *Sander* calls the year 1997 a landmark [*Zäsur*] in this respect: Sander 16f.

the Commission[384] and the legislator have preferred using more 'pertinent' Treaty provisions as legal bases,[385] eg what is now Article 114 TFEU. Only where it could not find a legal basis in the Treaty specifically referring to the field of operation of the agency to be established,[386] it continued to make use of the flexibility clause.[387] The Court clarified that the legislator in principle has the power to establish a European agency on the basis of a Treaty provision other than Article 352 TFEU – which is by no means evident –, at least with regard to Article 114 TFEU.[388] According to this judgement, in combination with the Court's confirmation that what is now Article 352 TFEU 'may be used as the legal basis for a measure only where no other provision of the Treaty [provides] … the necessary power to adopt it',[389] the legislator's current practice even seems to be a legal dictate. This does not, however, relieve the legislator of its duty to ensure in each and every case that the establishment of an agency with a certain set of powers is actually covered by the policy-related competence clause at issue. If not, recourse has to be made to Article 352 TFEU. The introduction of a general Treaty base for the establishment of agencies was proposed already in 2002,[390] but has not been realised so far.

Also on the level of secondary law there is no equivalent to the 'Comitology Decisions', no framework regulation sketching the essentials of European agencies, such as organisation, tasks and procedures or mechanisms of control. These are subject to each and every founding regulation of European agencies and related secondary law. There are, however, a couple of (non-binding)

---

384   See Commission, COM (2002) 718 final, 7.

385   See examples given by Wittinger 612; endorsing this new approach: Majone, Dilemmas 92.

386   With regard to the prerequisites for making use of (now) Article 352 TFEU see eg *European Parliament v Council* [1992], paras 11–20.

387   See, for that matter, Recital 31of Council Regulation 168/2007. This suggestion finds its confirmation in Commission, COM (2002) 718 final, 7; see also Craig, EU (#2) 147, for the ramifications for the EP of this paradigm shift, see ibid. 150f; Vetter 728f. For a table of European agencies, their founding regulations and their respective legal bases in the Treaty, see Griller and Orator, Everything 32ff. Critically as regards the merits of Article 352 TFEU as a legal base for European agencies: Kirste 273f; in favour of introducing a common legal base: Bodiroga-Vukobrat and Martinović 79 with further references.

388   See case *UK v Parliament/Council*, para 44: '[N]othing in the wording of Article [114 TFEU] implies that the addressees of the measures adopted by the Community legislature on the basis of that provision can only be the individual Member States. The legislature may deem it necessary to provide for the establishment of a Community body responsible for contributing to the implementation of a process of harmonisation in situations where, in order to facilitate the uniform implementation and application of acts based on that provision, the adoption of non-binding supporting and framework measures seems appropriate'; critically: the Opinion of AG *Kokott* in the above case; Ohler 732ff; Sander 16ff; critically, as it regards the establishment of the ESAs, Häde 663f; even dismissive Hertig et al. 193.

389   *European Parliament v Council* [2006], para 36 with reference to the ECJ's older case law.

390   See European Convention, CONV 375/1/02, 15 and 17.

Commission papers dealing with agencies in the EU.[391] These papers do not set the legal requirements of agencies from scratch. Rather, they attempt to systematise agencies already existing, at places proposing some reforms.[392] More recently, a Common Approach[393] was adopted that also provides some guidance for the future shape and role of European agencies.

In this respect the development of agencies is similar to that of comitology. There has been an outright rank growth of agencies so far, which the Commission recently has tried to catch by rendering papers dealing with the pivotal principles of European agencies. This is an attempt to conceptually grasp the phenomenon of agencies and to thereby sort what has become an intricate network. The 'Comitology Decisions' convey a similar picture: After decades of a rather unfettered evolution a decision was adopted in order to reduce this much disputed unfolding.[394] While the two developments move on similar lines, there are also crucial differences. First, comitology has – at least since the entry into force of the SEA – a much-more explicit legal basis in the Treaties. Secondly, the 'Comitology Decisions' in the first place regulated the comitology procedures, and only *en passant* the organisation of the committees. The Commission papers on agencies, on the contrary, give guidelines on what institutionally characterises European agencies.[395] The Commission does not deal with the question whether and, if so, when and by whom agencies ought to be consulted and what procedural implications their (positive or negative) opinion should have. This again is subject to the founding regulations of each agency or related secondary law. This leads us to the more general – conceptual – difference between comitology committees and European agencies, which shall be addressed in the following paragraphs.

2.   Rationale

Having compared the respective legal foundations, we shall now confront the respective rationale of these two systems – comitology committees and agencies – with each other: What was the *calculatio* of the policy-makers in the Community/Union to establish comitology committees on the one hand, and agencies on the other hand? [396]

---

391   See Commission, COM (2002) 718 final; Commission, COM (2005) 59 final; Commission, MEMO 08/159; Commission, COM (2008) 135 final.
392   Eg a new approach towards the composition of agencies' administrative boards; see Commission, COM (2002) 718 final, 9.
393   Parliament/Council/Commission, Joint Statement (with an annexed Common Approach).
394   See eg Hustedt et al. 107.
395   See, for example, Commission, COM (2008) 135 final, 4.
396   See Everson, Constitutionalisation 285ff; cf Schout, Framework 363, who claims that 'comitology was not a trustworthy alternative when agencies were created in the 1990s'.

From its historical origin comitology has been conceptualised by the legislator and the Commission as a means of MS control of the Commission in its exercise of implementing powers.[397] Since implementing acts regularly are rather technical, their understanding requires a certain expertise. For this reason, comitology committees have been composed of experts from the bureaucracies of the MS, the argument being the following: It would not be possible for the MS to adequately represent their interests, could they not send well-informed individuals to the committees, which were at the same time bound by the (political) instructions of their respective ministers. In other words, sound ('expert knowledge') representation ('bound by instructions') of MS' interests has been standing in the foreground,[398] not (objective) technical/scientific control.[399] The latter is – if at all – a merely collateral effect of the practice of comitology.[400]

Agencies have been – from their institutional appearance – conceptualised as something different from comitology committees. In spite of Commission and above all MS' representatives[401] sitting in their management boards[402] (for exceptions see 3. below) they are 'largely shielded from explicitly political processes' by virtue of their legal personality, their organisational structure – which resembles that of international organisations[403] –, their permanent staff,[404] their decentralised location and their budgetary leeway.[405] Also, in terms of the tasks and competences they may be vested with, agencies are – for lack of a clear Treaty base – the more versatile bodies. However, as regards the scientific committees of agencies, if they have any,[406] there may be links to

397 See Vos, Rise 223, who perceives comitology against the background of a 'functional understanding of the notion of the balance of powers', thereby encompassing MS.

398 See, with further references, Hustedt et al. 118–121.

399 See *TU München*, para 22, as an illustrative example; see also Everson and Majone 54, pointing to 'national representation …, the primacy of the Commission's policy initiative and the reference to scientific and technical expertise' as the main purposes of comitology.

400 The factors depending on which the work of comitology committees is rather 'political' or rather 'scientific' are addressed by Hustedt et al. 121.

401 On the varying degrees of preparation for meetings of MS' representatives see Busuioc, Agencies 725.

402 See Fischer-Appelt 226; on the varying composition of agencies' administrative boards see Comte 76.

403 Traditionally, international organisations have had a plenary policy-making and a non-plenary administrative organ; on the agency level, the management board (or similar designation) corresponds to the plenary, the executive director (or similar designation) to the non-plenary organ. Similar to the development on the international level, more recently established agencies, in addition to that, dispose of other non-plenary organs, mostly preparing the work of the plenary organ, eg the Administrative Board of the ACER; see Schermers and Blokker § 385 with regard to international organisations; Orator, Möglich-keiten 138 with regard to European agencies.

404 Compared with the Commission, European agencies are more flexible regarding their staff policy. In other words, agencies can both hire and fire staff more easily; see Suvarierol et al. 917.

405 See Everson, Constitutionalisation 286 with further references.

406 The early agencies Cedefop and EUROFOUND, for example, have not had any scientific committee.

comitology committees. The following examples may serve as an illustration: EU-OSHA, the EU Agency for Safety and Health at Work founded in 1994, is supported by the Advisory Committee on Safety, Hygiene and Health Protection at Work, which was founded in 1974 as a comitology committee. From the pool of members of this committee the members of the Governing Board of the agency are appointed: members representing the government, members representing the employers' organisations, members representing the employees' organisations – one member each from each MS.[407] In addition to that, three members representing the Commission are appointed.

The EMA, which was founded in 1993, disposes of a variety of committees.[408] The composition of three of them shall be described here.[409] The Committee for Medicinal Products for Human Use (CHMP) is composed of one member per MS (plus one member per EFTA state). They are complemented by up to five co-opted members that the committee may appoint on the basis of scientific competence from among the experts nominated by the MS or the EMA.[410] The Committee for Medicinal Products for Veterinary Use (CVMP), established in 1981 as a comitology committee,[411] is composed and its members are appointed accordingly.[412] For the Committee for Orphan Medicinal Products (COMP), established in 2001, one member is nominated by each MS, three members are nominated by patients' organisations, another three by the Commission on the EMA's recommendation, and one each by Iceland, Liechtenstein and Norway. In addition to that, the Commission sends one of its representatives. There may also be general observers.[413]

With EMCDDA, the agency monitoring drugs and drug abuse, founded in 1994, the setting is different. The Scientific Committee of the EMCDDA is composed of a maximum of 15 'well-known scientists' who are chosen and appointed by the Management Board on the basis of scientific excellence and independence.[414]

This exemplary selection of so-called 'second-wave agencies' shows that for some agencies – not for all – there is a strong connection with (former) comitology committees: as predecessors[415] and/or as constitutive elements of agencies. The EMCDDA with its concentration on excellence, thereby neglecting the national origin of candidates, being the exception, the

407 Article 8 paras 1f of Council Regulation 2062/94 as amended. The EU-OSHA's founding regulation is currently being reviewed, and also a reduction of the Governing Board's size is considered; see <http://ec.europa.eu/smart-regulation/roadmaps/docs/2015_empl_012_osha_en.pdf>.

408 For the predecessors of the EMA – committees – see Majone, Europeanization 200ff; for the EMA itself see Fischer-Appelt 245ff.

409 For the other EMA committees see Hustedt et al 186.

410 Article 1 of the RoP of the CHMP.

411 Council Directive 81/851/EEC.

412 Article 1 of the RoP of the CVMP.

413 Article 1 of the RoP of the COMP. See for the EMA's committees in general Majone, Europeanization 201.

414 Article 13 of Regulation 1920/2006.

415 See Hustedt et al. 155; critically, Joerges 28.

representation of MS' interests in scientific agency committees still appears to be a major objective.[416] In that sense, comitology committees and agencies are, at places, intertwined in that the committees – technically not to be called 'comitology committees' any more, but *de facto* composed the same way – persist within the organisational structure of agencies. But also within the system of different committees there is a considerable overlap, both personally and regarding the content.[417] Concerning the genesis of delegated and implementing acts, it was pointedly said that sometimes a group of persons gathers as a comitology committee in the morning and as a committee consulting the Commission in an Article 290-procedure in the afternoon.[418] In accordance with that, in the field of financial services, the Commission has declared to continue to consult experts appointed by the MS also in Article 290-procedures.[419]

3.   Independence

Independence is a popular buzzword also in European political rhetoric – the more independent, the better.[420] In the course of a more differentiated approach, however, the political actors ought to be clear and precise about the following: From whose influence should – *de lege ferenda* – the body at issue be protected? Especially in the EU with its multitude of different administrative actors, its '"composite" executive power',[421] it is imperative to be clear about whose independence from whom is at issue. Second, does the legislator want as unlimited an independence as possible, or does it prefer 'instances of control' – another tool of political diction? We should be very much aware of the (evident) truth that both, independence and control, are exclusionary concepts. In practice, however, instances of both concepts need to be set in place in order to prevent a body from confusing independence with impeccability. On a temporal scale, *Busuioc* differentiates three types of control: *ex ante* control, simultaneous (on-going) control and *ex post* control (ie accountability).[422] According to her, the only form of control compatible with independence is accountability.[423]

---

416   Cf Majone, Delegation 330.
417   See Hustedt et al. 111.
418   Blanck-Putz. This practice can be criticised for increasing the problem of lack of plurality of opinions; cf Bücker and Schlacke 225.
419   See Declaration No 39.
420   On the merits of non-majoritarian/independent actors in general see Schelkle 719; on the roots of regulatory independence in particular see Bernhard Müller 263–266.
421   Chiti, EU 15.
422   See Busuioc, Accountability 606; see also Bovens 449 with further references, generally criticising the undifferentiated use of the term 'accountability'; with regard to European agencies: see Everson, Governance 142.
423   Busuioc, Accountability 609: 'Instead of "independence" and "control", "independence" and "accountability" … can co-exist'. Among the two remaining forms of control, *ex ante* and ongoing control, it appears that the latter is more detrimental to independence.

Comitology committees are set up by an act of secondary law, institutionally that means by the Council or the Council and the EP. This act also determines the comitology procedure to be applied and the scope of the implementing powers to be exercised by the Commission. Comitology committees are chaired by a representative of the Commission and assist the latter in its decision-making.[424] Their members are designated by the MS pursuant to their internal rules.[425] These characteristics show that in a merely formal perspective the legislator, the MS and the Commission have an influence on comitology. The legislator decides whether they shall be established in the first place and, if so, in which way their opinion is to be considered by the Commission. The MS decide who is going to sit in the committee, and the Commission – to which comitology committees are organisationally assigned[426] – can exert influence by chairing the committee meetings.

More difficult to measure – but at the same time also more significant – is the substantial independence of comitology committees. The most prominent issue in this context is that the members of comitology committees are bound by the (political) instructions from their respective ministries.[427] Accordingly, the Court in its famous *Pfizer* judgement emphasised that a comitology committee 'must be regarded as a political body representative of the Member States and not as an independent scientific body' the output of which 'cannot be regarded as scientific advice based on the principles of excellence, transparency and independence'.[428] While independence from the MS obviously is not intended, a reliable statement on the committees' substantial independence in particular from the Commission would require extensive field research on the voting behaviour of each member of comitology committees during the meetings – which are not accessible for the public. In general, personal independence has a lot to do with the people in charge and their individual understanding of how best to perform their role and is therefore very difficult to measure.[429] While a systematic assessment on unwanted influence – that is to say from the Commission and the legislator – is therefore not possible here, there are examples of when accepted influence, that is to say from the MS, led to unwanted results.[430] In this context the BSE crisis is to be mentioned, in the course of which the competent committees were accused of having overemphasised the interests of national food industries in beef trade (can be regarded as MS interests), thereby neglecting the health concerns raised by experts.[431] It does not therefore come as a surprise that the founding

---

424 In the current legal framework this is laid down in Article 3 para 2 of *Comitology III*.
425 Parliament, E-2022/2008.
426 See Schmidt-Aßmann 18 with further references.
427 Critically with regard to that and to the lacking expertise of committee members: Schmid.
428 *Pfizer*, paras 283 and 285.
429 Cf Bücker and Schlacke 225.
430 On '"national-minded bureaucrats"' in agencies' management boards see Busuioc, Rule-Making 120f with further references.
431 See Lavrijssen and Ottow 426; Vos, EU 249.

regulation of the EFSA – the agency operating in the field of food safety that was established in the aftermath of the BSE crisis – does away with MS' representation. Instead of one representative per MS, one or more Commission representatives and possibly other institutions' and organisations' representatives, the Management Board of the EFSA is composed of one Commission representative and 14 individuals proposed by the Commission and appointed by the Council (having consulted the Parliament).[432] Four of these individuals 'shall have their background in organisations representing consumers and other interests in the food chain'.[433]

As regards the agencies' institutional position in the EU, there are arguments in favour of their greater independence from the Commission as compared with comitology committees: They have legal personality, they are held accountable also by the Parliament and the Council[434] (which increases their independence from the Commission) and they are decentralised – they have, as *Craig* put it, the advantage of 'not being in Brussels'.[435] In some cases, however, the Commission is involved in the selection of the agencies' Executive Directors,[436] and regularly has one or more of its representatives sitting in their administrative boards. Between the majority of agencies and the respective competent Commission DGs ('parent- or partner-DGs') there are regular meetings and other forms of exchange of information and views.[437]

With respect to the selection of scientists for the various scientific advisory boards, agencies sometimes do not, as we have seen, take a fundamentally different approach than committees have done in the past.[438] This relativises the Commission's claim that '[t]he independence of their [the agencies'] technical and/or scientific assessments is, in fact, their real raison d'être'.[439]

---

432 See Dehousse, Politics 19f with reference to the EFSA, the EIGE and the ACER which – with regard to their administrative boards – do not follow the political 'one representative per MS'-rule. The ACER, however, has a Board of Regulators composed of representatives of the national competent authorities from all MS.

433 Article 25 para 1 of Regulation 178/2002. See also Vos, Independence 124. As regards independence/credibility, the EFSA was criticised for instances of undue proximity to the food industry; see <http://diepresse.com/home/meinung/kommentare/leitartikel/744444/Zugelt-die-EUAgenturen-bevor-es-zu-spaet-ist>.

434 See reference in Egeberg et al. 10f.

435 Craig, EU (#2) 143. Exceptions, such as the European GNSS Agency, which actually is situated in Brussels, do not repeal the principle of decentralisation and geographical separation from the Commission. For the disadvantages of this decentralisation see Commission, COM (2002) 718 final, 7. See, however, Everson, Constitutionalisation 286, who places agencies 'under the Commission's institutional umbrella'. See also Lavrijssen and Ottow 441f, stressing that a certain degree of Commission influence is required to maintain the institutional balance.

436 See Orator, Möglichkeiten 343.

437 For the Commission DGs and the agencies assigned to them see Egeberg et al., 13f; for MoUs concluded between them see EU working group, No 31, 1.

438 The Commission seems to be aware that with regard to the selection of experts there is room for improvement: see Commission, Guidelines 7f.

439 Commission, COM (2002) 718 final, 5; on the practice of ensuring MS' representation through advisory bodies see EU working group, No 5, 5.

Sometimes, however, the independence of the advisory committees is explicitly laid down in the founding regulations.[440] What is more, the composition of most agencies' main decision-making organs opens the door for influence especially from the MS.[441] The founding regulations more and more stress the independence of the members of the agencies' management boards from instructions of the MS.[442] In spite of the representatives of other institutions, in particular the Commission, regularly not having voting power, the *de facto* influence[443] – in *Busuioc*'s scheme this would be called on-going control – these individuals may exert on other members of the management board should not be underestimated, either.[444] The Commission itself conceded that in the context of European agencies '[t]he weight of the Commission is [...] clearly beyond its formal powers'.[445]

In addition to that, *ex post* control (accountability) is exercised by different institutions and on different levels, above all: legally by the review of binding decisions/rules of agencies by their Boards of Appeal (if existent) and by the CJEU; politically via agencies' reporting duties towards the EP and other information rights of the EP and the Council;[446] financially via a discharge procedure (EP)[447] and the Court of Auditors' supervision; and administratively via the European Ombudsman's interventions.

4. Excursus: the legal status of expert opinions

An 'appropriate relationship ... between law and science'[448] is an important condition for a well-functioning society, in particular in view of the enormous

---

440 See eg Recital 40 of Regulation 178/2002; Article 61 para 6 of Regulation 726/2004 stipulating that 'Member States shall refrain from giving committee members and experts any instruction which is incompatible with their own individual tasks or with the tasks and responsibilities of the [EMA]'. That means that in principle instructions are allowed. For a list of agencies (not) having in place a conflict of interest regime for experts see Commission, Guidelines 14–16.

441 See Busuioc, Agencies 729; Tarrant and Kelemen 31; see also Commission, COM (2002) 718 final, 9. The Commission has argued in favour of smaller administrative boards with a significantly higher percentage (up to 50 per cent) of Commission representatives; see ibid.

442 See eg Article 37 para 1 of Regulation 178/2002 (EFSA) and Article 88 of Regulation 1907/2006 (ECHA), both with a more cautious wording, and Article 12 para 7 of Regulation 713/2009 (ACER) and Article 46 of Regulation 1093/2010 (EBA), which are more explicit and comprehensive (arguably also because in the field of electricity and banking market supervision/regulation already the respective national authorities are not bound by instructions).

443 Similarly, Curtin, Power 155ff with further references; Vos, Independence 123.

444 Cf Busuioc, Accountability 602f; Chiti, Part 1399f; Van Ooik 145. With regard to the difficulty to measure this influence see Thatcher, Agencies 49.

445 See reference in Egeberg et al., 9f.

446 See Orator, Möglichkeiten 347–349.

447 For cases in which the EP refused to discharge agencies see <http://diepresse. com/home/politik/eu/744479/Die-verschwenderischen-EUAgenturen>.

448 Everson, Tales 347.

importance expert opinions have gained in legislative and other political decision-making processes.[449] Expert opinions are of pivotal importance in both administrative regimes (selectively) compared with each other in this chapter: comitology[450] and European agencies.[451] For this reason, the legal status of expert opinions – which, in principle, applies to both regimes – shall now be addressed as an excursus following this comparison.

The legal status of expert opinions in EU law essentially can be addressed with three questions. 1) Are EU administrative bodies bound by expert opinions – and if so, to what extent? 2) Which remedies do natural or legal persons have that are adversely affected by an expert opinion? 3) Can bodies issuing such expert opinions make sure that they are duly considered in the course of the adoption of an EU measure, and if so how?

As regards the first question, it ought to be stressed that the Commission – while having to consult an expert body where the legislation so provides – is not bound by expert opinions,[452] but that it has 'a power of appraisal' in this respect.[453] The Court held that an expert opinion from an agency[454] is only to be considered 'a preparatory measure which does not definitely lay down the Commission's position'.[455] While the Commission is not bound by the results of an expert opinion, it has to ensure that '[its] decisions are taken in light of the best scientific information available'.[456] Especially where the opinion is the only source of information for the Commission, the Commission must ensure that the body issuing this opinion actually is composed of experts. If this is not provided for, and if therefore the opinion is not sound, the Commission by following this opinion '[infringes] its obligation to examine carefully and impartially all the relevant aspects of the case in point'.[457] Summing up, the Commission has to make sure to be provided with sound scientific information. While disposing of a certain room for appraisal, it must nevertheless give the reasons why it has decided one or the other way.[458] Failure to duly

---

449   See Wittinger 621f.
450   While comitology committees render their own opinions, the legal effects of which depend on the procedure to be applied, they may themselves ask external experts for their opinion (and so may the Commission, also when deciding in the course of a comitology procedure); see Article 7 of the Commission's Standard RoP for committees; see also Bücker and Schlacke 222f.
451   On legal protection against expert opinions in the context of European agencies see also Pabel 73–76.
452   See, with regard to the Commission, *FMC Chemical* [2008], para 66; see also Opinion of AG *Alber* in *Monsanto*, paras 133–135.
453   *TU München*, para 13.
454   For a critical view on the regulation of the (scientific) output of European agencies see decisions of the German *Bundesrat*, Drucksache 134/08, para 27, and Drucksache 228/08, para 23; see also Gundel, Rechtsschutz 391.
455   *Fern Olivieri*, para 53.
456   *Angelopharm*, para 33; *Alpharma*, para 171; *Pfizer*, para 158; *Schräder*, para 61; *Schniga*, para 81; for other procedural restrictions see Curtin et al. 19.
457   *TU München*, paras 21f.
458   *Pfizer*, para 199; see also Article 296 TFEU that, however, only refers to 'opinions required by the Treaties'.

consider an expert opinion – the Court is 'entitled' to limit its review to manifest errors of assessment[459] – may render the final decision unlawful.[460] For other administrative bodies, for example European agencies, which have to take decisions in a field where expert opinions are provided, the Court's case law applies *per analogiam*. Comitology committees are not bound, either, by the opinion of experts they may have consulted.[461] What is more, they are not explicitly obliged to give the reasons for their opinions.[462] However, with the minutes and a summary record to be created for each meeting,[463] the motives uttered therein are disclosed to the Commission. The legal status of the committees' own opinion – binding or non-binding for the Commission – depends on the procedure to be applied (see II.2. above).

The answer to the second question is connected to the first. An opinion, for its lack of producing binding effects[464] and as a 'preliminary or purely preparatory measure[ ]',[465] cannot be made subject to an action for annulment according to Article 263 para 4 TFEU.[466] The Court may nevertheless consider such opinions under certain circumstances. Where the content of the opinion forms an integral part of the final decision, the Court must examine that opinion where an (admissible) action for annulment has been launched against the decision.[467] The Court cannot replace the expert opinion by its own opinion, but it can review the composition,[468] the 'proper functioning [of the scientific body], the internal consistency of the opinion and the statement of reasons contained therein' to the extent of whether it allows to ascertain the considerations on which the opinion is based and whether a comprehensible link between the scientific finding and the conclusions is established.[469] In that context, the Court describes its role as to make sure that 'scientific risk assessment [is] carried out as thoroughly as possible on the basis of scientific advice founded on the principles of excellence, transparency and independence ... [in order to] ensure the

459   *Schräder*, para 77.
460   For the effects on the person concerned by this decision see *Zhejiang Xinshiji*, para 104.
461   Article 7 of the Commission's Standard RoP for committees.
462   See, however, Türk 347f, who seems to affirm that committees – as Union bodies – are obliged to reason their opinions.
463   Article 10 of the Commission's Standard RoP for committees.
464   While in the examination procedure the opinion of the committee does have binding effects, these effects do, procedurally speaking, concern only the Commission. For the applicant in a procedure that provides for the examination procedure to be applied, only the final Commission decision is binding – which can be made subject to an action for annulment according to Article 263 para 4 TFEU; see Türk 347.
465   However: the *publication* of an opinion in the European Public Assessment Report according to Article 13 para 3 of Regulation 726/2004 might trigger such legal effects; see Saurer 1027.
466   *FMC Chemical* [2007], para 53 with further references; *Fern Olivieri*; critically Saurer 1023 with further examples of relevant case law; cf Alemanno and Mahieu 328ff.
467   *Fern Olivieri*, para 55; see also *Artegodan*; Saurer 1026; Storr 91.
468   *TU München*, para 22.
469   *Artegodan*, paras 199f; see also Alemanno and Mahieu 329f; Craig, EU (#2) 648f.

scientific objectivity of the measures adopted and preclude any arbitrary measures'.[470]

In short, natural or legal persons adversely affected by an expert opinion cannot submit an action for annulment of that opinion, but only of the final decision, which is (at least in part) based on that opinion. In the course of the annulment procedure they may raise the point that the decision-making body has infringed Union law by not ensuring the expertise of the body issuing the opinion or by following an opinion, which lacks consistency and/or a proper reasoning. In addition to that, EU law may provide for the possibility of a re-examination of a committee opinion upon request (eg of a MS or the applicant in the respective procedure) already in the administrative procedure.[471]

As regards the third question, it must be stressed that the means of ensuring that an EU body duly considers an expert opinion are – for the originator of this opinion – limited. Where the originator has not provided its scientific opinion as (part of) a body of the EU (EU-external originator), and where contractual liability does not apply, an action for non-contractual liability of the Union according to Article 340 para 2 TFEU is – in principle – possible. However, it is difficult to think of a damage for the originator caused by the non-consideration of an opinion. And even if damage and causality can be proved, such an action would probably fail for lack of infringement of a 'Schutznorm', that is to say a provision which is intended (also) to confer a relevant right on the originator.[472] The consideration of an expert opinion may be – as explained above – a procedural duty of an EU decision-making body, but is regularly not, at the same time, a right of the originator of this opinion. If the expert opinion was rendered by an EU-internal originator with legal personality, eg an agency, it may launch an action for annulment against the respective legal act.[473] However, as non-privileged claimants, agencies would have to prove that the legal act is of direct (and individual, if applicable) concern to them, according to Article 263 para 4 TFEU.

For both EU-internal and EU-external originators (being citizens of or seated in the EU) a complaint to the European Ombudsman, eg against the Commission, according to Article 228 TFEU may be an option. In practice, however, EU bodies do not send complaints to the Ombudsman.

---

470   *Alpharma*, para 183.
471   See eg Article 69 para 5 of Regulation 1907/2006, regarding the re-examination of the list of substances; Article 9 para 2 of Regulation 726/2004, regarding the authorisation procedure of medicinal products. Other means for MS to oppose a scientific opinion are laid down eg in Article 114 paras 4f TFEU.
472   Cf *Gascogne*, para 96 with reference to *Bergaderm*, para 42.
473   In principle this would also be possible for the originator of the opinion.

V. THE CRISIS: ALTERNATIVE WAYS OF RISK GOVERNANCE

About the creation of European agencies it was aptly said that '[i]n certain cases the occurrence of a crisis that has aroused public sensitivity is the basis of the decision to create the agency'.[474] This holds true for instance for the EMCDDA[475] and the EFSA.[476] This certainly holds true also in the case of the financial market authorities.[477]

The financial and economic crisis[478] has effected an enormous amount of reforms, both on the EU and on the MS level.[479] In this chapter, three prominent examples of such reforms – the EFSM/EFSF/ESM, the SSM and the Fiscal Compact, which were said to 'endanger[ ] the legal and institutional unity of the EU'[480] – shall be assessed with a view to their institutional ramifications for the EU. More particularly, it shall be examined whether these measures – which all do not make use of the 'agency option' – can be interpreted as a trend reversal of agencification.

1. The EFSM/EFSF/ESM and the Troika

The Troika (now referred to as 'the institutions') – in this context describing the cooperation of the Commission, the ECB and the IMF in granting financial aid to euro-MS – is a complex construct that sits strikingly outside the EU legal order. The prerequisite for the formation of the Troika was the establishment of the EFSM/EFSF in May 2010 and its successor, the ESM, in October 2012. These instruments provide the funds to be distributed to ailing euro-MS, following a certain procedure including negotiations between the Troika and the MS concerned, in the form of financial aid. Since the aid essentially comes from two sources – the IMF and (now) the ESM – two separate (though aligned[481]) decisions to grant/not to grant are taken: one by the IMF and one by the ESM, more precisely: its Board of Governors. The ESM's Board of Governors is composed of the finance ministers of the euro-MS. Hence it is in its composition equivalent to the Eurogroup – an (informal) body of the Eurozone. This may be qualified as an instance of a

---

474 Group 3a, para 8; cf Majone, Delegation 329.

475 See EMCDDA, 38ff.

476 See Everson, Agencies 128.

477 Cf Schaefer 117.

478 There is abundant literature available by now on the causes, triggers and ramifications of the debt crisis which has developed into an economic crisis: see eg Arestis et al.; Bloss et al.; Gjerstad and Smith. See also *de Larosière* Report 6ff; for the crisis of the European banking sector in particular see Dragomir 21–25.

479 See overview provided in Commission, 81 Standard Eurobarometer.

480 Chiti and Teixeira 685.

481 The alignment of approaches is, at places, difficult due to the institutional and operational differences between the EU part of the Troika and the IMF; see Pisani-Ferry et al. 113–115.

de facto 'lending' of organs[482]; *de facto* only, because it is not 'the Eurogroup', which is empowered, but its single members as combined in the Board.

The role of the two EU institutions within the Troika – the Commission and the ECB – is, in cooperation and coordination with the IMF, to assess the financial situation of the applying MS and, in case of a positive grant decision by the ESM and the IMF, to negotiate the respective conditions. The negotiations with the Commission and the ECB result, if led successfully, in a Financial Assistance Facility Agreement between the ESM and the respective MS (and its relevant bodies[483]). This agreement refers to a MoU (now referred to as 'programme') in which the conditions for the single instalments of the financial aid are laid down.[484]

While it was supposed that Article 125 TFEU forbade the establishment of an instrument by means of which MS can financially support other MS,[485] the ECJ in its (in)famous judgement in the *Pringle* case confirmed the legality of the ESM. The Court took over the arguments of the European Council, the MS and the Commission that the new Article 136 para 3 TFEU (which was intended to legalise the ESM and, at the time the judgement was rendered, still pending ratification by some of the MS) was a merely declaratory provision that confirms the euro-MS' power to establish a stability mechanism, but does not confer any new powers to the EU.[486]

With regard to the leading question of this chapter it can be assumed that establishing a European agency would not have been a good alternative in this case. The ESM is an instrument based on international law (intended to be in accordance with EU law). The establishment of a European agency under international law is, by definition, not possible. The 'lending' of a newly established European agency, which would have been the first Eurozone-agency, appears complicated – which would be the EU-specific remit of such an agency? – and also seems to contribute little to enhancing the ESM's legitimacy. Providing public funds for other countries essentially is a political issue, which is why the Board of Governors is composed of *politicians*. The second collegiate decision-making organ of the ESM, the Board of Directors, however, is composed somewhat similarly to the administrative board of a European agency, namely first and foremost of high-ranking bureaucrats from

---

482   Cf Dehousse, Politics 22f with respect to the Eurogroup which he perceives as a means of evading governance by the Commission.

483   In the case of Spain, for example, these were the Spanish central bank and a Spanish guarantee fund; see <www.google.at/url?sa=t&rct=j&q=&esrc=s&source=web&cd=2& ved=0CCcQFjAB&url=http%3A%2F%2Fwww.esm.europa.eu%2Fpdf%2FFFFA%2520Spain_ Main%2520Agreement_Execution%2520Version.pdf&ei=6kOWVd6WJMOpyQPN14HA Ag&usg=AFQjCNF5pxmEhe6790xgcMRLECAuDVhy_A&bvm=bv.96952980, d.bGQ>.

484   For the MoU with Ireland see DG ECOFIN 59ff.

485   On the legal background of the ESM more generally see Tomkin 66–68.

486   *Pringle*, para 72f.

each MS.[487] Nevertheless, in view of its political importance and its exceptionality, the lending of enormous funds to ailing MS is certainly not everyday EU administration and hence not comparable to the European agencies' usual remit.[488]

2. The Single Supervisory Mechanism: empowering the ECB

In November 2014 the SSM became operative. This mechanism is one of the legislative reactions to the banking crisis that is – due to the rescue measures taken by various MS – strongly connected to the state debt crisis in the Eurozone. Since the foundation of the EBA, which mainly has coordinating and *de facto* rule-making powers but only few true supervisory powers,[489] has proved to be insufficient,[490] the mechanism now shifts essential microprudential supervisory powers from the national to the EU level. The mechanism and the powers it entails shall be discussed below in detail. In the given context, the focus shall be laid on the fact that the legislator did not vest the EBA with these new supervisory powers, but the ECB. This is remarkable. The EBA as a relatively young agency was set in place in 2011 as an attempt to better coordinate, regulate and – to a limited extent – supervise the EU's banking sector. Now the Commission, less than two years later, in September 2012, proposed to shift in particular supervisory powers from the national to the EU level. The expected candidate to receive new banking supervisory powers in such a case certainly would be the EBA.[491] However, the Commission – the EBA being favoured only by some[492] – eventually proposed and the legislator decided to tread new paths[493] and make the ECB the central EU banking supervisory authority. The reasons for this decision are multiple. One of these reasons may be that the SSM is in the first place envisaged as a Eurozone project (with other MS having the opportunity to join, if they

---

487 According to Article 6 para 1 ESM Treaty, the Governors are relatively free in deciding whom they appoint as Director ('from among people of high competence in economic and financial matters'). The actual composition of the Board of Directors, however, shows that the Governors have above all appointed bureaucrats; see <www.esm.europa. eu/about/governance/board-of-directors/index.htm>.

488 The management of the SRF by the SRB – a European agency – could be brought forward as a counter-argument. However, with the ESM being substantially heavier than the SRF, and with the ESM, as opposed to the SRF, being funded by taxpayers' money, these two instruments do not seem to be similar.

489 On the distinction between banking regulation and banking supervision see Kohtamäki 7–9.

490 Cf Dehousse, Politics 26.

491 See also Chang 10f; differently Gurlit 14; on the pre-SSM discussions on a single European banking supervisory authority see Kohtamäki 89f.

492 See Ferran and Babis 2.

493 The legal basis for conferring specific supervisory tasks on the ECB had already been introduced in the then new TEC by the Treaty of Maastricht, but up until the SSM had remained unused.

submit to the supervisory powers of the ECB).[494] During the banking crisis, it was the ECB that took rescue and support measures to provide – directly or indirectly via the MS – ailing Eurozone banks with liquidity.[495] In that sense, the ECB seemed to be sufficiently involved to also exercise banking supervisory powers.[496] Another reason may be that the powers at issue in the SSM were deemed to be too far-reaching for a European agency (*Meroni*). Also the legal basis for vesting the ECB with supervisory powers, Article 127 para 6 TFEU, is – in spite of its malleable wording and its limits – more explicit than the (hypothetical) legal basis of an empowerment of the EBA, Article 114 TFEU. In addition to that, the powers transferred to the ECB under the SSM aim at a further Europeanisation of banking supervision, not at the approximation of laws. Therefore the EBA could not have been empowered on the basis of Article 114 TFEU.[497]

The SSM is an exceptional measure that requires a high degree of legitimacy which – for the above reasons – the ECB is in a better position to provide. The empowerment of the ECB under the SSM does not appear to be a signal that agencification has come to a halt. To the extent that powers are not conferred on the Commission, but on a decentralised EU body, the ECB, the SSM even seems to foster the aims of agencification. For organisational similarities (eg the legal personality), some even consider(ed) the ECB a special kind of European agency.[498] Being elevated to an 'institution of the EU'[499] by the Treaty of Lisbon,[500] the ECB formally cannot (any more) be considered a European agency. But also in a less formalistic perspective, the process of empowering the ECB under the SSM due to the peculiar Treaty base is not too similar to the conferral of powers to European agencies regularly based on more general provisions, in particular Article 114 TFEU and (earlier) the flexibility clause.

3.   The Fiscal Compact

Another crisis measure is the Fiscal Compact,[501] which was concluded in March 2012. The Fiscal Compact that aims at strengthening the budgetary discipline of its signatories is an international treaty agreed on by 25 of the

494   Cf Selmayr, para 62.
495   For rescue measures early during the crisis see Stolz and Wedow 11f.
496   See Dehousse, Politics 26.
497   See Sacarcelik 356.
498   See Chiti, Agencies 94; Everson, Independent Agencies 187–189; see also Majone, Dilemmas 101, stressing the greater independence of central banks (including the ECB) compared with regulatory agencies.
499   Critical with regard to the ECB's status as an institution of the EU: Dörr, para 18.
500   Cf Barbier 217f.
501   Treaty on Stability, Coordination and Governance in the Economic and Monetary Union.

then 27 MS.[502] Since the UK[503] refused to agree on a Treaty revision, the remaining MS – except the Czech Republic[504] – evaded the system of Union law and based their agreement on international law.[505] In 2014, the Czech Republic eventually joined the Fiscal Compact. In the given context, it is the 'lending' of EU institutions by the regime of the Fiscal Compact that is of interest.

Under the Fiscal Compact, the Commission,[506] the Council[507] and the Court[508] are assigned a variety of tasks.[509] An ordinary Treaty revision according to Article 48 TEU was not possible for lack of consensus of all MS. By means of involving EU institutions in its functioning, it was intended to bring the system of the Fiscal Compact as close to the EU legal and institutional order as possible.

The lending of organs, more particularly EU institutions, has already been laid down in other international treaties, but only with the agreement of all MS.[510] In the case of the Fiscal Compact no such agreement was reached. With a view to our research question here, that is to say whether the crisis has led the Commission and the legislator to seek/take modes of governance alternative to agencification, we may conclude as follows: Since a consensus between all MS could not be found, a Treaty revision was legally impossible. As an alternative – a Plan B, as it were – the 25 MS that did agree concluded an international treaty, thereby employing EU institutions. This is a politically dubitable evasion of Treaty provisions (in particular Article 48 TEU). Hence it is not surprising that the 25 MS, striving for legitimacy, made recourse to an established procedure – the Treaty infringement procedure as a role model for Article 8 of the Fiscal Compact – and to EU institutions instead of European agencies. In the field of fiscal surveillance political institutions of a high authority are called for, not newly established agencies. In a legal perspective, such an 'agency solution' would infringe the central role of the Commission in monitoring the budgetary situation and the public debt of the

---

502   For an overview of its content and an analysis of selected legal issues see Baratta 31.

503   For the details of the UK's position see Hancox.

504   For the details of the Czech Republic's position see Dumbrovsky.

505   On the increased use of intergovernmental instruments by the EU during the crisis see Chiti and Teixeira 702.

506   See eg the time-framing of MS' convergence according to Article 3 para 1 lit b of the Fiscal Compact.

507   See eg receiving MS' reports on their public debt issuance plans according to Article 6 of the Fiscal Compact.

508   See eg the imposition of fines in case of a MS' non-compliance with a pertinent judgement according to Article 8 para 2 of the Fiscal Compact.

509   For a legal assessment of the Fiscal Compact (referring to the statements of *Giuliano Amato* and *Paul Craig*) see House of Lords, Euro, paras 75ff; for a critique of its economic ramifications see eg Schulmeister.

510   See Fischer-Lescano and Oberndorfer 10 (footnote 6); for the lending of Community organs by the pre-Lisbon EU see Stadlmeier 386.

MS laid down in Article 126 para 2 TFEU. What is more, there would be no legal basis for the establishment of a fiscal surveillance agency other than Article 352 TFEU – which again requires the unanimity in the Council that, in view of the above, seemed unlikely to be reached.[511] In that sense there was no ousting of the agency concept. In this case setting up an agency was neither a legal nor a political option in the first place.

---

511   In addition to that, since 2009 a German law is required in order for the German representative to agree to or abstain from voting with regard to a legislative proposal based on Article 352 TFEU (§ 8 of the German *Integrationsverantwortungsgesetz* in conjunction with Article 23 para 1 of the German *Grundgesetz*).

3 The European System of Financial Supervisors

I. THE DEVELOPMENT OF A FINANCIAL MARKET SUPERVISORY SYSTEM

1. The Committee of Wise Men and its reports

1.1. Genesis and main ideas

In its Financial Services Action Plan 1999[1] the Commission proposed an 'ambitious ... legislative agenda'[2] to complete integration in the field of financial services within the EU. The Lisbon European Council in March 2000 approved this Plan, thereby setting a five-year deadline for its implementation. In order to meet the tough deadline, the long-winded legislative procedure, which applied (also) in the field of financial services regulation had to be fast-tracked.[3] With a view to gather concrete proposals, in July 2000 the ECOFIN-Council appointed a group of seven experts chaired by *Alexandre Lamfalussy*, the so-called Committee of Wise Men, to work out an initial report on the regulation of the European securities markets. In particular, the Committee was asked to assess the current conditions for implementation of the regulation in this sector and to make proposals on how to ensure greater convergence and cooperation in day-to-day implementation, considering the current legal framework of the EU, more tellingly: without having to amend the Treaties.[4]

In its final report, the Committee *inter alia* dealt with the main obstacles to an integrated European securities market, concluding that the most important of these obstacles were 'legal differences' in general, that is to say different legal traditions in the MS, and – among the 'specific obstacles' – a lack of

---

1 The Financial Services Action Plan was based on the findings published in Commission, COM (1998) 625 final. For a summary of the legislative endeavours for harmonisation in the field of financial services regulation in the E(E)C/EU since the 70s see Moloney, Frontiers 809ff; Tridimas 784ff.
2 Dragomir 87.
3 See Alford 390.
4 Cf Committee of Wise Men, Initial Report 1.

unified securities legislation.[5] It concluded that the then current regime was 'too slow'[6] and 'too rigid', that it 'produce[d] too much ambiguity' and that it 'fail[ed] to distinguish between core, enduring, essential framework principles and practical, day to day, implementing rules'.[7] This critique has to be understood against the background of the long-lasting practice of minimum harmonisation in the field of financial market regulation, which was promoted especially by the Commission.[8]

In order to tackle the detected difficulties, the Committee proposed a four-level regulatory framework in the field of European securities markets regulation.[9]

- **Level 1 – framework principles:** Directives or Regulations should only contain framework principles, leaving the implementing powers to the next level (level 2). The framework principles are an expression of the essential political choices made by the Commission, the Council and the EP. However, they shall also 'clearly specify the nature and the extent of the technical implementing measures' to be taken at the second level.[10] Level 1 legislation is adopted in the ordinary legislative procedure. Commission, Council and EP give the directions, but leave the details of how to follow these directions to the actors on the next, the comitology-level of regulation.[11]
- **Level 2 – implementing the details:** On the second level of the new regulatory structure, the operating actors are the Commission, a committee of high-level representatives of the MS (ESC), and a committee of national securities regulators (ESRC).

    The ESC serves a multiple purpose: It can act as a regulatory committee within the comitology framework,[12] and it can advise the Commission, in particular, on level 1 legislation and on level 2 mandates for the ESRC.[13] The ESC shall be prepared to report to the EP on a regular basis.[14]

---

5   *Lamfalussy* Report 102.
6   For the duration of procedures in financial market legislation prior to the introduction of the *Lamfalussy* regime see Kohtamäki 40f.
7   *Lamfalussy* Report 14f.
8   For the drawbacks of this practice see N Raschauer, Strukturprobleme 317; Dragomir 113f.
9   *Lamfalussy* Report 19ff.
10   Ibid., 23.
11   For examples illustrating the conceptual difference between level 1 and level 2 regulation, respectively, see ibid. 23f. See also Wymeersch 247, who claims that level 1 measures – in contradiction to the concept according to the *Lamfalussy* process – often contain many details, which renders them 'inflexible and sometimes even ill conceived'.
12   See Chapter 2 II.2. above; the regulatory procedure was abolished by *Comitology III*. For the respective transitional provisions for existing regulatory committees see Articles 13f *leg cit*.
13   *Lamfalussy* Report 29.
14   Ibid., 31.

The ESRC plays the role of an advisory committee in level 2 decision-making, and – in level 3 – of an independent committee of national regulators ensuring consistent implementation of level 1 and level 2 legislation. In level 2 the ESRC shall be composed of the heads of the MS' authorities for securities regulation and/or supervision designated by the MS. The EP shall be entitled to request a report from the ESRC periodically.[15]

In short, the decision-making procedure on level 2 is envisaged as follows: The Commission consults the ESC as well as the ESRC on the details of a planned implementing measure. The Commission then draws up a proposal, and forwards it to the ESC for a vote (comitology). If the ESC approves it and neither the EP nor the Council consider it to exceed the implementing power defined on level 1,[16] the proposal is adopted by the Commission.

- **Level 3 – strengthened cooperation between regulators to improve implementation:** In order to ensure strengthened cooperation on level 3 the Committee proposed to build up a network of national regulators, which shall agree on joint protocols for improving implementation and on a peer review procedure to ensure consistent implementation.[17]

  As indicated above, also on level 3, the ESRC comes into play. At this stage of the process it shall be composed of one representative for each MS designated by the national supervisory authority. Its main tasks on level 3 are to issue guidelines, agree on joint interpretation recommendations and set common standards 'regarding matters not covered by EU legislation'. This shall go hand in hand with an ongoing comparison and assessment of regulatory practices in the MS and – on the basis of its findings – an ongoing definition of best implementation practice.[18]

- **Level 4 – enforcement:** On level 4 the most important goal of the proposals made by the Committee is strengthening the enforcement. All actors of the four-level regime are involved here, above all the Commission in its role as the guardian of the Treaties. The Commission monitors whether, and – if required – enforces that the rules are implemented correctly and in due time. The Commission is therefore greatly dependent on information about any potential infringement, delivered in particular by the MS, the national regulators, the EP and the private sector.[19]

1.2. *From theory to practice – the implementation of the* Lamfalussy *Report*

The European Council welcomed the final report and asked the Commission to set in place a new regulatory framework that should be operational by 2002

---

15 Ibid., 32.
16 See now Article 11 of *Comitology III*.
17 *Lamfalussy* Report 37.
18 Ibid.
19 Ibid.

at the latest, and be subject to 'full and open review' in 2004.[20] Also the EP endorsed the four-level regulatory framework.[21] In June 2001 the Commission, essentially following the final report, set up the ESC and – slightly changing the word order of the ESRC – the CESR.[22]

Despite the fact that the merits of the *Lamfalussy* process have not been fully assessed by then,[23] the Commission had been convinced of the four-level approach and – upon invitation by the Council – decided to extend the new regulatory framework to the two other financial market sectors, namely banking and insurance and occupational pensions. For this purpose, in November 2003 the founding decisions for four new committees were adopted: the EBC and the EIOPC[24] – the equivalents of the ESC – on the one hand, and – as pendants of the CESR – the CEBS and the CEIOPS, on the other hand.[25]

The secondary legislation referring to the predecessors of the above committees was adapted by Directive 2005/1/EC. This Directive also – in particular in its Recitals – demonstrates the legislator's approval of the *Lamfalussy* framework that until then had – with the establishment of the respective committees – mainly been implemented by the Commission.[26] Where the *Lamfalussy* procedure shall be applied beyond the scope of the provisions adapted by this Directive, the basic act explicitly needs to provide for the applicability of the four-level regime.[27]

2.   The committees within the *Lamfalussy* framework

2.1.   *The level 2 committees: ESC, EBC, EIOPC*

The ESC, the EBC and the EIOPC[28] are the comitology committees in their respective field. They are Union bodies[29] without legal personality, composed of high-level representatives of the MS, mostly officers from the respective

---

20   European Council, Presidency Conclusions 2001, para 8.
21   EP, 2002/2061.
22   ESC-Decision and CESR-Decision.
23   Commission, SEC (2004) 1459, para 27; for one of its drawbacks, namely the dramatic increase of norms in the field of capital market law, see Korinek 88. The Commission considered the preliminary experience made with the committees in the field of securities 'very positive'; see Commission, MEMO/03/220, 2.
24   EBC-Decision and EIOPC-Decision.
25   CEBS-Decision and CEIOPS-Decision. At the same time CESR's remit was extended so as to include advice on draft implementing measures concerning UCITS by virtue of Commission Decision 2004/7/EC.
26   See Schmolke 439; N Raschauer, Strukturprobleme 317f; for an early account of the regime see Moloney, Lamfalussy.
27   See N Raschauer, Strukturprobleme 318.
28   See ESC-, EBC- and EIOPC-Decision; see also Directive 2005/1/EC.
29   See Türk 348.

ministries of finance,[30] and chaired by a representative of the Commission. The chair convenes the meetings – usually a couple of times per year – on his own initiative or at the request of a simple majority of committee members, and draws up the agenda for each meeting.[31] Each MS delegation is considered to be one member of the committee.[32] The chairpersons of the level 3 committees (now: the ESAs) participate in the meetings of the respective level 2 committee as an observer, and so do, for example, representatives of the EFTA countries Iceland, Liechtenstein and Norway. Further experts may be invited by the committee.[33]

The main task of the level 2 committees is to control the Commission in their role as comitology committees. Where a committee issues an opinion in the course of the examination procedure, qualified majority voting – analogously to the Council – applies.[34] Also apart from the comitology procedures the committees shall advise the Commission on policy matters as well as on draft measures in their respective field of expertise.[35]

The *Lamfalussy* procedure can be described as a subset of comitology-supported regulation in the broader sense, which is applied in the field of financial market regulation.[36] This is not to say that it is the exclusive procedure in this field. As *Raschauer* has exemplified, both the *Lamfalussy* procedure and traditional comitology procedures are provided for in the respective basic acts.[37]

The practice of ordinary comitology entails 1) basic legislation; 2) implementing acts by the Commission laying down – controlled by committees of MS representatives – uniform conditions for implementing the basic act; and

---

30   In the new committees, unlike with their predecessors, national supervisors are not represented; see Commission, MEMO/03/220; see Kohtamäki 78.

31   Articles 1 para 1 and 2 para 1 of the ESC-RoP; Article 1 para 1 of the EBC-RoP; Article 1 para 1 of the EIOPC-RoP.

32   Article 6 para 1 of the EBC-RoP

33   Articles 1 para 3 and 8 of the EBC-RoP. Article 3 of the EBC-Decision allows for 'the Commission' to invite experts and observers 'to attend its meetings'. The parallel provision in the ESC-Decision allows for the 'Committee' to invite experts or observers. It would be impractical and non-system to allow the Commission (as a collegiate body) to invite guests for a committee. If at all, it would be the representative of the Commission chairing the committee, since he regularly is best informed about the needs of the committee. However, there is no indication for this argument in the Decision. The wording 'may invite experts and observers to *its* meetings' (emphasis added) suggests that the Commission in its Decision wanted to entitle the committee to invite guests. The fact that the Commission made the same typing mistake in the EIOPC-Decision does not challenge the validity of these arguments.

34   Article 5 para 1 of the ESC-RoP; Article 5 para 1 of the EBC-RoP; Article 5 para 1 of the EIOPC-RoP.

35   Article 2 of the ESC-Decision; Article 5 and Recitals 6f of the EBC-Decision: The EBC thereby takes over the advisory tasks of the Banking Advisory Committee (founded in 1979); Recital 15 of Directive 2005/1/EC; see also Dragomir 215.

36   See von Danwitz 633; to get an idea of the trade-off between Council and Parliament in the context of the *Lamfalussy* procedure see Hofmann et al. 273f.

37   N Raschauer, Strukturprobleme 318f, giving examples from the field of banking supervision.

3) supervision by the Commission (the 'guardian of the Treaties') of the implementation by the MS. Under the *Lamfalussy* regime a four-step procedure is envisaged. In level 1 the framework principles are set by the legislator, on which basis the technical implementing measures are adopted by the Commission – controlled by the ESC, the EBC and the EIOPC respectively – in level 2. While ordinary comitology committees are regularly set up by the respective basic act, the *Lamfalussy* committees have been established by Commission decisions. In level 3 – and this is the level that is missing in ordinary comitology-supported regulation – committees of representatives of national supervisory authorities cooperate in order to improve implementation, thereby using their soft law powers. These level 3 committees also act as advisors in level 2. In level 4 it is first and foremost the Commission that supervises the implementation of the rules adopted and, if need be, enforces them.[38]

2.2.　*The level 3 committees: CESR, CEBS and CEIOPS*

The CESR, the CEBS and the CEIOPS on level 3 were the pendants of the ESC, the EBC and the EIOPC on level 2. They were conceptualised as independent Union bodies without legal personality.[39] Only their respective secretariats were organised as legal entities under the respective private law. The committees were composed of representatives of the national supervisors (and invited experts), which advised the Commission when requested to do so or on their own initiative, in particular regarding the preparation of draft implementing measures in the respective field of financial market supervision.[40] As a form of supervisory cooperation, including the exchange of information, the committees contributed to the consistent implementation of Community (Union) directives and to the convergence of MS' supervisory practices.[41]

The CESR was set up in June 2001. Its secretariat is organised as a nonprofit organisation ('association loi 1901') seated in Paris.[42] The CESR's predecessor was the FESCO, which was established in December 1997 as an

---

38　Level 4 of the *Lamfalussy* procedure and level 3 of the ordinary comitology practice both – apart from soft law measures promoting compliance – above all address the competence of the Commission to initiate infringement proceedings against MS according to Article 258 para 1 TFEU. The role of the Commission here is not principally different from its role as it regards the supervision of the implementation by the MS of any other legislative act; see N Raschauer, Strukturprobleme 320.

39　On the CEBS' legal status see European Ombudsman, 2497/2010/FOR, paras 13–16. These considerations do, *mutatis mutandis*, also apply to the CESR and the CEIOPS; see also Kohtamäki 73.

40　For the European supervisory system prior to the *Lamfalussy* structure see Lannoo, System 243.

41　Recital 9 of the CESR-Decision; Article 2 of the CEBS- and of the CEIOPS-Decision. On the cooperation of financial market supervisory authorities in the EU see N Raschauer, Behördenkooperation.

42　See Commission, SEC (2009) 54, 4f.

'intergovernmental consultative body'.[43] The CESR took over all understandings, standards, commitments and wc⋅k agreed within the FESCO.[44] Originally, it was financed only by the supervisory authorities of the MS themselves.[45] The committee had to convene at least four times a year.[46]

The cooperation of national banking supervisors in the EEA dates back to 1972 when the so-called Groupe de Contact was established as an informal working group of European banking supervisors, in which they – confidentially – discussed practical problems in everyday supervision.[47] The Commission attended the meetings only irregularly and only as an observer.[48] The CEBS, which was established in November 2003 (with no concrete predecessor[49]), intended to benefit from this treasure trove of experience of European cooperation in the banking sector, not least by considering the Groupe de Contact[50] its 'main expert group'.[51] The CEBS' secretariat was organised as a limited company by guarantee without share capital under UK law, situated in London.[52] It was financed by the regulatory supervisory authorities of the MS. The committee was supposed to meet regularly and whenever the situation so demanded, but at least three times a year.[53]

Also in the insurance and occupational pensions sector the Commission established a committee of supervisors. The CEIOPS, which was preceded by relevant international cooperation,[54] in particular the Conference of Insurance Supervisory Authorities of the MS, was established in November 2003. Its secretariat was a private non-profit organisation registered in Germany ('eingetragener Verein'), seated in Frankfurt am Main and financed by contributions from the MS supervisory authorities.[55] All agreements, standards, commitments and work agreed within the Conference of Insurance Supervisory Authorities of the MS were taken over by it.[56] The CEIOPS was supposed to convene at least three times a year.[57]

43　Lannoo, System 241. Also the CESR was established under national law, but was later recognised and largely determined by EU legislation (see below); see Wymeersch 248.

44　Article 10 para 1 of the CESR-Charter.

45　Article 9 para 2 of the CESR-Charter. With the 2009 reform (see 3. below), the legislator, in addition to that and only for specific actions of the committees, allowed for contributions from the then Community budget; Decision 716/2009/EC.

46　Article 5 para 1 of the CESR-Charter.

47　See Dragomir 254.

48　See Kolassa, para 6.

49　See Dragomir 218.

50　On the tasks of the Groupe de Contact see Kohtamäki 77.

51　Article 5 para 4 of the CEBS-Charter; see Dragomir 217.

52　See Commission, SEC (2009) 54, 4f.

53　Article 5 para 1 of the CEBS-Charter. ⸱

54　For a summary of cooperation between national supervisors on the EC and on the international level prior to the introduction of the *Lamfalussy* procedure see Braumüller 616ff.

55　See CEIOPS, Annual Report 2010, 88f.

56　Article 3 para 3 of the CEIOPS-Charter.

57　Article 7 para 2 lit a of the CEIOPS-Charter.

The CESR and the CEIOPS were both composed of high-level representatives from the national public authorities competent in the field of securities, and insurance and occupational pensions, respectively – one representative designated by each MS.[58] Other experts and observers could be invited to attend the meetings.[59] In addition to that, representatives of the Commission and of Norway, Iceland and Liechtenstein were entitled to attend the meetings in the role of observers.[60] Each committee elected a Chairperson by secret ballot from among its members for a period of two years.[61] The Chair organised, set the agenda of and chaired the meetings of the committee. The Chair represented the committee externally and was, in case of the CESR, responsible for public relations, for the supervision of the committee's secretariat and for the execution of all other tasks delegated to him by the committee.[62] A Secretary General was appointed by both committees,[63] in case of the CESR for a renewable period of three years. As regards the CESR, the Secretary General headed the secretariat of the committee, which was staffed by and worked under the responsibility of the Chair. It assisted both the committee and its groups and the Chair and the Vice Chair(s) with respect to their representative functions.[64] The CEIOPS-Charter foresaw a peculiar steering organ, the Managing Board, which was composed of the Chair, the Vice Chair and four further members of the total number of the MS authorities' representatives ('Members' Meeting'). The Managing Board was responsible *inter alia* for the preparation of the Members' Meeting, the implementation of its resolutions and the reporting to the EP.[65] The Members' Meeting convened at least three times a year. It was responsible for the fulfilment of the mandate of the CEIOPS more generally, for the election and dismissal of the Managing Board and for the creation and compilation of the sub-committees of the CEIOPS.[66]

The CEBS was composed of one senior representative from the banking supervisory authority of each MS (national central bank or other supervisory authority). Where the national central bank was not the competent authority, a senior representative of the central bank was designated by the MS to attend the meeting (without voting rights).[67] Additionally, one senior representative of the ECB and one representative of the Commission were joining the group as observers. The CEBS itself added to the list of observers high-level

---

58   The different composition of the CESR (ESRC) depending on whether it operates in level 2 or in level 3, as envisaged by the *Lamfalussy* Report, has not been picked up by the Commission.

59   Article 1 para 1 of the CESR-Charter; Article 9 para 3 of the CEIOPS-Charter.

60   Article 1 para 2 of the CESR-Charter; Article 7 para 5 of the CEIOPS-Charter.

61   Article 2 para 1 of the CESR-Charter; Article 6 para 2 of the CEIOPS-Charter.

62   Article 2 of the CESR-Charter.

63   Article 8 para 1 of the CESR-Charter; Article 7 para 1 lit g of the CEIOPS-Charter.

64   Article 8 of the CESR-Charter.

65   Article 6 paras 1, 2 and 4 of the CEIOPS-Charter.

66   Article 7 para 1 of the CEIOPS-Charter.

67   Article 1 para 1 of the CEBS-Charter.

representatives of the banking supervisory authorities of the EEA-countries Iceland, Liechtenstein and Norway,[68] the chairs of the BSC of the ESCB and of the Groupe de Contact.[69] The CEBS was free to invite further experts or observers to attend its meetings.[70] The CEBS by consensus (if not possible: by a two-thirds majority) elected a Chairperson and a Vice Chair from among its voting members for a period of two years.[71] The Chair organised and chaired the meetings of the CEBS, was responsible for the external representation of the committee and the supervision of the secretariat, and executed all other tasks delegated to him by the committee.[72] The Chair, the Vice Chair and up to four further members who advised and assisted the Chair together formed the Bureau. The task of the Bureau essentially was to advise and assist the Chair.[73] The CEBS' secretariat assisted the committee and its expert groups[74] in their functions and executed all other functions assigned to it by the committee or by the Chair.[75] A Secretary General was appointed by the committee upon a proposal of the Chair for a renewable period of three years. The Chairman appointed other permanent or seconded staff.

The level 3 committees' tasks were to advise the Commission either upon request or on their own initiative, particularly for the preparation of draft implementing measures in the respective field of financial market law.[76] Before launching an opinion to the Commission, the committees had to adequately consult market participants, consumers and end-users.[77] The committees furthermore contributed to the consistent application of Community (Union) directives and the convergence of MS' supervisory practices by improving the supervisory cooperation between the MS' authorities – including the exchange of information.[78] As regards level 3 measures (guidelines, recommendations, standards etc.), the committees' Charters provided that MS ought to comply with them, although they were not legally binding.[79] In their versions of

68   Article 1 para 2 of the CEBS-Charter.
69   Article 1 para 4 of the CEBS-Charter.
70   Article 3 of the CEBS-Decision.
71   Article 2 para 1 of the CEBS-Charter.
72   Article 2 para 2 of the CEBS-Charter.
73   Article 2 para 3 of the CEBS-Charter.
74   Eg the Expert Group on Prudential Regulation or the Expert Group on Financial Information; see Kohtamäki 74.
75   Article 7 para 2 of the CEBS-Charter.
76   Preamble to and Article 6 para 3 of the CESR-Charter; Article 4 paras 1 and 2 of the CEBS-Charter; Article 1 para 2 of the CEIOPS-Charter. For the CESR since 2003 this includes the UCITS. For the CESR's role in the regulation and supervision of UCITS see CESR, CESR/03-378b.
77   Article 5 of the CESR-Decision; Article 5 of the CEBS-Decision. For a list of the consultative instruments see Article 5.10 of the CEBS-Charter; Article 5 of the CEIOPS-Decision.
78   Preamble to the CESR-Charter; Article 2 of the CEBS-Decision; Article 1 para 3 of the CEIOPS-Charter.
79   For a sample of CESR measures and the respective compliance rates in the MS see Maggetti and Gilardi, in particular 836f; on the legal quality of these soft law measures see also Kohtamäki 75 with further references.

2008/09, the Charters listed circumstances in which MS were explicitly allowed not to apply a level 3 measure. This was the case where a) the measure was incompatible with the respective national law or for lack of competence due to legal impediments; b) vital political or technical impediments for the measure were expected; or c) the objectives of the measure were met through other means or where the measure would have been disproportionate in the context of the local market. If a MS refused to comply with a level 3 measure for one of these reasons, it had to fully state its reasons, clarifying in detail the legal, political or technical impediment ('comply or explain' approach). This justification was to be published and included in the level 3 reports to the institutions.[80]

The committees principally adopted their decisions by consensus. Since 2008/09 the committees' Charters had provided for qualified majority voting analogously to the voting in the Council.[81] Up until then qualified majority voting had been allowed only where the committees were giving advice to the Commission. Dissenting opinions of individual members were recorded in one or the other way.[82]

The committees had to convey to the Commission an annual report.[83] In addition to that, they had to report to the EP periodically.[84] The chairs of the level 3 committees were supposed to work in close cooperation with each other[85] and to maintain close operational links with the Commission and their pendant level 2 committees.[86]

---

80 Article 6 para 4 of the CESR-Charter; Article 5 para 7 of the CEBS-Charter; Article 8 para 9 of the CEIOPS-Charter; cf Tridimas 787. This 'comply or explain' mechanism was recommended by the IIMG 18.

81 Article 6 para 1 of the CESR-Charter (see CESR, Annual Report 2008, 3); Article 5 para 6 of the CEBS-Charter (see CEBS, Annual Report 2004, 10); Article 8 para 3 of the CEIOPS-Charter (see CEIOPS, Annual Report 2004 and Work Programme 2005, 9). An adaptation of the majority requirements from consensus to qualified majority voting was considered necessary due to the accession of ten new MS in the course of the Eastern Enlargement of 2004; see Council, 15698/07, 21; see also Karpf et al. 7 (footnote 18).

82 Article 6 para 3 lit d of the CESR-Charter; Article 5 para 6 of the CEBS-Charter; Article 8 para 7 of the CEIOPS-Charter.

83 Article 7 para 1 of the CESR-Charter; Article 6 para 1 of the CEBS-Charter; Article 7 para 1 lit e of the CEIOPS-Charter.

84 Article 6 of the CESR-Charter; Article 6 para 2 of the CEBS-Charter; Article 6 para 4 of the CEIOPS-Charter.

85 Article 3 para 1 of the CESR-Charter; Article 6 para 5 of the CEBS-Charter; less clear in the CEIOPS-Charter, but may be read into its Article 1 para 3 subpara 3; see Karpf et al. 14 with further references. On the leading role of the CESR see Maggetti and Gilardi 835.

86 Articles 3 and 7 para 2 of the CESR-Charter; Articles 7 para 3 and 6 para 2 of the CEBS-Charter; eg CEIOPS, Annual Report 2004, 14.

2.3.   *The* Lamfalussy *process: its rationale and the role of committees*

The introduction of the *Lamfalussy* process has served a twofold purpose. First, it accelerated the decision-making process in a market that requires timely legislative responses to ever-changing circumstances – the considerable increase in the number of regulatory acts (and hence a very high complexity of the legal framework) being the collateral damage of this effect.[87] Second, it provides for new bodies on the EU level that shall facilitate a coherent application of law throughout the Union and – to a limited extent[88] – improve financial market supervision.[89] Through various means of cooperation between these bodies, the Commission and the national supervisory authorities, the two spheres 'regulation' and 'supervision' are intermingled with each other. The level 2 committees advise the Commission already in the legislative drafting stage of level 1. The level 3 committees are consulted by the Commission already in level 2, when it comes to the adoption of implementing measures. The level 2 and 3 committees cooperate closely and on a regular basis with each other. This compacted structure is intended to enhance the consistency of regulation and supervision and to improve the conformity of the latter with the former.

The national authorities' competences largely remained untouched in this context. While denying a need for an alignment of competences of national supervisors – they 'do not need to have identical supervisory powers to implement both EU directives and level 3 standards/guidelines' – the Commission claimed that 'they should have the necessary and sufficient minimum powers and tools (including sanctions) to fulfil their obligations'.[90]

But while the financial markets have become more and more integrated, the approximation of national supervisory practices has been lagging behind this development.[91] The implementation of the four-level *Lamfalussy* procedure has not only led to an acceleration of the legislative procedure as regards financial services legislation. It has also fostered the cooperation between national supervisors, the mutual exchange of information and the coordination of supervisory practices. The measures adopted in this context are mainly soft measures (standards, guidelines, best practices, etc.),[92] however – as the Committee of Wise Men stated with reference to the level 3 committees – clearly they 'carry considerable authority' and contribute strongly to a harmonisation of MS authorities' supervisory practices.[93]

---

87   See also B Raschauer, Verfahren 17.
88   See eg Dragomir 92, stressing that the *Lamfalussy* regime has neglected 'stability concerns'.
89   See Gause, para 327; see also Tsatsaronis 681.
90   Commission, COM (2007) 727 final, 10.
91   See Alford 396.
92   On soft law in Union law generally see Schwarze; with a focus on economic law see T Müller.
93   *Lamfalussy* Report 38.

In the *Lamfalussy* process, two types of committees can be differentiated. The first kind of committee is conceptualised as a body allowing for MS representation. It is regularly composed of one representative per MS, which may be complemented by additional experts and observers. Its function is twofold: first, the committee fulfils the function of a comitology committee – which essentially means voting on implementing measures proposed by the Commission, and, second, it advises the Commission on policy issues and Commission proposals in its respective field.[94] In both its functions – control and advisory function – the committee serves as a means of ensuring MS' participation in the decision-making process of the EU – 'a form of Council of Ministers writ small',[95] not least because the representatives are regularly bound by the instructions given by their respective minister.[96] However, concerns have been uttered frequently over time as regards the extent of the Commission's influence, since the committee, institutionally speaking, is part of the Commission, which finds its expression in the fact that it is regularly chaired by a representative of the Commission who is the agenda setter.[97] As regards the possibility of undue Commission influence, the level 2 committees' position is not any different from that of regular comitology committees (see Chapter 2 IV.3. above).

On the other hand, we have the type of a committee of independent supervisors. This kind of committee is conceptualised as an independent assembly of the MS' supervisory authorities. The rule 'one representative per MS' does not alter the fact that the link between the members of the committees and the respective MS is – on a whole – relatively weak. Independent expertise – both theoretical knowledge and practical experience – stays in the foreground,[98] whereas the representation of MS interests might be at issue at times, but ideal-typically does not play a role in this forum. Whereas the level 2 committees are 'political', the level 3 committees are 'neutral'.[99] Their independence has, according to the Commission, four main aspects: an institutional, a regulatory, a supervisory and a budgetary aspect.[100] This type of committee shall serve as a platform for the exchange of information and experience and shall help improve cooperation in the interest of better implementation. It emphatically 'does not have any regulatory powers at Community [Union] level'[101] but is limited to soft powers: It shall *inter alia* issue guidelines for the consistent application of legislation and implementing measures by the MS, agree on joint interpretative recommendations[102] and

---

94   See, eg, Article 2 of the EBC-Decision; cf N Raschauer, Strukturprobleme 323.
95   Hertig and Lee 8, with respect to the ESC.
96   Critically, N Raschauer, Strukturprobleme 336.
97   For the pivotal role the chair of a comitology committee plays see Falke 73.
98   Cf Hummer 112f.
99   Moloney, Frontiers 815, with respect to the ESC and the CESR.
100   Commission, COM (2007) 727 final, 10.
101   Recitals 9, 10 and 11 of the level 3 committees' founding decisions.
102   On the interpretative role of the CESR see Kalss 609–611.

set common standards 'regarding matters not covered by EU legislation'.[103] The latter task especially is a tool of creeping integration beyond the letter of the law – by means of soft measures reinforced by peer pressure.[104]

In terms of risk analysis, the competences of the level 3 committees can be assigned to risk assessment. Through their advisory role in levels 1 and 2 they did participate in risk management, but there they merely advised, which is to say they presented their assessments that the risk managers (the legislator, the Commission and the comitology committees) could then take as a basis for their decisions/opinions. The considerable *de facto* influence on risk management these assessments had, however, corroborates the assumption that they also acted as risk managers.[105] Since their advice was regularly published on their respective website they even had their share in risk communication.[106]

While the conceptual difference between the two types of committees is relatively clear, it ought to be stressed that both of them (also) play(ed) an advisory role. Here the level structure of the *Lamfalussy* regulatory framework steps back. Good advice does not know a hierarchy: The Commission takes expert advice in different stages of the decision-making process and from different committees.

Also regarding the voting mode, both types of committees operate(d) under the same conditions. Level 2 committees can give advice by a qualified majority of the votes. The same was true for level 3 committees. In both cases qualified majority means/meant the same, that is to say a weighing of votes according to the voting rules in the Council.[107]

3. The 2009 reform

3.1. *Room for improvement*

The *Lamfalussy* procedure has been subject to a variety of reviews, which all – in principle[108] – defended the four-level regulatory structure.[109] In February 2005 the ECB published an assessment[110] and especially in autumn 2007 evaluations were launched by the Commission, the IIMG[111] and the European Council.[112] The final report of the IIMG stated that the relevant actors on

---

103   *Lamfalussy* Report 37; CESR, Action Plan 3f; cf Schmolke 435.
104   See II.3.4.4. below.
105   See N Raschauer, Strukturprobleme 335; for examples see Kreisl and Raschauer 279ff.
106   See Weismann, EU-Finanzmarktaufsicht 808f.
107   For the respective weights assigned to each MS see Article 3 of Protocol No 36.
108   The Parliament repeatedly raised concerns about a democratic deficit of the *Lamfalussy* procedure; see Schmolke 446; for a differentiated view as regards the democratic deficit in the given context see von Bogdandy 200.
109   See, for example, Karpf et al. 6 with further references; on the 'political drawbacks' of the new committee structure see Commission, MEMO/03/220, 3f.
110   ECB, Review.
111   IIMG 4.
112   European Council, 7652/1/08 Rev 1, paras 30ff.

both level 1 and level 2 should exercise 'regulatory self-restraint', since the output on both levels has a tendency towards containing too much detail.[113] The IIMG furthermore proposed that level 1 legislation and level 2 implementing measures should be drafted in parallel with the implementing measures being finalised only after the adoption of level 1 legislation. Consultation, particularly with the level 3 committees, should take place on all levels but should be better coordinated in order to avoid overlaps. With respect to the level 3 committees it proposed to extend qualified majority voting.[114] As regards enforcement, the IIMG recommended regulatory additions by the MS in their respective implementation processes to be reduced.[115] To this end, MS should be required to report on regulatory additions they intend to adopt. Furthermore, convergence of practices should be reached by means of peer pressure.

The Commission in its review from November 2007 reported criticism on 'too much detail in the Level 1 texts'.[116] Furthermore, it held that the missions of the three level 3 committees were inconsistent.[117] Like the IIMG, the Commission, while acknowledging the 'considerable weight' of decisions taken by consensus, also argued in favour of more frequent use of qualified majority voting within the level 3 committees.

The European Council in its critique – with regard to the supervisory part of the *Lamfalussy* architecture – essentially demanded better cooperation between the supervisory authorities in the MS, enhanced exchange of information and improved convergence of supervisory practices. To that end, the European Council proposed, an 'EU dimension' should be included in the mandates of national supervisors.[118]

3.2.   *Extension of competences*

In the aftermath of the review process outlined above, and given the explicit invitation by the ECOFIN-Council to revise the Commission decisions establishing the committees of supervisors,[119] the Commission adopted new founding decisions vesting the committees of supervisors with enhanced and more clearly sketched tasks – based on the results of the review process – thereby repealing the old founding decisions, which provided for only a very

---

113   IIMG 4; see also Vitkova 167; cf Schmolke 432.
114   IIMG 5.
115   On MS' gold-plating practices see Kohtamäki 62f.
116   Commission, COM (2007) 727 final, 4.
117   Ibid., 8.
118   European Council, 7652/1/08 Rev 1, para 33. According to this document, the question of what exactly the inclusion of such an 'EU dimension' entails can only remain subject to speculations. In its Note 8515/3/08 Rev 3 the Council is more to the point regarding the EU dimension.
119   Council, Note 8515/3/08 Rev 3.

rough outline of the committees' tasks.[120] The Charters of the respective committees – autonomous statutes that were more explicit as regards composition and competences of the committees – applied (partly in a renewed version) also under the reformed regime.

In order to contribute to the 'common and uniform implementation and consistent application' of Union law – a remit which the CESR, contrary to the CEBS and the CEIOPS, has not had under the old regime – the committees of supervisors were now explicitly entitled to issue guidelines, recommendations and standards.[121] But the committees should also develop 'new practical convergence tools' to foster a common supervisory approach.[122]

According to Article 4 of the founding decisions the committees had to carry out the following tasks in order to enhance cooperation between the supervisory authorities in the MS and to improve convergence of their supervisory practices:

'(a) mediate or facilitate mediation between supervisory authorities in cases specified in the relevant legislation or at the request of a supervisory authority;

(b) provide opinions to supervisory authorities in cases specified in the relevant legislation or at their request;

(c) promote the effective bilateral and multilateral exchange of information between supervisory authorities subject to applicable confidentiality provisions;

(d) facilitate the delegation of tasks between supervisory authorities, in particular by identifying tasks which can be delegated and by promoting best practices;

(e) contribute to ensuring the efficient and consistent functioning of colleges of supervisors in particular through setting guidelines for the operational functioning of colleges, monitoring the coherence of the practices of the different colleges and sharing best practices;

(f) contribute to developing high-quality and common supervisory reporting standards; and

(g) review the practical application of the non-binding guidelines, recommendations and standards issued by the Committee.'

The committees had to monitor and assess the developments in their respective sector of the financial market and, where necessary, to inform the respective other level 3 committees, the Commission and – in case of 'potential or

---

120 For the partly correspondent recommendations of the *de Larosière* Group see 4.2. below.

121 Article 3 of the level 3 committees' founding decisions. Under the pre-2009 regime, the founding decisions did not *expressis verbis* provide for such competences, but the committees of supervisors themselves called upon these entitlements; see examples of such soft law output (of the CESR) given by Maggetti and Gilardi 836.

122 Article 4 para 3 of the level 3 committees' founding decisions.

imminent problems' – the MS' finance ministries and their central banks.[123] In order to also cover cross-sectoral developments, the committees had to cooperate closely with each other, and with the BSC of the ESCB.[124] Where appropriate, they should facilitate a 'joint assessment amongst supervisors' (CEIOPS: 'common position').[125]

Each committee was required to send an annual work programme to the Council, the EP and the Commission by the end of October each year. The committees had to regularly, and at least annually, inform these institutions of their performance of the activities envisaged in the latest work programme.[126] Also they should have regular contact with their sister comitology committees (ESC, EBC, EIOPC) and the competent committee of the EP.[127]

The CEBS and the CEIOPS cooperated in the area of supervision of financial conglomerates in a Joint Committee on Financial Conglomerates. In this Joint Committee also the CESR was allowed to participate. The Commission and the ECB were to be invited to attend the meetings of the Joint Committee as observers.[128]

Decisions of the committees were principally adopted by consensus. Only where consensus could not be reached, qualified majority voting applied. This was a general rule applying to all kinds of committee output.[129]

Members of the committees that did not follow the guidelines, recommendations, standards and other measures issued by the committees were asked to give the reasons for this deviance ('comply or explain' approach; see already 2.2. above).[130]

As regards the financial means, the legislator for specific actions of the level 3 committees allowed for contributions from the then Community budget.[131]

The reform of 2009 has to be understood as a compromise between those MS which promoted a new institutional order in the field of financial market supervision and those – eg the British[132] – which favoured further improvement of cooperation within the (limits set by the) then current institutional supervisory system.[133] As a result of the reform, the competences of the level 3 committees were put more precisely and in greater detail, for example as regards the competence to issue guidelines and recommendations in order to achieve more coherent supervision among the national authorities. At the

---

123   Article 5 para 1 of the level 3 committees' founding decisions.
124   Article 5 para 4 of the level 3 committees' founding decisions.
125   Article 5 para 3 of the level 3 committees' founding decisions.
126   Article 13 of the level 3 committees' founding decisions.
127   Article 9 para 1 of the level 3 committees' founding decisions.
128   Article 11 of the level 3 committees' founding decisions.
129   Article 14 of the level 3 committees' founding decisions.
130   Article 14 of the level 3 committees' founding decisions.
131   See Decision 716/2009/EC.
132   See Kohtamäki 93.
133   See Fischer zu Cramburg 64. For the diverging views on that matter see IIMG 18f; for a report on the changes in the CEBS due to the 2009 reform see af Jochnik.

same time, the committees were vested with new competences, for example the competence to mediate between supervisory authorities if provided for in the legislation or at the request of a supervisory authority, or the competence to facilitate the delegation of tasks between the supervisory authorities.

4. The *de Larosière* Report

4.1. Overview

The next step in the development of the European financial market supervisory architecture[134] was heralded by the *de Larosière* Report.[135] The *de Larosière* Group, a committee of eight experts (mainly economists) chaired by *Jacques de Larosière*, former managing director of the IMF, was mandated by the Commission in particular to work on the following questions: How should the financial market supervision – irrespective of questions of competence – best be organised in order to ensure 'the prudential soundness of institutions, the orderly functioning of markets and ... the protection of depositors, policy-holders and investors'? How can cooperation on a European-wide financial stability oversight, early warning mechanisms and crisis management (including cross-border and cross-sectoral risks) be strengthened? How should the EU's financial market supervisory bodies 'cooperate with other major jurisdictions to help safeguard financial stability at the global level'?[136]

The *de Larosière* Report evokes memories of the *Lamfalussy* Report. The mandates for both reports essentially consisted in issuing recommendations for the improvement of the functioning of the financial market via an improvement of its regulation and supervision. But while what has become famous as the *Lamfalussy* Report was requested in order to complete the integration of the financial market as envisaged in the Financial Services Action Plan of 1999, the *de Larosière* Report was ordered as a result of the crisis of the financial market starting in summer 2007[137] – also to repair the weaknesses of the principally successful *Lamfalussy* system.[138] This is why the *de Larosière* Report is more exhaustive in presenting the then current – extraordinary – economic circumstances and in drawing conclusions for institutional and operational reform in the field of financial market regulation and supervision. The *de Larosière* Committee begins its Report by giving an account of the

---

134 On Commission attempts to build up an EEC banking supervision as early as in the 60s see Burgard and Heimann, para 5 with further references. On the characteristics of a 'European financial market' see Ladler, Finanzmarkt 114ff.

135 *de Larosière* Report. For a summary of the developments after the break-out of the crisis see eg Kolassa, paras 8ff.

136 *de Larosière* Report 69.

137 For an extensive – economic – account of the reasons for the financial crisis see Friedman; *de Larosière* Report 6ff.

138 See Kämmerer, Finanzaufsichtssystem 1283.

crisis and its causes at some length. Suffice it here to have a word on the Committee's findings as they regard the financial market regulatory and supervisory system. The Committee draws the conclusion that the crisis was facilitated not only by FI, but also by 'those who regulated and supervised them'.[139] The regulators and supervisors of the financial markets have, according to the Committee, overestimated 'the ability of financial firms as a whole to manage their risks', and correspondingly have underestimated the importance of sufficient capital resources.[140]

In its second chapter the *de Larosière* Report dwells on 'regulatory repair' and makes proposals on how best to reform the substantive law regulating the financial market both on an international level and on the EU level. Starting with a consideration of Basel II (recommendations 1 and 2), it then goes on to deal with CRA that – in light of their 'pivotal and quasi-regulatory role' – ought to be regulated effectively in order to ensure independent, objective and high-quality ratings.[141] The Report here refers to a legislative proposal of the Commission.[142] The sharing of competences between home and host authorities envisaged in this proposal the Committee deemed to be 'too cumbersome' and 'likely to lack effectiveness and efficiency'.[143] It would be more reasonable instead to entrust a strengthened CESR with the licensing and monitoring – and, if need be, with the limitation of activities or even withdrawal of the licences[144] – of CRA (recommendation 3).

Recommendations 4 and 5, which regard accounting rules and insurance, are mentioned here for the sake of completeness, but shall not be elaborated further. Recommendation 6 suggests that the EU supervisory bodies should be equipped with 'sufficient' supervisory powers including sanctions. The following recommendations (7–9) are on the 'parallel banking system' (hedge funds, investment banks, various off-balance sheet items, etc.[145]), on securitised products and derivatives markets and on investment funds.

Recommendation 10 regards the establishment of a 'truly harmonised set of core rules' in the field of financial market regulation in the EU, which would, according to the Committee, be another step in the attempt to prevent future financial crises.

The improvement of corporate governance is subject to the next few pages of the Report – the result of this analysis being recommendation 11. Risk management within FI is dealt with in recommendation 12. The recommendations 13–15 touch upon the harmonisation of crisis management and the harmonisation of deposit guarantee schemes (burden-sharing).

---

139   *de Larosière* Report 8.
140   Ibid.
141   Ibid., 19.
142   Commission, COM (2008) 704 final. The regulation and supervision of CRA is now laid down in Regulation 1060/2009; see also Sonder 239.
143   *de Larosière* Report 19.
144   Ibid., 20.
145   Ibid., 23.

The next chapter of the *de Larosière* Report ('EU Supervisory Repair') is of pivotal importance here, since it contains the proposals for a new EU supervisory structure in the field of financial markets.

An important distinction drawn by the *de Larosière* Report right from the beginning of this chapter is the distinction between micro- and macroprudential supervision. Microprudential supervision is concerned with paying attention to the robustness of individual FI (eg to whether they meet their capital requirements), thereby also protecting the customers of the institution at issue. Macroprudential supervision, on the contrary, is the supervision of the financial system as a whole. The holistic perspective allows for a better perception of systemic risks and is therefore immensely important for the prevention of financial crises comparable to the last one – since such crises are more likely to emerge as the result of risks that affect the system as a whole, than as a result of the failure of one single financial institution.[146]

In the view of the *de Larosière* Group macroprudential supervision has been neglected so far. This and other supervisory shortcomings have – among many other factors – facilitated the emergence of the crisis.[147] Under the new regime financial supervision shall be exercised in a micro- as well as in a macroprudential way, since these two subsets of supervision are interdependent. Sound microprudential supervision requires macroprudential information and *vice versa*.[148] Especially in the macroprudential supervision EU bodies shall be involved more strongly. The Report recommends the ECB, and the ESCB respectively, to be entrusted with this task,[149] thereby refusing views according to which the ECB should also be involved in microprudential supervision.[150] The Group lists the reasons for this refusal, the most important of them being: a) the ECB is primarily responsible for monetary stability; b) the ECB's independence could be at risk in case of a crisis, when the ECB is involved in political discourse with the national providers of financial support (typically the finance ministries); c) the ECB is not responsible for the monetary policy of MS that are not part of the Eurozone; d) the ECB, according to the Treaty, is not competent to deal with insurance companies.[151]

---

146 Ibid., 38; for this terminology in more detail see Kohtamäki 10–14; Ladler, Finanzmarkt 134f.

147 Although the *de Larosière* Group is anxious not to offend the financial supervisors in the EU, and although it deems lacking supervision 'not [to be] one of the primary causes behind the crises', it stresses the fact that there have been 'real and important supervisory failures' (39).

148 *de Larosière* Report 38.

149 Ibid., 40.

150 Ibid., 42f.

151 Ibid., 43f; under the more recent SSM, however, the ECB has been vested with powers in the field of microprudential supervision (see Chapter 4 II.1. below).

The Report lists further drawbacks in the context of financial market supervision. The system lacks effective early warning mechanisms. The macroprudential supervision by the ECB/ESCB, as proposed by the Group, shall be coupled with an effective and enforceable mechanism to ensure that the EU advisory bodies as well as the national supervisors react to the systemic risks identified by the macroprudential supervision.[152]

Another point of criticism regards the role of home supervisors when the FI are operating across the borders of their home country. This can create significant risks for the host countries – the Group mentions the case of the Icelandic banks. Therefore, host countries shall have the possibility to challenge decisions of the respective home supervisors.[153] More generally, the Group recommends that a high level of minimum competences of the supervisory authorities in all MS shall be established.[154] In addition to that, binding mediation mechanisms shall be put in place in order to settle conflicts of competence between supervisors of different MS in cross-border cases.

Furthermore, the information flow between the national supervisors shall be improved and the resources as well as the powers of the level 3 committees shall be increased.[155]

A comparably short chapter of the Report is dedicated to the topic 'Global Repair'. It shall not be discussed here.

The Group concludes its proposals with the loaded words: 'This report sets out the regulatory, supervisory and global reforms that the Group considers are needed. Work must begin immediately.'[156]

4.2.   *The reform of microprudential supervision*

Having reviewed the financial market supervisory architecture, the *de Larosière* Group comes to the conclusion that the level 3 committees 'have contributed significantly to the process of European financial integration'.[157] In that sense, the reform proposals could be themed 'more of the same', since they envisage further enhanced cooperation between supervisory authorities – especially as it regards the exchange of information – within an EU institutional framework, and more competences attributed to this framework. The national supervisory structures shall – leaving apart the shift of competences from the national to the EU level – remain untouched, since they 'have been chosen for a variety of reasons and it would be impractical to try to harmonise them'.[158]

---

152   *de Larosière* Report 40.
153   Ibid., 40f.
154   Ibid., 41.
155   Ibid., 41f.
156   Ibid., 68.
157   Ibid., 46.
158   Ibid., 48.

The Group proposes the establishment of a European System of Financial Supervisors (ESFS). This system is a frame within which national as well as enhanced level 3 committees ('authorities') shall operate.[159] The new EU supervisory authorities shall be vested with a 'defined number' of supervisory competences, especially with respect to large cross-border institutions – which are most likely to pose systemic risks.[160] These competences shall be exercised by them, but shall be executed by the respective national authority. In other words, national authorities shall still be the 'first point of contact' for the supervised undertakings, but – as regards cross-border undertakings – they shall perform the will of the EU authorities, work as their extension, as it were. As regards the question of independence and accountability of the new framework, and the tensions between these two requirements, the Group contents itself with the lapidary recommendation that it must be 'independent from the political authorities, but fully accountable to them'.[161]

The Group aims at more than just changing the institutional structure of financial market supervision. Rather, it wants to bring together regulation, supervision and crisis management and resolution.

For the implementation of the proposals, the Group recommends a two-stage approach. In Stage 1 (2009–2010) the ESFS shall be prepared; in Stage 2 (2010–2011) it shall be established.

As part of Stage 1 the MS and the EU shall make every effort to improve the quality of supervision. On the MS level these efforts shall include the harmonisation of supervisors' competences to the most comprehensive system in the EU – in particular, a sound minimum of supervisory sanctioning powers shall be reached in all MS[162], the increase of supervisors' remuneration, the facilitation of personnel exchanges between the private sector and the supervisory authorities and ensuring a modern and attractive personnel policy within the authorities. On the EU level, the level 3 committees shall contribute to a strong European supervisory culture by intensifying their efforts as regards the training and the exchange of personnel.[163] Still in Stage 1, the level 3 committees shall be equipped with a larger budget, the intercommittee cooperation shall be intensified, and their role in identifying problems and proposing solutions shall become more 'pro-active' – in particular by making use of qualified majority voting. In addition to that, the weak peer review processes within each committee shall be developed towards becoming binding mediation procedures.[164] Besides, the Commission shall, in cooperation with the level 3 committees, examine the degree of independence of the national supervisory bodies and, based on an assessment thereof, make

---

159 Anticipating the trend towards more centralisation of competences on the EU level expressed in the *de Larosière* Report: Lastra 7ff.
160 *de Larosière* Report 47.
161 Ibid.
162 Ibid., 50f.
163 Ibid., 49.
164 Ibid., 51.

concrete recommendations for improvement.[165] Also, more abundant use of supervisory colleges shall be made. By the end of 2009 it is recommended that such colleges are established for all major cross-border firms.[166]

On the regulatory front, the EU institutions and the level 3 committees shall initiate a 'determined and concerted effort' to put on track a consistent set of core rules regulating the EU financial sector, thereby approximating the regulatory approaches of all MS. The legislative proposals shall be adopted by the beginning of 2013. In this context a harmonisation of the supervisory sanctions regime shall be attempted.[167]

With a view to crisis management and resolution, the Commission shall make legislative proposals in particular in the fields of company and insolvency law (for example winding-up, transferability of assets, bankruptcy) in order to make it possible for the EU to deal with future crises more effectively and more cost-efficiently.[168]

In Stage 2 the level 3 committees shall finally be upgraded to authorities proper. The Group describes the role of the new authorities[169] as follows: In addition to the tasks of the level 3 committees, the authorities shall, *inter alia*, be able to solve disputes of competence between national supervisors in case of cross-border institutions in a legally binding way; be allowed to take part in on-site inspections carried out by national supervisors; ensure the consistency of prudential supervision; and be competent to prudentially assess pan-EU mergers and acquisitions.

The authorities shall furthermore be competent to license and directly supervise specific EU-wide institutions, such as CRA and post-trading infrastructures. In the area of both hard and soft regulation, the authorities shall – on level 3 – play a decisive role in the technical interpretation of level 1 and level 2 measures and in the development of level 3 technical standards. The interpretation shall become 'legally valid'.

The authorities shall also define common supervisory practices and arrangements for the functioning of the colleges of supervisors[170] and shall perform ongoing evaluations of the structure, the processes, the performance and the independence of the national supervisory authorities through peer reviews. As a result of these evaluations, concrete recommendations for improvement shall be launched.

In addition to that, the authorities shall ensure the national supervisors' compliance with 'necessary standards'. To this end, they shall be able to issue 'rulings' *vis-à-vis* the national supervisors. If the national supervisors addressed fail to correspond with such rulings, the authorities shall be able to impose sanctions, including fines – which shall leave untouched the Commission's

---

165   Ibid., 49.
166   Ibid., 51.
167   On the respective legislative efforts see eg Commission, MEMO/13/774.
168   Ibid., 52; see now eg Directive 2014/59/EU (see Chapter 4 III.1. below).
169   For the following description of the authorities' role see *de Larosière* Report 52ff.
170   See II.3.6.3.4. below.

right to launch infringement procedures against the respective MS. In exceptional circumstances the authorities shall be allowed to 'acquire the duties which the national supervision is failing to discharge'.[171]

As regards the authorities' cooperation with a new European Systemic Risk Council,[172] binding cooperation and information-sharing procedures shall be introduced. In crisis situations, the authorities shall facilitate cooperation and information exchange between all supervisors. They shall verify this information, and mediate between the supervisors, if needed.

Also on an international level the authorities shall play a role – by preparing equivalence decisions with respect to the supervisors of third countries – and by taking part in bilateral and multilateral discussions with third countries pertaining to financial market supervision.

Sub titulo 'governance and budget'[173] the Group envisages the personal composition and the financing of the authorities. Each authority shall have a Governing Board comprising 'the highest level representatives' of the national supervisory authorities. Chairpersons and Directors General shall be full-time independent professionals, chosen and appointed by the Board; this shall not exclude the appointment of an external high-calibre person.[174] The Commission, the Council and the EP shall confirm the respective appointment. The tenure shall be eight years for each of the offices.

The Board shall take decisions applying qualified majority voting as a general rule. The authorities shall have 'the highest degree of independence'. The European institutions shall in no way interfere in the internal processes and decisions of the authorities. However, accountability towards the Council, the Parliament and the Commission shall be ensured, primarily through reports of the authorities to these institutions.

The authorities shall have their own autonomous budget, which could be fed by contributions from the industry and/or the public sector (including the EU budget).

Finally, the Group is dealing with the authorities' competences in extreme circumstances, which is to say in case of another crisis. The crisis management and resolution measures[175] to be taken by the authorities are outlined by the Group as maintaining and rebuilding, respectively, the market participants' trust in the European supervisory architecture as a whole, which is to say in the national regimes as well as in the EU framework. The Group believes that the implementation of its proposals would put the authorities in a better position than its predecessors, the committees of supervisors, to work against future crises, or – if a crisis has emerged, nevertheless – to manage and resolve it accordingly.

---

171 *de Larosière* Report 54.
172 See 4.3. below.
173 *de Larosière* Report 54f.
174 The Chairpersons of the level 3 committees were always selected from the respective committee members; see, with regard to the CEBS, Kohtamäki 74.
175 *de Larosière* Report 55.

The Group proposes a monitoring of the ESFS including a careful assessment of its effectiveness. A full review should then be performed within three years from the starting of Stage 2 (recommendation 24).

The Group claims that it does not want to anticipate the outcome of the reviewing process. However, *à la longue* it recommends a so-called Twin Peaks Approach, a system of only two authorities on the EU level.[176] One authority should be competent for banking and insurance matters – the merging of these two competences in one body would cater for more effective supervision of financial conglomerates – as well as for all other concerns regarding financial stability (eg hedge funds with systemical importance). The second authority should deal with the conduct of business and market issues, operating cross-sectionally, which is to say across the three main financial sectors (banking, insurance, securities). As regards the idea of a centralisation of the full supervision over cross-border institutions in one EU body, the Group is very cautious. Such a project, the Group holds, can only be attempted once the EU has decided to strive for greater political integration.[177]

4.3.   *The reform of macroprudential supervision*

In the *de Larosière* Report the Group proposes to explicitly and formally mandate the ECB/ESCB to assess – as part of the supervision of the financial system – high-level macrofinancial risks to the system and, if needed, to issue warnings. Within the organisation of the ESCB these tasks shall be assigned to a European Systemic Risk Council (ESRC), which shall replace the then current BSC. The ESRC shall be composed of the President and the Vice President of the ECB, the Governors of the then 27 central banks, the Chairpersons of the level 3 committees (and the successors of these bodies respectively) and one representative of the Commission. The Governors shall be able to choose to be represented by the head of the appropriate national supervisory authority, where the respective central bank does not have supervisory competences, or where it is deemed necessary in order to provide for a wider presence of insurance and securities supervisors.[178]

In order for this new system of macroprudential supervision to work effectively, a 'proper flow of information' between the national supervisors, the microprudential supervisory bodies on the EU level and the ECB/ESCB shall be ensured. The ESRC shall pool and analyse this information with a view to macroeconomic conditions and to macroprudential developments in all financial sectors (recommendation 16). As a subset of improved exchange of information, an effective early warning mechanism ought to be

---

176   See also Kohtamäki 68; for the spreading of the twin peaks system around the world see Michael 2.

177   *de Larosière* Report 58.

178   Ibid., 44.

established. All actors of the financial market supervision (micro- and macroprudential) shall be informed of detected signs of weaknesses of the system. If the weakness is limited to one or few MS, the ESRC shall liaise with the relevant central banks and/or supervisory authorities, give advice to them and monitor their actions taken on the basis of this advice. If need be, the ESRC may give further advice. Where the shortcomings are related to fiscal matters, the ESRC shall immediately contact the Economic and Financial Committee (EFC), a committee of representatives of the national administrations/central banks the ECB and the Commission set in place to discuss economic and financial issues of the EMU.[179] If the detected weakness is related to a global dysfunction of the system, the ESRC shall direct its warnings to the global supervisory system, notably to the IMF, the Financial Stability Forum and the Bank for International Settlements.

4.4. The resonance of the de Larosière Report in scholarship and in politics

The feedback on the proposals of the *de Larosière* Group, and especially on its legislative implementation, was mixed.[180] In the legal and economic literature, the response, as it regards the new supervisory architecture, can be summarised with the words 'Yes, but…'. While the enhanced 'Europeanisation' of financial market regulation and supervision was principally welcomed, for many the reform proposals did not go far enough.[181] Criticism was also passed on the tripartite supervisory regime,[182] on the geographical dispersion of the ESAs, and on the predominance of central bank representatives in the European Risk Board. *Praet*, a representative of the ECB, described the crisis resolution mechanism as proposed in the *de Larosière* Report as its 'weakest point'.[183] *Lannoo* predicted a 'duplication of tasks and confusion in the allocation of responsibilities'.[184] *Moloney* feared a repetition of institutional mistakes of the past.[185]

Many of the critics favoured a supervisory design that the then new Commissioner for Internal Market and Services, *Michel Barnier*, has proposed, and which both the Commission and the EP supported, which is to say the establishment of one supervisory authority which is competent to supervise all

---

179 See Council Decision 98/743/EC and Council Decision 1999/8/EC.
180 See, for example, Dullien and Herr; Zentraler Kreditausschuss 2ff.
181 See references in Kohtamäki 100.
182 See Dullien and Herr 14.
183 EurActiv.
184 Lannoo, Road.
185 Moloney, Crisis 2274.

sectors of the financial market.[186] However, this proposal was not picked up due to the resistance in the Council (ie of the MS).[187]

Some scholars acknowledged that the reform based on the *de Larosière* recommendations has considerably changed the *Lamfalussy* system,[188] but it is agreed that – compared with other reform proposals[189] – it is evolutionary rather than revolutionary.[190]

The Commission described the *de Larosière* Report as 'a balanced and pragmatic vision for a new system of European financial supervision'.[191] Shortly after the Group launched its final report in February 2009, the Commission – largely based on the recommendations contained therein – proposed a reform of the supervisory system that was, eventually and with some changes,[192] adopted by the legislator. Also this indicates both the Commission's and the legislator's strong appreciation of the recommendations, even though the details of the proposals were, at places, controversial.[193] In particular, the Commission supported the strong role remaining for the national supervisors and confirmed the need for an upgrading of the existing level 3 committees.[194]

II.   THE EUROPEAN SYSTEM OF FINANCIAL SUPERVISORS

1.   Introduction

The European System of Financial Supervisors (ESFS) encompasses most actors engaged in financial market supervision in the EU and in the MS. It comprises the European Systemic Risk Board (ESRB), the three ESAs (EBA, EIOPA, ESMA) – the successors of the former level 3 committees[195] – the Joint Committee of the ESAs and the competent supervisory authorities. In

---

186   See Dullien and Herr; Speyer 15; for the views of the Commission see COM (2009) 114 final, 5ff. In the last decade or so on the national level a trend towards integrating in one single authority the supervision of the different sectors of the financial market could be observed; cf the developments eg in Belgium, Germany or Ireland. See tables in Beju et al. 495f; see Elsen 119.

187   See Kohtamäki 100.

188   See, for example, Häde 662; Hofmann et al. 275; Kämmerer, Finanzaufsichtssystem 1286; Part and Schütz; Rötting and Lang 14; Wymeersch 254.

189   See Hertig et al.

190   See Kohtamäki 97.

191   Commission, COM (2009) 252 final, 2.

192   On the respective legislative procedures see Kohtamäki 103–112.

193   See Ferran and Alexander 763.

194   Commission, COM (2009) 114 final, 6.

195   Cf Article 8 para 1 lit l of the ESAs' founding regulations, according to which the ESAs shall 'take over, as appropriate, all existing and ongoing tasks' from their respective level 3 committee.

case of banking supervision, this shall also include the ECB acting within the SSM.[196] In the following, the functioning of the ESFS and its components on the EU level shall be presented.

Table 3.1 Simplified graphic representation of the ESFS

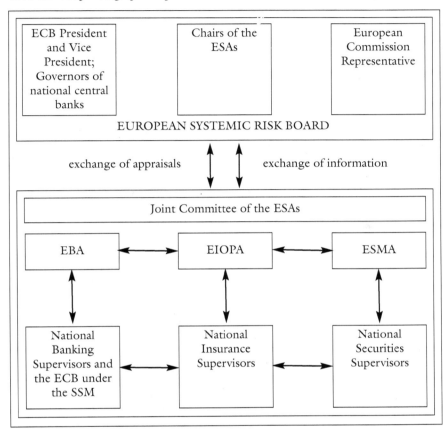

2. The European Systemic Risk Board (ESRB)

2.1. Tasks

The ESRB is responsible for the macroprudential oversight of the financial system of the EU. In that sense, it is to 'contribute to the prevention or mitigation of systemic risks to financial stability'.[197] In order to reach this

---

196 Article 1 para 3 of the ESRB-Regulation in conjunction with Article 1 para 2 of the EBA-Regulation as amended, and Article 9 para 1 of the SSM-Regulation.
197 Commission, COM (2014) 508 final, 4.

objective, Article 3 para 2 of the ESRB-Regulation sets out a list of concrete tasks. According to this provision the ESRB shall:

- determine and/or collect and analyse all the relevant and necessary information;
- identify and prioritise systemic risks;
- issue warnings where such systemic risks are deemed to be significant and, where appropriate, make those warnings public;
- issue recommendations for remedial action in response to the risks identified and, where appropriate, make those recommendations public;
- issue a confidential warning addressed to the Council pursuant to Article 18 of the ESA-Regulations;[198]
- monitor the follow-up to warnings and recommendations;
- cooperate closely with all the other parties to the ESFS, in particular with the ESAs;
- participate, where appropriate, in the Joint Committee;
- coordinate its actions with those of international financial organisations (in particular IMF and FSB) and the relevant bodies in third countries on matters related to macroprudential oversight; and
- carry out other related tasks as specified in Union legislation.

2.1.1.   Collection and exchange of information (Article 15)

Access to as complete a set of information as possible is the basis for a sound risk assessment. Therefore, the ESRB-Regulation provides for a wide net of sources for the ESRB to tap: the ESAs, the ESCB, the Commission, the national supervisory authorities and national statistics authorities (para 2). Information from the ESAs may principally be requested only in summary or aggregate form such that individual financial institutions/financial market participants (FI/FMP) cannot be identified (para 3).[199] If the information is not (made) available (in a timely manner), the ESRB may turn to the ESCB, the national supervisory authorities or the national statistics authorities, or – if the ESRB is still not successful – to the MS concerned without prejudice to the prerogatives of the Council, the Commission (Eurostat), the ECB, the Eurosystem and the ESCB in the field of statistics and data collection (para 5). This cascade of 'places to go' does not alter the fact that – under Union law and principally – the provision of the information requested by the ESRB is obligatory.[200]

---

198   See 3.4.3.2. below.
199   The provision only refers to 'financial institutions', but it can be assumed that it shall also include FMP; for the exceptions see Article 15 para 6 of the ESRB-Regulation.
200   See also Ferran and Alexander 773f.

2.1.2. Warnings and recommendations and their follow-up (Articles 16 to 18)

When the ESRB identifies significant risks to the achievement of its main objective (Article 3 para 1), it shall issue warnings and, where appropriate, recommendations for remedial action (including for legislative initiatives). Such warnings or recommendations may be general or specific, and shall be addressed 'in particular' to the Union as a whole, to one or more MS, to one or more of the ESAs, to one or more of the national supervisory authorities – in the latter case the respective MS shall be informed, accordingly – or to the Commission (as regards the relevant legislation). Recommendations shall contain a specified timeline for the requested policy response.[201]

Warnings or recommendations shall always also be transmitted – pursuant to strict rules of confidentiality – to the Council, the Commission and, if national supervisory authorities are addressed, to the ESAs.

The General Board shall decide on a case-by-case basis, and after having informed the Council in advance, whether a warning or a recommendation shall be made public. If it has decided in the affirmative, it shall inform the addressees in advance. The addressees are then free to publish their views and reasoning in response thereto. If the General Board has decided not to publish the warning or recommendation at issue, the addressees and, if applicable, the Council and the ESAs shall take all the measures necessary to maintain its confidentiality.[202]

Where a recommendation is addressed to one of the actors mentioned in Article 16 para 2 except for the 'Union as a whole', the addressee shall communicate to the ESRB and to the Council the actions taken in response to the recommendation and the justification for inaction, respectively. If need be, the ESRB shall, subject to strict confidentiality, inform the ESAs of the answers received. If the ESRB deems that its recommendation has not been followed or that the addressee has not brought forward adequate justification for its inaction, it shall – confidentially – inform the addressee, the Council and, where relevant, the ESA concerned. If the ESRB has made such a decision with respect to a recommendation that has been made public according to Article 18 para 1, the EP may invite the Chair of the ESRB to present that decision and the addressees may – upon their request – participate in an exchange of views.[203]

The warnings and recommendations the ESRB may issue are non-binding. This allows the ESRB to 'interact freely … and ensure[s] greater scope in the formulation of any recommendations'.[204] In order to ensure compliance it

---

201 Article 16 para 2 of the ESRB-Regulation.
202 Article 18 of the ESRB-Regulation.
203 Article 17 of the ESRB-Regulation.
204 Commission, COM (2014) 508 final, 4.

relies – reasonably successfully[205] – on 'moral suasion and peer pressure'.[206] While stakeholders in principle have approved of this soft law-toolkit of the ESRB, some complained about the still long-winded process of issuing a recommendation and called for complementing the set of soft powers by more flexible tools such as 'letters' or 'public statements'.[207] While these soft instruments may ensure timely decision-making and while high compliance rates suggest their functionality, the legitimacy in particular of such powerful soft law is – in terms of reviewability (remedies), and with the fast-track measures demanded also content-wise – remarkably low.

2.2.   Organisation

The ESRB, legally based on Article 114 TFEU[208] and seated in Frankfurt am Main, unites in one body – not: legal person[209] – the most important sources of information on the situation of the financial market.[210] Congruously, the General Board, the main decision-making organ of the ESRB, is composed of the President and the Vice President of the ECB, the Governors of the national central banks and the Chairpersons of the three ESAs. Members of the General Board are furthermore a member of the Commission, the Chair and the two Vice Chairs of the Advisory Scientific Committee (of the ESRB) and the Chair of the Advisory Technical Committee (of the ESRB). Members without voting rights are: one high-level representative per MS of the competent national supervisory authorities[211] and the President of the EFC.[212] All members of the Board shall perform their duties impartially pursuant to Article 7 of the ESRB-Regulation, solely in the interest of the Union as a whole, and bound by professional secrecy.[213] The General Board meets at least four times a year.[214] It takes its decisions by a simple majority of the voting members present, with the exception of adopting a recommendation and

---

205   See eg the follow-up of ESRB-recommendations by the ESAs addressed in: Parliament, Review 1 44.

206   Commission, COM (2014) 508 final, 6. Sceptical: Ladler, Finanzmarkt 170f.

207   Commission, COM (2014) 508 final, 7, 10f.

208   On the appropriateness of Article 114 TFEU as a legal basis for the establishment of a Union body in general see 3.1. below; for the ESRB in particular see Ferran and Alexander 768–770.

209   On the reasons for establishing the ESRB as a body without legal personality see Ferran and Alexander 766.

210   Commission, COM (2014) 508 final, 5.

211   See Article 6 para 3 of the ESRB-Regulation for further information.

212   Article 6 para 1 and 2 of the ESRB-Regulation; some argue that the Board has too many members in order to function smoothly and in order to ensure the confidentiality of the information exchanged; Parliament, Review 1 59f; on the need for a better exchange of information see Commission, COM (2014) 508 final, 10; Sibert 6; more cautious: Ferran and Alexander 765.

213   Article 8 of the ESRB-Regulation.

214   Article 9 para 1 of the ESRB-Regulation.

making public a warning or a recommendation. For these decisions a two-thirds majority of the votes cast is required.[215] In a survey undertaken by the Commission relevant stakeholders approved of the functionality of these voting modalities.[216]

The ESRB's external representatives are the Chair and, as his substitutes, the two Vice Chairs.[217] For a term of five years following the entry into force of the ESRB-Regulation, which is to say until 16 December 2015, the President of the ECB shall act as the Chair of the ESRB.[218] For the time afterwards, the Commission has not yet published information as to who shall be the Chair of the ESRB. Reportedly, the Commission plans to restructure the ESRB in the near future. Meanwhile, the President of the ECB shall remain in office as the Chairman of the ESRB even after 16 December 2015.[219] The first Vice Chair shall be elected by and from among the members of the General Council of the ECB for a term of five years, which is renewable once. The second Vice Chair shall be the Chair of the Joint Committee.[220] The Chair or, if he is unable to attend the meeting, one of his Vice Chairs presides at the meetings of the General Board and the Steering Committee.[221]

The ESRB's management organ is the Steering Committee. It is composed of the Chair and the first Vice Chair of the ESRB, the Vice President of the ECB, four other members of the General Board who are at the same time members of the General Council of the ECB (that means four Governors of national central banks), a member of the Commission, the Chairpersons of the three ESAs, the President of the EFC and the Chairs of the Advisory Scientific and of the Advisory Technical Committee.[222] It shall convene at least quarterly, before the meetings of the General Board in order to support their preparation.[223]

In addition to these semi-political organs, the ESRB comprises one expert committee – the Advisory Scientific Committee – and one committee, by means of which another link to the national central banks and (other) national supervisory authorities is created, namely the Advisory Technical Committee. Both committees shall advise and assist the ESRB at the request of the Chair of the ESRB.[224]

---

215 Article 10 paras 2f of the ESRB-Regulation.
216 Commission, COM (2014) 508 final, 5.
217 Article 5 para 8 of the ESRB-Regulation.
218 Article 5 para 1 of the ESRB-Regulation. On calls for the ECB President to be ESRB Chairperson *ex officio* see Ferran and Alexander 764.
219 Information provided by the ESRB via e-mail. Against the ECB President as the ESRB Chairperson: Parliament, Review 2 11.
220 Article 5 paras 2f of the ESRB-Regulation; see 3.5.5 below.
221 Article 5 paras 5f of the ESRB-Regulation.
222 Article 11 para 1 of the ESRB-Regulation.
223 Article 11 para 2 of the ESRB-Regulation.
224 Article 12 para 3 and Article 13 para 3 of the ESRB-Regulation.

The ESRB does not have a budget of its own. Rather the ECB provides the human and financial resources for the secretariat of the ESRB.[225]

3.   The European Financial Market Supervisory Authorities

3.1.   *Legal basis*

The legal basis of the ESAs' founding regulations 1093, 1094[226] and 1095/2010[227] is Article 114 TFEU. Article 114 TFEU is the general legal basis for the approximation of laws and hence – in spite of its being residual compared with more specific competence clauses[228] – the core competence clause as regards the internal market domain.[229] Article 114 TFEU is worded in malleable terms. Its para 1 allows for the adoption of 'measures for the approximation of [the law of the MS] which have as their object the establishment and functioning of the internal market'. The internal market is defined in Article 26 para 2 TFEU as an 'area without internal frontiers in which the free movement of goods, persons, services and capital is ensured in accordance with the provisions of the Treaties'.

In view of this broad concept, a multitude of different measures may be taken on the basis of Article 114 under the heading 'harmonisation'.[230] While emphasising that this Treaty provision does not confer on the legislator 'a general power to regulate the internal market',[231] in the *ENISA* case it affirmed that legislative measures on the basis of Article 114 may also include the establishment of a specific body facilitating harmonisation. It held that '[t]he legislature may deem it necessary to provide for the establishment of a Community body responsible for contributing to the implementation of a process of harmonisation in situations where … the adoption of non-binding supporting and framework measures seems appropriate'.[232] Whereas earlier the flexibility clause (now Article 352 TFEU) was the most common legal

---

225   See Council Regulation 1096/2010, in particular its Article 3 para 1. Also otherwise – namely in terms of administration, information and analysis – the link to the ECB is particularly strong; see Commission, COM (2014) 508 final, 5.

226   See Gal 336f, discussing the argument that Article 127 para 6 (and also para 5) TFEU as *lex specialis* (*leges speciales*) may prevent the establishment/empowerment of the EIOPA.

227   EBA-Regulation; EIOPA-Regulation; ESMA-Regulation. Taken collectively, these Regulations shall be referred to as 'ESA-Regulations'.

228   See eg Craig and de Búrca, EU 616.

229   For those Treaty provisions allowing for such approximations in specific policy fields see Tietje, para 2.

230   For the specific meaning of the term 'harmonisation' in EU law see Klamert 266.

231   *Germany v Parliament/Council* [2000], para 83; see Fahey 587f with regard to this case and its ambiguous follow-up case law.

232   *UK v Parliament/Council*, para 44; on the background of this case see Skowron 250f.

basis for the establishment of European agencies,[233] Article 114 appears to have become the legislator's 'first choice' (see Chapter 2 IV.1. above).[234] Since, according to the legislator, the 'purpose and tasks of [the ESAs] … are closely linked to the objectives of the Union acquis concerning the internal market for financial services', it deemed Article 114 TFEU – which, in *Moloney's* words, thereby has become the 'workhorse of the EU's crisis-era institutional reforms'[235] – to be the pertinent Treaty base also for the establishment of the ESAs.[236] In that sense, the legislative intention of the establishment of the ESAs was the 'improvement of the conditions for the establishment and functioning of the internal market'.[237]

Whether or not measures based on Article 114 TFEU need to comply with the principle of subsidiarity is a contested issue.[238] The Commission and the legislator support the applicability of this principle, and – with regard to the establishment of the ESAs – unsurprisingly confirm its being complied with.[239] In view of the supervisory blunders prior to the crisis and the respective *de Larosière* recommendations, it does indeed not seem undue to confirm that the objectives of the proposed action – which essentially correspond to the objectives of the ESAs (see 3.2. below) – cannot be sufficiently achieved by the MS, but can rather be achieved at Union level. As regards proportionality, it appears that the ESAs' regime – including their strong *ultima ratio* powers (see 3.4.3. below) – does not go beyond 'what is necessary to achieve the objectives of the Treaties'.[240]

When discussing the legal basis of the founding regulations, we have to bear in mind that they vest the ESAs with considerable powers, in particular

---

233   From a strategic point of view, Article 352 TFEU may seem inappropriate because of its unanimity requirement (Council) and the requirement of an agreement/involvement of eg the German *Bundestag* (§ 8 of the *Integrationsverantwortungsgesetz* in conjunction with Article 23 para 1 of the *Grundgesetz*) or the British *Houses of Parliament* (section 8 of the European Union Act 2011); see Häde 665. With regard to the ESAs, Article 352 TFEU was discussed as a possible legal basis; see Kohtamäki 157 with further references.

234   Commission, COM (2002) 718 final, 7; see also Vetter 722; critically, Sander 26f. By now there are quite a few decision-making agencies whose legal Treaty base is not Article 352 TFEU, eg the EASA (Article 80 para 2 TEC; now: Article 100 para 2 TFEU) or the ECHA (Article 95 TEC; now: Article 114 TFEU).

235   Moloney, Union 1655.

236   Recital 17 of the ESA-Regulations. See also Herdegen 142; Siekmann 56–60; Rötting and Lang 9.

237   *Germany v Parliament/Council* [2000], para 84; see also *Germany v Parliament/Council* [2006], para 80.

238   See Tietje, paras 58f with further references; in the affirmative: Michel, Gleichgewicht 204f.

239   See Recital 66 of the ESA-Regulations, also with regard to proportionality; critically, Michel, Gleichgewicht 205.

240   Article 5 para 4 TEU; see also Siekmann 61f; pointing at the importance not only of the legislation, but also of its application *in praxi*: Kohtamäki 163; critically Moloney, Securities 219.

with decision-making powers *vis-à-vis* third parties and with a strong involvement in rule-making. The legality of a conferral of such powers to European agencies can be contested, in particular if it is not based on what is now Article 352 TFEU.[241] In the *ESMA* case the ECJ appears to principally allow for a conferral of decision- and rule-making powers to European agencies on the basis of Article 114 TFEU (see above Chapter 2 III.4.).[242] In addition to that, the Court in this judgement re-defined the *Meroni* doctrine so as to allow for the conferral of considerable powers (see Chapter 2 I.7. above). In that sense, the hurdles for the conformity with primary law of the establishment of a European agency based on Article 114 TFEU are low. The ESAs indeed, as the ECJ requires, contribute 'to the implementation of a process of harmonisation'[243] in the field of financial services. While the wording of Article 114 TFEU remains vague,[244] it must be conceded that, in the liberal interpretation of the ECJ – whether or not it is to be approved – the provision does serve as a reasonable legal basis for the ESA-Regulations.[245] A detailed analysis of the ESAs' powers below shall show whether or not the founding regulations do comply with new *Meroni*.

3.2.   Seat, legal status, scope and objectives

The ESAs are Union bodies with legal personality and seated in London (EBA), Frankfurt am Main (EIOPA) and Paris (ESMA).[246] The ESAs and the respective seat MS shall lay down the accommodation of the ESA and the facilities to be made available by the MS in so-called Headquarters Agreements.[247] In each MS, it enjoys the most extensive legal capacity accorded to legal persons under national law.[248] This shall include, in particular, the acquisition or disposal of movable and immovable property, and the capacity

---

241   See Herdegen 143 with numerous further references.

242   See Moloney, Union 1655–1659; Weismann, Neues 127.

243   *UK v Parliament/Council*, para 44.

244   *Moloney* described it as 'a somewhat shaky competence for a radical institutional reform'; Moloney, EU 1341.

245   In the affirmative also Gal 333; Ladler, Finanzmarkt 201; Pötzsch 2370f; B Raschauer, Leitlinien 35 with further references; Siekmann 56–60; critically with regard to the EBA, Fahey 593, claiming the EBA's powers to be 'too limited *and* too broad for the purposes of Article 114 TFEU'.

246   Article 7 of the respective ESA-Regulation.

247   Article 74 of the ESA-Regulations. The ESAs and the respective seat states shall also lay down the specific rules applicable in the respective seat state to the Executive Director, the members of the Management Board, the staff of the Authority and the members of their families. Seat MS are furthermore obliged to provide 'the best possible conditions to ensure the proper functioning of the [ESAs], including multi-lingual, European-oriented schooling and appropriate transport connections'. See, for example, the UK's Headquarters Agreement with the EBA <www.official-documents.gov.uk/document/cm83/8363/8363.pdf>.

248   See eg Article 3 of the Headquarters Agreement of 8 May 2012 between the UK and the EBA <www.official-documents.gov.uk/document/cm83/8363/8363.pdf>.

to be a party to legal proceedings. The ESAs are represented by their Chairpersons.[249] Their internal working language is English.[250]

Article 1 para 2 of the respective ESA-Regulation determines the scope within which the ESAs are entitled to act. This scope is, apart from the respective ESA-Regulation, contained:

- for the EBA:[251] in Directives 94/19/EC[252] ('on deposit guarantee schemes') and 2002/87/EC ('on the supplementary supervision of credit institutions, insurance undertakings and investment firms in a financial conglomerate'), Regulations 1781/2006 ('on information on the payer accompanying transfers of funds') and 575/2013 ('on prudential requirements for credit institutions and investment firms'), Directive 2013/36/EU ('Capital Requirements Directive IV') and to the relevant parts of Directives 2002/65/EC ('concerning the distance marketing of consumer financial services'), 2005/60/EC ('on the prevention of the use of the financial system for the purpose of money laundering and terrorist financing'), 2007/64/EC ('on payment services in the internal market') and 2009/110/EC ('on the taking up, pursuit and prudential supervision of the business of electronic money institutions'), including all directives, regulations and decisions based on these acts, and of any further legally binding Union act, which confers tasks on the EBA.[253] The EBA shall also act in accordance with Council Regulation 1024/2013 ('SSM-Regulation').

  Furthermore, the EBA shall act in the field of activities of credit institutions, financial conglomerates, investment firms, payment institutions and e-money institutions, even where these issues are 'not directly covered' by the acts referred to above, including matters of corporate governance, auditing and financial reporting – provided the EBA's actions are 'necessary to ensure the effective and consistent application of those acts';[254]

- for the EIOPA: in Directives 2009/138/EC ('Solvency II Directive') with exception of its Title IV, 2002/92/EC ('on insurance mediation'), 2003/41/EC ('on the activities and supervision of institutions for occupational retirement provision'), 2002/87/EC ('on the supplementary supervision of credit institutions, insurance undertakings and investment firms in a financial conglomerate'), 64/225/EEC ('on the abolition of restrictions on freedom of establishment and freedom to provide services

---

249 Article 5 of the ESA-Regulations.
250 See Article 73 of the ESA-Regulations in conjunction with Article 1 of the ESAs' Decisions EBA DC 003, EIOPA-MB-11/003, ESMA/2011/MB/3.
251 See also Michel, Gleichgewicht 199f.
252 This Directive is repealed with effect from 4 July 2019; see Article 21 of Directive 2014/49/EU, recasting Directive 94/19/EC.
253 Eg Directives 2014/92/EU, 2014/17/EU, 2014/59/EU and Regulation 806/2014.
254 Article 1 para 3 of the EBA-Regulation.

in respect of reinsurance and retrocession'), 73/239/EEC ('on the coordination of laws, regulations and administrative provisions relating to the taking-up and pursuit of the business of direct insurance other than life assurance'), 73/240/EEC ('abolishing restrictions on freedom of establishment in the business of direct insurance other than life assurance'), 76/580/EEC (amending Directive 73/239/EEC), 78/473/EEC ('on the coordination of laws, regulations and administrative provisions relating to Community co-insurance'), 84/641/EEC (amending Directive 73/239/EEC), 87/344/EEC ('on the coordination of laws, regulations and administrative provisions relating to legal expenses insurance'), 88/357/EEC ('on the coordination of laws, regulations and administrative provisions relating to direct insurance other than life assurance and laying down provisions to facilitate the effective exercise of freedom to provide services'), 92/49/EEC ('on the coordination of laws, regulations and administrative provisions relating to direct insurance other than life assurance'), 98/78/EC ('on the supplementary supervision of insurance undertakings in an insurance group'), 2001/17/EC ('on the reorganisation and winding-up of insurance undertakings'), 2002/83/EC ('concerning life assurance'), 2005/68/EC ('on reinsurance') on the one hand, and in the relevant parts of Directives 2005/60/EC ('on the prevention of the use of the financial system for the purpose of money laundering and terrorist financing') and 2002/65/EC ('concerning the distance marketing of consumer financial services'), on the other hand, including all directives, regulations and decisions based on these acts, and of any further legally binding Union act that confers tasks on the EIOPA. Furthermore, the EIOPA shall act in the operative field of insurance and reinsurance undertakings, financial conglomerates, institutions for occupational retirement provision and insurance intermediaries, in relation to issues 'not directly covered' by the acts referred to above, including matters of corporate governance, auditing and financial reporting, provided that the taking of actions by the EIOPA is 'necessary to ensure the effective and consistent application of those acts';[255]

- for the ESMA: in Directives 97/9/EC ('on investor-compensation schemes'),[256] 98/26/EC ('on settlement finality in payment and securities

---

255 Article 1 para 3 of the EIOPA-Regulation.

256 Two such schemes are in place in the field of competence of the EBA (European system of deposit guarantee schemes) and the ESMA (European system of national Investor Compensation Schemes). Here, the respective ESAs are required to ensure the correct application of the respective legal bases, if need be, also by issuing guidelines and recommendations or by developing RTS/ITS (Article 26 of the EBA- and of the EIOPA-Regulation). The EIOPA, in the field of competence of which such a guarantee scheme does not yet exist, may facilitate the assessment of the need for a European network of national insurance guarantee schemes (Article 26 of the EIOPA-Regulation); see also the mandate of the Task Force on Insurance Guarantee Schemes EIOPA-TFIGS-11/001 (May 2011).

settlement systems'), 2001/34/EC ('on the admission of securities to official stock exchange listing and on information to be published on those securities'), 2002/47/EC ('on financial collateral arrangements'), 2003/6/EC ('on insider dealing and market manipulation (market abuse)'), 2003/71/EC ('on the prospectus to be published when securities are offered to the public or admitted to trading'), 2004/39/EC ('on markets in financial instruments'), 2004/109/EC ('on the harmonisation of transparency requirements in relation to information about issuers whose securities are admitted to trading on a regulated market'), 2009/65/EC ('on the coordination of laws, regulations and administrative provisions relating to undertakings for collective investment in transferable securities (UCITS)') and 2006/49/EC ('on the capital adequacy of investment firms and credit institutions'), without prejudice to the competence of the EBA in terms of prudential supervision, Directive 2011/61/EC ('on Alternative Investment Fund Managers') and Regulation 1060/2009 ('on credit rating agencies') on the one hand; in the relevant parts of Directives 2002/87/EC ('on the supplementary supervision of credit institutions, insurance undertakings and investment firms in a financial conglomerate'), 2005/60/EC ('on the prevention of the use of the financial system for the purpose of money laundering and terrorist financing'), 2002/65/EC ('concerning the distance marketing of consumer financial services'), on the other hand, including all directives, regulations and decisions based on these acts, and of any further legally binding Union act which confers tasks on the ESMA.[257] Furthermore, the ESMA shall act in the operative field of market participants in relation to issues 'not directly covered' by the acts referred to above, including matters of corporate governance, auditing and financial reporting, provided that the taking of action by the ESMA is 'necessary to ensure the effective and consistent application of those acts'. The ESMA shall also take appropriate action in the context of take-over bids, clearing and settlement and derivative issues.[258]

Article 1 para 3 of the ESA-Regulations is to be understood as an instruction for a wide teleological interpretation of the acts referred to above. It provides for a non-exhaustive list of fields, which are 'not directly covered' by the acts referred to above, but in which the ESAs shall act, nevertheless. It allows for the ESAs to assess what 'effective and consistent' application of the acts referred to above requires. This 'authorisation' by the legislator is – above all with a view to the rule of law – a questionable tool of law-making.

In this context the (legal) persons subject to supervision by the ESAs ought to be listed: According to the relevant provisions of the legal acts referred to

---

257 Eg Article 5 para 3 of Regulation 236/2012.
258 Article 1 para 3 of the ESMA-Regulation.

in Article 1 para 2 of the EBA-Regulation, the term 'financial institution' encompasses credit institutions,[259] investment firms[260] and financial conglomerates.[261] If the EBA acts within the scope of Directive 2005/60/EC, however, the term 'financial institution' includes both credit and financial institution as defined in Article 3 paras 1 and 2 of this Directive.[262]

According to Article 4 para 1 of the EIOPA-Regulation, the Regulation applies to all undertakings, entities and natural and legal persons subject to any of the legislative acts referred to in its Article 1 para 2 ('financial institutions'). If the EIOPA acts under Directive 2005/60/EC, however, 'financial institution' means only insurance undertakings and insurance intermediaries as defined in Article 3 para 2 lit a and e of this Directive.

In the ESMA-Regulation the term 'financial market participant' is defined as 'any person in relation to whom a requirement in the legislation referred to in Article 1(2) or a national law implementing such legislation applies'.[263] The term 'key financial market participant' means a 'financial market participant whose regular activity or financial viability has or is likely to have a significant effect on the stability, integrity or efficiency of the financial markets in the Union'.[264]

The objectives of the ESAs are summarised as the protection of 'the public interest by contributing to the short, medium and long-term stability and effectiveness of the financial system, for the Union economy, its citizens and businesses'. More exhaustively this means that the ESAs shall contribute to:

'(a)   improving the functioning of the internal market, including, in particular, a sound, effective and consistent level of regulation and supervision;

(b)   ensuring the integrity, transparency, efficiency and orderly functioning of financial markets;

(c)   strengthening international supervisory coordination;

(d)   preventing regulatory arbitrage and promoting equal conditions of competition;

---

259   The term 'credit institution' is now defined in Article 4 para 1 subpara 1 of Regulation 575/2013 as meaning 'an undertaking the business of which is to take deposits or other repayable funds from the public and to grant credits for its own account'; see also Dragomir 30–32, still with reference to the definition contained in Directive 2006/49/EC.

260   'Investment firms' are defined in Article 4 para 1 subpara 2 of Regulation 575/2013, referencing to Directive 2004/39/EC, as 'any legal person whose regular occupation or business is the provision of one or more investment services to third parties and/or the performance of one or more investment activities on a professional basis'; see also the identical definition in Directive 2014/65/EU, which shall repeal the former Directive by 3 January 2017.

261   An elaborate definition of the term 'financial conglomerate' is given in Article 2 para 14 of Directive 2002/87/EC.

262   Article 4 of the EBA-Regulation.

263   Article 4 para 1 of the ESMA-Regulation.

264   Article 4 para 2 of the ESMA-Regulation.

(e) ensuring the taking of credit and other risks are appropriately regulated and supervised; and

(f) enhancing customer protection'.

In order to achieve these aims, the ESAs shall 'contribute to ensuring consistent, efficient and effective application' of the relevant Union law and 'foster supervisory convergence, provide opinions to the European Parliament, the Council, and the Commission and undertake economic analyses of the markets'.[265] In particular, the ESAs shall pay attention to systemic risks that might be posed by FI/FMP, the failure of which may impair the functioning of the financial system or the real economy, in other words: FI/FMP which are 'too big to fail'.[266]

The ESAs shall act independently, objectively and exclusively in the interest of the Union.[267]

3.3. The ESAs' tasks – an overview

The ESA-Regulations in their Articles 8 and 9 distinguish between tasks and powers. Whereas the tasks describe what all the ESAs have to do, the powers form the tools by means of which the tasks may be completed.[268]

In the following, a short overview of the ESAs' tasks[269] as set out in Articles 8f of the ESA-Regulations shall be given, listing them under the following summarising headlines. Since some of the tasks serve more than one objective, certain overlaps cannot be avoided. While most of the tasks are laid down in Article 8 para 1 and Article 9 of the ESA-Regulations, the ESAs shall fulfil any other specific tasks set out in the ESA-Regulations or in other legislative acts.[270]

3.3.1. Unification of regulatory and supervisory practices (including the application of Union law; Article 8 para 1)

- by contributing to the establishment of high-quality common regulatory and supervisory standards and practices (single rulebook[271]; lit a), and, as regards the EBA, by creating a European supervisory handbook[272];

---

265 Article 1 para 5 subpara 2 of the ESA-Regulations.

266 For the 'too big to fail dilemma' see Pflock 15.

267 Article 1 para 5 subpara 4 of the ESA-Regulations; on the risk of politicisation with respect to the EBA see Babis, Rulebook 35f.

268 On the distinction between tasks and powers (in the context of German environmental law) see Brandt 88–90.

269 For a condensed summary of the ESAs' tasks see Burgard and Heimann, paras 28–30.

270 Article 8 para 1 lit j of the ESA-Regulations.

271 See Recital 21 of the EIOPA-Regulation and Recital 22 of the EBA- and the ESMA-Regulation.

272 With regard to both the single rulebook and the European supervisory handbook see Michel, Gleichgewicht 192f.

- by contributing to the consistent application of legally binding Union acts (common supervisory culture[273]; lit b);
- by stimulating and facilitating the delegation of tasks and responsibilities among competent authorities[274] (lit c); and
- by organising and conducting peer-review analyses of competent authorities in order to strengthen consistency in supervisory outcomes (lit e).

3.3.2.   *Provision of a sound information flow (Article 8 para 1)*[275]

- by cooperating closely with the ESRB, in particular by providing it with the necessary information for the achievement of its tasks and by ensuring a proper follow-up to the warnings and recommendations of the ESRB (lit d); and
- by publishing on their websites regularly updated information relating to its field of activities on registered FI/FMP, in order to ensure information is easily accessible by the public (lit k).

3.3.3.   *Long-term monitoring of the market with a view to systemic risks (Article 8 para 1)*

- by monitoring and assessing market developments in the area of their competence (lit f);
- by undertaking economic analyses of markets to inform the discharge of the ESAs' functions (lit g); and
- by contributing to the consistent and coherent functioning of the colleges of supervisors, the monitoring, assessment and measurement of systemic risk,[276] the development and coordination of recovery and resolution plans (thereby providing a high level of depositor and investor protection throughout the Union[277]) and developing methods for the resolution of failing FI/FMP and an assessment of the need for appropriate financing instruments (lit i).

3.3.4.   *Protection of stakeholders (Articles 8 and 9 para 1)*

- by fostering depositor and investor protection (Article 8 para 1 lit h);
- by promoting transparency, simplicity and fairness in the market for consumer financial products or services across the internal market, including by:
  - collecting, analysing and reporting on consumer trends (Article 9 para 1 lit a);

---

273   See also Article 29 of the ESA-Regulations.
274   See also Article 28 of the ESA-Regulations.
275   See also Article 35 of the ESA-Regulations.
276   See also Article 23 of the ESA-Regulations.
277   See 3.3.4. below.

- reviewing and coordinating financial literacy and education initiatives by the competent authorities (Article 9 para 1 lit b);
- developing training standards for the industry (Article 9 para 1 lit c); and
- contributing to the development of common disclosure rules (Article 9 para 1 lit d).

3.3.5. Tasks related to financial activities (Article 9)

- monitoring new and existing financial activities with a view to promoting the safety and soundness of markets and convergence of regulatory practice (para 2);
- issuing warnings in the event that a financial activity poses a serious threat to the objectives laid down in Article 1 para 5 of the ESA-Regulations (para 3);
- establishing a Committee on financial innovation with a view to achieving a coordinated approach to the regulatory and supervisory treatment of new or innovative financial activities and by providing advice for the ESAs to present to the EP, the Council and the Commission (para 4); and
- prohibiting or restricting certain financial activities that threaten the orderly functioning and integrity of financial markets or the stability of the whole or part of the financial system in the Union according to the legislative acts referred to in Article 1 para 2 (see 3.2. above) and to the procedure laid down in Article 9 para 5 of the ESA-Regulations.

3.4. The ESAs' powers

3.4.1. Regulatory technical standards (RTS)

3.4.1.1. GENERAL REMARKS

As has been outlined above (see Chapter 2 II.3.), the Lisbon Treaty has introduced a new regime of derived rule-/decision-making, differentiating between delegated acts (Article 290 TFEU) and implementing acts (Article 291 TFEU). Both Article 290 and Article 291 are directly applicable, but *Comitology III* further concretises Article 291. Unlike prior to the entry into force of the Treaty of Lisbon, primary law does not oblige the Commission any more to consult comitology committees (representatives of the national bureaucracies) when adopting delegated acts under Article 290 TFEU. However, the Commission has announced that it will continue to consult MS' experts.[278]

---

278 Commission, COM (2009) 673 final, 6f; see also Declaration No 39. These voluntary consultations, of course, do not have binding effects and are, in that sense, comparable to opinions launched in the course of an advisory procedure (see Chapter 2 IV.4. above).

In EU financial market law, rule- and decision-making by the Commission – supported by expert committees – already has a long tradition.[279] RTS according to Article 10 of the ESA-Regulations are (a special kind of[280]) delegated acts, which is to say 'non-legislative acts of general application to supplement or amend non-essential elements of the legislative act'.[281] RTS shall be 'technical' and shall not imply 'strategic decisions or policy choices', and their content shall be delimited by the legislative act on which they are based.[282] With the adoption of RTS the Commission shall ensure the timely and flexible regulation of the details of financial market law, which leads to a relief of the legislator.[283] In practice, most of the RTS adopted by the Commission specify (ie 'supplement') certain terms or conditions set in the respective legislative acts.[284] This 'executive interpretation'[285] of legislative acts by the Commission serves the aim of a uniform application of Union law and – in the long run – of a detailed 'single rule book'.[286]

3.4.1.2.   GENESIS: COOPERATION BETWEEN THE COMMISSION AND THE ESAS

While the Commission is the delegate, which is competent to adopt the RTS, the ESAs fulfil an important preparatory role.[287] The ESAs' role it is to conduct open public consultations on a draft RTS and to make a cost-benefit analysis of its effects – unless this would be disproportionate in relation to the scope and impact of the draft concerned or in relation to the particular urgency of the matter.[288] In the course of the consultations, the ESAs shall also request an opinion from the respective stakeholder group.[289] The respective ESA may then submit its draft to the Commission, which shall immediately forward it to the EP and to the Council.[290] Within three months of the receipt of the draft, the Commission shall decide whether or not to

---

279   See N Raschauer, Verfahren 159 with further references.
280   See Kahl, Aufsichtsbehörden 57.
281   Article 290 para 1 TFEU. For the differentiation 'essential' and 'non-essential' see Baur and Boegl 182; for an analysis of the terms 'supplementation' and 'amendment' see Kahl, Aufsichtsbehörden 70.
282   Article 10 para 1 of the ESA-Regulations.
283   See Nettesheim, Art. 290, para 12. Provisions which may be subject to an RTS are, for example, Article 2 paras 11 and 17 of Directive 2002/87/EC. For the authorisation of the Commission see Article 21a of this Directive.
284   See eg the EBA work programme for 2012 and the list of RTS to be adopted contained therein <www.eba.europa.eu/documents/10180/15748/EBA-BS-2011-137-Final-EBA-work-programme-for-2012-FINAL.pdf/cbe1d67b-c5fd-400c-ab4c-23fb5279a3f9>; see also examples given by N Raschauer, Verfahren 160.
285   As opposed to the 'authentic interpretation' of legislative provisions by the legislator itself.
286   See Commission, COM (2014) 509 final (Annex I), 3; see also Baur and Boegl 182.
287   Article 10 para 1 subpara 1 of the ESA-Regulations; see also Kahl, Aufsichtsbehörden 57.
288   Article 10 para 1 subpara 3 of the ESA-Regulations.
289   Article 37 para 1 of the respective ESA-Regulation. On the role of stakeholders in decision-making processes in the field of banking regulation see Dragomir 234–236.
290   Article 10 para 1 subpara 4 of the ESA-Regulations.

endorse it.[291] The Commission may decide to adopt only parts or an amended version of the draft.[292]

If the Commission intends not to endorse the draft at all, or to endorse it only in part or with amendments, it shall send the draft back to the ESA, explaining its respective intention. The ESA then has the possibility to amend the draft on the basis of proposals of the Commission[293] and to resubmit it to the Commission in the form of a formal opinion within six weeks. The ESA shall furthermore send a copy of the formal opinion to the EP and to the Council.[294] If, after the six weeks, the ESA has not duly considered (arg 'consistent with') the proposals of the Commission in its formal opinion, or if it has not submitted a formal opinion at all, the Commission may itself amend the draft accordingly and then adopt the RTS – or reject the draft.[295] If the Commission does not endorse the draft as proposed by the ESA – either by amending or by fully rejecting it – the Commission has to inform the ESA, the EP and the Council, thereby giving the reasons for its decision.[296] The EP or the Council may then, 'where appropriate' and within one month, invite the Commissioner in charge and the Chairperson of the respective ESA for an *ad hoc* meeting of the competent committee of the EP or the Council to present and explain their – differing – views.[297]

In Article 10 para 1 subpara 8 the legislator makes it clear that the procedure sketched above is obligatory if the Commission wants to have the draft amended. The Commission is emphatically not allowed to shorten the procedure by just amending the ESA-draft itself, which means 'without prior coordination with the Authority'. With this provision it shall be ensured that the ESA does have a say twice in the drafting of the RTS. First, in its role as the author of the first draft; and secondly, if the Commission does not fully agree with the first draft, by having the chance to issue a formal opinion. The ESA may consider the proposals of the Commission and may adapt its draft accordingly, but it may also rebut the Commission's objections in the formal opinion and try to convince it of the ESA's own considerations.

Where the ESA has not submitted a draft RTS within the time limit set in the respective basic act, the Commission may,[298] upholding its request, set a

---

291   This deadline, at places, for the Commission has been difficult to meet; see Commission, COM (2014) 509 final (Annex I), 3f.

292   Article 10 para 1 subpara 5 of the ESA-Regulations.

293   '[O]n the basis' means 'consistent with'; see Article 10 para 1 subpara 7 of the ESA-Regulations.

294   Article 10 para 1 subpara 6 of the ESA-Regulations.

295   Article 10 para 1 subpara 7 of the ESA-Regulations.

296   Article 14 para 1 of the ESA-Regulations.

297   Article 14 para 2 of the ESA-Regulations.

298   If the Commission still wants to adopt an RTS, it is obliged to set a new time limit – 'may' means 'must' in this context; see Article 10 para 3 of the ESA-Regulation: 'in accordance with paragraph 2'; see Kahl, Aufsichtsbehörden 62.

new time limit.[299] If the ESA does not meet the extended deadline either, the Commission may adopt a RTS drafted without the help of the ESA.[300] If the Commission drafts the RTS, the same requirements as with ESA being the drafter apply: open public consultations, cost-benefit analysis (unless disproportionate; see above) and consultation of the respective stakeholder group.[301] Equally, the Commission shall immediately forward the draft regulatory standard to the EP and the Council.[302] And again, even if the draft stems from the Commission, it has to be sent to the respective ESA, which then within six weeks may propose amendments in the form of a formal opinion to the Commission. The formal opinion shall also be sent to the EP and the Council.[303]

If the ESA fails to submit an amended draft within the six-week period, the Commission may adopt its RTS.[304] If the ESA has submitted an amended draft in due time, the Commission has two options. It may either adopt the RTS as amended by the ESA or, if it does not consider (all of) the ESA's proposals relevant, adopt it without any or only with some of the amendments proposed by the ESA. Again, it is explicitly provided that the Commission may not adopt RTS without 'prior coordination' with the ESA.[305]

As regards the legal form of RTS, para 4 provides that they shall take the form of regulations or decisions. They shall furthermore be published in the OJ and shall enter into force on the date stated therein.[306]

Where the drafting of an RTS falls within the area of competence of more than one ESA (cross-sectoral RTS), the ESAs concerned shall attempt to reach an agreement on its content and adopt the draft – which is then sent to the Commission – in parallel, as appropriate.[307]

3.4.1.3.   DELEGATION OF POWER AND ITS REVOCATION

As has been mentioned above, the power to adopt delegated acts is conferred on the Commission by the legislator. In the case of RTS according to Article 10 of the ESA-Regulations, the delegated power was initially conferred on the Commission for a period of four years only, starting from 16 December

299   Article 10 para 2 of the ESA-Regulations.
300   Article 10 para 3 subpara 1 of the ESA-Regulations.
301   Article 10 para 3 subpara 2 of the ESA-Regulations.
302   Article 10 para 3 subpara 3 of the ESA-Regulations.
303   Article 10 para 3 subpara 4 of the ESA-Regulations.
304   Article 10 para 3 subpara 5 of the ESA-Regulations.
305   Article 10 para 3 subpara 6 of the ESA-Regulations.
306   Article 10 para 4 of the ESA-Regulations.
307   Article 56 para 2 of the ESA-Regulation; see also Article 8 para 1 of the RoP of the Joint Committee 2014.

2010.[308] The delegation of powers was extended automatically for another period of four years, since the legislator has not revoked it.[309]

Specific delegations can be revoked at any time by the EP or by the Council.[310] The institution that has initiated the respective internal procedure shall inform the respective other institution and the Commission thereof and of the delegated powers at issue, within a reasonable time before the final decision is taken. If not specified otherwise in the decision, the revocation of delegated powers shall take immediate effect. It puts an end to the delegation of the powers revoked, but leaves untouched the validity of the RTS already in force. The decision to revoke delegated powers shall be published in the OJ.[311]

3.4.1.4.   OBJECTIONS BY THE EP AND/OR THE COUNCIL

Article 13 is elaborating what is envisaged already in Article 290 para 2 lit b TFEU, which is to say the right of the EP and the Council to object to a delegated act. Either institution may object to an RTS within three months from the date of notification of its adoption – which may be extended by another three months.[312] There is one exception to this deadline: If the Commission adopts an RTS exactly in the version of the draft proposed by the respective ESA, then the period in which either of the two institutions can object is reduced to one month from the date of notification – extendible by another month.[313] The rationale behind this exception is that here the ESA and the Commission have agreed on the content of the standard, and that – since the draft has not been changed after the ESA has submitted it to the Commission, the EP and the Council (see 3.4.1.2. above) – the institutions have had sufficient time to consider the draft. If neither of the legislative institutions has objected to the standard within the respective period, it enters – after publication in the OJ – into force.[314] If, prior to the expiry of the period, both legislative institutions have informed the Commission of their 'intention not to raise objections', it can be published and enter into force even earlier.[315]

---

308 The adoption of such a 'sunset clause' on level 2 was pushed through by the EP in the course of the negotiations on the legislative implementation of the *Lamfalussy* process; see Hofmann et al. 274.

309 See Article 11 para 1 of the ESA-Regulations.

310 This is generally provided for in Article 290 para 2 lit a TFEU as an option for the legislator, and regulated in detail in Article 12 of the ESA-Regulations; see Sohn and Koch 19.

311 Article 12 of the EBA-Regulation. See Ruffert, Art. 290, para 15.

312 Article 13 para 1 subpara 1 of the ESA-Regulations.

313 Article 13 para 1 subpara 2 of the ESA-Regulations.

314 Article 13 para 2 subpara 1 of the ESA-Regulations.

315 Article 13 para 2 subpara 2 of the ESA-Regulations.

If either legislative institution raises objections to an RTS within the respective period, thereby stating the reasons in accordance with Article 296 TFEU, it shall not enter into force.[316]

3.4.1.5.   THE ESAS' ROLE IN THE MAKING OF RTS – AN APPRAISAL

The drafting of RTS allows the ESAs to play a pivotal role. While it is clear that the Commission formally adopts the RTS, the ESAs regularly prepare the draft.[317] The Commission is highly dependent on the ESAs' expertise.[318] This expertise ensures a certain quality of the draft. The picture of the Commission as a 'blind driver' and the agency as 'directions-giving passenger', which has been created in the context of the relationship Commission-EFSA,[319] may be excessive with regard to RTS, but it scenarises well that the RTS are *de facto* made by the ESAs.[320] This assumption is underpinned by the Commission, which in 2014 reported that so far it has endorsed the majority of draft RTS. Where it considered amendments necessary, it sent the drafts back to the respective ESA.[321]

From the text of the relevant Articles it is clear that the legislator has intended close cooperation between the Commission and the ESAs. The ESAs can bring in their expertise in the drafting process. Even if they failed to provide for a draft they still can utter their opinion on the Commission's draft in the form of a formal opinion. There is a 'strong assumption, both legally and politically, ... that these [drafts] will be accepted by the Commission'.[322] If the Commission, however, does not want to follow the ESAs' proposals it has to state the reasons for that. While it is the Commission's general duty to reason its legal acts[323] (see Chapter 2 IV.4. above), the duty of consideration of the ESAs' opinions in combination with the procedural corset that Articles 10 and 14, in particular, provide certainly goes beyond that.[324]

Article 290 TFEU allows for the power to adopt delegated acts to be conferred on the Commission only. To the extent that the legislator entrusted the Commission in this context, it complied with Article 290 TFEU. At the same time it obliged the Commission to consider the opinion of another body, the respective ESA. Whether or not such an obligation of the Commission is

---

316   Article 13 para 3 of the ESA-Regulations.
317   On the consideration of systemic risks when drafting RTS see Article 22 para 3 subpara 2 of the ESA-Regulations.
318   Cf Craig, EU 151.
319   Vos and Wendler 122.
320   Critically, Busuioc, Rule-Making 117; with regard to the ESMA: Schammo 1883.
321   Commission, COM (2014) 509 final (Annex I), 3.
322   Craig, EU 172; cf Recital 23 of the ESA-Regulations, according to which the ESAs' drafts shall be amended by the Commission 'only in very restricted and extraordinary circumstances'; see also Kahl, Aufsichtsbehörden 61; Lutter et al., para 301.
323   Article 296 para 2 TFEU.
324   Cf Baur and Boegl 182.

allowed under Article 290 TFEU is contested.[325] The Commission itself has expressed 'serious doubts' as regards the compliance with Article 290.[326] Since the legislator, according to the Treaty, shall explicitly lay down 'objectives, content, scope and duration of the delegation', it appears that this also includes the right to oblige the Commission to consider certain opinions – with one exception: In view of the fact that Article 290 – contrary to Article 291 TFEU – does not provide for instances of MS control, laying down a comitology-like regime also for the adoption of delegated acts seems unlawful.[327] As has been elaborated above (see I.2.3.), the level 3 committees were not conceptualised as bodies ensuring MS representation (nevertheless, *de facto* they do ensure a limited degree of MS representation; see 3.4.2. below). This holds true also for their successors, the ESAs. Therefore the legislator with the RTS-procedure has not set in place a comitology-like regime. If we compare the role of the ESAs' opinions in the RTS-procedure on the one hand, and of the committees' opinions under the comitology regime, on the other hand, the following can be said: The legal relevance of the ESAs' opinions is higher than the committees' opinions in the advisory procedure and lower than the committees' opinions in the examination procedure. Recently, the Commission has proposed an Inter-Institutional Agreement with the EP and the Council[328] in which it also addressed the adoption of delegated acts. While agreeing on wide consultation where necessary, the Commission proposed that the legislator should 'refrain from adding … procedural requirements, sui generis procedures or additional roles for committees [other than those set out in *Comitology III*]'.[329]

In terms of the *Lamfalussy* system, the drafting and adoption of RTS falls under level 2 ('implementing the details').[330] While the Commission on a voluntary basis may consult the level 2 committees,[331] it is nevertheless the successors of the level 3 committees that play the most prominent role in this procedure. This is due to the fact that the Treaty of Lisbon has created a new regime of derived rule-/decision-making by the Commission. Since it was not possible for the legislator to oblige the Commission to consult the respective level 2 committee due to the exclusion of comitology under Article 290 TFEU, it installed the upgraded level 3 committees, the ESAs, as a source of expertise. With the ESAs' task to review the application of RTS they, for the rest, also take part in level 4 ('enforcement').[332]

325　See Sohn and Koch 17f.
326　Council, 5455/11, 14; see also Michel, Gleichgewicht 233f; Schammo 1884 with further references; on how the relationship between the Commission and the ESAs in the RTS- and ITS-procedures may look like in practice see Busuioc, Rule-Making 122–124.
327　See Sohn and Koch 17.
328　Commission, COM (2015) 216 final.
329　Ibid., 7f; see also the Common Understanding 3.
330　*Lamfalussy* Report 28ff.
331　See Declaration No 39.
332　Article 29 para 1 lit d of the ESA-Regulations.

3.4.2.   Implementing technical standards (ITS)

Apart from the RTS, the ESAs are also competent to draft ITS.[333] With the former they have in common their 'technical' nature,[334] which does 'not imply strategic decisions or policy choices'.[335] But while RTS as quasi-legislative acts[336] supplement or amend legislative acts, ITS (as executive acts[337]) shall 'determine the conditions of application' of legislative acts.[338] Whereas RTS resemble delegated acts according to Article 290, ITS resemble implementing acts according to Article 291 TFEU. The implementation of legally binding Union acts principally is the task of the MS. Only where uniform conditions for the implementation of legal acts are required, those acts shall confer implementing powers on the Commission, or, exceptionally, on the Council (see Chapter 2 II.3. above).[339] But while the adoption of ordinary implementing acts is subject to control by the MS via comitology committees, the ESA-Regulations provide for experts' participation via the ESAs in the case of ITS.[340] The respective MS' committees may be heard, as well, but on a voluntary basis only. The decision-making process of ITS – the 'most accomplished case'[341] of agencies participating in the adoption of implementing acts – is largely regulated equivalently to that of RTS (for the deviations, especially regarding the different role of the legislative institutions, see below).[342] This is why Article 15 of the ESA-Regulations is structured very similarly to Article 10. In order to keep repetitions to a minimum, the procedure shall be outlined only shortly.

Once the preparatory consultations and appraisals are done, the respective ESA shall submit a draft ITS, which the Commission shall immediately forward to the legislative institutions. Within three months, which the

---

333   On the consideration of systemic risks when drafting ITS see Article 22 para 3 subpara 2 of the ESA-Regulations.

334   Ordinary implementing acts may also have a non-technical ambit; see Wojcik, para 87.

335   Article 15 para 1 of the ESA-Regulations.

336   See N Raschauer, Verfahren 160.

337   See Kahl, Aufsichtsbehörden 63.

338   Provisions that are subject to ITS by the Commission are, for example, Article 7 para 2 and Article 8 para 2 of Directive 2002/87/EC. For the authorisation of the Commission see Article 21a para 2 of this Directive. See eg the EBA work programme for 2012 and the list of ITS to be adopted contained therein, <www.eba.europa.eu/documents/10180/15748/EBA-BS-2011-137-Final-EBA-work-programme-for-2012-FINAL.pdf/cbe1d67b-c5fd-400c-ab4c-23fb5279a3f9>.

339   See recently *Spain v Parliament/Council*, para 77.

340   See N Raschauer, Verfahren 163f.

341   Chiti, Agencies 96.

342   Cf Article 12 para 2 lit b of Regulation 1592/2002. This provision merely stipulates that the Commission shall not change the EASA's draft measures for the implementation of the Regulation 'without prior coordination with the Agency'; see Riedel, Gemeinschaftszulassung 132f.

Commission may extend by one month,[343] it may endorse[344] the standard in full, in part, or with amendments. Where the Commission intends not to endorse a draft ITS at all, or only in part or in an amended version, it shall notify the ESA stating the reasons for its intention. The ESA may reply within six weeks in the form of a formal opinion, which is again sent to the legislative institutions; if it fails to do so, the Commission may adopt the ITS in the version it considers best, or reject it. The coordination with the ESA as described here is obligatory.[345]

If the ESA fails to submit a draft within the (extended) deadline, the Commission may draft an ITS itself – on the basis of consultations and appraisals as laid down in para 3 subpara 2. This draft shall be sent to the ESA and the legislative institutions. Within six weeks the ESA may amend the draft and send it as a formal opinion to the Commission and the legislative institutions. The Commission may then adopt the standard, and is free to include the amendments possibly proposed by the ESA.

The ITS shall take the form of regulations or decisions – not: directives (which appear to be a less appropriate means to lay down a final and unified solution for questions of detail). They shall be published in the OJ and shall enter into force on the date stated therein.[346]

As is the case with RTS, where the drafting of the ITS falls within the area of competence of more than one ESA (cross-sectoral scope), they shall – trying to find an agreement on its content – draft the ITS in parallel, as appropriate.[347]

As we have seen, the genesis of ITS is very similar to that of RTS – in spite of their different character. ITS – like RTS – belong to level 2 of the *Lamfalussy* procedure. According to the *Lamfalussy* procedure as proposed in the renowned report, level 2 is the stage where comitology committees come into play. Originally this was only the ESC, but with the extension of the scope of the procedure the EBC and the EIOPC were created. Also to the ESAs' predecessors – CESR, CEBS and CEIOPS – an advisory role was assigned,[348] but their main field of operation was level 3 (eg the issuing of guidelines and

---

343 The provision according to which the Commission is entitled to extend the deadline does not find its equivalent in Article 10 of the ESA-Regulations.
344 In the German version of the ESA-Regulations there are – *prima vista* – two modes of endorsement. Draft RTS are sent to the Commission for its 'Billigung', whereas draft ITS seek the Commission's 'Zustimmung'. If used advisedly these two terms do have a different meaning, but they can also be interpreted as having the same meaning. The fact that in the English version – which is equally authentic – the word 'endorsement' is used in both cases has a lot to commend that we are merely dealing with an editorial error here. See Rötting and Lang 10 who do not consider this issue.
345 Article 15 para 1 subpara 7 of the ESA-Regulations.
346 Article 15 para 4 of the ESA-Regulations.
347 Article 56 para 2 of the ESA-Regulations.
348 *de Larosière* Report 29.

recommendations).[349] This traditional allocation of roles – and hence the entire *Lamfalussy* procedure – has changed apparently,[350] the comitology committees being marginalised in level 2 in favour of the ESAs. EP and Council – compliant with the system of Article 291 – do not have a right to revoke implementing power or to object to an ITS. Instead, they have a right to scrutiny as laid down in Article 11 of *Comitology III*.[351]

These differences raise the question of what the relationship is between ITS according to Article 15 of the ESA-Regulations on the one hand, and implementing acts according to *Comitology III* on the other, both having their primary legal basis in Article 291 TFEU. Is Article 15 of the ESA-Regulations to be understood as a *lex specialis* of the procedures laid down in *Comitology III*?[352] The fact that both regulations were drafted around the same time and that both of them regulate the adoption of implementing acts suggests that the ESA-Regulation shall prevail over the more general comitology procedures laid down in *Comitology III*. Article 5 para 4 lit a of *Comitology III* refers to implementing acts in the field of financial services, which *prima vista* appears to counter the *lex specialis* argument.[353] However, we have to be aware of the fact that there are still basic acts in EU financial market law providing for a comitology procedure to be applied.[354] Therefore it can be argued that this provision refers only to them, and that in the case of ITS *Comitology III* does not apply. In any event, it is striking that neither regulation explicitly acknowledges the existence of its respective *vis-à-vis*.[355]

In a second step we may examine whether the simultaneous existence of both regimes – Article 15 of the ESA-Regulations and the comitology procedures laid down in *Comitology III* – is in accordance with primary law, in particular with Article 291 para 3 TFEU. This provision stipulates that the legislative institutions 'shall lay down in advance the rules and general principles concerning mechanisms for control by Member States of the Commission's exercise of implementing powers'. Hence we have to scrutinise whether such mechanisms are in place. The two regimes differ in terms of the bodies acting and in terms of procedures. Under *Comitology III*, we have the respective comitology committee controlling the content of the implementing

---

349   On the ESAs role in level 4 ('enforcement') see Article 29 para 1 lit d of the ESA-Regulations.

350   Cf N Raschauer, Verfahren 165.

351   Since this provision is worded in general terms and does not depend on the application of a comitology procedure, it also applies with regard to ITS; see also Kahl, Aufsichtsbehörden 63f.

352   In the affirmative: Kahl, Aufsichtsbehörden 64.

353   See N Raschauer, Verfahren 164f.

354   Ibid., 163 and see examples given by Granner, para 141. Where both regimes – comitology and Article 15 of the ESA-Regulations are referred to – *Granner* proposes to apply both regimes in a complementary way; see also Kahl, Aufsichtsbehörden 64 with further references.

355   The ESA-Regulations which were adopted prior to *Comitology III* do not mention earlier *Comitology I* or *II*, either; see Kahl, Aufsichtsbehörden 64.

acts of the Commission, either in the advisory or in the examination procedure. Under the regime of Article 15 of the ESA-Regulations it is the ESAs playing this role, not the level 2 committees.[356] The Article 15-procedure – in spite of the non-bindingness of the ESAs' opinions,[357] but due to the more strict consulting procedure – assigns greater authority to the ESAs' opinions than the advisory procedure according to *Comitology III* assigns to the committees' opinions. The weight attached to the committees' opinions in the examination procedure, however, is much higher than in the Article 15-procedure. The right to propose the initial draft (which comitology procedures lack) again strengthens the position of the ESAs.

In terms of the composition of the acting bodies, we can state the following: whereas a comitology committee is composed of members of the national ministries that may be subject to directions given by their minister, the Board of Supervisors of the ESAs – which is competent to decide on draft ITS – is composed of members of the respective national supervisory authorities that have, if they are not fully independent anyway, a much weaker link to the respective minister (of finance; see Chapter 2 IV.2. above).[358] This is a hardly deniable fact. Whether the Article 15 regime therefore does not provide for MS representation at all is less clear.[359] Article 291 para 3 TFEU only demands that 'the rules and general principles concerning mechanisms for control by Member States' are set in advance. If we entirely deny the representative character of the ESAs (and their Boards of Supervisors), Article 15 of the ESA-Regulations would amount to a violation of primary law. Article 291 para 3 TFEU neither lays down the way in which, nor the extent to which, MS shall be represented. At the time when the Treaty of Lisbon entered into force, on 1 December 2009, the prevailing image of MS' participation in the context of what is now called 'implementing acts' was the comitology system. Hence it is probable that this is what the Treaty makers had in mind when requiring the legislative institutions to lay down the mode of MS control. By no means is this indicated in the wording of Article 291 para 3 TFEU, though. In my view the ESAs do – to a limited extent – represent MS' interests[360] (even though the main purpose of their Boards of Supervisors' composition is the pooling of expertise). Beyond doubt, the control mechanisms contained in *Comitology III* are, in terms of the acting bodies and (if the examination procedure applies) in terms of procedure, stronger. Nevertheless, Article 15 provides a mechanism for (some) control by MS, as required in Article 291 para 3 TFEU.

---

356 Critically, Granner, para 139.
357 See Article 15 para 3 subpara 6 of the ESA-Regulations.
358 See Rötting and Lang 8.
359 In the affirmative: N Raschauer, Verfahren 165. For the concept of comitology committees as a means of ensuring MS representation see Chapter 2 IV.2. above.
360 Cf Lavrijssen and Ottow 439f.

While the relation between comitology and Article 15 of the ESA-Regulations is far from clear[361] and it is agreed that this unsatisfactory situation should – *de lege ferenda* – be remedied, the coexistence of the two regimes appears to be in compliance with Article 291 para 3 TFEU. This provision does not prevent the legislator from setting in place different regimes at the same time.[362] That, apart from the lack of clarity the existence of two systems entails, the merits of a different treatment of implementing acts in financial market law on the one hand, and the remaining fields of law, on the other, are dubitable, and that a related justification of the legislator is required, is a different issue.

3.4.3.   Binding decisions[363]

The ESAs' power to issue binding decisions, either *vis-à-vis* competent authorities or *vis-à-vis* FI/FMP, is much disputed.[364] While the ESAs may be empowered to render decisions also by the secondary legislation referred to in Article 1 para 2 of the respective ESA-Regulation – eg the EMSA's decision-making powers in the context of the registration of CRA[365] – the focus of this chapter shall lie on the decision-making powers provided for in the ESA-Regulations themselves. The three fields of action are entitled '[b]reach of Union law' (Article 17), '[a]ction in emergency situations' (Article 18) and '[s]ettlement of disagreements between competent authorities in cross-border situations' (Article 19). In this context, it ought to be mentioned that the ESAs may issue (non-binding) opinions to the competent authorities on any

---

361   Critically also N Raschauer, Verfahren 165; see also Wojcik, para 87 differentiating between 'technical' ITS and other ('non-technical') implementing acts.

362   An indication for this interpretation is the wording 'acting by means of regulations' in Article 291 para 3 TFEU.

363   This sub-chapter on the ESA's power to issue binding decisions is partly influenced by the following article. Suffice it to cite it once with effect for the entire sub-chapter: Paul Weismann, 'The European Financial Market Supervisory Authorities and their Power to Issue Binding Decisions' (2012) 12 Journal of International Banking Law and Regulation 495. All rights reserved. No part of this publication may be reproduced or transmitted in any form or by any means, or stored in any retrieval system of any nature without prior written permission, except for permitted fair dealing under the Copyright, Designs and Patents Act 1988, or in accordance with the terms of a licence issued by the Copyright Licensing Agency in respect of photocopying and/or reprographic reproduction. Application for permission for other use of copyright material including permission to reproduce extracts in other published works shall be made to the publishers. Full acknowledgement of author, publisher and source must be given. Thomson Reuters and the Thomson Reuters Logo are trademarks of Thomson Reuters. Sweet & Maxwell ® is a registered trademark of Thomson Reuters (Professional) UK Limited. Reproduced by permission of THOMSON REUTERS (PROFESSIONAL) UK LIMITED.

364   See eg Moloney, EU 1368f.

365   Articles 16-20 of Regulation 1060/2009 as amended; cf Board of Appeal, Decision BoA 2013–14; see also ESMA, Annual Report 2014, 24–26.

subject within their scope of competence and at any time.[366] In view of the – generally speaking – strong effect of the ESAs' soft law output (see 3.4.4. below), the issuing of such an opinion may ensure compliance (of a competent authority or – via the respective competent authority – of a FI/FMP), rendering unnecessary the initiation of one of the decision-making procedures discussed here. That procedures under Article 17, 18 and 19 are hardly ever initiated in general, is attributed to the current governance structure of the ESAs and to the dissuasive effect of the respective powers.[367]

As a preliminary, the general decision-making rules set out in Article 39 shall be looked at. Before taking a binding decision, the ESAs have to inform any named addressee of their intention to adopt a decision. In order to allow the addressee to express its views on the matter, it shall set a time limit, 'taking full account of the urgency, complexity and potential consequences of the matter'.[368] The decision – which the Boards of Supervisors, the ESAs' main decision-making organs, regularly take by a simple majority of their members[369] – shall state the reasons on which they are based and inform the addressee of the legal remedies available under the respective ESA-Regulation.[370]

The identity of the addressee and the main content of all decisions issued under Article 17, 18 or 19 shall be made public, unless such publication would conflict with the legitimate interests of FI/FMP (protection of business secrets) or could 'seriously jeopardise the orderly functioning and integrity of financial markets or the stability of the whole or part of the financial system of the Union'.[371]

3.4.3.1.   BREACH OF UNION LAW (ARTICLE 17)

Where a competent authority has not or not correctly applied the acts referred to in Article 1 para 2, including the respective RTS and ITS,[372] the ESA is provided special powers (para 1). On its own initiative or upon request of one

---

366   Article 29 para 1 lit a of the ESA-Regulations. Apparently, the ESMA intends to launch an opinion according to this provision before initiating an Article 17-procedure. In other words: It attempts to solve a conflict softly, before starting a process that may end with a binding measure; see Parliament, Review 1 101.

367   Commission, COM (2014) 509 final, 7.

368   Article 39 para 1 of the ESA-Regulations.

369   Article 44 para 1 of the ESA-Regulations.

370   Article 39 paras 2f of the ESA-Regulations. See also the 'Code of Good Administrative Behaviour', which the Management Board of each ESA has adopted: EBA DC 006; EIOPA-MB-11/043; ESMA/2011/MB/6. This Code, by means of which the ESAs legally oblige themselves, stipulates in greater detail rights, and duties respectively, of 'good administration', eg the right to be heard (Article 16), the duty to state the grounds of decisions (Article 18) and the indication of the possibilities to appeal (Article 19). The Code is essentially a copy of the 'European Code of Good Administrative Behaviour' adopted by the European Ombudsman in 2005. For a critical account of the concept of 'good administration' see Nehl 322 with numerous further references.

371   Article 39 para 5 of the ESA-Regulations.

372   See also Article 29 para 1 lit d of the ESA-Regulations.

or more competent authorities, of one of the legislative institutions, the Commission or the respective stakeholder group, an ESA may – at its discretion[373] – investigate an alleged breach of Union law.[374] Such an investigation begins with informing the authority of the matter, and allowing it to be heard within a reasonable time.[375] It is not clear which investigatory powers Article 17 shall include.[376] The fact that specific powers are not even hinted at suggests a restrictive interpretation and hence the negation of strong investigatory powers. Article 17 rules that the authority concerned is obliged to provide the respective ESA with all the information it, the ESA, considers necessary for its investigation (para 2 subpara 2). This certainly includes the forwarding of relevant files to the ESA. Whether it also comprises the interrogation of members of the competent authority is dubitable. I would suggest that the breach of Union law finds its expression in a written document, eg a decision, – or its lack – most of the time anyway – but that is a pragmatic, not a legal answer. While the ESAs are, for lack of a clear legal basis,[377] certainly not entitled to perform formal hearings, the duty to comprehensively inform the ESAs could – also against the background of the duty of sincere cooperation according to Article 4 para 3 TEU – be interpreted in a way that obliges the competent authorities (ie their employees) to serve as 'informants' (not: formal witnesses) for the ESAs, though.[378]

Within two months from the start of the investigation, the ESA may address a recommendation to the competent authority, depicting 'the action necessary to comply with Union law' (para 3 subpara 1). The authority addressed, on the other hand, shall – within ten working days of receipt of the recommendation – inform the ESA of the steps it has taken or intends to take, if any, to ensure compliance with Union law (para 3 subpara 2).

If the competent authority has not complied with the recommendation within one month from its receipt, the Commission may issue a formal opinion requiring the authority to take the action necessary to comply with Union law, thereby taking into account the ESA's preceding recommendation (para 4 subpara 1). The Commission has discretion on whether or not to

---

373   See eg EBA, EBA/DC/2014/100 in whose Annex 2 the factors speaking for or against the initiation of an investigation are listed; see also Board of Appeal, BoA 2013-008, paras 30–34 and the General Court in *SV Capital*, para 47; sceptical, Korinek 94.

374   Any natural or legal person may propose to the ESA to initiate proceedings on its own initiative. The refusal to act by the ESA addressed does not constitute a decision which may be appealed; *SV Capital*, para 45. On the unclear opinion of the Board of Appeal see BoA 2014-C1-02, paras 32–34 and 80(1) on the one hand, and BoA 2014 05, para 51, on the other hand.

375   See Article 39 para 1 of the ESA-Regulations.

376   See Michel, Bankenaufsichtsbehörde 732 (footnote 85).

377   See Hofmann et al. 430; see, eg, Article 19 of Regulation 1/2003, setting out an explicit '[p]ower [of the Commission] to take statements'.

378   Article 8 para 3 of the ESAs' RoP for investigation of breach of Union law merely states that the Chairperson of the ESAs 'may request ... information from any ... relevant person'. Coercive measures are not mentioned in any way; decisions of the EBA: EBA/DC/2014/100; EIOPA: EIOPA-BoS-11-017; ESMA: ESMA/2012/BS/87; see Hofmann et al. 430f.

render a formal opinion.[379] If it decides to render a formal opinion, however, it shall do so within three, occasionally four, months after the adoption of the recommendation (para 4 subpara 2). For that purpose both the ESA as well as the competent authority shall provide the Commission with all the necessary information (para 4 subpara 3). Upon receipt of the formal opinion, the competent authority addressed again has ten working days to inform the Commission and the ESA of the steps it has taken or intends to take, if any, in order to comply with that opinion (para 5).

Where the competent authority does not comply with the formal opinion within the time limit set therein, where the relevant requirements of the relevant Union law are directly applicable to FI/FMP[380] and where timely compliance is necessary in order to 'maintain or restore neutral conditions of competition in the market or ensure the orderly functioning and integrity of the financial system', the ESA may adapt a decision addressed to a FI/FMP in conformity with the formal opinion (para 6). The introduction of these conditions emphasises the decision's character as an *ultima ratio* measure.[381] Such a decision shall overrule the decisions the competent authority may have rendered on the same matter (para 7 subpara 1; see below). The 'sinner' authorities, and FI/FMP respectively, that is to say those that have not complied with formal opinions and decisions respectively, shall be listed in the respective ESA's annual report[382] – another item in the 'naming, blaming, and shaming' toolkit of the ESAs.[383]

While, doctrinally speaking, the formal opinion of the Commission can be qualified as a (soft) instruction,[384] a decision addressed to a FI/FMP by the ESA under Article 17 is the expression of an evocation, at least of an evocation '*à l'européenne*' (emphasis in the original).[385] The ESA exercises a power that principally falls within the power of the competent authority. *Kämmerer*[386] assumes that this evocation mechanism was inspired by the system applied in the area of competition law, more precisely the system of Article 11 para 6 of Council Regulation 1/2003. Under this regime, national competition authorities are 'relieved of' their competence to apply what are now Articles 101 and 102 TFEU, once the Commission itself has initiated the respective proceedings. Some consider the *modus operandi* provided for in Article 17 para 6 subpara 1 of the ESA-Regulations an execution by substitution,[387] but

---

379 Arg 'may'; cf the respective discussion as regards Treaty infringement procedures: eg Cremer, paras 40ff with further references.

380 For considerations on what to do if a MS failed to adequately transpose a Directive into national law, and, in particular, if the Directive (or provisions thereof) cannot be directly applied, see Kämmerer, Finanzaufsichtssystem 1286.

381 Similarly, Kämmerer, Finanzaufsichtssystem 1285; Rötting and Lang 11.

382 Article 17 para 8 in conjunction with Article 43 para 5 of the ESA-Regulations.

383 See Weismann, EU-Finanzmarktaufsicht 812f.

384 See also Witte 97f.

385 Kämmerer, Finanzaufsichtssystem 1285; see also Weismann, EU-Finanzmarktaufsicht 812.

386 Kämmerer, Finanzaufsichtssystem 1285 with further references.

387 See Lehmann and Manger-Nestler 91; Rötting and Lang 11; Walla, para 47.

this provision is about the competence to render a substantive decision, not about the execution (procedurally understood) of an action.[388]

It remains unclear whether the ESA's evocation – like the mechanism of competition law just mentioned – excludes the powers of the competent authority. In my view, the competence of the respective authority persists. A decision on the same matter of the competent authority, even if its content is contrary to the ESA-decision, continues to be the decision of a competent authority – it only gets 'substantially superposed' by the ESA-decision.[389] In other words, the ESA-decision does not render decisions of the competent authority invalid, but only non-applicable.[390] There is no indication of a withdrawal of competence or of an invalidating effect of the ESA-decision in the Regulation, and, what is more, such effects (by virtue of Union law[391]) would be inconsistent with primary law, particularly with the principle of supremacy. As clarified by the ECJ in the *Simmenthal* case,[392] the supremacy of Union law merely requires the non-application of conflicting national law by the competent authority (including courts), not its invalidation.[393] The same effect applies where the competent authority renders a non-accordant decision *after* the ESA has issued its decision under Article 17 para 6. Although the ESA-Regulations do not *expressis verbis* so provide or rather seem to exclude it (arg 'previous decision'), it can be deduced from Article 17 para 7 subpara 2 that stipulates that '[w]hen [= whenever] taking action' in relation to issues that are dealt with in an ESA-decision (or a formal opinion of the Commission), the competent authority (including the ECB) shall comply with it. As regards decisions of national competent authorities this also follows from the principle of supremacy. In the *Simmenthal* case just mentioned, the Court held that what back then was Community law prevails over national law – 'whether prior or subsequent to the Community rule'.[394]

Under the SSM-Regulation the ECB works as a 'competent authority' according to Article 4 para 2 of the EBA-Regulation. In case of an EBA-decision rendered in accordance with Article 17 and an ECB-decision on this matter, the ESA-decision prevails *qua* Article 17 para 7, but the ECB-decision continues to legally exist (unless it is revoked by the ECB itself).

---

388 Similarly, Kämmerer, Finanzaufsichtssystem 1285.
389 See Weismann, EU-Finanzmarktaufsicht 812; pointing at the legal uncertainties such a situation entails: Moloney, Securities 202.
390 This conforms to the general effects of the supremacy of EU law; see eg *IN.CO.GE.*, para 21 with reference to *Simmenthal*.
391 National laws may, of course, provide for such effects, thereby going beyond the effects of the supremacy of Union law.
392 *Simmenthal*, para 24.
393 See the recent case *Filipiak*, para 82 with further references.
394 *Simmenthal*, para 21. See also Craig and de Búrca, EU 269f with references to the more recent case law.

From a legal certainty perspective, the Article 17-regime leaves something to be desired. In a worst case scenario we have at least one decision by a competent authority conflicting with another decision, rendered by the ESA. Then the FI/FMP is confronted with two conflicting decisions from two different authorities, out of which only one is to be complied with, and hence only one is worth appealing against – given it is disadvantageous for the FI/FMP at issue.[395] This scenario, however unlikely it is to come true in practice, is remarkable, not least because it is a *novum* in the field of financial market supervisory law.[396] MS (and, in case of the ECB, the Council) are advised to introduce special provisions in their respective regulations in order to clarify these questions.[397]

The system of ensuring compliance with Union law envisaged in Article 17 raises the question of its relation to the Commission's discretion to launch infringement proceedings against a MS. Article 17 para 6 subpara 1 lapidarily stipulates that the Article 17 regime is '[w]ithout prejudice to the powers of the Commission pursuant to Article 258 TFEU'. This means that either procedure – Article 17 of the ESA-Regulations or Article 258 TFEU – may be initiated regardless of the respective other. It appears that the breach of Union law by one recalcitrant competent authority can be remedied in a more appropriate and timely manner according to Article 17,[398] but – from a legal point of view, and where a national authority (that is to say: not the ECB) is concerned – there is no argument to prevent the Commission from launching Treaty infringement proceedings instead of rendering a formal opinion under Article 17 of the ESA-Regulations. It is also possible to do both. Once an Article 17-procedure has been closed with an ESA-decision addressed to the FI/FMP concerned – and given that the competent authorities in the MS execute it accordingly, if need be – the infringement is remedied and the Commission will not be successful before the ECJ any more.[399] Summing up, Article 17, untechnically speaking, may be perceived as a *lex specialis* (not in a derogating sense, of course) of Article 258 TFEU, and it is therefore more pertinent to use this *lex specialis* in order to remedy the instances of a breach of Union law covered by this provision.[400]

395 Critical with regard to the ESAs' influence on the procedure in which EU law is enforced in general: Korinek 95f.
396 Ibid.
397 Cf, for example, § 21b of the Austrian *Finanzmarktaufsichtsbehördengesetz* that provides for the expiry of decisions rendered by the Austrian supervisory authority *Finanzmarktaufsichtsbehörde* in case one of the ESAs has issued a decision according to Article 17 para 6, Article 18 para 4 or Article 19 para 4 directly to a financial institution (para 1). In case of a recommendation, formal opinion or decision according to Article 17 to 19, the *Finanzmarktaufsichtsbehörde* may amend its decisions accordingly – even, and thereby this provision is deviating from the general rule of the Austrian law of administrative procedure, if it is to the disadvantage of a party concerned (para 2).
398 See Moloney, Securities 201.
399 Cf Smith 566; for an interdisciplinary approach see Börzel et al.
400 Similarly, Korinek 95.

The 'three-step-mechanism'[401] of Article 17 of the ESA-Regulations is to be understood as an attempt to facilitate a gradual decision-making process, in which the ESAs' expertise is combined with the Commission's political legitimacy.[402] The output by its respective name gets more and more authoritative: recommendation, formal opinion and, finally, as an *ultima ratio*, a decision. The procedure ensures the continuity of administrative output, starting with an ESA-recommendation, which might then be reinforced by a formal opinion of the Commission, and eventually concluding with an ESA-decision directly addressed to the FI/FMP concerned. The duty to take into account the respective preceding output arguably is tiered. Whereas the Commission only has to 'take into account' (para 4 subpara 1) the ESA's recommendation when rendering a formal opinion, the ESA's subsequent decision, if it is issued at all, shall be 'in conformity with' the formal opinion (para 6 subpara 2). This means that the Commission has considerable leeway when drafting its formal opinion, and even the ESA is given room for an at least partly autonomous decision – as long as it does not conflict with the formal opinion.

Where the remedying of a breach of Union law by a competent authority falls within the area of competence of more than one ESA, the competent ESAs shall adopt their decisions in parallel – as a common act –, as appropriate.[403]

In case of the EBA, under Article 17 an independent panel composed of the Chairperson and six other disinterested members of the Board of Supervisors proposes draft decisions to the Board for a vote.[404]

So far, the Article 17-regime has been applied sparingly.[405] Only one recommendation under Article 17 has been launched so far.[406]

3.4.3.2.   ACTION IN EMERGENCY SITUATIONS (ARTICLE 18)

The powers assigned to the ESAs under Article 18 are genuine emergency powers, which shall be exercised only where extraordinary economic circumstances so suggest. More precisely, Article 18 provides a tripartite structure. Whereas para 1 constitutes an action regime of its own, para 2 sets out the prerequisites for the exercise of certain powers, which are defined in paras 3–5 in greater detail.

---

401   Commission, COM (2009) 501 final, 16.
402   The legislator might have deemed mandatory the involvement of the Commission in light of the ECJ's delegation case law; see *International Film*, para 52 with reference to the *Meroni* judgement.
403   Article 56 para 2 of the ESA-Regulations.
404   Article 41 paras 1a and 3 of the EBA-Regulation.
405   See Parliament, Review 1 68, 84.
406   EBA, EBA/REC/2014/02.

Para 1 subpara 1 stipulates that in case of:

> adverse developments which may seriously jeopardise the orderly functioning and integrity of financial markets or the stability of the whole or part of the financial system in the Union, the [ESAs] shall actively facilitate and, where deemed necessary, coordinate any actions undertaken by the relevant ...[407] competent supervisory authorities.

This subparagraph leaves plenty of room for the respective ESA's appraisal of when it deems adverse developments to be capable of seriously jeopardising what could be circumscribed as an intact financial market (arg 'may'). If the ESA's appraisal is positive, it shall 'actively facilitate' and, if necessary, 'coordinate' the actions taken by the competent authorities. Subpara 2 stipulates that the ESA shall be 'fully informed' of any relevant developments, and that it shall be invited to participate in any relevant gathering by the competent authorities as an observer. Both demands are addressed to the competent authorities. Para 1 does not mention any concrete powers fleshing out the ESAs' competence to facilitate, and to coordinate respectively, but limits itself to urging the competent authorities to intensify the bottom-up information flow. Consequently, the ESAs have to make use of the powers laid down in other provisions in order to meet the objective of para 1, which is the active facilitation and coordination of any actions undertaken by the competent authorities.

The remaining paragraphs of Article 18 build up a different regime. Here, new output-related powers – emergency powers – are conferred upon the ESAs. The prerequisite for this regime to apply is that the Council formally states that there is an emergency situation.[408] To that end it shall consult with the Commission and the ESRB and, where appropriate, the ESAs, and issue, with a qualified majority, a decision 'determining the existence of an emergency situation for the purposes of this Regulation' (para 2 subpara 1). Such a decision can only be launched upon request by one of the ESAs, the Commission or the ESRB. If one of the ESAs or the ESRB consider that an emergency situation may arise, they shall send a confidential recommendation to the Council and attach an assessment of the situation. Irrespective of the Council's final decision, in which it is – once the decision is requested and in spite of the required consultations – 'entirely unrestrained',[409] all actors in this process shall handle the information confidentially (para 2 subpara 2). If the Council decides to state that an emergency situation within the meaning of

---

407   Whereas the respective passages in the EIOPA- and the ESMA-Regulation are still worded 'relevant national competent supervisory authorities', the amended EBA-Regulation – in order to include the ECB as a supervisory authority under the SSM – has dropped the word 'national'.

408   Critically with regard to the involvement of the Council: Inwinkl 333; see also Kohtamäki 189 with reference to the Commission that proposed to be vested with this power itself, and the EP having preferred the ESRB.

409   Adamski 822.

Article 18 para 2 subpara 1 exists, it shall without delay inform the EP and the Commission (para 2 subpara 3).

The Council shall review its decision at appropriate intervals, at least once a month. If the Council does not renew its decision at the end of the one-month period it shall automatically expire. The Council may declare the discontinuation of the emergency situation at any time (para 2 subpara 1).

The proceedings described above essentially provide for two important players: the body requesting the decision, and the body making the decision, ie the Council. The Council is not free to determine that an emergency situation exists and hence to trigger the emergency power regime of Article 18 paras 3–5. Rather, it is bound by the condition that an expert body (ESAs, ESRB) or the Commission requests this decision. This setting obviously is an attempt to strike a balance between political decision-making and MS representation on the one hand, and independent expertise on the other hand. The question arises why the Commission – which is operating in many fields, but which is definitely not the primary expert in the field of financial market supervision – is among those entitled to request an Article 18-decision by the Council. Presumably this is to enhance the political legitimacy of the Article 18-regime. An Article 18-decision triggers ('activates'[410]) the applicability of a given piece of legislation, namely paras 3–5. Hence the involvement of the Commission that is – in the system of the Treaties – the primary initiator of legislation seems appropriate to enhance the regime's legitimacy, not least in view of the fact that the EP is – arguably in the interest of timely decision-making – excluded.[411]

The powers, which the above Council decision triggers, are laid down in paras 3 and 4. For the emergence of new powers para 3 requires a Council decision pursuant to para 2 and the existence of exceptional circumstances where coordinated action by the competent authorities[412] is necessary to respond to 'adverse developments which may seriously jeopardise the orderly functioning and integrity of financial markets or the stability of the whole or part of the financial system in the Union'.[413] Hence para 3 cumulatively requires a Council decision pursuant to para 2 and 'exceptional circumstances…'.[414] Once these conditions are met, the ESAs are empowered to

---

410   Kämmerer, Finanzaufsichtssystem 1284 with references to a similar mechanism in the German *Grundgesetz*.

411   See Michel, Bankenaufsichtsbehörde 733, who criticises the weak participation of the Commission and calls for more influence for it in the Article 18-procedure in order to make sure the Union interest is duly considered.

412   On these processes see the EBA's Code of Conduct of July 2012 addressed to the national competent authorities referred to in Parliament, Review 1 71f.

413   This wording is also used in para 1.

414   It is true that the wording of the first sentence of para 3 allows for reading the Council decision and the 'exceptional circumstances' as alternative prerequisites. However, this would counteract the purpose of the Council decision, since it would allow the ESAs to appraise the economic situation themselves and, were they to take 'exceptional circumstances…' as a given, to make use of the powers contained in paras 3f. A look at, for example, the German version of the Regulation confirms the cumulative reading.

adopt individual decisions requiring competent authorities – apparently the legislator thought of decisions addressed to a plurality of (all) competent authorities to be most adequate in order to take the 'necessary action' – to take certain action in accordance with the legislation referred to in Article 1 para 2 of the ESA-Regulations, eg the prohibition of certain practices of FI/FMP, say the dealing with certain hazardous financial products. In other words, the ESAs can give formal instructions to the competent authorities on how to make use of their powers laid down in the respective Union law.[415]

Para 4 lays down the consequences of a competent authority failing to comply with an ESA-decision rendered pursuant to para 3. Such a failure to comply comprises non-application and evidently incorrect application ('manifest breach'). In such a case, the ESA may, where the relevant legal provisions are directly applicable to FI/FMP, adopt an individual decision *vis-à-vis* a FI/FMP (instead of the competent authority). The ESA can thereby require the FI/FMP to comply with its respective obligations (this may include the cessation of any practice). The ESAs shall only apply this competence 'where urgent remedying is necessary to restore the orderly functioning and integrity of financial markets or the stability of the whole or part of the financial system in the Union' (para 4).

Like with regard to Article 17, the mechanism applied in para 4 is to be qualified as an evocation. ESA-decisions rendered according to para 4 shall 'overrule' any previous – and also any successive – decisions adopted by the national authorities on the same matter (para 5 subpara 1; see 3.4.3.1. above).

Decisions rendered pursuant to paras 3 or 4 shall be reviewed 'at appropriate intervals' by the ESA.[416] If the adoption of decisions pursuant to Article 18 falls within the area of competence of more than one ESA, the competent ESAs shall adopt their decisions in parallel – as a common act –, as appropriate.[417]

The ESAs shall ensure that no decision adopted pursuant to Article 18 impinges on the fiscal responsibilities of the MS.[418] Where a MS deems an ESA-decision taken in accordance with Article 18 para 3 to impinge on its fiscal responsibilities, it may notify the respective ESA, the Commission and the Council within three working days after notification of the ESA-decision to the competent authority that it will not be implemented by it. In the case of such notification the ESA-decision shall be suspended. Now the Council may, within ten working days and by a simple majority of its members, take a decision as to whether or not the ESA-decision is revoked. Where the Council, having considered the issue, does not take a decision to revoke the ESA-decision, its suspension shall be terminated.[419] In the latter case, the MS may notify the Commission and the respective ESA and request the Council to

---

415   See Kämmerer, Finanzaufsichtssystem 1284; Weismann, EU-Finanzmarktaufsicht 813.
416   Article 39 para 4 of the ESA-Regulations.
417   Article 56 para 2 of the ESA-Regulations.
418   Article 38 para 1 of the ESA-Regulations.
419   Article 38 para 3 of the ESA-Regulations.

re-examine the issue, explaining why it still considers its fiscal responsibilities to be impinged upon by the ESA-decision. Within four weeks from the notification – possibly extended to eight weeks – the Council shall either confirm its decision or take a new decision pursuant to Article 38 para 3.[420]

According to Article 38 para 5, any abuse of this provision (in particular by the MS) shall be prohibited as incompatible with the internal market.

The Article 18-procedure – which has never been applied so far – shall be without prejudice to the Commission's powers under Article 258 TFEU (para 4).

3.4.3.3.   SETTLEMENT OF DISAGREEMENTS BETWEEN COMPETENT AUTHORITIES IN
            CROSS-BORDER SITUATIONS (ARTICLE 19)

Article 19 provides for a regime under which competent authorities may turn to the ESAs in order to have differing legal opinions clarified in a more or less authoritative way. At the request of one or more of the competent authorities, the respective ESA may assist the authorities in reaching an agreement (para 1 subpara 1). Only legal questions of the acts referred to in Article 1 para 2 are at issue, not, however, questions of competence (arg 'competent authorities').[421] Where a disagreement between competent authorities within the scope of the acts referred to in Article 1 para 2 can be determined on the basis of objective criteria, the ESA also on its own initiative may become active in the above-mentioned sense (para 1 subpara 2).

First of all, the ESA sets a time limit for conciliation between the authorities concerned, thereby considering any relevant deadlines set in the acts referred to in Article 1 para 2, and the complexity and urgency of the matter. In this phase of the procedure, the ESA shall act as a mediator (para 2).[422] This means that it shall facilitate the communication between the parties without interfering in the substance of the matter.[423] Only where the parties fail to reach an agreement within the above 'conciliation phase', the ESA may step in, this time in the role of an arbitrator, and take a decision requiring the parties to take specific action or to refrain from action. Such a decision[424] has binding effects on all parties and shall 'settle the matter' (para 3).[425]

Where one of the competent authorities fails to comply with the ESA-decision, and thereby fails to ensure that a FI/FMP complies with requirements directly applicable to it by virtue of the acts referred to in Article 1 para 2, the ESA may adopt an individual decision addressed to that FI/FMP,

---

420   Article 38 para 4 of the ESA-Regulations.
421   See also Kämmerer, Finanzaufsichtssystem 1284.
422   A similar mediation mechanism was already applied by the ESAs' predecessors CEBS, CEIOPS and CESR; see Wymeersch 260 with further references.
423   For an account of the nature of mediation see Roberts and Palmer 153ff.
424   On the majority requirements in the Boards of Supervisors for such a decision to be taken see Article 44 para 1 subparas 3f of the ESA-Regulations.
425   For the details of the procedure see the respective RoP, eg EBA/DC/2014/091 and EBA/DC/2014/093.

requiring the necessary action to comply with Union law (para 4). Such decisions 'overrule' any previous or successive decisions adopted on the same matter by the competent authority (para 5; see 3.4.3.1. above). This procedure shall be without prejudice to the Commission's powers under Article 258 TFEU.

In both cases in which the ESA is competent to render a binding decision (paras 3 and 4), it has discretion (arg 'may') whether or not to do so. Both times this discretion is limited by considerations of legal certainty and of *effet utile*.

An independent panel composed of the Chairperson and two (EBA: six) other disinterested members of the Board of Supervisors shall facilitate a settlement of the disagreement and propose decisions for adoption by the Board.[426]

In case of a cross-sectoral disagreement, that is to say a disagreement of two or more competent authorities supervising different sectors of the financial market, it shall be the Joint Committee that is competent to settle the disagreement.[427] The purpose of this provision clearly suggests that the whole process of Article 19, starting from the mediation phase, falls within the competence of the Joint Committee.[428] Decisions shall be adopted as a common act of the ESAs concerned.[429]

The nature and type of disagreements between competent authorities as well as the agreements reached and, where applicable, the settlement decisions shall be published in the report on the respective ESA's activities.[430]

Article 38 para 2 provides a safeguard regime for the fiscal responsibilities of the MS, which is similar to that set out for the Article 18-regime (see 3.4.3.2. above). The difference is that Article 38 para 2 provides for longer deadlines and for an involvement of the respective ESA (next to the Council) in the decision on whether or not the contested ESA-decision shall be revoked.

The Article 19-regime – in principle – pursues the same goal as Article 267 TFEU. Both systems provide for an authoritative clarification of a question of Union law by an EU body. The differences between these two mechanisms regard the body answering the question, the scope of the possible clarification, the 'standing', ie the right to refer to the respective EU body and the legal remedies available against the authoritative decision. As regards the scope it is

---

426   Article 41 paras 2f of the respective ESA-Regulation.
427   Article 20 of the ESA-Regulations.
428   See also Article 6 para 6 of the RoP of the Joint Committee 2014 (arg 'resolve', 'the procedure laid down in Article 19').
429   Article 56 of the ESA-Regulations; Article 8 para 3 of the RoP of the Joint Committee 2014.
430   Article 19 para 6 in conjunction with Article 50 para 2 of the ESA-Regulations; see for example the EBA's Annual Report 2014, 56.

apparent that the respective ESA can only decide on questions of interpretation of the acts referred to in Article 1 para 2 of the ESA-Regulations, whereas the ECJ pursuant to Article 267 TFEU is competent to decide not only on the interpretation of all Union law, but also on the validity of secondary Union law.

With a view to 'standing' we can see that under Article 19 it is not sufficient that a competent authority has doubts on the interpretation of one of the acts referred to in Article 1 para 2 in order to be entitled to turn to the ESA. Rather, a dispute between at least two competent authorities on the 'procedure or content of an action or inaction' of one of these authorities must have arisen. As opposed to the ECJ under Article 267 TFEU, it is possible for the ESA to get involved in such a dispute even without one of the parties so having requested – if a disagreement can be determined on the basis of 'objective criteria' (para 1 subpara 2). A preliminary reference to the ECJ, on the contrary, would be possible for a financial market supervisory authority only where it met the qualification of a 'court or tribunal' according to Article 267. As regards the legal remedies available, with an ESA-decision the competent authorities may appeal to the ESAs' Board of Appeal[431] and, subsequently, to the CJEU.[432] The judgement of the ECJ under Article 267 TFEU, on the contrary, is a decision of last resort. The Article 19-regime has been applied in only a few cases so far.[433]

3.4.3.4.   THE RELATIONSHIP BETWEEN THE REGIMES LAID DOWN IN ARTICLES 17, 18 AND 19

While the regimes under Articles 17, 18 and 19 in principle tackle different problems, their scopes do overlap to some extent. We may begin by comparing the modalities under Article 17 and under Article 18 paras 3f. In the first sentence of Article 18 para 4 the ESA is given the power to launch a decision directly addressed to a FI/FMP, given the fact that an authority does not comply with the instruction given by the ESA pursuant to para 3. In the second sentence this competence is made subject to a situation in which the competent authority does not or not correctly ('manifest breach') apply the acts referred to in Article 1 para 2. In addition to this requirement, 'urgent remedying [must be] necessary to restore the orderly functioning and integrity of financial markets or the stability of the whole or part of the financial system in the Union'. This raises the question of what it is that distinguishes the competences under Article 18 para 4 from those under Article 17 para 6. When comparing the prerequisites and implications which the two regimes establish with respect to an ESA-decision directly addressed to a FI/FMP, it is apparent that both regimes are without prejudice to the Commission's

---

431   Article 60 para 1 of the ESA-Regulations.
432   Article 61 para 1 of the ESA-Regulations in conjunction with Article 263 TFEU.
433   See eg EBA, Annual Report 2014, 56.

powers pursuant to Article 258 TFEU; both decisions are preceded by a 'preliminary output' – a formal opinion (Article 17) and a decision (Article 18), respectively, addressed to the respective competent authority.

Thus far for the similarities. As regards the differences we can see that a decision according to Article 17 para 6 must be 'necessary to remedy in a timely manner such non-compliance in order to maintain or restore neutral conditions of competition in the market or ensure the orderly functioning and integrity of the financial system', whereas a decision pursuant to Article 18 para 4 may be rendered 'where urgent remedying is necessary to restore the orderly functioning and integrity of financial markets or the stability of the whole or part of the financial system in the Union'. It is apparent that, although both of the latter conditions have a considerable overlap, the former is directed at maintaining fair competition and at ensuring the orderly functioning and integrity of the system 'in a timely manner', whereas the latter is directed at quickly ('urgent') restoring this very orderly functioning and integrity of the system. Whereas an Article 17-decision may react to an infringement of any of the acts referred to in Article 1 para 2, Article 18 para 4 limits its scope to the legislative acts referred to in Article 1 para 2 and the RTS and ITS adopted in accordance with these acts.[434] Also the procedural requirements are different. Whereas a decision under Article 17 is preceded by a recommendation of the ESA and a formal opinion of the Commission, for the ESA to render a decision according to Article 18 para 4 it is necessary that the Council has adopted a decision pursuant to para 2 and that a competent authoritiy does not comply with the ESA's instruction given in accordance with para 3.

Now there may be a situation in which the Council has rendered a decision according to Article 18 para 2 and where a competent authority acts in a way which is a) not in accordance with at least one of the acts referred to in Article 1 para 2 and b) contrary to the necessary action according to Article 18 para 3. Where the additional requirements of either regime are met, the question arises which procedure the Commission shall apply. In my view, it has to apply Article 18 para 4. While Article 18 para 4 requires an infringement of Union law, namely an ESA-decision rendered in accordance with para 3, it is – in these circumstances – the *lex specialis* compared with Article 17. After all, Article 18 – applicable only under extreme circumstances – provides for much faster decision-making and less *audiatur et altera pars*,[435] ie less regard to the competent authorities' views.[436] Article 17, on the contrary, lays down the

---

434   Since RTS and ITS are non-legislative acts (Article 289 para 3 TFEU *e contrario*), the word 'including' seems inadequate. It is clear, however, what the legislator meant to say: legislative acts *and* RTS and ITS.

435   See the respective minimum requirements according to Article 39 para 1, which apply to all ESA-decisions.

436   Also with regard to the ESA's power to temporarily prohibit or restrict certain financial activities referred to in Article 9 para 5, in the case of an emergency situation Article 18 has to be applied as a legal basis (*lex specialis*).

regular, ie the more general procedure to be applied in case of infringements of the relevant law. This relationship is, arguing *e contrario*, confirmed by Article 19 para 1 that explicitly provides that it shall apply '[w]ithout prejudice to the powers laid down in Article 17' – a clause which Article 18 lacks. Also compared with Article 19 – in a situation where the requirements for the initiation of either regime are met – Article 18 prevails as *lex specialis*. On the contrary, between Articles 17 and 19 there is no such prevalence.[437] In a situation where both regimes may lawfully be applied, the Commission has to decide which procedure it deems more adequate to remedy the situation.

All three regimes, as has been mentioned above, leave untouched the right of the Commission to initiate an infringement procedure according to Article 258 TFEU.[438]

3.4.4.   Guidelines and recommendations

Guidelines and recommendations 'on the application of Union law'[439] are another – increasingly used[440] – tool of the ESAs to ensure 'consistent, efficient and effective supervisory practices within the ESFS' as well as a 'common, uniform and consistent application of Union law'.[441] Although by definition not legally binding, the influence they can exert on competent authorities ought not to be neglected.[442] They can be addressed either to the competent authorities or to FI/FMP in areas 'not covered by [RTS/ITS]'.[443] Within the *Lamfalussy* system the issuing of guidelines and recommendations falls under level 3, which is to say strengthened cooperation between regulators to improve implementation.[444]

When drafting a guideline or a recommendation, the ESAs shall – as provided in the case of technical standards – conduct (proportionate) open public consultations, and a (proportionate) cost-benefit analysis. Where appropriate, the ESAs shall also request an opinion or advice from the respective stakeholder group.[445]

---

437   Article 19 para 1 of the ESA-Regulations.
438   Articles 17 para 6, 18 para 4 and 19 para 4 of the ESA-Regulations.
439   Recital 26 of the ESA-Regulations.
440   With regard to the ESMA: van Rijsbergen 120.
441   Article 16 para 1 of the ESA-Regulations. On the use of soft law in EU financial market law more generally see Ferran and Alexander 760f.
442   See *Alassini*, para 40 with further references; Michel, Bankenaufsichtsbehörde 732; B Raschauer, Verfahren 22f; Wymeersch 248f.
443   Recital 26 of the ESA-Regulations. In my view, only in a field where RTS/ITS have *actually* been adopted, the ESAs may not adopt guidelines and recommendations; cf van Rijsbergen 122.
444   *Lamfalussy* Report 37ff.
445   Article 16 para 2 of the ESA-Regulations; critical with regard to the generally weak proceduralisation in the creation of soft law by European agencies: van Rijsbergen 117f.

Para 3 provides that the competent authorities and the FI/FMP shall make 'every effort' to comply with such guidelines and recommendations.[446] Within two months of the issuance of the respective output, each competent authority has to fill in and send to the respective ESA a form indicating whether it complies or intends to comply, or whether it does not. In the latter case, it has to state the reasons ('act or explain'). The same applies, where a competent authority only partially 'confirms' a guideline or recommendation.[447]

The ESAs publish a list of all 'sinners', which is to say competent authorities that do not, or do not intend to comply with this ESA-output. It is at the discretion of the ESAs to incorporate in the list the reasons for (partial) non-compliance given by the competent authority. In any event, the competent authority shall be notified of the publication in advance.[448]

If a guideline or a recommendation, which is addressed to FI/FMP, so requires, the addressees have to report clearly and in detail whether or not they comply with it.[449]

In the annual reports on their activities, the ESAs shall inform the legislative institutions and the Commission of the guidelines and recommendations they have issued, of the competent authorities that have not complied with them and of the measures the ESAs intend to take in order to ensure they will meet the rules proposed therein in the future.[450]

All these measures, especially the 'naming and shaming'[451] mechanism – in combination with the factual authority of the ESAs – render the ESAs' competence to issue guidelines and recommendations a powerful tool. With a view to the 'act or explain' mechanism, it is to be noted that only the guidelines and recommendations are non-binding, whereas the duty of the authorities and FI/FMP, respectively, to justify is – as the term 'duty' suggests – binding.[452] The fact that the non-compliance with a non-binding measure triggers a legal obligation substantially relativises the soft character of the ESAs' guidelines and recommendations.

The ESAs' soft law output, especially guidelines, ought to help competent authorities and subsequently also FI/FMP interpret legal norms correctly – or at least the way ESAs want them to be applied. Given the fact that the ESAs could even 'execute' their legal opinion by issuing a (binding) decision *vis-à-*

---

446   According to *B Raschauer*, as regards the competent authorities this also follows from Article 4 para 3 TEU (loyalty principle); B Raschauer, Leitlinien 37.

447   Article 16 para 3 subpara 2 of the ESA-Regulations in conjunction with the 'Form for Confirmation' attached to the guideline or recommendation. See eg EBA, GL 45, 29f; see also a compliance table with respect to the EBA's GL 44.

448   Article 16 para 3 subpara 3 of the ESA-Regulations; see also van Rijsbergen 124f.

449   Article 16 para 3 subpara 4 of the ESA-Regulations.

450   Article 16 para 4 of the ESA-Regulations; see eg the EBA's Annual Report 2014, 110–112.

451   See Rötting and Lang 10 with further references.

452   If need be, the violation of this duty to justify can – as a breach of Union law – be stated by an ESA-decision according to Article 17 of the ESA-Regulations; *B Raschauer*, conversely, calls Article 16 para 3 a *lex imperfecta*; B Raschauer, Leitlinien 40.

vis an 'unruly' competent authority, eg under the breach of EU law-regime,[453] the ESAs' competences amount to a power that comes close to a proper decision-/rule-making power.[454] In other words: the competence to set supervisory standards combined with the ability to 'overrule' decisions of competent authorities allows the ESAs to establish a quasi-binding interpretation of certain provisions of EU law. It is true that the ESAs do not have the 'last word' in such a case, since its (binding) decisions can be made subject to an appeal before the Board of Appeal or of an action for annulment before the CJEU, but still it has an 'important word' to say.

Guidelines and recommendations may also be seen as measures, whereby the ESAs are uttering their interpretation of a certain provision or whereby they are predetermining how they will exercise their discretion in future – binding – decisions. The ESAs shall consider these expressions of legal opinion as binding upon themselves with a view to future decisions,[455] if they do not want to jeopardise their authority in the long run.[456] In that sense, also non-binding guidelines and recommendations have a certain legal effect[457] – or, as the ECJ has put it, 'they are not without any legal effect'.[458] The application of the guidelines and recommendations shall be reviewed by the ESAs.[459] In general there is a high degree of willingness among the competent authorities to follow the ESAs' guidelines and recommendations.[460]

For all these reasons, the ESAs' guidelines and recommendations can be described as soft law with great *de facto* authority.[461] Whether this kind of soft law must be seen as an instance of an entirely new regulatory approach ('persuasion and information'), whether it is just 'command and control' with a new ('soft') look[462] or whether it is something in between, remains to be discussed.[463]

---

453 Article 17 of the ESA-Regulations; see 3.4.3.1. above.

454 Similarly Busuioc, Rule-Making 119.

455 See *Dansk Rørindustri*, para 211.

456 See Thomas 430f.

457 Groß 23; Michel, Bankenaufsichtsbehörde 732; T Möllers 289; N Raschauer, Verfahren 165 with further references; Storr 79. Comparing the legal effects of guidelines in general with those of recommendations and opinions: Thomas 424; see also B Raschauer, Verhaltenssteuerungen 685.

458 See *Alassini*, para 40. Differently, Herdegen 114; see also Thomas 424; see already *Grimaldi*, para 18, in which the Court held that 'national courts are bound to take recommendations into consideration in order to decide disputes submitted to them, in particular where they cast light on the interpretation of national measures adopted in order to implement them or where they are designed to supplement binding Community provisions'.

459 Article 29 para 1 lit d of the ESA-Regulations.

460 See Herdegen 114, still with respect to CEBS recommendations.

461 See Busuioc, Rule-Making 113f; with regard to the role such output of European agencies plays on the national level see N Raschauer, Aufsicht 76; more generally Majone, Delegation 332.

462 Cf Dragomir 106; pointing at 'uncertainties relating to the concrete scope and nature' of certain of the ESAs' soft law measures: Commission, COM (2014) 509 final, 5.

463 On these two regulatory approaches see Majone, Agencies 267–269.

3.4.5. Legal protection against ESA-output

The variety of forms of administrative output the ESAs may produce raises the question of what mechanisms of legal protection the persons concerned may avail themselves of. Already in *Meroni* the ECJ has held that the delegation of powers principally requires the maintenance of equivalent legal protection.[464] The Court has clarified in particular in its *Sogelma* judgement[465] that also binding acts of European agencies can principally be made subject to a review by the Court.[466] For the ESAs (as for some other agencies) the legislator, in addition to that, has provided for a Board of Appeal.[467] The installation of an appellate body, which principally must be addressed prior to launching an action before the CJEU, serves the purpose of disburdening the chronically overstrained Court[468] and thereby contributes to 'a more fluid functioning of the Single Market'.[469] Another, maybe more important purpose is to provide legal protection by a group of experts in the respective field (air safety, chemicals, financial market supervision, etc.) – which a majority of the judges at the CJEU are not.[470] This trend towards a specialisation of bodies of appeal finds its expression also in the Treaty, more precisely in Article 257 TFEU, which provides for the possibility to establish specialised courts attached to the General Court.[471]

The Board of Appeal (BoA) of the ESAs is composed of independent experts appointed by the respective Management Board (for the details of the composition see 3.5.6. below). As a 'joint body of the ESAs'[472] it is competent to deal with appeals submitted by natural or legal persons (including competent authorities) against any decision adopted by the ESAs in accordance with the Union acts referred to in Article 1 para 2, which is addressed or otherwise of direct and individual concern to that person.[473] These standing requirements correspond to those laid down in Article 263 para 4 TFEU for an action for annulment before the Court,[474] although the wording of Article 60 para 1 of the ESA-Regulations is still closer to that of the predecessor provision in the Treaty (ie Article 230 para 4 TEC). If a decision is addressed to a FI/FMP, its standing before the Board of Appeal is indubitable. However,

---

464 *Meroni* 150. For the applicability of *Meroni* also in the case of the legislator conferring powers on an EU body see Chapter 2 I.5. above.

465 *Sogelma*, in particular paras 56f; on the congruity with the up to then case law see Riedel, Rechtsschutz 565f.

466 Cf Pabel 66 with reference to Article 47 CFR.

467 For the different models ensuring legal protection applied with European agencies see Görisch 215ff; Siegel 142ff.

468 See Magiera and Weiß 515.

469 Parliament, Review 1 113.

470 See also Pabel 82.

471 See Wegener, para 7.

472 Article 58 para 1 of the ESA-Regulations.

473 See van Cleynenbreugel 157, criticising the unclear wording of Article 60 para 1 of the ESA-Regulations.

474 See Board of Appeal, BoA 2013-008, para 24.

under the regimes of Articles 17-19 – which shall be focused on here – this is the most extreme case that can only happen where the competent authority has failed to implement the formal opinion of the Commission (Article 17) or the ESA-decision (Articles 18, 19). In the reverse case, that is when the competent authority addresses a decision, according to the Commission's formal opinion or the ESA-decision, to the FI/FMP, the question arises whether or not the FI/FMP can, apart from appealing against the competent authority's decision, challenge the acts of the Commission and the ESA respectively. Since the Commission's formal opinion is, *qua* its non-bindingness, not 'intended to produce legal effects vis-à-vis third parties' in accordance with Article 263 para 1 TFEU, it cannot be challenged, neither before the BoA[475] nor before the CJEU. As regards the ESA-decisions rendered under Article 18 para 3 and Article 19 para 3, according to the Court's case law on a) direct and b) individual concern, the FI's/FMP's standing – at first before the BoA – depends on the following: a) whether the decision addressed to the competent authority leaves no discretion as regards its implementation[476]; b) whether 'that decision affects them by reason of certain attributes which are peculiar to them or by reason of circumstances in which they are differentiated from all other persons and by virtue of these factors distinguishes them individually just as in the case of the person addressed' (*Plaumann* test).[477] As regards direct concern, no general remark can be made as to whether an ESA-decision leaves discretion to the respective competent authority as to its implementation (in which case it would not be of direct concern), but it would need to be assessed case by case. As regards individual concern, this qualification may be affirmed where one or a small number of FI/FMP are affected by virtue of a sort of *differentia specifica*. Where an ESA-decision affects all FI/FMP in the EU in the same way, in particular due to an ESA-decision addressed to all competent authorities in accordance with Article 18 para 3, they are not individually concerned.[478]

The appeal, stating the grounds, has to be filed in writing with the respective ESA within two months of the date of notification of the decision to the person concerned, or, in the absence thereof, of the day of its publication by the ESA.[479] Within two months of the appeal being lodged, the Board shall scrutinise the legality – not: the expediency[480] – of the respective ESA-decision.[481]

---

475   Article 60 para 1 of the ESA-Regulations: 'decision'.
476   See Craig and de Búrca, EU 515–517 with references to the pertinent case law.
477   *Plaumann.*
478   See also Michel, Bankenaufsichtsbehörde 734.
479   Article 60 para 2 subpara 1 of the ESA-Regulations. The 'day on which [the decision] came to the knowledge of the [person concerned]' is, unlike with Article 263 para 6 TFEU, not a relevant point in time.
480   See Storr 86f.
481   Article 60 para 2 subpara 2 of the ESA-Regulations. The duty to publish all decisions taken under Articles 17–19 is laid down in Article 39 para 5.

Principally, an appeal does not have suspensive effect.[482] However, the Board may, if it deems that circumstances so require, suspend the application of the appealed decision.[483] The parties to the appeal proceedings shall be invited to make their submissions, and are entitled to make oral representations.[484] The BoA has two opportunities: It may either confirm the decision under appeal, or remit the case to the respective ESA. In the latter case the ESA has to decide afresh, thereby being bound by the legal opinion of the BoA expressed in its appeal decision.[485] However, where the law provides for discretion, the Board must not impose its own discretionary view on the ESA.[486] It is not clear from the wording of Article 60 para 5 (or from the BoA's RoP) whether the Board, if it does not confirm it anyway, actually annuls the decision under appeal. Neither is the, to date only, BoA-decision remitting the case to the ESA explicit in this regard.[487] Since the principle of *res iudicata* prohibits two decisions being rendered on the same matter, the BoA's competence to 'remit the case' to the ESA concerned according to Article 60 para 5 is to be understood as having a cassatory effect.

The question arises whether it is possible to initiate proceedings before the CJEU without having turned to the BoA before. This question is to be answered in the negative.[488] Article 61 para 1 provides that only 'in cases where there is no right of appeal before the Board of Appeal' may an action be brought before the Court against an ESA-decision – otherwise such an action can only be brought against a BoA-decision. This mediatisation of legal protection from the CJEU via the BoA is in accordance with primary law since Article 263 para 5 TFEU explicitly allows for '[a]cts setting up ... agencies ... [to] lay down specific conditions and arrangements concerning actions brought by natural or legal persons against acts of these ... agencies intended to produce legal effects in relation to them'.[489] While Article 61 para 2 – taken literally – stipulates that MS, the Union institutions and 'any natural or legal person' may turn to the CJEU *direttissima* this provision, as far as 'any natural or legal person' is concerned, has to be read in conjunction with para 1. Understood that way, it is apparent that para 2 applies only 'where there is no right of appeal before the Board of Appeal'. MS and the Union institutions,

---

482 Critically Michel, Bankenaufsichtsbehörde 734. Cf Article 91 para 2 of Regulation 1907/2006, according to which an appeal before the Board of Appeal does have suspensive effect.

483 Aritcle 60 para 3 of the ESA-Regulations. Cf Article 278 TFEU as regards actions brought before the CJEU.

484 Article 60 para 4 of the ESA-Regulations.

485 Article 60 para 5 of the ESA-Regulations.

486 See Craig, EU (#2) 434f regarding the pertinent case law of the Court on its own scope of scrutiny which ought to be applied *per analogiam*.

487 Board of Appeal, BoA 2013-008.

488 With regard to the OHIM's system of legal protection similarly: Dammann 24f; Fischer-Appelt 314; more generally Pabel 79; sceptical: Parliament, Review 1 112 with further references.

489 See also Magiera and Weiß 515; Sonder 11.

however, cannot appeal before the Board – they may initiate proceedings only before the CJEU.[490]

An ESA's failure to act can be exclusively remedied before the CJEU in the course of proceedings according to Article 265 TFEU.[491] The ESA shall take the necessary measures to comply with a judgement of the CJEU, regardless of whether it was issued according to Article 263 or Article 265 TFEU.

Exceptionally, the ESAs may be allowed to render binding acts of a general application. The most prominent example is the ESMA's power to prohibit the short-selling of financial products according to Article 28 of Regulation 236/2012, which was at issue in the *ESMA* case (see Chapter 2 I.7. above). Since these acts can only be regulatory acts within the meaning of Article 263 para 4 TFEU,[492] natural or legal persons may institute proceedings against them before the CJEU where they are of direct concern to them and do not entail implementing measures. Regulatory acts arguably cannot be brought before the BoA, since Article 60 para 1 only refers to decisions of direct and individual concern to the applicant.[493]

For ESA-output without binding effects legal protection is weak. Preparatory acts, eg drafts for RTS/ITS, may be challenged incidently in the course of an action for annulment against the final act.[494] For guidelines and recommendations there are no remedies available.[495] Only where they exceptionally – and unlawfully – do have binding effects, in legal scholarship the admissibility of an action according to Article 263 TFEU is affirmed.[496]

Competent authorities that do not have the status of legal persons cannot bring an action before the CJEU themselves, but this may only be done by the legal person to which the respective authority is subordinated.

3.5.   *Organisation: tasks and composition of the ESAs' organs*

The ESAs each comprise of four main organs: the Chairperson, the Executive Director, the Board of Supervisors and the Management Board. Additionally,

---

490   See Storr 84.
491   See Article 61 para 3 of the ESA-Regulations; see also van Cleynenbreugel 156.
492   *Tapiriit Kanatami* [2011], paras 40ff; confirmed by *Tapiriit Kanatami* [2013], para 61.
493   Cf Commission, COM (2014) 509 final, 5.
494   See Michel, Bankenaufsichtsbehörde 734.
495   Critically, van Cleynenbreugel 158.
496   See Michel, Gleichgewicht 278f; B Raschauer, Leitlinien 37f with reference to Storr 83; Russ and Bollenberger 809–811; in the affirmative also: Commission, COM (2014) 509 final, 5. On shortcomings with regard to the legal protection against warnings issued by the Austrian financial market supervisory authority (*Finanzmarktaufsichtsbehörde*) see judgement of the Austrian constitutional court (*Verfassungsgerichtshof*), collection number 18747.

there are at least two joint organs composed of members of all three ESAs, namely the Joint Committee and the Board of Appeal.[497]

3.5.1. *The Chairperson*

3.5.1.1. TASKS

As Union bodies with legal personality, the ESAs are each represented by one full-time independent Chairperson.[498] His independence does not allow him to seek or take instructions from Union institutions or bodies, from MS governments or from any other public or private body. Neither shall any of these bodies seek to influence him.[499] According to Article 49a of the EBA-Regulation, the Chairperson has to 'make public meetings held and hospitality received'. Even after leaving service, the Chairperson continues 'to be bound by the duty to behave with integrity and discretion as regards the acceptance of certain appointments or benefits'.[500] Apart from representation tasks the Chairperson is responsible for preparing the work of the Board of Supervisors and chairing the meetings of both the Board of Supervisors and the Management Board. Only in the Management Board the Chairperson also – exceptionally – has the right to vote, more precisely to give his casting vote.[501]

The Chairperson also has reporting duties *vis-à-vis* the Council, and in particular *vis-à-vis* the Parliament.[502]

3.5.1.2. APPOINTMENT AND DISMISSAL

The Chairperson is – following an open selection procedure – appointed by the Board of Supervisors 'on the basis of merit, skills, knowledge of [FI/FMP] and markets, and of experience relevant to financial supervision and regulation'.[503] The EP may object to the designation up to one month after the selection by the Board of Supervisors, before the Chairperson has taken up his duties.[504] The Board of Supervisors also elects an alternate of the

---

497 For the different types of organisation of European agencies and their development in a historical retrospective see Görisch 193ff; for an organigramme of the ESAs (internal organisation) see <www.eba.europa.eu/about-us/organisation/organisation-chart> (EBA), <https://eiopa.europa.eu/Publications/Administrative/EIOPA%20Organigram%202015%2011.pdf> (EIOPA), <www.esma.europa.eu/system/files/organigramme_2.pdf> (ESMA).
498 Article 5 para 3 of the ESA-Regulations.
499 Article 49 paras 1f of the ESA-Regulations.
500 Article 49 para 3 in conjunction with Article 16 para 1 of Council Regulation 31/62.
501 See 3.5.4.2. below.
502 See Article 50 of the ESA-Regulations.
503 Article 48 para 2 subpara 1 of the ESA-Regulations.
504 Article 48 para 2 subpara 2 of the ESA-Regulations.

Chairperson from among those members of the Board of Supervisors who are not at the same time members of the Management Board.[505]

The Chairperson's term of office is five years and may be extended once.[506] In the course of the nine months preceding the end of his (first) term of office, the Board of Supervisors has to evaluate the results achieved in the term of office as well as the ESA's duties and requirements in the coming years. With a view to this evaluation, the Board of Supervisors may extend the term of office of the Chairperson – which is again subject to the EP's confirmation.[507]

Also the removal from office of the Chairperson is subject to a decision of the Board of Supervisors and subsequent confirmation – which then is the formal act of removal – by the EP.[508] The Chairperson shall not prevent the Board of Supervisors from discussing matters relating to him (in particular: his removal) and shall not be involved in its deliberations on such matters.[509]

3.5.2.   The Executive Director

3.5.2.1.   TASKS

The Executive Director is a full-time independent professional.[510] He is in charge of managing the ESA and of preparing the work of the Management Board.[511] Managing the ESA encompasses the implementation of the annual work programme of the ESA under the guidance of the Board of Supervisors and under the control of the Management Board. It also encompasses ensuring the functioning of the ESA, eg by adopting internal administrative instructions and by publishing notices, for example vacancy notices.[512] The Executive Director furthermore shall prepare an annual as well as a multi-annual work programme to be adopted by the Management Board, draw up a preliminary draft budget of the ESA and also implement its budget, once

---

505   Article 48 para 2 subpara 3 of the ESA-Regulations.

506   Article 48 para 3 of the ESA-Regulations. The *de Larosière* Group has proposed a tenure of eight years; *de Larosière* Report 54.

507   Article 48 para 4 of the ESA-Regulations. The Parliament can prevent a renewal of the Chairperson's term of office by refusing its confirmation, but it cannot push through a renewal against the will of the Board of Supervisors. In the latter case another candidate is selected, whose appointment by the Board of Supervisors may then be subject to objection by the Parliament (Article 48 para 2 subpara 2).

508   The Parliament may maintain the *status quo* by refusing to remove the Chairperson – against the will of the Board of Supervisors. It may not, however, remove the Chairperson against the will of the Board of Supervisors, since it is only asked to decide on a removal 'following a decision of the Board of Supervisors'.

509   Article 48 para 5 of the ESA-Regulations.

510   Article 51 para 1 of the ESA-Regulations. For the conception of the director of more traditional European agencies see Fischer-Appelt 238ff.

511   Article 53 para 1 of the ESA-Regulations.

512   See, for example, Vacancy Note EBA CA 06/2012R <www.eba.europa.eu/documents/10180/58901/CA—06-2012-FG-IV—Accounting—Assistant_draft.pdf>.

adopted by the Board of Supervisors (Article 63 para 5), draft an activity report and handle staff affairs as laid down in Article 68 and the legal acts referred to therein.[513]

The Executive Director has to exercise his tasks independently. This independence is – according to the ESA-Regulations – equal to that of the Chairperson (see 3.5.1.1. above).[514]

3.5.2.2.   APPOINTMENT AND DISMISSAL

The Board of Supervisors appoints the Executive Director after confirmation by the Parliament. Following an open selection procedure he is chosen on the basis of merit, skills, knowledge of FI/FMP and markets, and experience relevant to financial supervision and regulation and managerial experience.[515]

The Executive Director's term of office is five years and may be extended once. In order to be able to take an informed decision on the renewal, the Board of Supervisors shall – within the nine months preceding the end of the Executive Director's (first) term of office – evaluate in particular the results achieved and the way they were achieved, as well as the ESA's duties and requirements in the coming years. In the case of the Executive Director, unlike that of the Chairperson, it is the Board of Supervisors alone that decides on the renewal – a confirmation by the EP is not required.[516]

The Board of Supervisors can remove the Executive Director from office upon a decision. The Parliament does not have a say here, either.[517]

3.5.3.   *The Board of Supervisors*

3.5.3.1.   TASKS

The Board of Supervisors is the main decision-making organ of, and hence of primary importance for, each of the ESAs.[518] This is expressed by the words that it 'shall give guidance to the work of the [ESA]',[519] but it can also be deduced from its status as a collegiate body, composed *inter alia* of the heads of the respective financial market supervisory authorities of all MS – a fact that contributes greatly to the professional legitimacy of the Board.

---

513   Article 53 paras 4-8 of the ESA-Regulations.
514   Cf Article 49 (Chairperson's independence) with Article 52 (Executive Director's independence) of the ESA-Regulations.
515   Article 51 para 2 of the respective ESA-Regulation.
516   Article 51 para 4 of the ESA-Regulations.
517   Article 51 para 5 of the ESA-Regulations.
518   See Schaefer 111.
519   Article 43 para 1 of the ESA-Regulations.

The Board of Supervisors adopts the opinions, recommendations and decisions, and issues the advice referred to in chapter II of the ESA-Regulations, ie Articles 8 to 39.[520] Furthermore the Board is in charge of appointing the Chairperson and the Executive Director (see above). Over both officials the Board shall exercise disciplinary authority,[521] the removal of inappropriate office holders being the most powerful item in its toolkit. The Board adopts, before 30 September of each year, the ESA's work programme for the coming year on the basis of a proposal by the Management Board. The Board shall furthermore adopt a multi-annual work programme. Both work programmes are then transmitted to the Parliament, the Council and the Commission for the sake of information, and are finally made public.[522] The counterpart of the prospective work programme is the – retrospective – annual report on the ESA's activities. This is a statement of accounts by means of which it can be checked whether the work programme of the respective year has been fulfilled; it also includes information on the performance of the Chairperson's duties. The annual report on the ESA's activities is adopted on the basis of a proposal from the Management Board. It shall be adopted and forwarded to the Parliament, the Council, the Commission, the Court of Auditors and the European Economic and Social Committee by 15 June each year, before it is made public.[523]

The Board is competent to adopt the ESA's budget in accordance with Article 63.[524]

3.5.3.2.   COMPOSITION AND DECISION-MAKING

The Board of Supervisors is composed of a number of actors from EU institutions and bodies: the Chairperson (who also acts as the Chair of the Board of Supervisors), one representative each of the Commission, of the ESRB and of the two other ESAs. In the Board of Supervisors of the EBA also one representative nominated by the ECB's Supervisory Board[525] shall be sitting as a member. Neither of them has any voting rights within the Board. Also the Executive Director, who is free to participate in the meetings of the Board, does not have a right to vote.[526] Apart from the Chairperson and the Executive Director (and, for the EBA, the representative nominated by the ECB's Supervisory Board), non-voting members and observers are, apparently for reasons of confidentiality, not allowed to attend any discussion of the

---

520   Article 43 para 2 of the ESA-Regulations.
521   Article 43 para 8 of the ESA-Regulations.
522   Article 43 paras 4 and 6 of the ESA-Regulations.
523   Article 43 para 5 of the ESA-Regulations.
524   For the budget see 3.6.5. below.
525   On the 'significant role' this representative may play in shaping the views within the Board of Supervisors see Ferran 36f.
526   Article 40 para 6/7 subpara 2 of the respective ESA-Regulation.

Board related to individual FI/FMP.[527] The remaining group in the Board is composed intergovernmentally;[528] it consists of the heads of the national public (financial market) supervisory authorities of each MS.[529] For the EBA the following rule applies: Where this authority is not the MS' central bank, the member of the Board may be accompanied by a non-voting representative of the central bank[530] to facilitate that the central bank's views consideration of. Safe for discussions according to Article 44 para 4, the representative nominated by the ECB's Supervisory Board may be accompanied by a representative of the ECB with expertise on central banking tasks. The representatives of the MS' authorities are the only ones who have voting power. For those MS that have more than one supervisory authority in the respective field, Article 40 para 5 (EBA-Regulation), and Article 40 para 4 (EIOPA- and ESMA-Regulations), respectively, provide that the authorities shall agree on a common representative. If an issue discussed in the Board does not fall within the competence of the authority the respective member of the Board represents, that member may bring a – non-voting – representative from the relevant other national authority in order to be in the position to take an informed and advised vote. A similar mechanism applies in the cases laid down in Article 40 para 6 of the EBA-Regulation (deposit guarantee schemes; bank recovery and resolution) and 40 para 5 of the ESMA-Regulation (investor compensation schemes).

Each competent authority shall nominate a high-level alternate from its authority to replace its head in the Board in case he is prevented from attending.[531] Further observers may be admitted upon decision by the Board.[532]

As a general rule, the Board of Supervisors takes its decisions by a simple majority of its members (with a right to vote), each of them having one vote.[533] There are two groups of exceptions. First, qualified majority as in the Council[534] applies in the following cases: the adoption of RTS/ITS and of guidelines and recommendations (Articles 10 to 16); the adoption of the decision whether or not to maintain a decision temporarily prohibiting or restricting certain financial activities[535] upon request by a MS according to

---

527 Article 44 para 4 of the respective ESA-Regulations. For the exceptions from this rule the *lex citata* refers to Article 75 para 3 and to the acts referred to in Article 1 para 2.

528 Cf Kirste 279, who differentiates between predominantly intergovernmentally and predominantly supranationally organised administrative boards of European agencies.

529 This distinguishes the ESAs from the traditional model of the European agency. The latter conceptualised the main decision-making body (the 'administrative board') as a group of MS' representatives, not of the representatives of regularly independent MS authorities (see Chapter 2 III.2. above); see Fischer-Appelt 226ff, for different representative concepts in particular 227.

530 Article 40 para 4 of the EBA-Regulation.

531 Article 40 para 3 of the ESA-Regulations.

532 Article 40 paras 6/7 subpara 1 of the respective ESA-Regulation.

533 Article 44 para 1 subpara 1 of the ESA-Regulations. On different thresholds in the main decision-making body of European agencies see Fischer-Appelt 225.

534 See Article 16 para 4 TFEU.

535 See Article 9 para 5 subpara 1 of the ESA-Regulations.

Article 9 para 5 subpara 3; the adoption of the annual budget and all other decisions rendered under chapter VI of the ESA-Regulations. In case of the EBA, such a qualified majority shall include at least a simple majority each of those voting members of the Board representing authorities of MS partici-pating and of MS not participating in the SSM/SRM (see Chapter 4 I. below).[536]

Second, the following kind of decisions can be taken by a simple majority, unless it is rejected by a blocking minority of votes as defined in the provisions on qualified majority voting: decisions to be taken by the 'group supervisor' (EIOPA), and the 'consolidating supervisor' (ESMA), respectively, in accordance with Article 19 para 3.[537] For all other decisions taken pursuant to Article 19 para 3, a simple majority shall adopt the decision proposed by the panel.[538] In case of the EBA, decisions according to Articles 17 and 19 shall be adopted (as proposed by the panel) by a simple majority that shall include a simple majority each of members representing authorities of participating and of non-participating MS.[539] Decisions according to Article 18 paras 3f, as well, shall be adopted by simple majority, which shall include the two simple majorities referred to above.[540]

With the EBA, the Board of Supervisors shall proceed to a vote at the request of the Chairperson or any member of the Board with the right to vote. A quorum of two-thirds of the members with the right to vote shall be present in order for the Board to be able to vote. If this quorum is not met, the Chairperson may convene an extraordinary meeting at which decisions can be taken without a quorum.[541] Also the EIOPA- and the ESMA-Regulation require a two-thirds quorum.[542] Voting normally is done openly. The Chair-person may propose to vote in a written procedure.[543]

---

536   Article 44 para 1 subpara 2 of the EBA-Regulation.
537   See Directive 2013/36/EU ('Capital Requirements Directive IV') and Directive 2009/138/EC ('Solvency II'). Cf Herdegen 115ff. It can be criticised that qualified majority voting according to Article 16 para 4 TEU is applied in an expert body, since qualified majority in the EU means a (political) weighing of votes, either explicitly or, since 1 November 2014, implicitly. However, an explanation as to why the legislator has chosen to politicise the voting on some of the issues to be decided by the ESAs can be found in the character of these very issues. The adoption of draft rules (RTS/ITS) as well as the adoption of a budget are inherently 'political' decisions, which means decisions that are traditionally taken by political bodies. Arguably that is why the legislator has brought in the weighing of votes also in this context.
538   Article 44 para 1 subpara 4 of the EIOPA- and the ESMA-Regulation.
539   Article 44 para 1 subpara 3 of the EBA-Regulation (exception: subpara 4); see also subpara 6 on the panel.
540   Article 44 para 1 subpara 7 of the EBA-Regulation.
541   Article 3 paras 2f of the RoP of the EBA Board of Supervisors.
542   Article 4 para 17 of the RoP of the EIOPA Board of Supervisors; Article 4 para 1 of the RoP of the ESMA Board of Supervisors.
543   Article 3 para 12 of the RoP of the EBA Board of Supervisors; Article 4 para 11 of the RoP of the EIOPA Board of Supervisors; Article 4 para 7 of the RoP of the ESMA Board of Supervisors.

Meetings of the Board are convened by the Chairperson at his own initiative or at the request of at least one third of its members.[544] The dates of the meetings are determined by the Board on a proposal of the Chairperson before the start of each calendar year. The determination of the frequency of Board meetings lies within the discretion of the ESAs. Meetings of the Board shall take place at least four (EBA), three (EIOPA), and two (ESMA) times a year, respectively.[545]

The Board shall meet with the respective stakeholders (EBA: Banking Stakeholder Group; EIOPA: Stakeholder Groups; ESMA: Securities and Markets Stakeholder Group) at least twice a year.[546]

The voting members of the Board of Supervisors and the Chairperson have to exercise their tasks independently.[547] In this context, however, recently concerns have been uttered that it is national views which dominate the discussions within the Boards of Supervisors.[548]

3.5.3.3. INTERNAL COMMITTEES AND PANELS

The Board of Supervisors is free to delegate certain clearly defined tasks and decisions to – existing or to be established – internal committees or panels, to the Management Board or to the Chairperson.[549] One example of such a panel is the EIOPA's review panel, established in 2008 still under the CEIOPS regime,[550] whose task it is to 'periodically organise and conduct peer reviews of some or all of the activities of competent authorities, to further strengthen consistency in supervisory outcomes'.[551] The panel is composed of representatives of the respective competent authorities and chaired by a member of the Board of Supervisors.[552] Also the two other ESAs have established their respective review panels.[553]

Another panel is the independent panel set in place to facilitate an impartial settlement in case of disagreements according to Article 19 of the ESA-Regulations[554] or the one to be convoked by the EBA in Article 17-cases.[555]

---

544   Article 44 para 2 of the ESA-Regulations.
545   Article 1 para 1 of the RoP of the EBA Board of Supervisors; Article 5 para 1 of the RoP of the EIOPA Board of Supervisors; Article 5 para 8 of the RoP of the ESMA Board of Supervisors.
546   Article 40 para 2 of the respective ESA-Regulations.
547   In Article 42 para 3 of the EBA-Regulation it is added that this independence shall be without prejudice to the tasks conferred on the ECB under the SSM.
548   See Commission, COM (2014) 509 final, 9.
549   Article 41 para 1 of the ESA-Regulations.
550   In May 2011, the panel's existence was confirmed by Decision EIOPA-RP-11/005.
551   Article 3 para 1 of the Decision EIOPA-RP-11/005; for the peer reviews see 3.6.3.3. below.
552   Article 4 para 3 of the Decision EIOPA-RP-11/005.
553   Decision EBA DC 035; Decision ESMA/2001/BS/229.
554   See 3.4.3.3. above.
555   See 3.4.3.1. above.

In addition to that, a variety of committees have been established – either by the ESAs themselves or by their predecessors CEBS, CEIOPS and CESR. Within the organisation of the EIOPA, for example, the Quality Control Committee, the Equivalence Committee and the Financial Stability Committee are – *inter alia* – operative.[556]

3.5.4.   *The Management Board*

3.5.4.1.   TASKS

The Management Board indeed acts as the 'manager' of the respective ESA. What distinguishes it from the typical management organ of an undertaking is the fact that it hardly has any external decision-making power. Its tasks are mainly limited to, still important, preparatory work. In general terms, the Management Board shall ensure that the ESA 'carries out its mission and performs the tasks assigned to it'.[557]

In greater detail, the duties of the Management Board can be listed as follows. It shall propose for adoption an annual and multi-annual work programme to the Board of Supervisors; it shall exercise its budgetary powers (Articles 63f); it has certain tasks in the area of staff policy; it shall adopt practical measures for the application of Regulation 1049/2001 (access to ESA documents)[558]; it shall propose an annual report on the ESA's activities, including on the Chairperson's duties, based on the Executive Director's draft,[559] to the Board of Supervisors for approval; it shall appoint and remove the members of the Board of Appeal in accordance with Article 58 paras 3 and 5.[560]

3.5.4.2.   COMPOSITION AND DECISION-MAKING

The Management Board is composed of the Chairperson and six other members, which are elected by and from among the voting members of the Board of Supervisors (ie the heads of the competent authorities in the MS).[561] Other than the Chairperson, each member shall have an alternate. The term of office of the members elected by the Board of Supervisors is two and a half years and may be extended once. The Management Board's composition shall be 'balanced and proportionate and shall reflect the Union as a whole'.[562] The EBA's Management Board shall include at least two representatives of

---

556   See <https://eiopa.europa.eu/Pages/About-EIOPA/Organisation/Committees/Committees.aspx>.

557   Article 47 para 1 of the ESA-Regulations.

558   Cf the ESAs' decisions of the Management Boards on access to documents: EBA DC 036; EIOPA-MB-11/051; ESMA/2011/MB/69.

559   See 3.5.2.1. above.

560   Article 47 paras 2 to 6 and para 8 of the ESA-Regulations.

561   Critical with regard to this composition: Busuioc, Rule-Making 120f.

562   Article 45 para 1 subpara 3 of the ESA-Regulations.

authorities of MS not participating in the SSM/SRM.[563] At first sight this formula might appear cryptic, since it does not in any way hint at whether balance, proportionality and reflection of the Union as a whole are to be achieved with a view to gender, nationality, age, experience, field of expertise, etc. Given the fact that six out of seven voting members of the Management Board are heads of the competent authorities of the MS,[564] the question of experience and field of expertise is already predetermined. Age – or rather: seniority – might be a factor, but – in light of the fact that all voting members of the Board of Supervisors are equally ranked – does certainly not stay in the foreground; neither does the question of gender. What actually is meant is the 'nationality' of the authority that a person is representing: the 'authority of origin' as it were. The Management Board shall be composed of a mix of people from authorities of big, small, and medium-sized MS, of Northern, Eastern, Western and Southern MS, and of politically powerful and less powerful MS – thus far for the intention of the legislator.[565] The provision is a *lex imperfecta* and hence only to be considered as a guideline: In the end, the voting members of the Board of Supervisors are free to elect whomever they want without anybody being in the position to remedy the result – given that the procedural requirements have been complied with. Mandates shall be overlapping and rotate appropriately – also the latter words are arguably related to the members' 'authority of origin'.

The Management Board adopts a decision by simple majority of the members present,[566] given one vote assigned to each member and a quorum of at least two-thirds of the voting members. In case of a tie, the Chairperson has a casting vote (EBA). If the quorum is not met, the Chairperson may convene an extraordinary meeting at which decisions can be taken irrespective of the quorum (EBA),[567] or a provisional decision is taken which can then be ratified by written procedure (EIOPA, ESMA).[568]

Meetings of the Management Board, which are convened by the Chairperson on his own or on the initiative of at least one-third of its members, shall be held prior to every meeting of the Board of Supervisors and – otherwise – as often as the Management Board deems necessary; however, at

---

563 Article 45 para 1 subpara 3 of the EBA-Regulation.
564 Article 40 para 1 lit b of the ESA-Regulations.
565 For the importance of 'equitable geographical representation' in non-plenary organs see – with a view to bodies of international law – Schermers and Blokker, § 276. With regard to the current Management Boards, the composition of the EBA's Board – with the representatives coming from Germany, Italy, Spain, Poland, the Netherlands and the United Kingdom – does not seem to adequately represent all different 'categories' of MS, <www.eba. europa.eu/about-us/organisation/management-board/members>; see Dehousse, Politics 25f.
566 Article 45 para 2 subpara 1 of the ESA-Regulations.
567 Article 3 para 1 of the RoP of the EBA Management Board.
568 Article 4 para 4 of the RoP of the EIOPA Management Board; Article 4 para 1 of the RoP of the ESMA Management Board.

least five times a year.[569] The respective dates shall be agreed on in advance. Also teleconferencing is allowed.[570] The Executive Director of the respective ESA and a representative of the Commission shall attend the meetings of the Management Board without a right to vote.[571] Only in budgetary matters shall the Commission representative have the right to vote.[572]

Advisors or experts may be invited by the Management Board to attend its meetings and assist its members in their deliberations.[573] Apart from the Executive Director, the non-voting members shall, apparently for reasons of confidentiality, not attend any discussion of the Management Board related to individual FI/FMP.[574]

The Management Board has to exercise its tasks independently. This independence is described similarly to that of the Chairperson and the Executive Director, respectively.[575]

3.5.5.   *The Joint Committee of the ESAs*

The Joint Committee is, as its name suggests, a joint body of the three ESAs. It is composed of the Chairpersons of the ESAs[576] and of the Chairperson of any Sub-Committee and shall meet at least once every two months.[577] The Joint Committee shall serve as a forum in which the ESAs shall cooperate 'regularly and closely' with each other in order to ensure cross-sectoral consistency of their actions. The idea of such institutionalised cooperation was already taken up in 2005 by the ESAs' predecessors CEBS, CEIOPS and CESR, and has been followed since then.[578] According to the ESA-Regulations, cooperation shall take place in particular with regard to: financial conglomerates, accounting and auditing, microprudential analyses of cross-sectoral developments, risks and vulnerabilities for financial stability, retail investment products, measures combating money laundering, information exchange with the ESRB and – more generally – developing the relationship between the ESRB and the ESAs.[579] The Committee shall also identify and

---

569   Article 45 para 3 of the ESA-Regulations.
570   Article 3 para 3 of the RoP of the EBA Management Board; Article 5 para 2 of the RoP of the EIOPA Management Board; Article 5 para 3 of the RoP of the ESMA Management Board.
571   Article 45 para 2 subpara 2 of the ESA-Regulations.
572   Article 45 para 2 subpara 3 of the ESA-Regulations.
573   Article 45 para 4 of the ESA-Regulations in conjunction with Article 2 para 5 of the RoP of the EBA Management Board; Article 5 para 4 of the RoP of the EIOPA Management Board; Article 1 para 3 of the RoP of the ESMA Management Board.
574   Article 45 para 4 of the ESA-Regulations.
575   Article 46 of the ESA-Regulations; cf Articles 49 and 52.
576   The Chairpersons of the ESAs work as Chairperson of the Joint Committee in annual alternation; Article 55 para 3 of the ESA-Regulations.
577   Article 55 para 4 subpara 2 of the ESA-Regulations.
578   Recital 1 of the (meanwhile revisited) RoP of the Joint Committee 2011.
579   Article 54 para 2 of the ESA-Regulations.

propose further areas for joint work and tasks of cross-sectoral relevance.[580] The Committee shall be provided with dedicated staff, which shall build up its secretariat, as well as with adequate resources (from the ESAs) to administrative, infrastructure and operational expenses (the 'budget').[581] Where at least two ESAs are competent, according to Articles 10–15 and 17–19 in conjunction with one of the acts referred to in Article 1 para 2 of the ESA-Regulations, to render a certain act, the Joint Committee shall prepare a proposal for a common act.[582]

For this purpose a Sub-Committee on Financial Conglomerates, composed of the members of the Joint Committee and one high-level representative from the current staff of the competent authority of each MS, shall be established.[583] It shall elect a Chairperson from among its members who shall also be a member of the Joint Committee.[584] The Joint Committee may establish further Sub-Committees.[585]

The Executive Directors of the three ESAs, a representative of the Commission and one of the ESRB shall be invited as observers to the meetings of the Joint Committee and of any Sub-Committee.[586]

The ESAs agree that the Joint Committee facilitates coordination. However, its work is said to be 'largely unknown to stakeholders'.[587]

3.5.6. The Board of Appeal

With the Board of Appeal the ESA-Regulations – 'for reasons of efficiency and consistency'[588] – create another joint body of the ESAs.[589] It is competent to decide on appeals against decisions of the ESAs. This main task was presented and discussed above in the context of legal protection against the ESAs' binding decisions. In order to avoid repetition here, let it suffice to refer to 3.4.5. above. The BoA shall be independent from the administrative and regulatory structures of the ESAs – organisationally (not affiliated to any of the

---

580 Article 6 para 2 of the RoP of the Joint Committee 2014.
581 Article 54 para 3 of the ESA-Regulations in conjunction with Article 23 of the RoP of the Joint Committee 2014.
582 Article 6 para 5 of the RoP of the Joint Committee 2014.
583 This sub-committee has taken over the tasks of the former European Financial Conglomerates Committee; see also Dragomir 196.
584 Article 57 para 3 of the ESA-Regulations.
585 Article 57 para 4 of the ESA-Regulations. On the Joint Committee's organisation (including Sub-Committees and Sub-Groups) see Parliament, Review 1 108.
586 Article 55 para 2 of the ESA-Regulations. The provision reads 'a representative of the Commission and the ESRB'. It can be assumed that the legislator intended to say 'one of the Commission and one of the ESRB'.
587 Parliament, Review 1 111.
588 Recital 58 of the ESA-Regulations.
589 Article 58 para 1 of the ESA-Regulations. For the Board of Appeal model applied in some European agencies see Siegel 142ff.

ESAs or their respective organs) and substantially (not bound by instructions, impartial administration).[590]

The BoA shall be equipped with adequate operational and secretarial means by the ESAs through the Joint Committee.[591] It shall be composed of six members of 'high repute with a proven record of relevant knowledge and professional experience', including supervisory experience in the ESAs' fields of operation.[592] In addition to that, six alternates, also with an according professional profile, shall be appointed. Current staff of the ESAs, of the competent authorities, and of any other national or Union institution involved in the activities of the ESAs, shall be excluded. The last sentence of Article 58 para 2 subpara 1 goes: 'The Board of Appeal shall have sufficient legal expertise to provide expert legal advice on the legality of the [ESAs'] exercise of [their] powers'. This means that not each and every member of the Board must have a legal background, but that the Board taken as a whole shall be in the position to scrutinise the legality of a decision under appeal. From the current 'manning' – six members and six alternates – at least eight officials have a professional legal background.[593] The BoA designates its President who shall convene the Board whenever necessary.[594]

The Management Board of each ESA appoints two members of the BoA and two alternates from a short-list proposed by the Commission, following a public call for expressions of interest in the OJ and after consulting the respective Board of Supervisors.[595]

The term of office of the members and – for lack of a special rule – *per analogiam* also for the alternates is five years and may be extended once.[596] A member of the Board and, again *per analogiam*, an alternate shall not be removed during his term of office, unless he has been found guilty of serious

---

590   Recital 58 in conjunction with Article 59 of the ESA-Regulations. For the limits of the independence of members of agencies' Boards of Appeal more generally see Dammann 55ff; for the generally positive evaluation of European agencies' Boards of Appeal see EU working group, No 10, 3.

591   Article 58 para 8 of the ESA-Regulations.

592   Article 58 para 2 subpara 1 of the ESA-Regulations.

593   See biographies at <www.eba.europa.eu/about-us/organisation/joint-board-of-appeal/members>.

594   Article 58 para 2 subpara 2 and para 7 of the ESA-Regulations. In September 2012 the Board of Appeal appointed *William Blair* as its President.

595   Article 58 para 3 of the ESA-Regulations.

596   Article 58 para 4 of the ESA-Regulations.

misconduct.[597] The Management Board may then, after having consulted the Board of Supervisors, decide to remove him from office.[598]

The BoA takes its decisions by at least four of the six members. If the case at issue falls within the scope of the EBA-Regulation, at least one of the members appointed by the EBA shall be part of the deciding majority for there to be a decision. This rule applies accordingly also for the EIOPA and for the ESMA.[599]

The members of the Board shall undertake to act independently and in the public interest. In order to make sure that 'justice is not only done, but also seen to be done', as it were, the members of the Board have to make a declaration of commitments/interests. These declarations are made public, annually and in writing.[600]

In order to ensure impartiality, the members of the Board are not allowed to take part in appeal proceedings in which they have a personal interest, or in which they have previously been involved either as representative of one of the parties to the proceedings or as decision-maker.[601] If a member of the BoA considers that another member should not take part in certain appeal proceedings for one of these reasons, for lack of independence according to Article 59 para 1, or for any other reason, he shall inform the BoA. Parties to the appeal proceedings may object to the participation of a certain member of the Board for one of the reasons referred to in paras 1 and 2 (not: 'for any other reason'), or if suspected of bias. The nationality of a member cannot serve as a reason for objection. Furthermore, an objection is inadmissible if a party, while being aware of a reason for objection, has nevertheless taken a procedural step other than objecting accordingly.[602] In legal terms, such action leads to the preclusion of the right to object for the reason(s) the party was aware of when taking the procedural step. However, the possible impartiality of the member is not fully cured, since the BoA can still take action, possibly upon information by another member. In any case of suspected partiality, the BoA shall decide on the action to be taken without the participation of the member concerned. He shall be replaced by his alternate, or where the alternate is in a similar situation, by another available alternate as designated by the Chairperson.[603]

---

597 It is not entirely clear from the wording of this provision whether this requirement must have been confirmed in a conviction by a criminal court, or whether an according finding of the Management Board suffices. Given the fact that the members of the Board of Appeal exercise a judge-like function, their removal should be subject to enhanced requirements. In an understanding based on the rule of law the words 'found guilty' are to be interpreted as to require a conviction by a criminal court. Arguably this is not required in case of the Chair of the Supervisory Board of the ECB and the full-time members of the SRB ('guilty'); see Chapter 4 II.2. and III.2. below.
598 Article 58 para 5 of the ESA-Regulations.
599 Article 58 para 6 of the respective ESA-Regulation.
600 Article 59 para 6 of the ESA-Regulations. See <www.eba.europa.eu/about-us/organisation/joint-board-of-appeal/members>.
601 Article 59 para 2 of the ESA-Regulations.
602 Article 59 para 4 of the ESA-Regulations.
603 Article 59 para 5 of the ESA-Regulations.

So far, the Board has rendered five appeal decisions in two cases each against EBA- and ESMA-decisions, respectively, and in one case against an EIOPA-decision. Once the case was remitted to the ESA (the EBA), twice the appeal was dismissed and twice it was held to be inadmissible.

3.6.   *Information, networks and budget*

3.6.1.   *Preliminary remarks*

The preceding chapters have dealt with the ESAs' powers and their organisation. Now emphasis shall be laid on the informational and financial input, which is to say on how the ESAs are receiving the information and generating the knowledge necessary to take well-informed decisions, and on the amount and the composition of their financial resources. In the context of the former, it is the legal framework for the collection and assessment of information that is of interest, and the ESAs' network with the competent authorities, a variety of EU bodies, the MS and in third countries, which shall be investigated. This network is spun *ex lege*, namely by the ESA-Regulations,[604] but more importantly is fleshed out by the ESAs' networking practice.[605] Eventually, the ESAs' budget shall be discussed in law and in fact.

3.6.2.   *Risk assessment and risk management*

At the core of the ESAs' risk assessment and risk management tasks is 'dealing with' (identification, assessment, monitoring, etc.) systemic risks. According to Article 2 lit c of the ESRB-Regulation 'systemic risk' means

> a risk of disruption in the financial system with the potential to have serious negative consequences for the internal market and the real economy. All types of financial intermediaries, markets and infrastructure may be potentially systemically important to some degree.[606]

The ESAs shall address any risk of disruption in financial services that is a) caused by an impairment of all or parts of the financial system, and b) has the potential to have serious negative consequences for the internal market and the real economy.[607] For that purpose the ESAs shall also consider the respective findings of the ESRB (in particular warnings and recommendations).[608] At the same time, the ESAs shall ensure they have the 'specialised and ongoing

---

604   See also the respective ESA-output, eg EBA-decision EBA/DC/2015/130.
605   On the functioning in the context of other European agencies of networks connecting the EU and the national level see EU working group, No 11, 3–5; for the collateral effects of building up networks see Majone, Delegation 336 and Europeanization 206f.
606   On the multiplicity of definitions of systemic risk see Sibert 2.
607   Article 22 para 1 subpara 1 of the ESA-Regulations.
608   Article 22 para 1 subpara 2; see also para 2 subpara 1 of the ESA-Regulations.

capacity to respond effectively to the materialisation of systemic risks' and shall, in such a case, facilitate a 'coherent and coordinated crisis management and resolution regime' in the EU.[609]

One way for the ESAs to identify and measure systemic risks posed by FI/key FMP is to apply a stress-testing regime.[610] Those FI/FMP that may pose a systemic risk shall be made subject to 'strengthened supervision' and, if need be, to recovery and resolution procedures.[611] Part of this special treatment may also be additional guidelines and recommendations for FI/key FMP.[612] The EBA, in addition to that, may conduct peer reviews of the exchange of information and of the joint activities of the SRB and the national resolution authorities of the non-pMS.

Another way for the ESAs to find out about potential threats to the integrity of financial markets or the stability of the financial system, is to undertake an enquiry into a particular type of financial activity, type of product or type of conduct with the coordinating support of the Joint Committee.[613] The ESAs may request the competent authorities to provide the information necessary to carry out their duties under the respective ESA-Regulation – to the extent that the competent authorities have legal access thereto.[614] In order to avoid redundant requests for information, the ESAs shall first check whether existing statistics produced and disseminated by the European Statistical System and the ESCB already provide sufficient information.[615]

In case the necessary information is not available or is not made available by the competent authority in due time, the ESAs may turn to other supervisory authorities, the ministry of finance, the national central bank or the statistical office of the respective MS.[616] If also this does not work out, either because the information is not available or because it is not made available in due time, the ESAs may address the relevant FI/FMP directly.[617] All such requests (except for those directed to the competent authorities), be they addressed to MS bodies or directly to FI/FMP, shall be duly justified and give

609 Article 24 paras 1f of the ESA-Regulations.
610 Article 23 para 1 of the ESA-Regulations; for the EBA, see also Article 22 para 1a of the EBA-Regulation. While stress tests have been applied a number of times, the concrete modalities of the EBA's stress-testing are (still) being developed; see EBA, Annual Report 2014, 65–68.
611 Article 23 para 1; see also Article 25 of the ESA-Regulations and Parliament, Review 1 72, 86, 103.
612 Article 22 para 3 of the ESA-Regulations.
613 Article 22 paras 4f of the ESA-Regulations. The ESA may initiate such an enquiry on its own initiative, or upon request from a competent authority, the EP, the Council or the Commission.
614 Article 35 para 1 of the ESA-Regulations. The modalities of such requests are outlined in para 2.
615 Article 35 para 4 of the ESA-Regulations.
616 Article 35 para 5 of the ESA-Regulations.
617 Article 35 para 6 of the ESA-Regulations. For further addressees in case of the EBA see Article 35 para 6 of the EBA-Regulation.

the reasons why the requested information is necessary.[618] The relevant competent authority shall be informed of all such requests. If need be, the ESAs may also request the respective competent authority to assist them in collecting the information.[619] The ESAs may use confidential information only for the purposes of carrying out their duties according to the ESA-Regulations.[620]

While the ESAs are entitled to request information from the competent authorities, *vice versa* any competent authority may request from the ESAs the information necessary for it to carry out its tasks.[621]

On the basis of this information, the ESAs shall, within their respective area of competence, monitor and assess market developments and their possible impacts on FI/FMP. If need be, the ESAs shall inform each other and, at least once a year, the ESRB, the EP, the Council and the Commission about their – mainly microprudential – findings on trends, potential risks and vulnerabilities within their respective field and, if needed, recommend preventative or remedial actions.[622] Only in a synopsis of the data and analyses of all relevant actors can a macroprudential appraisal be undertaken. The coverage also of cross-sectoral developments, risks and vulnerabilities is facilitated by the Joint Committee, which serves as a forum for close cooperation between the ESAs.[623]

3.6.3.   *Relations with competent authorities*

3.6.3.1.   GENERAL REMARKS

As regards the cooperation of the ESAs with the competent authorities, the ESAs generally function as bodies that collect and disseminate information, promote the information flow between the competent authorities and take all appropriate measures to provide for a smooth cooperation between these authorities on the one hand, and between them and the ESAs, on the other.[624] For that purpose the ESAs can, upon request or on their own initiative, carry out non-binding mediation between competent authorities as provided in Article 31 lit c.[625] Since this provision is set up 'without prejudice to Article 19', it appears that the legislator intended a) to create a possibility for the ESAs to intervene in cases where there was no request from a competent authority and where therefore no Article 19-procedure – save for the case

---

618   Article 35 para 5 and para 6 subpara 1 of the ESA-Regulations.
619   Article 35 para 6 subparas 2 and 3 of the ESA-Regulations. For further means of ensuring compliance with the request in case of the EBA see Article 35 para 7a of the EBA-Regulation.
620   Article 35 para 7 of the ESA-Regulations.
621   Article 35 para 3 of the ESA-Regulations.
622   Article 32 paras 1 and 3 of the ESA-Regulations.
623   Article 32 para 4 of the ESA-Regulations.
624   See Article 31 of the ESA-Regulations. See also EBA, Annual Report 2014, 60.
625   See eg EBA, Annual Report 2014, 56.

described in Article 19 para 1 subpara 2 – could be initiated; b) to invite competent authorities to turn – in case of a disagreement – to the ESAs under Article 31 lit c, without having to fear the ESAs' final decision-making power under Article 19.

On the personnel front, the ESAs' tasks to establish sectoral and cross-sectoral training programmes, to facilitate personnel exchanges and to encourage competent authorities to intensify the use of secondment schemes and other tools ought to be mentioned.[626]

3.6.3.2. DELEGATION

Another prong in the ESAs' striving for smooth cooperation between the competent authorities is the facilitation of the delegation of tasks and responsibilities to the respective ESA or among the competent authorities themselves. In spite of the 'general rule that delegation should be allowed'[627] MS may set out specific arrangements regarding the delegation of responsibilities and may limit the scope of delegation to what is necessary for the effective supervision of cross-border FI/FMP or groups.[628] It is important to note that there may be a legislative wishing that delegation should be allowed, but in the given context MS or the competent authorities are certainly not obliged to delegate any of their tasks or responsibilities to the respective ESA or to other competent authorities. In that sense, MS/competent authorities are free to delegate or not to delegate, possibly constrained only by the very abstract principle of sincere cooperation between the Union and the MS (Article 4 para 3 TEU in conjunction with Article 78 of the ESA-Regulations) and – as regards the relationship between the ECB, as a competent authoritiy, and the ESA – between the Union institutions themselves (Article 13 para 2 second sentence TEU[629]). Nevertheless (or rather: because of this), ESAs are called upon to 'stimulate and facilitate' the delegation of tasks or responsibilities by identifying potential cases of application.[630] The delegation of tasks allows the delegated authority (competent authority or ESA) to carry out the delegated task, whereas the responsibility for supervisory decisions remains with the delegating authority. With the delegation of responsibilities, the delegated authority is entitled to decide upon a certain supervisory matter in its own name in lieu of the

---

626 Article 29 para 1 lit e of the ESA-Regulations. Whereas the ESAs do offer training seminars for officials from competent authorities (see eg EBA, Annual Report 2014, 58), in the field of staff exchange they merely serve as messengers between the competent authorities concerned (see eg ESMA, Work Programme 2015, 13).

627 Recital 39 of the ESA-Regulations.

628 Article 28 para 1 of the ESA-Regulations. For delegation under the pre-ESA regime and in other secondary legislation see Dragomir 263–265.

629 On the wide interpretation of the term 'institution' in Article 13 TEU see Nettesheim, Art. 13, para 7.

630 Article 28 para 2 of the ESA-Regulations.

delegating authority.[631] In the latter case the competence to render a certain decision is transferred to the delegated authority. It is the law of the MS of the delegated authority and, in case of the ESAs and the ECB, the law of the EU, which governs the procedure, enforcement and administrative and judicial review relating to the delegated responsibilities.[632]

The competent authorities shall inform the respective ESA of delegation agreements at least one month before they put them into effect. The ESA addressed may give an opinion thereon within one month of being informed. The ESA shall publish any delegation agreement concluded by competent authorities in order to ensure adequate publicity.[633]

It appears that the delegation of tasks and responsibilities at present plays a major role only in case of the ESMA.[634]

3.6.3.3.   PEER REVIEWS

In order to foster supervisory consistency within the network of financial supervisors, the ESAs shall periodically organise and conduct peer reviews on certain or all activities of the competent authorities.[635] The ESAs shall develop the methods allowing for an objective assessment and the comparability of these assessments.[636] Existing information and evaluations shall also be taken into account when conducting a peer review. The peer review shall *inter alia* cover an assessment of the effectiveness and the degree of convergence with regard to the enforcement of the provisions implementing EU law by the competent authorities.[637] Based on the results of a peer review, the ESAs may publish the best practices identified, issue guidelines and recommendations and draft RTS/ITS, accordingly.[638]

All three ESAs have established their respective review panels composed of representatives of the competent authorities,[639] which conduct peer reviews in a number of fields.[640] The Commission endorses an increased use of peer reviews by the ESAs.[641]

---

631   Recital 39 of the ESA-Regulations.
632   Article 28 para 3 of the respective ESA-Regulation.
633   Article 28 para 4 of the ESA-Regulations.
634   See ESMA, Work Programme 2016, 5f; see also related contribution to the ESMA's budget (see 3.6.5. below). As regards the EBA and the EIOPA, see Parliament, Review 1 65, 82.
635   See Recital 41 of the ESA-Regulations.
636   See eg EBA BoS 2012 107.
637   For further details see Article 30 para 2 of the ESA-Regulations.
638   Article 30 paras 3f of the ESA-Regulations.
639   See 3.5.3.3. above.
640   See EBA, Annual Report 2014, 56f; EIOPA, Annual Report 2014, 26; ESMA, Annual Report 2014, 54f.
641   See Commission, COM (2014) 509 final, 6.

The EBA may, in addition to that, organise and conduct peer reviews of the SRB and the national resolution authorities.[642]

3.6.3.4. COLLEGES OF SUPERVISORS

In case of banking or insurance groups, or financial conglomerates, operating in two or more MS and hence under the supervision of at least two competent authorities, disagreements between the authorities concerned (the home supervisor and the host supervisor(s)) on questions of supervision may be discussed, and ideally solved by a bilateral or multilateral agreement,[643] in so-called colleges of supervisors.[644] But even where there are no disagreements, the regular exchange of information and of viewpoints within the colleges shall enhance the efficiency and effectiveness of the supervision of cross-border groups or financial conglomerates,[645] for example by planning and coordinating supervisory on-site inspections, including joint supervisory examinations, or by reviewing and evaluating risks within the college.[646] Also the ESA-Regulations show reference to such groups of institutionalised cooperation, thereby referring to the pertinent secondary legislation. In one of these acts, namely the Solvency II Directive, colleges of supervisors are defined as 'a permanent but flexible structure for cooperation and coordination among the supervisory authorities of the Member States concerned'.[647]

It is the ESAs' task under the ESA-Regulations to promote and monitor the efficient, effective and consistent functioning of the colleges of supervisors referred to in the respective acts of secondary law.[648] For that purpose, staff from the ESAs shall be allowed to participate in the activities of the colleges of supervisors, including on-site examinations, carried out jointly by two or more competent authorities.[649] For these purposes the respective ESA shall be considered a 'competent authority' within the meaning of the relevant legislation.[650] Within the colleges of supervisors the respective ESA may function as a collector of and contact point for relevant information, initiate and coordinate Union-wide stress tests in accordance with Article 32, promote effective and efficient supervisory activities, oversee the tasks carried out by the competent authorities, and request further deliberations of a college where it

---

642 Article 25 para 1a of the EBA-Regulation.
643 Critical with regard to the struggle to reach a consensus: Herdegen 115.
644 The idea of establishing supervisory colleges dates back to the 1980s when such a college was established eg between the British and the Luxembourgish supervisors; see Kohtamäki 197.
645 See CEBS, GL 34, 3; Basel Committee on Banking Supervision.
646 CEBS and CEIOPS, CEBS 2008 124/CEIOPS-SEC-54/08, 4f.
647 Article 212 para 1 lit e of Directive 2009/138/EC.
648 Whereas Article 21 of the EBA- and the EIOPA-Regulation, respectively, refers to specific acts, namely Regulation 575/2013 and Directive 2013/36/EU, and Directive 2009/138/EC, respectively, the ESMA-Regulation refers generally to 'the legislative acts referred to in [its] Article 1(2)'.
649 Article 21 para 1 of the ESA-Regulations.
650 Article 21 para 2 subpara 2 of the ESA-Regulations.

deems the current result to entail an incorrect application of Union law or where this result would not contribute to the objective of convergence of supervisory practices. This includes the right of the ESA to require the home supervisor[651] to schedule, or add a point to the agenda of, a meeting of the college.[652] Also the ESAs' mediation role according to Article 19 applies in the context of colleges of supervisors.[653]

The ESAs may develop draft RTS/ITS with a view to ensure uniform conditions for the functioning of colleges of supervisors and issue guidelines and recommendations to promote convergence in the functioning of and best practices adopted by the colleges of supervisors.[654]

With the entry into force of the SSM, colleges of supervisors will be competent only for banking groups with a presence in non-SSM countries.[655] Before that, there were around 80 supervisory colleges, the effectiveness of which was improvable.[656]

3.6.4.   Reaction to ESRB warnings and recommendations

The ESRB's power to issue warnings and recommendations has been pointed out already.[657] It is the ramifications of these warnings and recommendations addressed to the ESAs or to competent national supervisory authorities that shall be explained in more detail here.

On receipt of a warning or recommendation addressed to one of the ESAs, the respective ESA shall convene a meeting of the Board of Supervisors, assess the implications of the ESRB-output for the fulfilment of the respective ESA's tasks and decide on the action to be taken. If it has decided not to act on a recommendation (not: warning), it shall communicate to the Council and to the ESRB the reasons for its decision.[658]

On receipt of a warning or recommendation addressed to a competent national supervisory authority, the ESA shall, where relevant, ensure a timely follow-up. Where the addressee intends not to follow an ESRB-recommendation, it shall inform and discuss with the Board of Supervisors the respective reasons. When informing the ESRB and the Council, according to Article 17

---

651   The term home supervisor is the generic term for 'consolidating supervisors' for banking groups, 'group supervisors' for insurance groups and 'coordinators' for financial conglomerates; see Herdegen 93.

652   Article 21 para 2 of the ESA-Regulations.

653   Article 21 para 4 of the ESA-Regulations.

654   Article 21 para 3 of the ESA-Regulations; see eg CEBS and CEIOPS, CEBS 2008 124/ CEIOPS-SEC-54/08; see CEBS, GL 34; see also EIOPA-BoS-12-004 and <www. eba.europa.eu/regulation-and-policy/colleges-of-supervisors/regulatory-and-imple menting-technical-standards-on-the-functioning-of-colleges-of-supervisors>.

655   <www.eba.europa.eu/supervisory-convergence/supervisory-colleges>. The entry into force of Directive 2014/59/EU, on the contrary, provides for new tasks for the colleges; see EBA, Annual Report 2014, 93; cf Article 32 lit b of the SSM-Regulation.

656   See Parliament, Review 1 64.

657   See 2.1.2. above.

658   Article 36 para 4 of the ESA-Regulations.

para 1 of the ESRB-Regulation, of the actions taken following an ESRB-recommendation, the competent national supervisory authority shall take due account of the views of the Board of Supervisors.[659]

Generally, in performing its tasks under the respective ESA-Regulation, the ESAs shall take 'the utmost account' of warnings and recommendations of the ESRB.[660] This arguably also includes that the ESAs shall interpret Union law in a way that is compatible with the ESRB-output and, consequently, affects, for example, the ESAs' exercise of their Article 17 powers ('breach of Union law'), which are applicable to both action and inaction of the competent authorities. This way, ESRB-output, even though it does not have binding effect, may be pushed through by the ESAs against competent authorities.

3.6.5.   *The ESAs' budget*

The ESAs' revenues are mainly supplied by a) obligatory contributions from the competent national supervisory authorities, b) a subsidy from the Union and c) any fees paid to the ESAs in the cases specified in the relevant instruments of Union law.[661]

By 15 February each year, the Executive Director launches a draft statement of estimates of revenue and expenditure for the following financial year as well as an establishment plan.[662] Once the Management Board approves the draft statement,[663] the Board of Supervisors shall produce the (final) statement of estimates of revenue and expenditure of the Authority for the following financial year. This statement shall, together with a draft establishment plan, be forwarded to the Commission by 31 March.[664] The Commission transmits the statement to the EP and the Council (which together form the 'budgetary authority'), together with the draft budget of the EU.[665]

On the basis of these calculations, the Commission shall enter in the draft budget of the EU the estimates it deems necessary with regard to the establishment plan and the amount of the subsidy to be charged to the general budget of the EU.[666] The budgetary authority shall then adopt the

---

659   Article 36 para 5 of the ESA-Regulations.
660   Article 36 para 6 of the ESA-Regulations.
661   Article 62 of the ESA-Regulations in conjunction with Article 147 of Regulation 966/2012. This Regulation is the successor of Council Regulation 1605/2002, which is still referred to in the ESA-Regulations.
662   The EBA's and the EIOPA's Financial Regulations provide for a 'provisional draft estimate' of revenue and expenditure to be sent to the Commission already by 31 January (EBA; Article 33 para 2), and 10 February (EIOPA; Article 27 para 2), respectively.
663   The Commission representative in the Management Board is allowed to vote in matters regarding the establishment of the ESA's budget; see Article 45 para 2 subpara 3 of the ESA-Regulations.
664   Article 63 para 1 of the ESA-Regulations.
665   Article 63 para 2 of the ESA-Regulations.
666   Article 63 para 3 of the ESA-Regulations.

establishment plan for the respective ESA and shall authorise the appropriations for the subsidy to it, as calculated by the Commission.[667] Then the Board of Supervisors adopts the budget of the ESA. The finality of the budget is subject to the final adoption of the general budget of the EU; it may be necessary to adjust the ESA's budget accordingly.[668]

If the respective ESA intends to implement any project that may have 'significant financial implications' for the funding of its budget (eg the acquisition of property), the Management Board shall notify the budgetary authority and inform the Commission. If either part of the budgetary authority – EP or Council – intends to issue an opinion, it shall notify the ESA thereof within two weeks. If there is no such notification within the above time limit, the ESA may proceed with the implementation of the project.[669]

It is the Executive Director who acts as an authorising officer and is in charge of implementing the ESA's budget.[670] By 1 March the ESA's accounting officer shall transmit to his counterpart with the Commission and to the Court of Auditors the provisional accounts of the last financial year, together with a report on budgetary and financial management during that period. The latter report shall furthermore be sent to the members of the Board of Supervisors, the EP and the Council by 31 March. The Commission's accounting officer shall then consolidate the provisional accounts of the ESA with the Commission's provisional accounts in accordance with what is now Article 147 of Regulation 966/2012.[671] Having received the observations of the Court of Auditors on the ESA's provisional accounts,[672] the Executive Director shall draw up the final accounts of the ESA and transmit them to the Management Board for opinion.[673] The Executive Director shall forward the final accounts and the opinion of the Management Board to the members of the Board of Supervisors, the EP, the Council, the Commission and the Court of Auditors by 1 July.[674] The final accounts shall then be published.[675]

At the Parliament's request, the Executive Director shall – as provided for in Article 165 para 3 of Regulation 966/2012 (with regard to the Commission) – provide it with any information necessary for the smooth application of the discharge procedure for the respective financial year.[676]

The Parliament shall, following a Council recommendation, grant a discharge to the ESA for the implementation of the budget comprising

---

667   Article 63 para 4 of the ESA-Regulations.
668   Article 63 para 5 of the ESA-Regulations.
669   Article 63 para 6 of the ESA-Regulations.
670   Article 64 para 1 of the ESA-Regulations.
671   Article 64 para 2 of the ESA-Regulations.
672   The Executive Director shall send a reply to these observations to the Court of Auditors by 30 September. A copy of this reply shall be sent to the Management Board and the Commission; Article 64 para 7 of the ESA-Regulations.
673   Article 64 para 3 of the ESA-Regulations.
674   Article 64 para 5 of the ESA-Regulations.
675   Article 64 para 6 of the ESA-Regulations.
676   Article 64 para 8 of the ESA-Regulations.

revenue from the general budget of the EU and from the competent authorities before 15 May, two years after the financial year at issue.

Table 3.2 Revenue and expenses of the ESAs in 2015

	EBA	EIOPA	ESMA
Total revenue 2015 (provisional)	33	20	37
Contributions from national supervisors	19.5	12	14
Contribution from general budget of the EU	13	8	10
Contributions from observers	0.5	–	0.4
Fees paid to the ESA	–	–	10
Contribution from national supervisors for delegated tasks	–	–	3
Total expense 2015 (provisional)	33	20	37
Main post: personnel costs	22	12	18

Note: Numbers in millions of euros.[677]

As regards the actual numbers, it is apparent that the budgets of the ESAs have increased enormously in the years since their establishment: from 13 (EBA), 11 (EIOPA), and 17 million euro (ESMA) in 2011, to 33 (EBA), 20 (EIOPA) and 37 million euro (ESMA), respectively.[678] This can be explained by the fact that the ESAs are still in their early years and hence developing strongly. This can exemplarily be demonstrated by looking at the increase in the ESAs' human resources in terms of staff: from 31 (EBA), 27 (EIOPA) and 35 (ESMA), respectively, in January 2011 when the ESAs started operating,[679] to 146 (EBA), 134 (EIOPA) and 167 (ESMA), respectively, late in 2014.[680]

According to a survey among stakeholders undertaken by the Commission, both the amount and the composition of the ESAs' budgets leave something to be desired. The Commission is currently discussing alternative funding models.[681]

677 Numbers taken from: EBA Budget for 2015; EIOPA Budget for 2015; ESMA Budget for 2015.
678 Numbers taken from: EBA Budget for 2011; EIOPA Budget for 2011; ESMA Budget for 2011.
679 Numbers taken from: EBA, Annual Report 2011, 36; EIOPA, Annual Report 2011, 17; ESMA, Annual Report 2011, 28.
680 Numbers taken from: EBA, Annual Report 2014, 83; EIOPA, Annual Report 2014, 8; ESMA, Annual Report 2014, 4. This strong increase of human resources in the first few years after establishment is not unusual and should be understood as 'teething problems'. Cf the ECHA's development in the field of human resources: While its General Report 2007 informs about 110 staff, this number rose to 219 in 2008 (General Report 2008, III), to 320 in 2009 (General Report 2009, fact sheet), and again to 541 in 2011. Since then it has gradually increased to 621 in 2014 (General Report 2014, 20).
681 Commission, COM (2014) 509 final, 11.

4.   Résumé

Before the most recent institutional developments in EU financial market risk governance are addressed in Chapter 4, a brief résumé on the ESFS shall be given, thereby incorporating the results of the comparative analysis of comitology and European agencies undertaken in Chapter 2. This résumé shall move along the lines of the three headings 'Expertise and MS representation', 'Hard law and soft law' and '*Meroni* and the EU's institutional balance'.

Expertise and MS representation: The comparison drawn in Chapter 2 between comitology and European agencies – two main risk governance regimes whereby, to varying degrees, MS representation, experience and expertise in EU administration is facilitated – has revealed an inter-connectedness with respect to organisation ([former] comitology committees as part or predecessors of European agencies), tasks (advice) and institutional development (unfettered growth in the beginning, and limits being set only after some time). The establishment of the ESAs has added another facet to this relationship. While the ESAs do not have their roots in comitology committees, but have transformed from level 3 committees,[682] a *sui generis* type of committee introduced by the *Lamfalussy* regime, they have marginalised the respective comitology committees in the sphere of implementing acts. Through the important and institutionalised role the ESAs play in the drafting of ITS, they have in fact taken over the tasks of the level 2 committees. The latter may still be consulted in addition to the ESAs, but on a merely voluntary basis. For lack of applicability of *Comitology III*, the Commission has no duty to hear them, let alone follow them to the extent provided in the examination procedure. In that sense, the special decision-making process of ITS has weakened MS representation in the field of implementing acts. With regard to the drafting of RTS, the strong role of the ESAs ensures a limited degree of MS representation where comitology – by virtue of Article 290 TFEU and hence by virtue of primary law – is excluded. On the assumption that the rationale of comitology committees is in the first place MS representation, whereas that of European agencies is primarily the pooling of expertise, we may say that the creation of special procedures for the adoption of RTS and ITS has – compared with regular delegated and implementing acts – structurally increased expertise at the cost of MS (and Commission[683]) representation. This conclusion is reinforced by the fact that, compared with

---

682   In this context *Kämmerer* has metaphorically uttered that the new authorities relate to the former level 3 committees 'like the butterfly (or only the moth?) relates to the caterpillar' [*wie der Schmetterling (oder doch nur die Motte?) zur Raupe*]; Kämmerer, Finanzaufsichtssystem 1282.

683   Whereas comitology committees are chaired by a Commission representative, the ESAs' Board of Supervisors is chaired by an independent Chairman. See also Article 4 para 3 subpara 4 of the SSM-Regulation for the (informal) influence the ECB may exert on the content of RTS/ITS.

other agencies' decision-making bodies, the ESAs' Board of Supervisors – due to its composition of representatives of mostly independent national authorities – is even better shielded from MS' influence.

Empirical evidence may attenuate these conclusions, eg the fact that comitology committees are regularly consulted by the Commission on a voluntary basis, both with respect to RTS and ITS,[684] or the fact that the representation of MS' interests cannot be excluded by institutional independence – the representatives of national authorities may pursue their respective MS' interest of their own accord.[685] The institutional development, however, cannot be denied.

Hard law and soft law: The ESRB was called a 'soft law body'.[686] This denomination refers to its lack of legal personality, but – more than that – to the fact that its output is limited to soft measures, namely warnings and recommendations. The scene looks different with respect to the ESAs. They dispose of both soft and hard powers. The adjectives 'hard' and 'soft' are not necessarily indicative of the powers' effectiveness or, more generally, their importance – neither in case of the ESRB nor in the case of the ESAs. While the malleable ambit of the ESRB allows it to 'interact freely … and ensure[s] greater scope in the formulation of any recommendations',[687] the compliance rates with ESRB output appear to be satisfactory, and the technique of 'moral suasion and peer pressure'[688] seems to work well. In the meantime, stakeholders have called for even more output flexibility of the ESRB.[689]

The ESAs also have a set of soft powers. While RTS/ITS remain for the Commission to be adopted, the ESAs exert a pivotal influence on their content in the drafting phase. The draft provided for by the ESAs is authoritative not only *qua* the ESAs' expertise (material authority), but also *qua* the requirements for its amendment by the Commission as laid down in the ESA-Regulations (formal authority).[690] That way, the ESAs take part in rule-making and, given the Commission's willingness to regularly accept the ESAs' drafts,[691] it is not an exaggeration to claim that they themselves dispose of a (soft) rule-making power.[692]

---

684 See Commission, COM (2009) 673 final, 6f and Declaration No 39 with regard to Article 290 TFEU.
685 See Busuioc, Rule-Making 120f with further references; see also Masciandaro.
686 Ferran and Alexander 766.
687 Commission, COM (2014) 508 final, 4.
688 Ibid., 6. Sceptical: Ladler, Finanzmarkt 170f.
689 See references in II.2. above.
690 See 3.4.1. and 3.4.2. above.
691 With regard to the RTS see Commission, COM (2014) 509 final (Annex I), 3.
692 See, in this context, the taxonomy of Griller and Orator 31.

Another of the ESAs' soft law competences is the power to issue guidelines and recommendations. With this output the ESAs can direct and harmonise the supervision on the national level. Non-compliance by the competent authorities is subject to a duty to justify towards the respective ESA ('comply or explain'). The possibility for the ESAs to publish a list of sinners is a typical – and powerful – sanction in the soft law toolkit.

The hard law powers conferred on the ESAs – in this work the decision-making powers according to Articles 17–19 of the ESA-Regulations were focused on – *in praxi* are much less relevant. Qualitatively speaking, however, the ESAs' decision-making powers – unprecedented among their institutional siblings – are highly significant.

The fact that the powers conferred on the ECB within the SSM, and the SRB within the SRM respectively (see chapter 4 below), are much more far-reaching ought not to obstruct our view on the importance of the ESAs' powers. With their supervisory and – more than that – regulatory powers they sustainably govern the actions of both the competent authorities and the supervised institutions.

Meroni and the EU's institutional balance: The *Meroni* doctrine still sets the threshold to be met by delegations of powers from EU institutions to other bodies within or outside the organisation of the EU. The ECJ has recently revisited *Meroni*, indicating a great generosity when it comes to assessing the compliance of Union acts, but at the same time leaving unclear its outer limits. The gist of *Meroni* remains the same: A delegation must be explicit, justified and may only encompass powers the exercise of which can be reviewed 'in the light of objective criteria'.[693] In addition to that, with regard to the institutional balance, the role of the Commission as the central EU authority[694] must stay intact, for which reason the delegation of powers to other bodies must remain to be the exception, rather than the rule.[695] This requirement cannot be dismissed as irrelevant in the case of European agencies, thereby pointing at the fact that the EU's agencification mostly has brought about a shift of competences from the MS to the EU level and hence has left the Commission's (existing) powers untouched. As an organic principle, the institutional balance needs to be held also when the total amount of EU competences changes.

Arguably as a result of *Meroni*, we have bodies such as the ESRB that have no legal personality and that may only render soft law output.[696] Since the warnings and recommendations to be rendered by the ESRB entail a relatively wide discretion with different politico-economic interests coming into play,[697]

---

693   *Meroni* 152.
694   See Article 17 TEU.
695   See Griller and Orator 28.
696   Probably this is also due to considerations of retaining the ECB's independence while granting in particular its President a pivotal role within the ESRB.
697   See Ferran and Alexander 767.

providing for binding ESRB-output would not have been compliant with *Meroni*. However, these measures – and also the ESAs' soft law acts – are far from being irrelevant (see above) and must also be taken into account when assessing the EU's institutional balance.

As the summarising account of European agencies and their powers has shown, there is a number of agencies exercising strong decision- and (soft or hard) rule-making powers, especially the more recently founded examples of the ECHA, ACER, the ESAs and the SRB. In that sense, we may say that – in a holistic perspective – the institutional equilibrium appears to be somewhat imbalanced at the cost of the Commission.

4 Institutional change through the Banking Union

I. SINGLE SUPERVISORY MECHANISM (SSM) AND SINGLE RESOLUTION MECHANISM (SRM): DEVELOPMENT, LEGAL BASIS AND SCOPE

As a political idea, the Banking Union was first proclaimed in June 2012, as a measure to produce stabilising effects on the banking sector and on the financial system of the EU and its MS as a whole.[1] In the midst of the euro-area sovereign debt crisis, the main objective was to sustainably remedy one of its main triggers, which is to say to disentangle the functioning of the euro-area banking sector and the fiscal conditions of the euro-MS. In the words of the euro-area heads of state or government: 'to break the vicious circle between banks and sovereigns'.[2] On 12 September 2012, the Commission launched its 'Roadmap towards a Banking Union' which was flanked by two legislative proposals – one for a regulation conferring new tasks on the ECB, the other one directed to amending the founding regulation of the EBA.[3] The quintessence of this Communication was the finding that with regard to the supervision of banks 'mere coordination is not enough'.[4] Since then, the Banking Union's regulatory framework has been fleshed out step by step. As of now, it is conceptualised as a banking regime comprising the three pillars: prudential supervision (SSM), recovery and resolution[5] (SRM), and regulation

---

1   On the political negotiations on the Banking Union, and in particular on the pivotal role played by the French President *Hollande*, see Chang 16–19.
2   <www.consilium.europa.eu/uedocs/cms_data/docs/pressdata/en/ec/131359.pdf>.
3   Commission, COM (2012) 510 final; COM (2012) 511 final; COM (2012) 512 final.
4   Commission, COM (2012) 510 final, 3.
5   For an overview of respective measures on the international level see Haentjens. For an early recommendation to set up resolution schemes on the EU level see *de Larosière* Report 52 (see also Chapter 3 I.4.2. above).

(single rulebook).[6] From the first two pillars – the SSM, operational since November 2014, and the SRM, fully operational since January 2016 – emanates substantial institutional change, which is why they shall be given special attention here. The internal market-wide single rulebook – a 'single set of harmonised prudential rules which institutions throughout the EU must respect'[7] –, on the contrary, shall be achieved by substantive legislative and subsequent rule-making activity,[8] not by establishing new bodies.

The SSM-Regulation vests the ECB with a wide range of powers in the field of prudential supervision in the Eurozone.[9] Those supervisory tasks that are not assigned to the ECB (or the EBA within the ESFS) remain for the respective national competent authorities to be fulfilled. Similarly, those recovery and resolution tasks not assigned to the SRB, the Commission or the Council within the SRM (or the EBA within the ESFS) remain for the respective national competent authorities to be fulfilled. As a complementary, the EU legislator has established a harmonised national bank recovery and resolution regime (including national resolution funds in non-pMS) to be applied on the national level, which is mainly laid down in the BRRD.

The SSM-Regulation is based on Article 127 para 6 TFEU, requiring unanimity in the Council and providing only for a consultative role of the EP.[10] According to this provision, the Council may confer 'specific tasks' upon the ECB 'concerning policies relating to the prudential supervision of credit institutions and other financial institutions with the exception of insurance undertakings'. While clearly the SSM does not cover insurance undertakings,[11] the compliance of the SSM with this Treaty clause can be contested with a view to the 'specific tasks'. As shall be shown, the ECB within the SSM disposes of a wide range of supervisory powers and – by giving instructions – predetermines supervisory actions taken by the national competent authorities. In the words of *Wolfers* and *Voland*, the ECB's supervisory powers are

---

6   <www.consilium.europa.eu/en/policies/banking-union>. For further EU, national and international measures strongly connected with the Banking Union see Moloney, Union 1625f and European Council, 104/2/13, 9f; for accompanying EU measures see Wolfers and Voland 1466f. The aim of a common deposit guarantee scheme – originally one of the pillars of the Banking Union – was dropped upon resistance from Germany in favour of merely harmonising the respective national regimes; see <www.reuters.com/article/2015/09/11/eu-deposits-germany-idUSL5N11H2WY20150911#jVRGhFX7k D3VAMPJ.97>; for the (unsuccessful) resistance of Germany already against Directive 94/19/EC on the harmonisation of deposit-guarantee schemes in the MS see *Germany v Parliament/Council* [1997].

7   <www.eba.europa.eu/regulation-and-policy/single-rulebook>.

8   See Ferran 8f; Kahl, Rulebook 21–23.

9   For arguments against setting in place the ECB as a microprudential supervisor see *de Larosière* Report 43f (see Chapter 3 I.4.1. above).

10   Nevertheless, the EP substantially influenced the decision-making process; see Moloney, Union 1625 (in particular footnote 72).

11   In the *de Larosière* Report, on the contrary, the establishment of a supervisory body competent for both the banking and the insurance sector was recommended (see Chapter 3 I.4.2. above).

'literally all-encompassing'.[12] It can be argued with good reason that the tasks of the ECB corresponding to this comprehensive set of possibilities to influence supervisory practice are not 'specific' any more.[13]

The SRM-Regulation establishing a new European agency – the SRB – is, like the ESRB- and the ESA-Regulations, based on Article 114 TFEU. However, the SRM (such as the SSM) commences as a euro-area measure only. Since it is open for non-euro-MS to join, it could be argued, with a view to Article 114, that it also is a (potential) internal market measure. By linking participation in the SRM with a participation in the SSM and *vice versa*, the legislator has consciously limited the SRM's scope, although it could have given it an internal market-wide scope from the outset. In view of the wide wording of this provision, given its liberal interpretation by the Court (see Chapter 3 II.3.1. above),[14] and in view of the arguably actual (not merely potential) risk of financial fragmentation due to decreasing cross-border banking activities referred to in Recital 1 of the SRB-Regulation, Article 114 para 1 TFEU seems to be an adequate legal basis.[15] That the establishment of a European agency on the basis of Article 114 is principally possible has already been confirmed by the Court (see Chapter 3 II.3.1. above). As regards the SRF, a resolution fund fed by contributions from the banks, it was generally deemed impossible to establish it under the Treaties – even under Article 114. Therefore – 'in order to avoid any risk of legal challenges'[16] – the Commission and the Council called for an Intergovernmental Agreement concluded between all MS[17] (except for Sweden and the UK) to lay down the MS' obligations to transfer the respective contributions to the Fund.[18] According to its Article 2, this agreement is to be applied and interpreted according to EU law. The ECJ has jurisdiction with regard to its interpretation and with regard to infringements by pMS.[19]

The territorial scope of both SSM and SRM principally is confined to the pMS,[20] that is to say the euro-MS and MS which have entered into a 'close

---

12   Wolfers and Voland 1470.
13   See Beutel 74f, still with regard to Article 105 TEC; Griller, Art. 127, para 60; Kämmerer, Bahn 836; Klaushofer 106–108; Weismann, Bankenaufsichtsmechanismus 270f; apparently also Wolfers and Voland 1486; differently: Moloney, Union 1631 with further references.
14   See Michel, Gleichgewicht 119.
15   See Weismann, Abwicklungsmechanismus 1016. See Selmayr, para 61 (footnote 146) with reference to the view of representatives of the German federal government that the creation of the SRM required a Treaty amendment or, at least, the application of Article 352 TFEU, and with further references.
16   Commission, MEMO/14/295, 2.
17   To those MS not (yet) participating in the SSM/SRM only some of the provisions of the agreement apply, eg Article 15 on compensation for contributions to non-contractual liability expenses with respect to the SRM regime.
18   Cf Ferran 7.
19   Article 14 of the Intergovernmental Agreement.
20   Article 4 para 1 of the SSM-Regulation; Article 4 para 1 of the SRM-Regulation.

cooperation'.[21] Such a close cooperation is established by a decision of the ECB upon a request of the respective MS.[22] In the notification of this request to the other MS, the Commission, the ECB and the EBA, the MS shall essentially indicate that its national competent authority shall abide by the relevant ECB-output and provide the relevant information to the ECB.[23] By entering a close cooperation, a MS comes within the scope not only of the SSM, but also of the SRM – to submit only to either of the two regimes is not possible.[24]

The personal scope of the SSM is twofold: as regards the authorisation and its withdrawal (Article 4 para 1 lit a) and as regards the assessment of the acquisition or disposal of qualifying holdings in credit institutions (Article 4 para 1 lit c) the ECB is competent for all credit institutions established in pMS and for credit institutions established in non-pMS which establish a branch or provide cross-border services in a pMS.[25] Otherwise the ECB shall only be competent for the institutions with 'significant relevance with regard to the domestic economy'.[26] This significance shall be assessed on the basis of size, importance for the economy of the EU or any pMS and the significance of cross-border activities.[27] For the time being, 120 credit institutions are being directly supervised by the ECB under the SSM.[28]

The personal scope of the SRM encompasses all significant or those credit institutions in relation to which the ECB has decided to exercise directly all the relevant powers, and other cross-border groups.[29] Where resolution action requires the use of the SRF, and where a MS so requests for its credit institutions, the SRB shall be responsible, irrespective of the institution's significance.[30]

---

21   See also Witte 95.

22   See also ECB-Decision 2014/434/EU.

23   Article 7 para 2 of the SSM-Regulation.

24   See, with regard to Bulgaria, <www.euinside.eu/en/analyses/bulgaria-banking-union-membership>. On the different considerations of non-euro-MS to join/not to join see Ferran 13–17 and 26–29.

25   Article 4 paras 1f in conjunction with Article 6 para 4 of the SSM-Regulation.

26   Recital 41 of the SSM-Regulation. On the central role of this recital – for lack of a corresponding provision – see Weismann, Bankenaufsichtsmechanismus 267; on the details of the classification of an institution as 'significant' see Articles 39ff of ECB Regulation 468/2014; on the classification in practice see Moloney, Union 1646; for an alternative way of determining a bank's systemic relevance see Article 131 of Directive 2013/36/EU.

27   Article 6 para 4 subpara 2 of the SSM-Regulation; for the details of the calculation see subparas 3ff and ECB Regulation 468/2014, in particular its Articles 39f and 43f; see also Weismann, Bankenunion 126–130. A list of significant institutions is provided and regularly updated by the ECB: <www.bankingsupervision.europa.eu/ecb/pub/pdf/list_sse_lsi.en.pdf?492828653da06f7b24babd65e9e3077c>. In 2014, before the SSM legally came into being, the ECB undertook a Comprehensive Assessment (ie a stress test) of 130 euro-area banks and banking groups, most of which now fall under the regime of the SSM; for the Comprehensive Assessments undertaken in 2015 see <www.bankingsupervision.europa.eu/banking/comprehensive/2015/html/index.en.html>.

28   <www.ecb.europa.eu/press/pr/date/2014/html/pr140904_2.en.html>.

29   Article 7 para 2 of the SRM-Regulation.

30   Article 7 para 3 subpara 2 of the SRM-Regulation.

Both mechanisms shall be reviewed by the Commission some time after their respective establishment: the SSM by 31 December 2015; the SRM by 31 December 2018.[31]

II.   THE ECB UNDER THE SSM

1.   Tasks and powers

The ECB's tasks are listed in Articles 4 and 5 of the SSM-Regulation. The most prominent microprudential task is the authorisation of credit institutions and its withdrawal.[32] This task and the assessment of the acquisition and disposal of qualifying holdings in credit institutions the ECB shall carry out itself. The other tasks mentioned in Article 4 of the SSM-Regulation shall be carried out by the national competent authorities under the guidance of, and with the possibility of an attraction of powers by, the ECB.[33] Apart from that, the ECB carries out the task of the competent authority of the home MS in case of a credit institution established in a pMS wishing to establish a branch or provide cross-border services in a non-pMS; ensures compliance of credit institutions with the rules in place in the field of corporate finance and corporate governance; carries out supervisory reviews, including where appropriate and in coordination with the EBA stress tests; carries out supervision on a consolidated basis over credit institutions' parents established in one of the pMS; participates in supplementary supervision of certain financial conglomerates and carries out supervisory tasks in relation to recovery plans and early intervention in case of certain credit institutions or groups.[34] With any act related to these tasks the national competent authorities are obliged to assist the ECB in its preparation and implementation.[35]

On the macroprudential side, most prominent is the power instead of the national competent authorities to apply higher requirements for capital buffers to be held by credit institutions at the relevant level and to apply more stringent measures aimed at addressing systemic or macroprudential risks at the level of credit institutions.[36]

In order to carry out its tasks, the ECB shall adopt guidelines and recommendations, and take decisions in accordance with the relevant Union law. It may also adopt regulations 'necessary to organize or specify the arrangements for the carrying out' of its tasks under the SSM-Regulation and shall

---

31   Article 32 of the SSM-Regulation and Article 94 of the SRM-Regulation.
32   Article 4 para 1 lit a of the SSM-Regulation.
33   See Article 6 paras 5f (in particular para 5 lit b) of the SSM-Regulation.
34   Article 4 para 1 lit b and d-i of the SSM-Regulation. See also para 2.
35   Article 6 para 3 of the SSM-Regulation; see Ladler, Finanzmarkt 225.
36   Article 5 para 2 of the SSM-Regulation. For the respective procedure in the course of which the national competent authorities may object see in particular paras 3–5.

contribute (informally) to the development by the EBA of draft RTS/ITS.[37] More specific powers are laid down in Chapter III of the SSM-Regulation, namely supervisory and investigatory powers. Article 9 provides for the ECB to act as a competent or designated authority in the pMS for the purpose of carrying out its tasks under Article 4 paras 1 and 2 and Article 5 para 2 of the SSM-Regulation. Where this Regulation does not confer on the ECB the powers necessary to carry out its tasks, it may instruct the relevant national authorities of pMS to make use of their respective powers under national law.[38]

Among the investigatory powers exists a comprehensive right to request and access information from credit institutions and holding companies established in the pMS, and from persons belonging to or to whom these entities have outsourced functions or activities. In case of obstruction of the investigation, the respective national competent authorities shall assist the ECB.[39] In addition to that, the ECB may, in accordance with Articles 12f, undertake on-site inspections in cooperation with the relevant national competent authorities.

As mentioned before, at the core of the ECB's *pouvoir* is its authorisation power. The application for an authorisation to take up the business of a credit institution established in a pMS shall be submitted to the respective national competent authority.[40] Where the applicant complies with all the relevant conditions laid down in the respective national law, the national competent authority shall take a draft decision to grant the authorisation and notify it to the ECB and the applicant.[41] Otherwise, the national competent authority shall reject the application.[42]

The draft decision shall be deemed to be adopted by the ECB, unless it objects within a period of ten (extendable to 20) working days. It shall object, thereby giving the reasons, only where the conditions for authorisation set out in the relevant Union law, or national law transposing relevant EU-Directives, are not met.[43] The ECB's decision shall be notified to the applicant by the national authority. While the decision to grant authorisation, and to reject the application respectively, legally originates from the national authority and can be remedied under the conditions of national law, the objection by the ECB can – as a decision according to Article 288 TFEU – be appealed before the CJEU according to Article 263 para 4 TFEU.[44] The ECB shall withdraw the authorisation in accordance with the relevant Union law, following an exchange of views with the national competent authority.[45]

---

37 Article 4 para 3 subparas 2–4 of the SSM-Regulation.
38 Article 9 para 1 of the SSM-Regulation.
39 Articles 10f of the SSM-Regulation.
40 Article 14 para 1 of the SSM-Regulation.
41 On the notification procedures within the organisation of the ECB see Article 13i of the ECB-RoP.
42 Article 14 para 2 of the SSM-Regulation.
43 Article 14 para 3 of the SSM-Regulation; see Witte 105f.
44 See Weismann, Bankenaufsichtsmechanismus 269.
45 Article 14 para 5f of the SSM-Regulation.

The second task directly exercised by the ECB for all credit institutions is the assessment of acquisition and disposal of qualifying holdings. Upon notification by a credit institution, the national competent authority shall assess the proposed *acquisition* and shall then forward to the ECB the notification and a proposal for a decision to oppose or not to oppose, based on the relevant Union law and national law transposing relevant EU-Directives, respectively. The ECB shall make the final decision.[46] The procedure regarding the *disposal* of qualifying holdings falls within the competence of the ECB, as well,[47] but is not regulated in detail.

The ECB has a number of further supervisory powers *vis-à-vis* credit institutions laid down in Article 16, eg to restrict or limit the business, operations or network of a credit institution or to request the divestment of activities that pose excessive risks to the soundness of the institution.[48]

Mention should also be made of the administrative penalties that the ECB may impose on credit institutions and holding companies – not: on other legal persons, or on natural persons[49] – for the intentional or negligent breach of the relevant directly applicable acts of Union law, where such sanctions are or shall be made available to competent authorities under Union law. The amount of the penalty and the details of the procedure are laid down in Article 18 of the SSM-Regulation.

Decisions taken by the ECB under the SSM-Regulation may, in accordance with Article 24 of the SSM-Regulation, be subject to an internal review by the Administrative Board of Review[50] upon request by a person addressed by the decision or otherwise directly and individually concerned.

2.   Organisation

When conceptualising a supervisory regime with the ECB as its main player, the predominant organisational difficulty is to ensure the ECB's independence as regards the exercise of its monetary policy functions. According to Article 127 para 1 TFEU the ESCB's (and hence also the ECB's) 'primary objective' is to maintain price stability. In exercising the respective (monetary policy) powers, the ECB shall be independent within the meaning of Articles 130 and 282 para 3 TFEU. While this independence does, as the ECJ implied, have certain limits,[51] the exercise of supervisory powers by the ECB may certainly pose a threat to the independence of its monetary policy.[52] After all, the supervision of banks and a monetary policy aiming at price stability may, at places, conflict with each other.[53] This is the reason why a number of

---

46   Article 15 paras 2f of the SSM-Regulation.
47   Article 4 para 1 lit c of the SSM-Regulation.
48   Article 16 para 2 lit e of the SSM-Regulation.
49   Recital 53 of the SSM-Regulation; see also Wolfers and Voland 1478.
50   See ECB-Decision 2014/360/EU.
51   *Commission v ECB*, in particular para 174.
52   On the reporting duties of the ECB in place under the SSM see Wolfers and Voland 1488f.
53   See Eriksson 42; Ladler, Finanzmarkt 219, both with examples.

commentators argued – in spite of Article 127 para 6 TFEU providing for this possibility – against such a double-hatting of the ECB.[54] The Council, however, has decided to ensure the ECB's independence in matters of monetary policy by creating a new organ of the ECB, the Supervisory Board, which is detached from its other organs.[55] Thereby a true separation of the ECB's supervisory powers under the SSM-Regulation from its monetary policy functions, as laid down in Article 25 of the SSM-Regulation, shall be ensured.[56] This is also expressed in Recital 12 of the SSM-Regulation, according to which the supervision within the SSM shall be 'unfettered by other, non-prudential considerations'.[57]

The Supervisory Board shall be composed of the Chair, the Vice Chair, four representatives of the ECB and one representative of each national competent authority of the pMS.[58] The Chair shall be a full-time professional and shall not hold any offices at national competent authorities. His term of office shall be five years (not renewable).[59] Both Chair and Vice Chair shall be appointed by the Council upon a proposal submitted by the ECB (after hearing the Supervisory Board) and approved by the EP. The Chair shall be chosen on the basis of a merit-based open selection procedure. Members of the Governing Council of the ECB shall be excluded as candidates. The Vice Chair shall be chosen from among the members of the Executive Board of the ECB.[60]

If the Chair no longer fulfils the conditions required for the performance of his duties or has been guilty of serious misconduct, the Council may, upon a proposal by the ECB (approved by the EP), remove the Chair from office. The Vice Chair may be removed according to the same procedure, following a compulsory retirement as a member of the Executive Board.[61]

The four representatives of the ECB shall be appointed by the Governing Council for a non-renewable period of five years.[62] They shall not perform duties directly related to the monetary function of the ECB.[63]

The Supervisory Board shall carry out preparatory works regarding the supervisory tasks of the ECB. It shall propose to the Governing Council of the

54　See Eriksson 42 with further references.
55　See Ladler, Finanzmarkt 216f, referring to Article 9.1 of the ECB-RoP on the ECB-internal establishment of committees.
56　See also ECB Decision 2014/723/EU.
57　Recital 12 of the SSM-Regulation.
58　Article 26 para 1 of the SSM-Regulation; Article 13b.1 of the ECB-RoP. Where the competent authority of a MS is not its central bank, a representative from this central bank may accompany the respective member of the Supervisory Board. This does not affect the voting power in any way.
59　Article 26 para 3 subpara 2 of the SSM-Regulation.
60　Article 26 para 3 subpara 1 of the SSM-Regulation.
61　Article 26 para 4 of the SSM-Regulation.
62　See Article 1 para 2 of ECB Decision 2014/427/EU, also with regard to the term of office for the initial appointment.
63　Article 26 para 5 of the SSM-Regulation.

ECB complete draft decisions (together with explanatory notes on the background and the main reasons of the proposal[64]) to be adopted by the latter. The Board shall take its draft decisions by simple majority. Only draft regulations pursuant to Article 4 para 3 shall be adopted by a qualified majority.[65] The draft decision shall be deemed adopted unless the Governing Council objects within ten working days (in emergency situations: a maximum of 48 hours).[66] Such objections shall be reasoned, and then be transmitted to the Supervisory Board and the national competent authorities. A pMS whose currency is not the euro may express its reasoned disagreement with a draft decision of the Supervisory Board by notifying the ECB within five working days of receiving the draft. The Governing Council shall take these reasons into account and decide on the matter within five working days.[67] A similar procedure applies where a pMS whose currency is not the euro disagrees with an objection of the Governing Council to a draft decision.[68] Within 30 days the Governing Council shall decide on whether it confirms or withdraws its objection. These procedures, by means of which a pMS whose currency is not the euro may influence this organ's decision to object/not to object, serve as a compensation for the non-representation of non-euro-MS in the Governing Council, which may lead to the inapplicability of a contested decision in that pMS, and/or termination of the close cooperation.[69]

The governance structure described above allows for the Board to prepare the draft decisions which shall formally be adopted by the Governing Council applying reverse majority voting.[70] However, with a view to Article 10 para 2 subpara 4 of the Statute of the ESCB/ECB, according to which the Governing Council '[s]ave as otherwise provided for in this Statute' shall act by a simple majority of the members having a voting right, it is dubitable whether Article 26 para 8 of the SSM-Regulation is in accordance with the Statute.[71]

While the requirements laid down in Article 130 TFEU do not encompass the ECB as a bank supervisor pursuant to secondary legislation based on Article 127 para 6 TFEU,[72] the decision-making mechanism just described aims at maintaining the independence of the ECB in the performance of its monetary policy functions. At the same time, the ECB's organisation as provided for in the TFEU and the Statute of the ECB/ESCB needs to be respected. Since the Supervisory Board is an organ of the ECB established by secondary legislation only, conferring external decision-making power to it

---

64   Article 13g para 1 of the ECB-RoP.
65   Article 26 paras 6f of the SSM-Regulation.
66   Article 13g para 2 of the ECB-RoP.
67   Article 7 para 8 of the SSM-Regulation; Article 13g para 3 of the ECB-RoP.
68   Article 13g para 4 of the ECB-RoP.
69   Article 7 paras 7f of the SSM-Regulation.
70   See in more detail Article 26 para 8 of the SSM-Regulation.
71   Cf Palmstorfer on the (in)compatibility with primary law of reverse majority voting of the Council laid down in secondary law.
72   See Klaushofer 110 with further references.

would conflict with the ECB's organigram as set out in the TFEU. This tension between requirements of independence on the one hand and organisational inelasticity, on the other, has led the legislator to adopt this questionable system. In order to further mitigate concerns regarding independence, the SSM-Regulation and the ECB-RoP stipulate a strict separation between supervisory and monetary policy functions of the ECB in terms of staff, meetings and agendas.[73] This is complemented by reporting duties of the ECB *vis-à-vis* the EP and the Council,[74] and by the creation of a mediation panel.[75]

The SSM-Regulation provides for an Administrative Board of Review composed of five experts (with two alternates) appointed by the ECB for a renewable period of five years. Current staff of the ECB and other national or Union institutions, bodies, offices and agencies involved in the carrying out of the tasks conferred on the ECB within the SSM shall be excluded.[76] Where the request is admissible, the Board of Review shall adopt a reasoned opinion on the matter, and remit the case to the Supervisory Board for preparation of a new draft decision. When doing so, the Supervisory Board shall take into account, but is not bound by, the opinion of the Board of Review.[77] The new draft decision, abrogating the original decision or replacing it by an identical or an amended version, shall become a decision where it is adopted by the Governing Council, again applying reverse majority voting. Such a decision cannot be made subject to a review by the Board of Review.[78] Irrespective of whether a decision of the ECB made under the SSM has been made subject to such a review, it can be appealed before the CJEU.[79]

III.   THE SRB UNDER THE SRM

1.   Tasks and powers

One of the main tasks of the SRB is drawing up resolution plans[80] for the entities and groups in accordance with Article 7 paras 2, 4 lit b or 5 of the SRB-Regulation, in consultation with the ECB and the relevant national competent authorities, including an assessment of resolvability.[81] To that end,

---

73   Critical with regard to the effectiveness of this separation: Gurlit 15.
74   See also the MoU between the Council and the ECB, in particular I. (Accountability) and the Interinstitutional Agreement between EP and ECB.
75   Article 25 para 5 of the SSM-Regulation; see Wolfers and Voland 1480.
76   Article 24 para 2 of the SSM-Regulation.
77   Article 24 para 7 of the SSM-Regulation.
78   Article 24 para 5 second sentence of the SSM-Regulation.
79   Article 24 para 11 of the SSM-Regulation. See also Wolfers and Voland 1481.
80   For the components of a (group) resolution plan see Article 8 paras 9–11 of the SRM-Regulation.
81   See Article 10 of the SRM-Regulation.

the SRB may require the national resolution authorities, and the group-level resolution authorities, respectively, to prepare a draft (group) resolution plan, and may, in that context, issue guidelines and address instructions to the resolution authorities.[82] The (draft) resolution plan shall 'set out options for applying the resolution tools and exercising resolution powers'.[83] Resolution plans shall be reviewed and where appropriate updated at least annually. The SRB shall transmit the resolution plans and the respective updates to the ECB or to the relevant national competent authorities.[84] For those entities and groups for which the SRB is not competent, the national resolution authorities shall adopt resolution plans themselves.[85]

Where an entity within the SRB's scope of competence a) is failing or likely to fail[86] – an assessment which is normally undertaken by the ECB[87] – and where b) there is no 'reasonable prospect that any alternative private sector measures … would prevent its failure within a reasonable timeframe' and c) a resolution action is necessary in the public interest,[88] the SRB shall adopt a resolution scheme that places the entity under resolution, determines the resolution tools to be applied and determines the use of the SRF (where necessary).[89] The resolution scheme is then transmitted to the Commission that shall, within 24 hours, endorse the resolution scheme or object to it 'with regard to the discretionary aspects of the resolution scheme'.[90] Exception: Where the Commission deems that a) the public interest criterion is not met[91] or b) a material (ie substantial) modification of the amount of the Fund is provided for in the resolution scheme, it 'may' (shall) propose within 12 hours to the Council to object in case of alternative a) and either to approve or object in case of alternative b). Where the Commission has objected on the discretionary aspects or where the Council has approved the Commission proposal for modification of the resolution scheme, the SRB shall, within eight hours, modify its resolution scheme accordingly. Where the Council objects for lack of public interest or with regard to a modification of the Fund, the resolution scheme shall not be adopted. Where no objection has been expressed either by the Commission or by the Council within 24 hours, the resolution scheme shall enter into force. Where the resolution involves SRF aid

82   Article 8 paras 2f of the SRM-Regulation.
83   Article 8 para 5 of the SRM-Regulation.
84   Article 8 paras 12f of the SRM-Regulation.
85   Article 9 of the SRM-Regulation.
86   For the details of this qualification see Article 18 para 4 of the SRM-Regulation.
87   Article 18 para 1 of the SRM-Regulation.
88   For the notion of 'public interest' see Article 18 para 5 of the SRM-Regulation.
89   Article 18 para 6 of the SRM-Regulation.
90   Article 18 para 7 subparas 1f of the SRM-Regulation.
91   In this case the entity shall be wound up in accordance with the applicable national law; Article 18 para 8 of the SRM-Regulation.

or state aid according to Article 107 para 1 TFEU the adoption of a resolution scheme is subject to a positive or conditional Commission decision on the compatibility of such aid with the internal market.[92]

The resolution scheme shall be implemented by the relevant national resolution authorities in accordance with the instructions addressed to them by the SRB.[93]

The resolution tools referred to above are a) the sale of business tool, b) the bridge institution tool, c) the asset separation tool and d) the bail-in tool. The sale of business means a transfer to a purchaser that is not a bridge institution of a) instruments of ownership issued by an institution under resolution or b) all or any assets, rights or liabilities of an institution under resolution.[94] Where the purchaser is in fact a bridge institution – that is to say 'an institution which is wholly or partially owned by one or more public authorities or controlled by the resolution authority'[95] – the bridge institution tool is at issue. The rationale of the bridge institution tool is to ensure that the entity under resolution – legally speaking: through the bridge institution – continues to provide essential financial services to its clients and to perform essential financial activities. It should be operated as a viable going concern and be put back on the market in due time or wound up if not viable.[96] The asset separation tool means 'the transfer of assets, rights or liabilities of an institution under resolution or a bridge institution to one or more asset management vehicles'.[97] An asset management vehicle is an at least partly public-owned legal person controlled by the resolution authority, in this case the SRB.[98] The asset separation tool should be used in combination only with other tools in order to prevent an undue competitive advantage for the failing institution.[99] The bail-in tool aims at a recapitalisation of the failing institute, in particular by involving its shareholders and its creditors.[100] The institute may also be recapitalised from the Fund, thereby indirectly involving the entities paying into the fund, that is to say the whole industry. However, where possible, the losses shall be borne first by shareholders and, secondly, by the creditors.[101] A recapitalisation from the Fund shall be an option of last resort.[102]

The SRB shall monitor the execution of the resolution scheme by the national resolution authorities and – where necessary – give instructions to

---

92   Article 19 para 1 of the SRM-Regulation; see Ferran 19f; for the conditions for the authori-
     sation of liquidation aid see the Commission, 2013/C 21b/01, notes 69ff.
93   Article 18 para 9 of the SRM-Regulation.
94   Article 24 para 1 of the SRM-Regulation.
95   Recital 65 of Directive 2014/59/EU.
96   Ibid.
97   Article 26 para 1 of the SRM-Regulation.
98   Article 42 para 2 of Directive 2014/59/EU.
99   Recital 66 of Directive 2014/59/EU.
100 Recital 67 of Directive 2014/59/EU.
101 Article 15 para 1 lit a and b of the SRM-Regulation.
102 See Article 92 para 2 lit a of the SRM-Regulation. For the possible use of the relevant
     deposit guarantee scheme see Article 79 of the SRM-Regulation.

them. In that context the national authorities shall cooperate with and assist the SRB and provide it with all the respective information.[103] In addition to that, the SRB has a set of investigatory powers with regard to the entities referred to in Article 2, their employees or third parties to whom they have outsourced functions or activities: It may, directly or through the national resolution authorities, request relevant information (Article 34); it may, directly or through the national resolution authorities, conduct the necessary investigation (examination of books and records, interviewing of persons, etc.) of the legal or natural persons referred to above, where they are established or located in a pMS (Article 35); and it may conduct necessary on-site inspections (Article 36).[104]

Under the heading 'Implementation of decisions ...' the SRM-Regulation provides for mechanisms aimed at ensuring compliance with SRB-decisions on the part of national resolution authorities and institutions under resolution, respectively. Article 29 para 1 stipulates that the national resolution authorities shall take the necessary action to implement decisions referred to in the SRM-Regulation and, more specifically, implement all decisions addressed to them by the SRB.[105] Where a national resolution authority has not (correctly) applied a decision of the SRB, the SRB may order an institution under resolution to adopt the action necessary to comply with the respective SRB-decision.[106] Before deciding to impose such a measure it shall notify the national resolution authorities concerned and the Commission thereof, normally not less than 24 hours before the measure shall take effect.[107] The institution under resolution shall comply with such a decision, which shall prevail over any previously (and subsequently; see Chapter 3 II.3.4.3.1. above) adopted decision by the national resolution authorities on the same matter.[108]

Where 'necessary to ensure the consistent application of high resolution standards',[109] the SRB may issue warnings to the national resolution authorities where it considers that a draft decision regarding an entity or group for which the national resolution authorities of the pMS are competent in accordance with Article 7 para 3 is not in compliance with the SRM-Regulation or a general instruction of the SRB. It may also decide to attract[110] the national resolution authorities' competences *vis-à-vis* non-significant credit institutions listed in Article 7 para 3.[111] In addition to that, the SRB – as was

---

103 Article 28 of the SRM-Regulation.
104 For the required judicial authorisation under national law see Article 37.
105 Article 29 para 1 of the SRM-Regulation.
106 Article 29 para 2 subparas 1f of the SRM-Regulation with further details.
107 Article 29 para 2 subparas 3f of the SRM-Regulation.
108 Article 29 para 3 of the SRM-Regulation.
109 Article 7 para 4 of the SRM-Regulation.
110 For lack of an express rule on this, the SRB is merely ousting the national authorities' competences, *qua* supremacy overruling any decision on the same matter of the respective national authority (a similar mechanism can be found in the ESA-Regulations; see Chapter 3 II.3.4.3. above).
111 Article 7 para 4 lit a and b of the SRM-Regulation.

hinted at above – may address to the national resolution authorities specific and general instructions as well as guidelines[112] and utter its views on national resolution authorities' draft decisions that they have to send to the SRB.[113]

The SRB may impose a penalty on an entity referred to in Article 2, where it has failed to comply with a request for information under Article 34, to submit to a general investigation under Article 35 or an on-site inspection under Article 36 or to comply with a decision addressed to it by the SRB under Article 29. The SRB may also impose periodic penalty payments to an entity referred to in Article 2 under the conditions laid down in Article 39.

2.   Organisation

The SRM-Regulation establishes a new European agency, the SRB.[114] It is composed of the Chair who represents the SRB, a Vice Chair, four other full-time members and one representative of the resolution authority of each pMS.[115] One representative each of the Commission and the ECB shall participate in the meetings of both executive and plenary sessions as permanent observers.[116] Following a merit-based open selection procedure, the candidates for the full-time members' positions are – after hearing the SRB in its plenary session (safe for the historically first selection procedure) – shortlisted by the Commission, which is sent to the EP and to the Council. In a next step the Commission proposes a list of candidates to the EP for approval. Following that approval, the candidates are appointed by the Council.[117] Their term of office shall be a non-renewable five years. Only the historically first Chair shall be appointed for a term of three years, which may be extended once by a period of five years.[118]

Where a full-time member of the SRB does no longer meet the conditions required for the performance of his duties or where he has been guilty of serious misconduct, the Council may – on a proposal from the Commission that has been approved by the EP – remove him from office.[119]

The SRM – 'in an uneasy compromise' between speedy decision-making and legitimacy[120] – decides in two kinds of sessions. In the executive session, which is composed of the Chair and the other four full-time members, with the respective representatives of the national resolution authorities of the pMS concerned and observers participating,[121] it shall essentially prepare the

---

112   Article 28 para 2 and Article 31 para 1 lit a of the SRM-Regulation.
113   Article 31 para 1 lit d of the SRM-Regulation.
114   Article 42 of the SRM-Regulation.
115   Article 43 para 1 in conjunction with Article 56 para 3 of the SRM-Regulation.
116   Article 43 para 3 of the SRM-Regulation.
117   Article 56 paras 4 and 6 of the SRM-Regulation.
118   Article 56 para 7 of the SRM-Regulation.
119   Article 56 para 9 of the SRM-Regulation.
120   Moloney, Union 1638.
121   Article 53 of the SRM-Regulation.

decisions (eg a resolution plan) to be adopted in the plenary session and take the decisions within its competence necessary to implement the SRM-Regulation (eg decisions regarding the budget of the Fund).[122] In its plenary session (including all members) the SRB shall – *inter alia* – adopt the SRB's annual work programme, adopt and monitor the annual budget and decide on the use of the SRF in excess of a certain threshold.[123]

3.   The Single Resolution Fund (SRF)

The SRF, owned by the SRB,[124] shall provide the necessary means for the efficient application of the resolution tools and the exercise of the resolution powers of the SRB. It is therefore 'an essential element without which the SRM could not work properly'.[125] The SRF shall be funded by all credit institutions in the pMS. The available funds shall, after an initial period of eight years, reach at least 1 per cent of the amount of covered deposits of all credit institutions authorised in the pMS, ie 55 billion euro.[126] The credit institutions' contributions shall be raised on the national level,[127] at least annually *ex ante* and, possibly and in addition to that, *ex post*.[128] They shall be calculated pro-rata to the amount of the institution's liabilities (excluding own funds) less covered deposits, with respect to the aggregate liabilities (excluding own funds) less covered deposits, of all of the institutions authorised in the territories of all pMS.[129] During the transitional period the contributions shall be assigned to different compartments corresponding to each pMS.[130] Eventually they shall be mutualised.

Non-pMS are required to establish their respective national resolution funds in accordance with Articles 100ff of the BRRD.

IV.   CONSEQUENCES FOR THE ESFS AND APPRAISAL

The fleshing out of the Banking Union, in particular the creation of the SSM and the SRM, has significant consequences for the functioning of the ESFS,

---

122   Article 54 of the SRM-Regulation.
123   Article 50 para 1 of the SRM-Regulation.
124   Article 67 paras 2f of the SRM-Regulation.
125   Recital 19 of the SRM-Regulation.
126   Article 69 para 1 of the SRM-Regulation.
127   Article 1 para 1 lit a of the Intergovernmental Agreement.
128   Articles 70f of the SRM-Regulation.
129   Article 70 para 1 of the SRM-Regulation. For the individual calculations undertaken by the SRB see Article 70 para 2 of the SRM-Regulation; for the methodology of these calculations see Council Implementing Regulation 2015/81.
130   Recital 20 of the SRM-Regulation. For the functioning of the compartments see Article 5 of the Intergovernmental Agreement.

above all of the EBA[131] whose function now also is to work as a 'bridge between SSM and non-SSM members'.[132] Positively, it can be said that the EBA's powers, which are mainly regulatory, thereby facilitating convergence, are now complemented by comprehensive supervisory powers, regularly allowing for direct intervention (in particular with regard to cross-border banking groups[133]), conferred on the ECB.[134]

While the concern about representatives of competent authorities of non-pMS being marginalised in the EBA Board of Supervisors has been tackled by introducing double-majority requirements (see Chapter 3 II.3.5.3.2. above), certain tensions in terms of hierarchy and cooperation remain. One example is the double function of the ECB as a micro- as well as a macroprudential supervisor. While the ECB exercises macroprudential tasks via its representation in the ESRB and, to a limited extent, under the SSM-Regulation,[135] it acts as microprudential supervisor within the SSM. Whether it can fulfil both functions with the same intensity remains to be seen.[136] While the ECB within the SSM certainly is the more powerful authority compared with the EBA,[137] there are nevertheless instances of the former having to submit to the authority of the EBA. This is *de facto* the case with RTS/ITS drafted by the EBA (and adopted by the Commission) and its guidelines and recommendations, and *de iure*, due to being confronted with a binding instruction and/or due to an ECB-decision being overruled in the context of the decision-making powers according to Articles 17–19 of the EBA-Regulation. In that sense, the relationship is problematic in terms of institutional balance.[138] On the other hand, conflicts may arise due to the fact that both actors, the EBA and the ECB within the SSM, have a comprehensive soft regulatory power that may, at worst, conflict with each other.[139] A similar argument can be brought forward against the existence of two stress test regimes – that of the EBA according to Article 22 of the EBA-Regulation and that of the ECB (Article 4 para 1f of the SSM-Regulation), which shall be applied in cooperation with the EBA.[140]

---

131 In spite of Article 3 para 3 of the SSM-Regulation, according to which the ECB shall carry out its tasks under the SSM-Regulation 'without prejudice to the competence and the tasks of EBA, ESMA, EIOPA and the ESRB'.

132 Parliament, Review 1 124. Critical with regard to an ousting of the EBA: Ladler, Finanzmarktregulierung 332.

133 See Parliament, Review 1 73.

134 See Moloney, Union 1621. On the differentiation between the terms 'banking supervision' and 'banking regulation' see Michel, Gleichgewicht 166–168.

135 See in particular Article 5 of the SSM-Regulation.

136 Sceptical: Ladler, Finanzmarkt 228.

137 Predicting that the EBA's actions will be substantially influenced by the ECB: Ferran 9f; see also Parliament, Review 1 74, calling for the EBA to be 'properly resourced' in order to be in a position to cooperate with the ECB on an equal footing.

138 Critically, Moloney, Union 1665f; Wolfers and Voland 1493.

139 See Gurlit 16f; Michel, Gleichgewicht 242f; Wolfers and Voland 1493.

140 For the methodological overlap of these two regimes see Moloney, Union 1667; see also Michel, Gleichgewicht 262f.

Within the SRM, the SRB, the Commission and the Council are subject to RTS/ITS drafted by the EBA (and adopted by the Commission) and shall make 'every effort' to comply with its guidelines and recommendations in accordance with Article 16 para 3 of the EBA-Regulation.[141] They shall cooperate with the EBA in terms of Article 25 (recovery and resolution procedures) and Article 30 (peer reviews of competent authorities) of the EBA-Regulation. The SRB shall also be subject to decisions according to Article 19 of the EBA-Regulation where the BRRD provides for such decisions.[142] National resolution authorities have a variety of reporting duties towards the EBA.[143]

From an institutional point of view the Banking Union has brought two new bodies, the Supervisory Board as a new organ within the ECB (and a couple of collateral ECB-internal organs) on the one hand, and the SRB as a European agency, on the other hand. The composition of both bodies reflects a strong dedication to the representation of national authorities' representatives in the pMS and thereby seems to follow the composition of the administrative boards of the more recently established agencies (ACER, ESAs). With around 800 new employees the supervisory branch of the ECB[144] has substantially more staff than the SRB, which intends to have recruited a total of 250 staff by 2017.[145] In terms of powers, it is apparent that the powers of the ECB and the SRB, over the respective competent national authorities, go far beyond the powers of the ESAs; with regard to the SSM it was even said that the 'transfer of national competences to a European institution ... is without precedent since the introduction of the euro'.[146] Both have comprehensive instruction rights towards their national counterparts, they are entitled to attract national authorities' powers and they have strong investigatory and enforcement powers.[147]

While in this respect, the set of powers of the two bodies is similar, it is clear that the ECB, as an institution of the EU, disposes of more discretionary powers than the SRB as a mere European agency. This can be exemplified by the latitude the ECB has in determining which credit institutions are 'significant' and – on the contrary – by the SRM's dependence on Commission/Council approval with regard to crucial elements of the resolution

---

141   See eg <www.eba.europa.eu/regulation-and-policy/recovery-and-resolution/guide lines-on-how-information-should-be-provided-under-the-brrd>. On the SRM's, the Commission's and the Council's being competent authorities see the new Article 4 para 2 of the EBA-Regulation as amended by Article 95 of the SRM-Regulation.

142   Article 5 para 2 subpara 2 of the SRM-Regulation.

143   See eg Article 4 para 7 of Directive 2014/59/EU. On the EBA's role in the establishment of the national resolution authorities see EBA, Annual Report 2014, 55f.

144   ECB, Annual Report 2014, 169; with regard to the increase in the ECB's administrative expenses by 150 million euro due to the SSM see ibid. 115.

145   <http://srb.europa.eu/>.

146   Chiti and Teixeira 691; similarly Chang 2.

147   See Moloney, Union 1642f.

scheme. The reservation of a decision-making competence of the Commission/Council is to be understood as an attempt of the legislator to comply with the *Meroni* doctrine[148] (see Chapter 2 I. above), which prohibits the delegation of wide discretionary powers to entities other than the institutions of the EU within the meaning of Article 13 TEU. The short time allowed for the Commission/Council to make their – reasoned[149] – decision, which is to make sure that a resolution scheme 'is adopted over a weekend while markets are closed',[150] strongly relativises their powers, given the fact that a resolution scheme in accordance with Article 8 of the SRM-Regulation is supposed to be a lengthy and complicated document. The SRB shall, where appropriate, modify the resolution scheme in accordance with the reasons expressed by the Commission/Council.[151] As regards the ECB's powers under the SSM *Meroni* is not to be applied. It is true that the Supervisory Board in its composition and also in terms of its accountability resembles other European agencies. The fact that the Supervisory Board is placed within the organisation of the ECB, however, cannot be neglected. It could be argued that *de facto* the Supervisory Board was the decision-maker, and that for its separation from the monetary policy organs of the ECB it was to be treated as an independent European agency, and hence *Meroni* were to be applied. However, the organisational construction laid down in the SSM-Regulation in principle was – for lack of a Treaty amendment – without an alternative. Article 127 para 6 TFEU allows for the ECB to be vested with powers of banking supervision. Article 130 TFEU (and other provisions) require(s) the ECB to be independent when exercising its monetary policy functions.[152] Assuming that Article 127 para 6 does not suggest or even require an amendment of the Treaties for it to be applied, the current organisational setting can in principle be read into this Treaty provision. It is *the ECB* as an institution of the EU that may be granted supervisory powers under Article 127 para 6 TFEU, and it is – according to the SSM-Regulation – *the ECB* making decisions within the SSM. In that sense, the requirements for an application of *Meroni* are not met.[153] This finding cannot, of course, do away with the concerns discussed above regarding the actual scope of the legal basis, the imperfect separation of banking supervision and monetary policy and the reverse majority voting applied in the Governing Council.

---

148 See also Moloney, Union 1660f.
149 Article 18 para 7 subpara 6 of the SRM-Regulation.
150 Moloney, Union 1640.
151 Article 18 para 7 subpara 8 of the SRM-Regulation.
152 With regard to the ECB's independence, it could be said that it has been threatened even before the introduction of the SSM: Where in a euro-MS the national central bank is at the same time the banking supervisory authority of that state, its governor, when voting in the Governing Council of the ECB, may always be at risk of being influenced by supervisory considerations.
153 Sceptical: Wolfers and Voland 1491f.

The mutualisation of losses through the SRF – whether or not one wants to call it 'an historic development'[154] – beyond doubt is one of the most substantial anti-crisis measures within the Banking Union and constitutes a step in the overall transformation of the EU from a 'community of mutual benefits' to a community of mutual benefits and burden-sharing.[155] The SRF was the most contested element of the SRM, in particular due to German resistance to a mutualisation of risks for bank failure.[156] The SRF in its final shape provides, as a compromise and for a transitional period of eight years, for the MS to collect the contributions from their banks and to transfer them to the respective national compartment of the Fund. These compartments shall gradually be mutualised until they cease to exist.[157]

---

154   Moloney, Union 1644.
155   Chiti and Teixeira 700f.
156   See Ferran 21.
157   Article 1 para 1 lit b of the Intergovernmental Agreement.

Conclusion

Summary

The review of the institutional development of both comitology and European agencies has disclosed a significant relationship between these two risk governance regimes. Both of them reflect the political struggle for MS representation on the one hand, and independent expertise on the other hand. As the comparison has shown, the two compromises – comitology committees and European agencies – differ from each other considerably. In case of comitology, MS representation and the link to the Commission stay in the foreground, whereas European agencies – dominated by representatives of the MS bureaucracies, as well – from their institutional position seem to prioritise independent expertise. The new system of Commission rule-making as laid down in Articles 290/291 TFEU has reduced the scope of comitology and also the fact that a number of European agencies was preceded by a comitology committee or has incorporated such a committee within its organisation indicates that the comitology regime is – far from being endangered – not the first option in risk governance any more. This is exemplified by the – admittedly exceptional – adoption procedure of RTS/ITS according to the ESA-Regulations.

This leads us to the ESAs. In terms of the *Lamfalussy* system, they exercise power on all levels: on the level of legislation ('framework principles'; level 1) as advisors; on the level of 'implementing the details' (level 2) as advisors/*de facto* decision-makers; on the level of cooperation (level 3) by monitoring and harmonising the competent authorities' actions; and on the enforcement level (level 4) by crossing – with soft or hard legal means – their respective interpretation of the relevant rules *vis-à-vis* the competent authorities. The quality of their powers – which is at risk of being relativised in view of the powers conferred in the context of the SSM and the SRM – in the history of the E(E)C/EU's agencification is without precedent.

The Banking Union is one component of a 'genuine economic and monetary union'.[1] The Commission and the legislator have conceptualised

---

1   Report by the President of the European Council <www.consilium.europa.eu/uedocs/cms_data/docs/pressdata/en/ec/131201.pdf>.

the two pillars of the Banking Union at issue in this work, the SSM and the SRM, as projects for the euro-area, but have left the door open for all other MS to enter into a close cooperation.

Are these developments another element in a two-speed EU?[2] Supposedly yes, but this direction has already been taken by allowing for a situation in which there are euro- and non-euro-MS in the EU. With the EU's own currency, the euro, being at risk, it is therefore not surprising that above all the MS of the euro-area are involved in the measures intended to reduce this risk. In that sense, the crisis has given a strong impetus to the further integration of the Eurozone (not so much of the rest of the EU), which entails a considerable separation.[3]

With the creation of the SSM, the legislator has made use of Article 127 para 6 TFEU and vested the ECB with far-reaching supervisory powers. With regard to the ECB's independence this may raise general democratic legitimacy concerns.[4] The legislator, however, rather seemed to be concerned with convincingly separating the ECB's monitory functions from its new supervisory powers. With a number of new internal organs, above all the Supervisory Board – which is not a European agency – a regime was created in which there is one powerful *de facto* decision-maker and the 'old' Governing Council deciding *de iure*.

Institutional placement

With a view to commonalities between the agencies operating in financial market risk governance, a final remark on the ESAs' decision-making powers under Articles 17–19 of the ESA-Regulations may be made. What makes them special is, in my view, the fact that they entail parallel competences of the respective ESA and the competent (regularly: national) authorities. The 'evocation *à l'européenne*'[5] creates a situation in which two authorities are in principle competent to render a decision. However, if the two decisions differ in substance, one of the decisions (here: the ESA-decision) 'overrules' the other one. It is not the supremacy of EU law expressed in this legal mechanism which is of interest here, but it is the fact that a European agency can dictate to a mostly national body the content of a decision that it, the national body, is competent to render in the first place. Only in case the competent body does not abide, the EU body shall – by means of the said evocation *à l'européenne* – render its own – supreme – decision. These competences clearly go beyond what European agencies have been entrusted with up until then. It would not be a valid legal argument against the significance of these competences to say that the ESAs will – in all likelihood – hardly ever render

2   See generally for this debate Piris.
3   Cf Chiti and Teixeira 692.
4   See Quaglia 114.
5   Kämmerer, Finanzaufsichtssystem 1285.

such an overruling decision anyway. Though the assumption – in light of the experience made so far – seems to be justified, the legal significance of competences cannot be mitigated by the fact that they will hardly be applied. What is more, it cannot be overlooked that the factual authority of the ESAs' instructions directed towards the competent authorities, and hence the competent authorities' willingness to abide, is increased considerably by the legal possibilities the ESAs have at hand, even if only as an *ultima ratio*.

The ECB within the SSM and the SRB within the SRM have even more far-reaching instruction powers *vis-à-vis* their national counterparts. With regard to this kind of 'composite decision making procedures'[6] the relationship of subordination is so strong that it comes close to the hierarchical structures known from national administrations. In that sense, what is referred to as '*Europäischer Verwaltungsverbund*'[7] has reached a new level of intensity.[8]

The comparison with other European agencies has shown that this power regime did not come as a surprise, but that the Commission and the legislator have become more and more willing to delegate powers to Union bodies, which were established for this purpose. It is, as *Craig* put it, 'increasingly common for EU agencies to be given strong quasi-regulatory powers'.[9] Another conclusion that can be drawn is that the operations of agencies – in particular when exercising their soft harmonisation powers – foster what was referred to above as 'creeping integration beyond the letter of the law' (see Chapter 3 I.2.3. above).

Considering the judgement of the Court in the *ESMA* case, it seems unlikely that it would declare any of the other powers the ESAs currently have to contravene the *Meroni* limits set to the delegation of powers. With the SRB this may be different. Although the legislator – by involving the Council and the Commission in the adoption of resolution schemes – has implicitly taken into account *Meroni* at places, the powers remaining for the SRB in *Meroni* terms still appear to be excessive. With regard to another, though connected, element of the *Meroni* judgement, the balance of powers (now: institutional balance[10]), the following can be said: The powers of the European agencies in the field of financial market risk governance in many ways resemble that of the Commission in the execution of competition law, eg as regards the SRB's investigatory powers,[11] the SRB's and – to a more limited extent – the ESAs' power to exercise competences which are principally exercised by the national competent authorities,[12] or the ESAs' enquiry into a particular type of financial

---

6   Hofmann, Decision 136ff.
7   See Schmidt-Aßmann.
8   Cf Majone: 'The new agencies could become the laboratories where new forms of regulatory co-operation among nations are developed' (Agencies 274).
9   Craig, EU (#2) 150.
10   See Michel, Gleichgewicht 74.
11   Cf Articles 17ff of Regulation 1/2003.
12   Article 11 para 6 of Regulation 1/2003.

activity with a view to detecting (suspected) threats to the financial system (see Chapter 3 II.3.6.2. above).[13] This underpins the argument that the institutional balance is at risk (see Chapter 3 II.4. above), because it shows that powers which have in the past – in the case of competition law – been conferred on the Commission, are now – in the case of financial market risk governance – conferred on European agencies.

Assessment and prospects

European agencies, as *Craig* put it, 'are here to stay', without any doubt.[14] Bearing in mind the momentum European agencies have gained over the past 40 years, the SRB builds up the provisional peak of this development. Vested with unprecedented powers, the SRB within the SRM represents the most recent legislative effort in paving the way towards a new generation of European agencies.

With respect to the US, *Majone* called agencies the 'fourth branch of government'.[15] As a way of expressing the importance of agencies this quotation is also valid in the context of EU institutional law, although the European agencies' tasks can comfortably be accommodated in the executive and – in a *de facto* perspective – partly also in the legislative branch. The EU, however, unlike the US, does not have a clear leader of the executive. Rather, the executive power is shared between the Council and the Commission, but also other bodies, in particular European agencies. This way, the EU's executive branch can be mapped with two main power centres in Brussels, and dozens of – inhomogeneously sized – smaller, but still power centres in many other locations of the EU.

Another lesson that European agencies, and the European agencies in the field of financial market risk governance in particular, are teaching us is that on the increasing relevance of soft law.[16] In this case influenced above all by the UK's style of rule-making, the EU has empowered its bodies, not least its agencies, to render soft law measures, such as guidelines, standards or recommendations.[17] Soft law rules can be as effective as or even more effective than hard law rules (given the authority of the ruler and/or the peer pressure are high enough), and hence the empowerment of the executive to render such rules further mitigates the (in the EU traditionally weak[18]) separation of powers.

---

13   Cf Article 17 of Regulation 1/2003.
14   Craig, EU (#2) 180.
15   Majone, Delegation 335. See also Follesdal and Hix (538), who – paraphrasing *Majone* – describe the EU as a whole as 'a glorified regulatory agency, a "fourth branch of government"' of the MS.
16   See also B Raschauer, Verhaltenssteuerungen 699f.
17   See B Raschauer, Verfahren 25.
18   Cf Simoncini 339.

The discussion of the topic 'agencification of the EU' boils down to the old conflict of technocracy *versus* democracy[19] – faster decision-making *versus* legitimate decision-making. In a similar vein the question 'independence or accountability' arises. So far the EU legislator – unsurprisingly – has tried to clear both concepts – technocracy *and* democracy, independence *and* accountability – by establishing agencies that provide independent expertise in principle, but at the same time are held accountable by a variety of checks and balances.

As has been mentioned earlier,[20] the conceptual difference between European agencies and the Commission is not apparent at first sight. And even at second sight European agencies and the Commission resemble each other in many respects. They are both fulfilling tasks in the executive and the legislative branch in a variety of policy fields, they are both policy-initiators and they are both non-majoritarian. This striking similarity poses the question why agencies have been established in the first place. Could not all the tasks and powers now being delegated to European agencies be fulfilled equally well under the organisational umbrella of the Commission,[21] and would not this solution be more in compliance with how the Commission was originally conceptualised, which is to say as *the* collector and provider of information and assessment, *the* policy-initiator and, not least, *the* executive authority in the EU? There are no compelling legal arguments against implementing such a traditional understanding of the EU's institutional landscape. The reasons for the popularity of European agencies among EU policy-makers are all political in nature.

Summing up the findings on the phenomenon of European agencies in general, and the example of those operating in financial market risk governance in particular, agencies appear as a perfect tool for fostering integration: They *de facto* or *de jure* set rules and thereby thicken the web of EU law, be it on the hard law or the soft law, the legislative or the executive front; they ensure compliance with these rules in a reasonably effective way[22] (peer pressure being an important asset in soft law 'enforcement'; instructions to national authorities being the hard law counterpart); and they spread the EU's authority throughout its territory in a way that is already geographically visible (decentralisation).[23]

---

19   Cf Wallace and Smith.
20   See Chapter 1 I. above.
21   Cf Schout, Environment 138f with regard to the EEA.
22   Certain difficulties with ensuring MS' compliance (see Moloney, Union 1645 with further references) should not be overemphasised.
23   Cf Majone, Europeanization 192.

References

Books, book contributions, journal articles and (presented) papers

Abbott, Kenneth, and Duncan Snidal, 'Hard and Soft Law in International Governance' (2000) 54 International Organization 421

Adamski, Dariusz, 'The ESMA Doctrine: A Constitutional Revolution and the Economics of Delegation' (2014) 6 European Law Review 812

af Jochnik, Kerstin, 'CEBS – Work Progress and Future Challenges' (2011) 4 Bankarchiv 243

Alemanno, Alberto, 'EU Risk Regulation and Science: The Role of Experts in Decision-making and Judicial Review' (2008) 6 CONNEX Report Series 37 <www.mzes.uni-mannheim.de/projekte/typo3/site/fileadmin/BookSeries/Volume_Six/NEU%20Chapter%202%20Alemanno.pdf> accessed 21 November 2015

Alemanno, Alberto, 'Unpacking the Principle of Openness in EU Law: Transparency, Participation and Democracy' (2014) 39 European Law Review 72

Alemanno, Alberto, and Stéphanie Mahieu, 'The European Food Safety Authority before European Courts' (2008) 5 European Food and Feed Law Review 320

Alemanno, Alberto, and Anna Meuwese, 'Impact Assessment of EU Non-Legislative Rulemaking: The Missing Link in "New Comitology"' (2013) 19 European Law Journal 76

Alford, Duncan, 'The Lamfalussy Process and EU Bank Regulation: Another Step on the Road to Pan-European Regulation?' (2006) 25 Annual Review of Banking and Financial Law 389

Arestis, Philip, Rogério Sobreira and José Luis Oreiro (eds), *The Financial Crisis: Origins and Implications* (Palgrave Macmillan 2010)

Babis, Valia, 'Single Rulebook for Prudential Regulation of Banks: Mission Accomplished?' (2014) 37 Legal Studies Research Paper Series 1

Babis, Valia, 'The Power to Ban Short-Selling: The Beginning of a New Era for EU Agencies?' (2014) 73 Cambridge Law Journal 266

Ballmann, Alexander, David Epstein and Sharyn O'Halloran, 'Delegation, Comitology, and the Separation of Powers in the European Union' (2002) 56 International Organization 551

Baratta, Roberto, 'Legal issues of the "Fiscal Compact". Searching for a mature democratic governance of the Euro' in B de Witte, A Héritier and A Trechsel (eds), *The Euro Crisis and the State of European Democracy. Contributions from the 2012 EUDO Dissemination Conference* (European University Institute 2013)

Barbier, Cécile, 'La prise d'autorité de la Banque centrale européenne et les dangers démocratiques de la nouvelle gouvernance économique dans l'Union européenne' in B de Witte, A Héritier and A Trechsel (eds), *The Euro Crisis and the State of European Democracy. Contributions from the 2012 EUDO Dissemination Conference* (European University Institute 2013)

Bartodziej, Peter, *Reform der EG-Wettbewerbsaufsicht und Gemeinschaftsrecht* (Nomos 1994)

Baur, Georg, and Martin Boegl, 'Die neue europäische Finanzmarktaufsicht – der Grundstein ist gelegt' (2011) 5 Zeitschrift für Bank- und Kapitalmarktrecht 177

Beju, Georgeta, Codruta Făt and Angela Filip, 'The Impact of European Integration and Financial Globalization on Prudential Supervision' (Working Paper 2008) <www2.lse.ac.uk/fmg/documents/specialPapers/2003/sp149.pdf> accessed 21 November 2015

Bergström, Carl, *Comitology: Delegation of Powers in the European Union and the Committee System* (Oxford University Press 2005)

Bergström, Carl, 'Shaping the new system for delegation of powers to EU agencies: United Kingdom v. European Parliament and Council (Short selling)' (2015) 52 Common Market Law Review 219

Berrisch, Georg, Peter Bogaert, Cándido García Molyneux, David Harfst, Lisa Peets and Wim van Velzen, 'Reform of the "Comitology" Procedure' (E-ALERT, February 2011) <www.cov.com/files/Publication/2e18f607-e38b-4398-ab72-bc21850c3c0a/Presentation/PublicationAttachment/1d78b48f-370b-4449-83ea-cd8e97be6074/Reform%20of%20the%20EU%20'Comitology'%20Procedure.pdf> accessed 21 November 2015

Beutel, Jochen, *Differenzierte Integration in der Europäischen Wirtschafts- und Währungsunion* (de Gruyter 2006)

Blanck-Putz, Kathrin, 'The Interplay of the Various Regulating Agencies on EU and MS Level' (The Banking Union, Vienna, 17 April 2015)

Blom-Hansen, Jens, 'The origins of the EU comitology system: a case of informal agenda-setting by the Commission' (2008) 15 Journal of European Public Policy 208

Blom-Hansen, Jens, 'The EU Comitology System: Taking Stock before the New Lisbon Regime' (2011) 18 Journal of European Public Policy 607

Bloss, Michael, Dietmar Ernst, Joachim Häcker and Nadine Eil, *Von der Subprime-Krise zur Finanzkrise. Immobilienblase: Ursachen, Auswirkungen, Handlungsempfehlungen* (R Oldenbourg 2009)

Bodiroga-Vukobrat, Nada, and Adrijana Martinović, 'European Decentralised or Regulatory Agencies – Quest for a Common Approach' in N Bodiroga-Vukobrat, G Sander and S Barić (eds), *Regulierungsagenturen im Spannungsfeld von Recht und Ökonomie. Regulatory Agencies in the Tension Between Law and Economics* (Verlag Dr. Kovač 2012)

Börzel, Tanja, Tobias Hofmann, Diana Panke and Carina Sprungk, 'Obstinate and Inefficient: Why Member States Do Not Comply With European Law' (2010) 11 Comparative Political Studies 1363

Bovens, Mark, 'Analysing and Assessing Accountability: A Conceptual Framework' (2007) 13 European Law Journal 447

Bradley, Kieran, 'Comitology and the Law: Through a Glass, Darkly' (1992) 29 Common Market Law Review 693

Bradley, Kieran, 'Halfway house: The 2006 comitology reforms and the European parliament' (2008) 31 West European Politics 837

Brandt, Edmund, *Umweltaufklärung und Verfassungsrecht* (Eberhard Blottner Verlag 1994)

Braumüller, Peter, *Versicherungsaufsichtsrecht. Internationale Standards, europäische Richtlinien und österreichisches Recht* (Springer 1999)

Bücker, Andreas, and Sabine Schlacke, 'Die Entstehung einer "politischen Verwaltung" durch EG-Ausschüsse – Rechtstatsachen und Rechtsentwicklungen' in C Joerges and J Falke (eds), *Das Ausschußwesen der Europäischen Union: Praxis der Risikoregulierung im Binnenmarkt und ihre rechtliche Verfassung* (Nomos 2000)

Burgard, Ulrich, and Carsten Heimann, 'Bankrecht' in M Dauses (ed), *EU-Wirtschaftsrecht* (CH Beck, 36th supplement 2014)

Busuioc, Madalina, 'Accountability, Control and Independence: The Case of European Agencies' (2009) 15 European Law Journal 599

Busuioc, Madalina, 'European Agencies and their Boards: Promises and Pitfalls of Accountability beyond Design' (2012) 19 Journal of European Public Policy 719

Busuioc, Madalina, 'Rule-Making by the European Financial Supervisory Authorities: Walking a Tight Rope' (2013) 19 European Law Journal 111

Chamon, Merijn, 'EU Agencies between Meroni and Romano or the Devil and the Deep Blue Sky' (2011) 48 Common Market Law Review 1055

Chang, Michele, 'The rising Power of the ECB: the Case of the Single Supervisory Mechanism' (2015) (European Union Studies Association Conference, Boston, 5–7 March 2015)

Chiti, Edoardo, 'An Important Part of the EU's Institutional Machinery: Features, Problems and Perspectives of European Agencies' (2009) 46 Common Market Law Review 1395

Chiti, Edoardo, 'EU and Global administrative Organizations' in E Chiti and B Mattarella (eds), *Global Administrative Law and EU Administrative Law: Relationships, Legal Issues and Comparison* (Springer 2011)

Chiti, Edoardo, 'Existe-t-il un modèle d'Agence de l'Union européenne?' in J Molinier (ed), *Les agences de l'Union européenne* (Bruylant 2011)

Chiti, Edoardo, 'Agencies' Rulemaking: Powers, Procedures and Assessment' (2013) 19 European Law Journal 93

Chiti, Edoardo, and Pedro Gustavo Teixeira, 'The Constitutional Implications of the European Responses to the Financial and Public Debt Crisis' (2013) 50 Common Market Law Review 683

Christiansen, Thomas, and Mathias Dobbels, 'Non-Legislative Rule Making after the Lisbon Treaty: Implementing the New System of Comitology and Delegated Acts' (2013) 19 European Law Journal 42

Comte, Françoise, '2008 Commission Communication "European Agencies – the Way Forward": What is the Follow-Up Since Then?' (2010) 3 Review of European Administrative Law 65

Craig, Paul, *EU Administrative Law* (Oxford University Press 2006)

Craig, Paul, 'Delegated Acts, Implementing Acts and the New Comitology Regulation' (2011) 36 European Law Review 671

Craig, Paul, 'Institutions, Power and Institutional Balance' in P Craig and G de Búrca (eds), *The Evolution of EU Law* (2nd edn, Oxford University Press 2011)

Craig, Paul, *EU Administrative Law* (2nd edn, Oxford University Press 2012)

Craig, Paul, and Grainne de Búrca, *EU Law. Text, Cases, and Materials* (6th edn, Oxford University Press 2015)

Cremer, Wolfgang, 'Zum Rechtsschutz des Einzelnen gegen abgeleitetes Unionsrecht nach dem Vertrag von Lissabon' (2010) 2 Zeitschrift für öffentliches Recht und Verwaltungswissenschaft 58

Curtin, Deirdre, 'Delegation to EU Non-majoritarian Agencies and Emerging Practices of Public Accountability' in D Geradin, R Muñoz and N Petit (eds), *Regulation through Agencies in the EU: A New Paradigm of European Governance* (Edward Elgar 2005)

Curtin, Deirdre, *Executive Power of the European Union: Law, Practices, and the Living Constitution* (Oxford University Press 2009)

Curtin, Deirdre, 'Holding (Quasi-) Autonomous EU Administrative Actors to Public Account' (2007) 13 European Law Journal 523

Curtin, Deirdre, and Renaud Dehousse, 'European Union agencies: tipping the balance?' in M Busuioc, M Groenleer and J Trondal (eds), *The agency phenomenon in the European Union. Emergence, institutionalization and everyday decision-making* (Manchester University Press 2012)

Curtin, Deirdre, Herwig Hofmann and Joana Mendes, 'Constitutionalising EU Executive Rule-Making Procedures: A Research Agenda' (2013) 19 European Law Journal 1

Curtin, Gerard, 'Regulation 1210/90: Establishment of the European Environment Agency' (1991) 14 Boston College International and Comparative Law Review 321

Daiber, Birgit, 'EU-Durchführungsrechtsetzung nach Inkrafttreten der neuen Komitologie-Verordnung' (2012) 2 Europarecht 240

Dammann, Amina, *Die Beschwerdekammern der europäischen Agenturen* (Peter Lang 2004)

Dawson, Mark, 'Three Waves of New Governance in the European Union' (2011) 36 European Law Review 208

Dehousse, Renaud, 'Constitutional Reform in the European Community: Are there Alternatives to the Majoritarian Avenue?' in J Hayward (ed), *The Crisis of Representation in Europe* (Frank Cass 1995)

Dehousse, Renaud, 'Regulation by networks in the European Community: the role of European agencies' (1997) 42 Journal of European Public Policy 246

Dehousse, Renaud, 'The Politics of Delegation in the European Union' (2013) 4 Les Cahiers Européens de Sciences Po. 1

Dehousse, Renaud, Ana Fernández Pasarín and Joan Plaza, 'How consensual is comitology?' (2014) 21 Journal of European Public Policy 842

Dobbels, Mathias, 'Non-Legislative Rule Making after the Lisbon Treaty: Implementing the New System of Comitology and Delegated Acts' (2013) 19 European Law Journal 42

Dörr, Oliver, 'Art. 263 AEUV' in E Grabitz, M Hilf and M Nettesheim (ed), *Das Recht der Europäischen Union* (CH Beck 2015)

Dragomir, Larisa, *European Prudential Banking Regulation and Supervision. The legal dimension* (Routledge 2010)

Dullien, Sebastian, and Hansjörg Herr, 'Die EU-Finanzmarktreform. Stand und Perspektiven im Frühjahr 2010' (2010) Friedrich Ebert Stiftung 1 <http://library.fes.de/pdf-files/id/ipa/07157.pdf> accessed 21 November 2015

Dumbrovsky, Tomas, 'Czech Republic' (EUI Project Constitutional Change through Euro Crisis Law) <http://eurocrisislaw.eui.eu/czech-republic/> accessed 21 November 2015

Egeberg, Morten, Jarle Trondal and Nina Vestlund, 'Situating EU Agencies in the Political-Administrative Space' (2014) ARENA Working Paper 6

Ehlermann, Claus-Dieter, 'Institutionelle Probleme im Bereich der Durchführung des abgeleiteten Gemeinschaftsrechts' (1971) 6 Europarecht 250

Ehlermann, Claus-Dieter, 'Die Errichtung des Europäischen Fonds für währungspolitische Zusammenarbeit' (1973) 8 Europarecht 193

Elsen, Jochen, 'Die Befugnisse und Tätigkeiten der deutschen Bundesanstalt für Finanzdienstleistungsaufsicht (BaFin) mit dem Schwerpunkt auf der Finanzmarktaufsicht und aktuelle Herausforderungen' in N Bodiroga-Vukobrat, G Sander and S Barić (eds), *Regulierungsagenturen im Spannungsfeld von Recht und Ökonomie.* [*Regulatory Agencies in the Tension Between Law and Economics*] (Verlag Dr. Kovač 2012)

Eriksson, Andrea, *Einheitlicher Europäischer Bankenaufsichtsmechanismus (EAM). Von den Vorschlägen der Kommission zur politischen Einigung im Rat* (Infobrief PE 6 – 3010 – 005/13 der wissenschaftlichen Dienste des Deutschen Bundestages 2013)

EurActiv (3 March 2009) <www.euractiv.com/financial-services/ecb-official-airs-doubts-larosire-report/article-179890> accessed 4 December 2012

Everson, Michelle, 'Independent Agencies: Hierarchy Beaters?' (1995) 1 European Law Journal 180

Everson, Michelle, 'The Constitutionalisation of European Administrative Law: Legal Oversight of a Stateless Internal Market' in C Joerges and E Vos (eds), *EU Committees: Social Regulation, Law and Politics* (Hart Publishing 1999)

Everson, Michelle, 'Good Governance and European Agencies: The Balance' in D Geradin, R Muñoz and N Petit (eds), *Regulation through Agencies in the EU: A New Paradigm of European Governance* (Edward Elgar 2005)

Everson, Michelle, 'Agencies: the "dark hour" of the executive?' in H Hofmann and A Türk (eds), *Legal Challenges in EU Administrative Law* (Edward Elgar 2009)

Everson, Michelle, 'Three intimate tales of law and science: hope, despair and transcendence' in M Everson and E Vos (eds), *Uncertain Risks Regulated* (Routledge Cavendish 2009)

Everson, Michelle, and Christian Joerges, 'Re-conceptualising Europeanisation as a public law of collisions: comitology, agencies and an interactive public adjudication' in H Hofmann and A Türk (eds), *EU Administrative Governance* (Edward Elgar 2006)

Everson, Michelle, and Giandomenico Majone, 'European Agencies Within the Treaties of the European Union' in G Majone (project director), *The Role of Specialised Agencies in Decentralising EU Governance* (Report Presented to the Commission, 1999)

Everson, Michelle, and Ellen Vos, 'The scientification of politics and the politicisation of science' in M Everson and E Vos (eds), *Uncertain Risks Regulated* (Routledge Cavendish 2009)

Fahey, Elaine, 'Does the Emperor Have Financial Crisis Clothes? Reflections on the Legal Basis of the European Banking Authority' (2011) 74 Modern Law Review 581

Falke, Josef, 'Komitologie – Entwicklung, Rechtsgrundlagen und erste empirische Annäherung' in C Joerges and J Falke (eds), *Das Ausschußwesen der Europäischen Union: Praxis der Risikoregulierung im Binnenmarkt und ihre rechtliche Verfassung* (Nomos 2000)

Ferran, Eilís, 'European Banking Union and the EU Single Financial Market: more differentiated integration, or disintegration?' (2014) 29 University of Cambridge Faculty of Law Research Paper 1

Ferran, Eilís, and Kern Alexander, 'Can Soft Law Bodies be Effective? The Special Case of the European Systemic Risk Board' (2010) 35 European Law Review 751

Ferran, Eilís, and Valia Babis, 'The European Single Supervisory Mechanism' (2013) 10 Legal Studies Research Paper Series 1

Fischer zu Cramburg, Ralf, 'Europäischer Rat beschließt Kompromiss zum Lamfalussy-Verfahren' (2008) 2 Neue Zeitschrift für Gesellschaftsrecht 64

Fischer-Appelt, Dorothee, *Agenturen der Europäischen Gemeinschaft* (Duncker & Humblot 1999)

Fischer-Lescano, Andreas, and Lukas Oberndorfer, 'Fiskalvertrag und Unionsrecht. Unionsrechtliche Grenzen völkervertraglicher Fiskalregulierung und Organleihe' (2013) 1–2 Neue Juristische Wochenschrift 9

Fleischer, Julia, 'Die europäischen Agenturen als Diener vieler Herren? Zur Steuerung und Rolle von EU-Agenturen' in W Jann und M Döhler (eds), *Agencies in Westeuropa* (VS Verlag für Sozialwissenschaften 2007)

Follesdal, Andreas, and Simon Hix, 'Why There is a Democratic Deficit in the EU: A Response to Majone and Moravcsik' (2006) 44 Journal of Common Market Studies 533

Friedman, Jeffrey (ed), *What Caused the Financial Crisis?* (University of Pennsylvania Press 2011)

Friese, Brigitte, 'Europäisches Zulassungssystem und gegenseitiges Anerkennungsverfahren' in P Dieners and U Reese (eds), *Handbuch des Pharmarechts* (CH Beck 2010)

Gal, Jens, 'Legitimationsdefizite und Kompetenzen der EIOPA im Lichte der Meroni-Rechtsprechung' (2013) 102 Zeitschrift für die gesamte Versicherungswissenschaft 325

Gause, Bernhard, 'Laufende Rechts- und Finanzaufsicht' in T Langheid and M Wandt (eds), *Münchener Kommentar zum Versicherungsvertragsgesetz*, vol I (CH Beck 2010)

Geradin, Damien, 'The Development of European Regulatory Agencies: Lessons from the American Experience' in D Geradin, R Muñoz and N Petit (eds), *Regulation through Agencies in the EU: A New Paradigm of European Governance* (Edward Elgar 2005)

Geradin, Damien, and Nicolas Petit, 'The Development of Agencies at EU and National Levels: Conceptual Analysis and Proposals for Reform' (2004) Jean Monnet Working Paper 1/2004 <http://jeanmonnetprogram.org/archive/papers/04/040101.pdf> accessed 21 November 2015

Gilardi, Fabrizio, 'Principal-Agent Models Go to Europe: Independent Regulatory Agencies as Ultimate Step of Delegation' (ECPR General Conference, Canterbury, September 2001) <http://citeseerx.ist.psu.edu/viewdoc/download?doi=10.1.1.202.2258&rep=rep1&type=pdf> accessed 21 November 2015

Gjerstad, Steven, and Vernon Smith, 'Monetary Policy, Credit Extension, and Housing Bubbles, 2008 and 1929' in J Friedman (ed), *What caused the Financial Crisis* (University of Pennsylvania Press 2011)

Gleske, Leonhard, 'Stand und Zukunftsperspektiven der Wirtschafts- und Währungsunion' (1974) 9 Europarecht 17

Görisch, Christoph, *Demokratische Verwaltung durch Unionsagenturen* (Mohr Siebeck 2009)

Granner, Georg, 'Unionsrechtliche Grundlagen der Wertpapieraufsicht' in M Gruber and N Raschauer (eds), *WAG-Wertpapieraufsichtsgesetz* (LexisNexis ARD Orac 2011)

Griller, Stefan, '"Verfassungsinterpretation" in der Europäischen Union' in G Lienbacher (ed), *Verfassungsinterpretation in Europa. Heinz Schäffer Gedächtnissymposion* (Jan Sramek Verlag 2011)

Griller, Stefan, 'Art. 127 AEUV' in E Grabitz, M Hilf and M Nettesheim (ed), *Das Recht der Europäischen Union* (CH Beck 2012)

Griller, Stefan, and Andreas Orator, 'Meroni Revisited – Empowering European Agencies between Efficiency and Legitimacy' (2007) 04/D40 NEWGOV <www.eu-newgov.org/database/DELIV/D04D40_WP_Meroni_Revisited.pdf> accessed 21 November 2015

Griller, Stefan, and Andreas Orator, 'Everything under control? The "way forward" for European agencies in the footsteps of the Meroni doctrine' (2010) 35 European Law Review 3

Groenleer, Martijn, *The Autonomy of European Union Agencies. A Comparative Study of Institutional Development* (Eburon 2009)

Groß, Thomas, 'Exekutive Vollzugsprogrammierung durch tertiäres Gemeinschaftsrecht?' (2004) 1 Zeitschrift für öffentliches Recht und Verwaltungswissenschaft 20

Gundel, Jörg, 'Rechtsschutz gegen Handlungen der EG-Agenturen – endlich geklärt?' (2009) 3 Europarecht 383

Gundel, Jörg, 'Die energiepolitischen Kompetenzen der EU nach dem Vertrag von Lissabon: Bedeutung und Reichweite des neuen Art. 194 AEUV' [2011] Europäisches Wirtschafts- und Steuerrecht 25

Gurlit, Elke, 'The ECB's relationship to the EBA' (2013) 1 Europäische Zeitschrift für Wirtschaftsrecht (Beilage) 14

Häde, Ulrich, 'Jenseits der Effizienz: Wer kontrolliert die Kontrolleure?' (2011) 17 Europäische Zeitschrift für Wirtschaftsrecht 662

Haentjens, Matthias, 'Bank Recovery and Resolution: An Overview of International Initiatives' (2014) 3 International Insolvency Law Review 255

Hancox, Emily, 'United Kingdom' (EUI Project Constitutional Change through Euro Crisis Law) <http://eurocrisislaw.eui.eu/uk/> accessed 21 November 2015

Harcourt, Alison, 'Institutionalizing Soft Governance in the European Information Society' in D Ward (ed), *The European Union and the Culture Industries. Regulation and the Public Interest* (Ashgate Publishing 2008)

Hardacre, Alan, and Michael Kaeding, 'Delegated & Implementing Acts: The New Comitology' (2011) EIPA Essential Guide (Version 3)

Harlow, Carol, *Accountability in the European Union* (Oxford University Press 2002)

Hart, Herbert, 'Positivism and the Separation of Law and Morals' (1958) 71 Harvard Law Review 593

Herdegen, Matthias, *Bankenaufsicht im Europäischen Verbund. Banking supervision within the European Union* (de Gruyter 2010)

Hertig, Gérard, and Ruben Lee, 'Four Predictions about the Future of EU Securities Legislation' (January 2003) 8 <www.oecd.org/finance/financial-markets/18469 147.pdf> accessed 21 November 2015

Hertig, Gérard, Ruben Lee and Joseph McCahery, 'Empowering the ECB to Supervise Banks: A Choice-Based Approach' (2010) 2 European Company and Financial Law Review 171

Hilf, Meinhard, *Die Organisationsstruktur der Europäischen Gemeinschaften* (Springer 1982)

Hofmann, Herwig, *Normenhierarchien im europäischen Gemeinschaftsrecht* (Duncker & Humblot 2000)

Hofmann, Herwig, 'Composite Decision Making Procedures in EU Administrative Law' in H Hofmann and A Türk (eds), *Legal Challenges in EU Administrative Law. Towards an Integrated Administration* (Edward Elgar 2009)

Hofmann, Herwig, Gerard Rowe and Alexander Türk, *Administrative Law and Policy of the European Union* (Oxford University Press 2011)

Hummer, Waldemar, 'Von der "Agentur" zum "Interinstitutionellen Amt"' in S Hammer, M Stelzer and B Weichselbaum (eds), *Demokratie und sozialer Rechtsstaat in Europa: Festschrift für Theo Öhlinger* (Wiener Universitätsverlag 2004)

Hustedt, Thurid, Arndt Wonka, Michael Blauberger, Annette Töller and Renate Reiter, *Verwaltungsstrukturen in der Europäischen Union. Kommission, Komitologie, Agenturen und Verwaltungsnetzwerke* (Springer 2014)

Ilgner, Theresa, *Die Durchführung der Rechtsakte des europäischen Gesetzgebers durch die Europäische Kommission. Art. 290 und Art. 291 AEUV und deren Auswirkungen auf die Komitologie* (Duncker & Humblot 2014)

Inwinkl, Petra, 'Zum geplanten Rechtsrahmen der neuen Europäischen Finanzaufsicht' (2010) 11 Zeitschrift für Recht und Rechnungswesen 330

Joerges, Christian, 'Die Europäische "Komitologie": Kafkaeske Bürokratie oder Beispiel "deliberativen Regierens" im Binnenmarkt' in C Joerges and J Falke (eds), *Das Ausschußwesen der Europäischen Union: Praxis der Risikoregulierung im Binnenmarkt und ihre rechtliche Verfassung* (Nomos 2000)

Joss, Simon, 'Public participation in science and technology policy- and decision-making – ephemeral phenomenon or lasting change?' (1999) 26 Science and Public Policy 290

Kaeding, Michael, and Alan Hardacre, 'The European Parliament and the Future of Comitology after Lisbon' (2013) 19 European Law Journal 382

Kahl, Arno, 'Das Single Rulebook als wesentlicher Bestandteil des Finanzmarktregulierungsverbunds im europäischen Mehrebenensystem nach dem Vertrag von Lissabon' (2011) publiclaw.at online publications 20

Kahl, Arno, 'Europäische Aufsichtsbehörden und technische Regulierungsstandards' in P Braumüller, D Ennöckl, M Gruber and N Raschauer (eds), *Die neue europäische Finanzmarktaufsicht. Band zur ZFR-Jahrestagung 2011* (LexisNexis ARD Orac 2012)

Kalss, Susanne, 'Kapitalmarktrecht' in K Riesenhuber (ed), *Europäische Methodenlehre* (de Gruyter 2010)

Kämmerer, Jörn, 'Das neue Europäische Finanzaufsichtssystem (ESFS) – Modell für eine europäisierte Verwaltungsarchitektur?' (2011) Neue Zeitschrift für Verwaltungsrecht 1281

Kämmerer, Jörn, 'Bahn frei der Bankenunion? Die neuen Aufsichtsbefugnisse der EZB im Lichte der EU-Kompetenzordnung' (2013) 13 Neue Zeitschrift für Verwaltungsrecht 830

Karpf, Alexander, Corina Weidinger-Sosdean and Karin Zartl, 'Die Integration der Finanzmärkte der EU – Die Rolle von CESR, CEBS und CEIOPS im Lamfalussy-Prozess' (2007) 1 Zeitschrift für Finanzmarktrecht 6

Kassim, Hussein, and Anand Menon, 'The principal-agent approach and the study of the European Union: promise unfulfilled?' (2003) 10 Journal of European Public Policy 121

Kelemen, Daniel, 'The Politics of "Eurocratic" Structure and the New European Agencies' (2002) 25 West European Politics 93

Kelemen, Daniel, and Andrew Tarrant, 'The Political Foundations of the Eurocracy'

(2011) West European Politics 922

Kenen, Peter, *Economic and Monetary Union in Europe: Moving beyond Maastricht* (Cambridge University Press 1995)

Kirste, Stephan, 'Das System der Europäischen Agenturen: Erläutert am Beispiel des Europäischen Innovations- und Technologieinstituts (EIT)' (2011) 2 Verwaltungsarchiv 273

Klamert, Marcus, 'Altes und Neues zur Harmonisierung im Binnenmarkt' (2015) 7 Europäische Zeitschrift für Wirtschaftsrecht 265

Klaushofer, Reinhard, 'Bankenaufsicht durch die EZB – ein primärrechtlicher Grenzgang' (2014) 22 Journal für Rechtspolitik 102

Kleine, Andreas, *Entscheidungstheoretische Aspekte der Principal-Agent-Theorie* (Physica-Verlag 1996)

Klinke, Andreas, 'Inclusive risk governance through discourse, deliberation and participation' in M Everson and E Vos (eds), *Uncertain Risks Regulated* (Routledge Cavendish 2009)

Knight, Frank, *Risk, Uncertainty and Profit* (Houghton Mifflin 1921)

Koenig, Christian, Sascha Loetz and Sonja Fechtner, 'Do we really need a European agency for market regulation?' (2008) 43 Intereconomics 226

Kohler-Koch, Beate, and Berthold Rittberger, 'The "Governance Turn" in EU Studies' (2006) 44 Journal of Common Market Studies 27

Kohtamäki, Natalia, *Die Reform der Bankenaufsicht in der Europäischen Union* (Mohr Siebeck 2012)

Kolassa, Doris, '§ 139. Fragen der praktischen Umsetzung' in H Schimansky, H-J Bunte, H-J Lwowski (eds), *Bankrechts-Handbuch* (4th edn, CH Beck 2011)

Korinek, Stephan, 'Praxisrelevante Tätigkeitsfelder von Agenturen: Finanzmarktrecht' in N Raschauer (ed), *Europäische Agenturen* (Jan Sramek Verlag 2012)

Kreher, Alexander, 'Agencies in the European Community – a step towards administrative integration in Europe' (1997) 4 Journal of European Public Policy 225

Kreisl, Rene, and Nicolas Raschauer, 'Vor- und Nachhandelstransparenz' in E Brandl, S Kalss, O Lucius, G Saria (eds), *Handbuch Kapitalmarktrecht*, vol III (Springer 2006)

Kröll, Thomas, 'Artikel 290 und 291 AEUV – Neue vertragliche Grundlagen der Rechtsetzung durch die Europäische Kommission' in A Debus, F Kruse, A Peters, H Schröder, O Seifert, C Sicko and I Stirn (eds), *Verwaltungsrechtsraum Europa* (Nomos 2011)

Kühling, Jürgen, 'Die Zukunft des Europäischen Agentur(un)wesens – oder: Wer hat Angst vor Meroni?' (2008) 5 Europäische Zeitschrift für Wirtschaftsrecht 129

Kuhn, Thomas, *The structure of scientific revolutions* (2nd edn, University of Chicago Press 1970)

Ladler, Mona, 'Finanzmarktregulierung in der Krise oder die Krise der Finanzmarktregulierung? Kritische Anmerkungen zur Übertragung der Banken- und Finanzaufsicht auf die EZB' (2013) 6 Zeitschrift für das Privatrecht der Europäischen Union 328

Ladler, Mona, *Finanzmarkt und institutionelle Finanzaufsicht in der EU* (Manz 2014)

Laffont, Jean-Jacques, and David Martimort, *The Theory of Incentives. The Principal-Agent Model* (Princeton University Press 2009)

Lannoo, Karel, 'Supervising the European Financial System' in P Cecchini, F Heinemann and M Jopp (eds), *The Incomplete Market for Financial Services* (Springer 2003)

Lannoo, Karel, 'The road ahead after de Larosière' (2009) 195 CEPS Policy Brief 5

Lastra, Rosa, 'The Governance Structure for Financial Regulation and Supervision in Europe' (2003) The London Financial Regulation Seminar (London School of Economics and Political Science) <www2.lse.ac.uk/fmg/documents/special-Papers/2003/sp149.pdf> accessed 21 November 2015

Lavrijssen, Saskia, and Annetje Ottow, 'Independent Supervisory Authorities: A Fragile Concept' (2012) 39 Legal Issues of Economic Integration 419

Lehmann, Matthias, and Cornelia Manger-Nestler, 'Die Vorschläge zur neuen Architektur der europäischen Finanzaufsicht' (2010) 3 Europäische Zeitschrift für Wirtschaftsrecht 87

Levi-Faur, David, 'Regulation & Regulatory Governance' (2010) Jerusalem Papers in Regulation & Governance 1/2010 <http://levifaur.wiki.huji.ac.il/images/Reg.pdf> accessed 21 November 2015

Lutter, Marcus, Walter Bayer and Jessica Schmidt, *Europäisches Unternehmens- und Kapitalmarktrecht* (5th edn, de Gruyter 2012)

Maggetti, Martino, and Fabrizio Gilardi, 'The policy-making structure of European regulatory networks and the domestic adoption of standards' (2011) 18 Journal of European Public Policy 830

Magiera, Siegfried, and Wolfgang Weiß, 'Alternative Dispute Resolution Mechanisms in the European Union Law' in D Dragos and B Neamtu (eds), *Alternative Dispute Resolution in European Administrative Law* (Springer 2014)

Majone, Giandomenico, 'The New European Agencies: Regulation by Information' (1997) 4 Journal of European Public Policy 262

Majone, Giandomenico, 'Two Logics of Delegation. Agency and Fiduciary Relations in EU Governance' (2001) 2 European Union Politics 103

Majone, Giandomenico, 'Delegation of Regulatory Powers in a Mixed Polity' (2002) 8 European Law Journal 319

Majone, Giandomenico, *Dilemmas of European integration. The ambiguities and pitfalls of integration by stealth* (Oxford University Press 2005)

Majone, Giandomenico, 'Managing Europeanization: The European Agencies' in J Peterson and M Shackleton (eds), *The Institutions of the European Union* (2nd edn, Oxford University Press 2006)

Marjosola, Heikki, 'Bridging the Constitutional Gap in EU Executive Rule-Making: The Court of Justice Approves Legislative Conferral of Intervention Powers to European Securities Markets Authority: Court of Justice of the European Union (Grand Chamber) Judgment of 22 January 2014, Case C-270/12, UK v. Parliament and Council (Grand Chamber)' (2014) 10 European Constitutional Law Review 500

Marjosola, Heikki, 'Case C-270/12 (UK v. Parliament and Council) – Stress Testing Constitutional Resilience of the Powers of EU Financial Supervisory Authorities – A Critical Assessment of the Advocate General's Opinion' (2014) 2 EUI Department of Law Research Paper

Masciandaro, Donato, 'The European Banking Authority: Are its governance arrangements consistent with its objectives?' (VOX 2011) <www.voxeu.org/index.php?q=node/6084> accessed 21 November 2015

Michael, Bryane, 'The "Twin Peaks" Regulatory Model: The Future of Financial Regulation' (2014) BankingTODAY (March/April 2014)

Michel, Katja, 'Die neue Europäische Bankenaufsichtsbehörde' (2011) 18 Zeitschrift für öffentliches Recht und Verwaltungswissenschaft 728

Michel, Katja, *Institutionelles Gleichgewicht und EU-Agenturen. Eine Analyse unter besonderer Berücksichtigung der European Banking Authority* (Duncker & Humblot 2015)

Möllers, Christoph, 'Durchführung des Gemeinschaftsrechts – Vertragliche Dogmatik und theoretische Implikationen' (2002) 4 Europarecht 483

Möllers, Thomas, 'Auf dem Weg zu einer neuen europäischen Finanzmarktaufsichtsstruktur. Ein systematischer Vergleich der Rating-VO (EG) Nr. 1060/2009 mit der geplanten ESMA-VO' (2010) 8 Neue Zeitschrift für Gesellschaftsrecht 285

Moloney, Niamh, 'New Frontiers in EC Capital Markets Law: From Market Construction to Market Regulation' (2003) 40 Common Market Law Review 809

Moloney, Niamh, 'The Lamfalussy Legislative Model: A New Era For The EC Securities And Investment Services Regime' (2003) 52 International and Comparative Law Quarterly 509

Moloney, Niamh, 'EU Financial Market Regulation after the Global Financial Crisis: "More Europe" or More Risks?' (2010) 47 Common Market Law Review 1317

Moloney, Niamh, 'The Financial Crisis and EU Securities Law-Making: A Challenge Met?' in S Grundmann, B Haar, H Merkt, P Mülbert and M Wellendorfer (eds), *Festschrift für Klaus J. Hopt zum 70. Geburtstag am 24. August 2010* (de Gruyter 2010)

Moloney, Niamh, 'The European Securities and Markets Authority and Institutional Design for the EU Financial Market – A Tale of Two Competences: Part (2) Rules in Action' (2011) 12 European Business Organization Law Review 177

Moloney, Niamh, 'European Banking Union: Assessing its Risks and Resilience' (2014) 51 Common Market Law Review 1609

Morand, Charles-Albert, *La législation dans les Communautés européennes* (Pichon & Durand-Auzias 1968)

Müller, Bernd, *Verwaltungsrecht. Schnell erfasst* (Springer 2004) <http://link.springer.com/chapter/10.1007/978-3-662-10789-8_1> accessed 21 November 2015

Müller, Bernhard, '"Agentur hat Konjunktur" – "Agencification" und demokratische Verwaltungslegitimation' in G Lienbacher and G Wielinger (eds), *Öffentliches Recht. Jahrbuch 2011* (Neuer Wissenschaftlicher Verlag 2011)

Müller, Thomas, 'Soft Law im europäischen Wirtschaftsrecht – unionsverfassungsrechtliche Grundfragen' (2014) 22 Journal für Rechtspolitik 112

Nehl, Hanns, 'Good administration as procedural right and/or general principle?' in H Hofmann and A Türk (eds), *Legal Challenges in EU Administrative Law* (Edward Elgar 2009)

Nettesheim, Martin, 'Art. 288 AEUV' in E Grabitz, M Hilf and M Nettesheim (ed), *Das Recht der Europäischen Union* (CH Beck 2012)

Nettesheim, Martin, 'Art. 290 AEUV' in E Grabitz, M Hilf and M Nettesheim (ed), *Das Recht der Europäischen Union* (CH Beck 2012)

Nettesheim, Martin, 'Art. 13 EUV' in E Grabitz, M Hilf and M Nettesheim (ed), *Das Recht der Europäischen Union* (CH Beck 2015)

Nickles, Thomas (ed), *Scientific discovery, logic, and rationality* (Reidel 1980)

Ohler, Christoph, 'Rechtmäßige Errichtung der Gemeinschaftsagentur ENISA' (2006) 17 Europäische Zeitschrift für Wirtschaftsrecht 369

Orator, Andreas, *Möglichkeiten und Grenzen der Einrichtung von Unionsagenturen* (doctoral thesis, University of Vienna 2011)

Orator, Andreas, 'Die unionsrechtliche Zulässigkeit von Eingriffsbefugnissen der ESMA im Bereich von Leerverkäufen' (2013) 22 Europäische Zeitschrift für Wirtschaftsrecht 852

Pabel, Katharina, 'Europäische Agenturen: Rechtsschutz' in N Raschauer (ed), *Europäische Agenturen* (Jan Sramek Verlag 2012)

Palmstorfer, Rainer, 'The Reverse Majority Voting under the "Six Pack": A Bad Turn for the Union?' (2014) 20 European Law Journal 186

Part, Sigrid, and Melitta Schütz, 'Reform der nationalen und EU-Finanzmärkte: Endlich effiziente Rahmenbedingungen?' (2010) 1 Bankarchiv 33

Pawlik, Martin, *Das REACH-System und die Meroni-Doktrin. Ein imperfekter Quantensprung im Europäischen Verwaltungsverbund* (Nomos 2013)

Pechstein, Matthias, and Carola Drechsler, 'Die Auslegung und Fortbildung des Primärrechts' in K Riesenhuber (ed), *Europäische Methodenlehre* (de Gruyter 2010)

Pelkmans, Jacques, 'Single Market: Deepening and Widening over Time' (2011) 2 Intereconomics 64 <www.intereconomics.eu/archive/year/2011/2/> accessed 21 November 2015

Pflock, Thomas, *Europäische Bankenregulierung und das 'Too big to fail-Dilemma'* (Berliner Wissenschaftlicher Verlag 2014)

Pierre, Jon, and B. Guy Peters, *Governance, Politics and the State* (Macmillan 2000)

Piris, Jean-Claude, *The Future of Europe. Towards a Two-Speed EU?* (Cambridge University Press 2012)

Pisani-Ferry, Jean, André Sapir and Guntram Wolff, *EU-IMF assistance to euro-area countries: an early assessment* (Bruegel Blueprint Series, vol XIX, 2013)

Pötzsch, Thorsten, 'Reform der Europäischen Finanzaufsichtsstrukturen' in S Grundmann, B Haar, H Merkt, P Mülbert and M Wellendorfer (eds), *Festschrift für Klaus J. Hopt zum 70. Geburtstag am 24. August 2010* (de Gruyter 2010)

Priebe, Reinhard, *Entscheidungsbefugnisse vertragsfremder Einrichtungen im Europäischen Gemeinschaftsrecht* (Nomos 1979)

Quaglia, Lucia, *Central Banking Governance in the European Union: A comparative analysis* (Routledge 2008)

Raschauer, Bernhard, 'Subnormative Verhaltenssteuerungen' in M Akyürek, G Baumgartner, D Jahnel, G Lienbacher and H Stolzlechner (eds), *Staat und Recht in europäischer Perspektive. Festschrift Heinz Schäffer* (Manz / CH Beck 2006)

Raschauer, Bernhard, 'Verfahren der Rechtsetzung im europäischen Finanzmarktrecht' in P Braumüller, D Ennöckl, M Gruber and N Raschauer (eds), *Die neue europäische Finanzmarktaufsicht. Band zur ZFR-Jahrestagung 2011* (LexisNexis ARD Orac 2012)

Raschauer, Bernhard, '"Leitlinien" europäischer Agenturen' (2013) Österreichische Zeitschrift für Wirtschaftsrecht 34

Raschauer, Nicolas, *Aktuelle Strukturprobleme des europäischen und österreichischen Bankenaufsichtsrechts* (Springer 2010)

Raschauer, Nicolas, 'Verfahren der abgeleiteten Rechtsetzung im EU-Finanzmarktrecht nach dem Vertrag von Lissabon' (2011) 4 Zeitschrift für Finanzmarktrecht 159

Raschauer, Nicolas, 'Europäische Behördenkooperation in der Finanzmarktregulierung' in M Holoubek and M Lang (eds), *Verfahren der Zusammenarbeit von Verwaltungsbehörden in Europa* (Linde 2012)

Raschauer, Nicolas, 'Aufsicht, Kontrolle und parlamentarische Verwaltung in der "Agency-Verwaltung"' (2015) Spektrum der Rechtswissenschaft 74

Remmert, Barbara, 'Die Gründung von Einrichtungen der mittelbaren Gemeinschaftsverwaltung' (2003) 1 Europarecht 134

Renn, Ortwin, *Risk Governance. Coping with Uncertainty in a Complex World* (Earthscan 2008)

Riedel, Daniel, *Die Gemeinschaftszulassung für Luftfahrtgerät. Europäisches Verwalten durch Agenturen am Beispiel der EASA* (Duncker & Humblot 2006)

Riedel, Daniel, 'Rechtsschutz gegen Akte Europäischer Agenturen' (2009) Europäische Zeitschrift für Wirtschaftsrecht 565

Riesz, Thomas, 'Europäische Gesundheitsagenturen – zugleich ein Beitrag zum Europäischen Arzneimittelzulassungssystem' in N Raschauer (ed), *Europäische Agenturen* (Jan Sramek Verlag 2012)

Risse, Thomas, 'The Political, the State, and Governance: Reflections on Essentially Contested Concepts' in W Steinmetz, I Gilcher-Holtey, H-G Haupt (eds), *Writing Political History Today* (Campus Verlag 2013)

Ritleng, Dominique, 'The dividing line between delegated and implementing acts: The Court of Justice sidesteps the difficulty in Commission v. Parliament and Council (Biocides)' (2015) 52 Common Market Law Review 243

Roberts, Simon, and Michael Palmer, *Dispute Processes: ADR and the Primary Forms of Decision-Making* (2nd edn, Cambridge University Press 2005)

Roller, Gerhard, 'Komitologie und Demokratieprinzip' (2003) 2 Kritische Vierteljahresschrift für Gesetzgebung und Rechtswissenschaft 249

Rötting, Michael, and Christina Lang, 'Das Lamfalussy-Verfahren im Umfeld der Neuordnung der europäischen Finanzaufsichtsstrukturen' (2012) 1 Europäische Zeitschrift für Wirtschaftsrecht 8

Ruffert, Matthias, 'Verselbständigte Verwaltungseinheiten: Ein europäischer Megatrend im Vergleich' in H-H Trute, T Groß, H Röhl and C Möllers (eds), *Allgemeines Verwaltungsrecht – zur Tragfähigkeit eines Konzepts* (Mohr Siebeck 2008)

Ruffert, Matthias, 'Art. 290 AEUV' in C Calliess and M Ruffert (eds), *EUV/AEUV. Das Verfassungsrecht der Europäischen Union mit Europäischer Grundrechtecharta* (4th edn, CH Beck 2011)

Ruffert, Matthias, 'Art. 291 AEUV' in C Calliess and M Ruffert (eds), *EUV/AEUV. Das Verfassungsrecht der Europäischen Union mit Europäischer Grundrechtecharta* (4th edn, CH Beck 2011)

Ruffert, Matthias, 'Art. 298 AEUV' in C Calliess and M Ruffert (eds), *EUV/AEUV. Das Verfassungsrecht der Europäischen Union mit Europäischer Grundrechtecharta* (4th edn, CH Beck 2011)

Russ, Alexander, and Raimund Bollenberger, 'Leitlinien der europäischen Aufsichtsbehörden im Rahmen des ESFS. Rechtsqualität und Auswirkung auf Kundenverträge' (2015) 11 Bankarchiv 806

Sacarcelik, Osman, 'Europäische Bankenunion: Rechtliche Rahmenbedingungen und Herausforderungen der einheitlichen europäischen Bankenaufsicht' (2013) 9 Zeitschrift für Bank- und Kapitalmarktrecht 353

Sander, Peter, 'Europäische Agenturen: Rechtsgrundlagen in und sonstige Berührungspunkte mit dem primären Unionsrecht' in N Raschauer (ed), *Europäische Agenturen* (Jan Sramek Verlag 2012)

Saurer, Johannes, 'Der Rechtsschutz gegen Entscheidungen und Fachgutachten der Europäischen Agenturen nach dem Sogelma-Urteil des EuG' (2009) 16 Deutsches Verwaltungsblatt 1021

Savino, Mario, 'The Constitutional Legitimacy of the EU Committees' (2005) 3 Les Cahiers Européens de Sciences Po. 1

Schaefer, Rupert, 'Neue Agenturen für die EU – die European Financial Supervisory Authorities' in N Bodiroga-Vukobrat, G Sander and S Barić (eds), *Regulierungsagenturen im Spannungsfeld von Recht und Ökonomie. Regulatory Agencies in the Tension Between Law and Economics* (Verlag Dr. Kovač 2012)

Schammo, Pierre, 'The European Securities and Markets Authority: Lifting the veil on the allocation of powers' (2011) 48 Common Market Law Review 1879

Scharf, Daniel, 'Das Komitologieverfahren nach dem Vertrag von Lissabon – Neuerungen und Auswirkungen auf die Gemeinsame Handelspolitik' (2010) 101 Beiträge zum Transnationalen Wirtschaftsrecht

Scharpf, Fritz, 'European Governance: Common Concerns vs. The Challenge of Diversity' (2001) 6 Max-Planck-Institut für Gesellschaftsforschung-Working Paper <www.mpifg.de/pu/workpap/wp01-6/wp01-6.html> accessed 21 November 2015

Schelkle, Waltraud, 'EU Fiscal Governance: Hard Law in the Shadow of Soft Law' (2007) 13 Columbia Journal of European Law 705

Schermers, Henry, and Niels Blokker, *International Institutional Law* (5th edn, Martinus Nijhoff Publishers 2011)

Scheunig, Dieter, Case Annotation 25/70 Einfuhr- und Vorratsstelle für Getreide und Futtermittel v Köster et Berodt & Co (1971) 6 Europarecht 145

Schlögl, Martina, 'Europäische Agenturen im Umweltrecht' in N Raschauer (ed), *Europäische Agenturen* (Jan Sramek Verlag 2012)

Schmid, Klaus-Peter, 'Die unerhörten Experten' Die Zeit (Hamburg, 21 June 1996)

Schmidt-Aßmann, Eberhard, 'Einleitung: Der Europäische Verwaltungsverbund und die Rolle des Europäischen Verwaltungsrechts' in E Schmidt-Aßmann and B Schöndorf-Haubold (eds), *Der Europäische Verwaltungsverbund* (Mohr Siebeck 2005)

Schmolke, Klaus, 'Die Einbeziehung des Komitologieverfahrens in den Lamfalussy-Prozess – Zur Forderung des Europäischen Parlaments nach mehr Entscheidungsteilhabe' (2006) 3 Europarecht 432

Scholten, Miroslava, 'The newly released "Common Approach" on EU agencies: Going forward or standing still?' (2012) 19 Columbia Journal of European Law online 2012

Schout, Adriaan, 'The European Environment Agency (EEA): Heading Towards Maturity?' in G Majone (project director), *The Role of Specialised Agencies in Decentralising EU Governance* (Report Presented to the Commission, 1999)

Schout, Adriaan, 'Framework for assessing the added value of an EU agency' (2011) 31 Journal of Public Policy 363

Schulmeister, Stephan, 'EU-Fiskalpakt: Strangulierung von Wirtschaft und Sozialstaat' <http://stephan.schulmeister.wifo.ac.at/fileadmin/homepage_schulmeister/files/Fiskalpakt_Misere__end_04_12.pdf> accessed 21 November 2015

Schusterschitz, Gregor, and Sabine Kotz, 'The Comitology Reform of 2006 – Increasing the powers of the European Parliament without changing the treaties' (2007) 3 European Constitutional Law Review 68

Schwarze, Jürgen, 'Soft Law im Recht der Europäischen Union' (2011) 1 Europarecht 3

Selmayr, Martin, 'Art. 127 AEUV' in H von der Groeben, J Schwarze and A Hatje (eds), *Europäisches Unionsrecht* (7th edn, Nomos 2015)

Senden, Linda, *Soft Law in European Community Law* (Hart Publishing 2004)

Shapiro, Martin, 'Independent Agencies: US and EU' (1996) 34 Jean Monnet Chair Papers 8

Shapiro, Martin, 'The problems of independent agencies in the United States and the European Union' (1997) 4 Journal of European Public Policy 276

Shapiro, Martin, 'Independent Agencies' in P Craig and G de Búrca (eds), *The Evolution of EU Law* (2nd edn, Oxford University Press 2011)

Shirvani, Foroud, 'New Public Management und europäische Agenturen: Transparenzfragen bei der Modernisierung der Verwaltungsorganisation' (2008) Die öffentliche Verwaltung 1

Sibert, Anne, Systemic Risk and the ESRB (Policy Department Economic and Scientific Policies of the EP 2009) <www.annesibert.co.uk/Dec2009.pdf> accessed 21 November 2015

Siegel, Thorsten, 'Die Widerspruchskammer im System des europäischen Verwaltungsrechtsschutzes – Wesen und Funktionsweise der Widerspruchskammer nach der neuen REACH-Verordnung für Chemikalien' (2008) 5 Europäische Zeitschrift für Wirtschaftsrecht 141

Siekmann, Helmut, 'Die Entstehung des neuen Europäischen Finanzaufsichtssystems' (2010) 40 IMFS Working Paper Series 1

Simoncini, Marta, 'The Erosion of the Meroni Doctrine: The Case of the European Aviation Safety Agency' (2015) 21 European Public Law 309

Skowron, Magdalena, 'Die Zukunft europäischer Agenturen auf dem Prüfstand' (2014) 2 Europarecht 250

Smismans, Stijn, 'Institutional balance as interest representation' in C Joerges and R Dehousse (eds), *Good Governance in Europe's Integrated Market* (Oxford University Press 2002)

Smith, Melanie, 'Inter-institutional dialogue and the establishment of enforcement norms: a decade of financial penalties under Article 228 EC (now 260 TFEU)' (2010) 16 European Public Law 547

Soell, Hermann, *Das Ermessen der Eingriffsverwaltung. Zugleich eine Studie zur richterlichen Ermessenskontrolle im Kartellrecht und zur Bedeutung des détournement de pouvoir im französischen Verwaltungs- und europäischen Gemeinschaftsrecht* (Carl Winter Universitätsverlag 1973)

Sohn, Klaus-Dieter, and Jessica Koch, *Kommentierung der Mitteilung der Kommission [KOM (2009) 673] über die Umsetzung von Artikel 290 des Vertrags über die Arbeitsweise der Europäischen Union* (cepKommentar 2010) <www.cep.eu/ Analysen_KOM/KOM_2009_673_Kommentar_ex-Komitologie/KOM_ 2009-673_Kommentar.pdf> accessed on 21 November 2015

Sonder, Nicolas, 'Die verwaltungsrechtliche Kontrolle von Ratingagenturen im neuen System der europäischen Finanzaufsicht' in A Debus, F Kruse, A Peters, H Schröder, O Seifert, C Sicko and I Stirn (eds), *Verwaltungsrechtsraum Europa* (Nomos 2011)

Speyer, Bernhard, 'Finanzaufsicht in der EU. Inkrementeller Fortschritt, Erfolg ungewiss' (2011) 84 EU-Monitor (Deutsche Bank Research) <www.dbresearch. de/PROD/DBR_INTERNET_DE-PROD/PROD0000000000278252.pdf> accessed 21 November 2015

Stadlmeier, Sigmar, 'Die "Implied Powers" der Europäischen Gemeinschaften' (1997) 52 Zeitschrift für öffentliches Recht 353

Steunenberg, Bernard, Christian Koboldt and Dieter Schmidtchen, 'Comitology and the Balance of Power in the European Union: A Game Theoretic Approach' in D

Schmidtchen and R Cooter (eds), *Constitutional Law and Economics of the European Union* (Edward Elgar 1997)

Stirling, Andy, 'Keep it complex' (2010) 468 Nature 1029

Stolz, Stéphanie, and Michael Wedow, 'Extraordinary measures in extraordinary times. Public measures in support of the financial sector in the EU and the United States' (2010) 117 Occasional Paper Series 1

Storr, Stefan, 'Agenturen und Rechtsschutz' in P Braumüller, D Ennöckl, M Gruber and N Raschauer (eds), *Die neue europäische Finanzmarktaufsicht. Band zur ZFR-Jahrestagung 2011* (LexisNexis ARD Orac 2012)

Suvarierol, Semin, Madalina Busuioc and Martijn Groenleer, 'Working for Europe? Socialization in the European Commission and Agencies of the European Union' (2013) Public Administration 908

Szapiro, Manuel, 'Comitology: the ongoing reform' in H Hofmann and A Türk (eds), *Legal Challenges in EU Administrative Law. Towards an Integrated Administration* (Edward Elgar 2009)

Tallberg, Jonas, 'Delegation to Supranational Institutions: Why, How, and with What Consequences?' (2002) 25 West European Politics 23

Tallberg, Jonas, 'Paths to Compliance: Enforcement, Management, and the European Union' (2002) 56 International Organization 609

Tarrant, Andrew, and Daniel Kelemen, 'Building the Eurocracy: The Politics of EU Agencies and Networks' (Biennial European Union Studies Association Convention, Montréal, 16–19 May 2007) <http://aei.pitt.edu/7931/1/kelemen-d-08h.pdf> accessed 21 November 2015

Thatcher, Mark, 'Delegation to Independent Regulatory Agencies: Pressures, Functions and Contextual Mediations' (2002) 25 West European Politics 125

Thatcher, Mark, 'Independent Regulatory Agencies and Elected Politicians in Europe' in D Geradin, R Muñoz and N Petit (eds), *Regulation through Agencies in the EU: A New Paradigm of European Governance* (Edward Elgar 2006)

Thomas, Stefan, 'Die Bindungswirkung von Mitteilungen, Bekanntmachungen und Leitlinien der EG-Kommission' (2009) 3 Europarecht 423

Tietje, Christian, 'Art. 114 AEUV' in E Grabitz, M Hilf and M Nettesheim (ed), *Das Recht der Europäischen Union* (CH Beck 2011)

Töller, Annette, *Komitologie. Theoretische Bedeutung und praktische Arbeitsweise von Durchführungsausschüssen in der Europäischen Union am Beispiel der Umweltpolitik* (Leske + Budrich 2002)

Tomkin, Jonathan, 'Contradiction, Circumvention and Conceptual Gymnastics: the Impact of the Adoption of the ESM Treaty on the State of European Democracy' in B de Witte, A Héritier and A Trechsel (eds), *The Euro Crisis and the State of European Democracy. Contributions from the 2012 EUDO Dissemination Conference* (European University Institute 2013)

Tridimas, Takis, 'EU Financial Regulation: Federalization, Crisis Management, and Law Reform' in P Craig and G de Búrca (eds), *The Evolution of EU Law* (2nd edn, Oxford University Press 2011)

Tsatsaronis, Kostas, 'The Supervision of an Integrating European Banking Sector: Theory, Practice, and Challenges' in X Freixas, P Hartmann and C Mayer (eds), *Handbook of European Financial Markets and Institutions* (Oxford University Press 2008)

Türk, Alexander, 'Comitology' in A Arnull and D Chalmers (eds), *The Oxford Handbook of European Union Law* (Oxford University Press 2015) van Asselt, Marjolein, Ellen Vos and Bram Rooijackers, 'Science, knowledge and uncertainty in EU risk regulation' in M Everson and E Vos (eds), *Uncertain Risks Regulated* (Routledge Cavendish 2009)

van Cleynenbreugel, Pieter, *Market Supervision in the European Union. Integrated Administration in Constitutional Context* (Brill Nijhoff 2015)

van Gestel, Rob, 'European Regulatory Agencies Adrift? Case C-270/12 United Kingdom of Great Britain and Northern Ireland v. Parliament and Council of the European Union, Judgment of 22 January 2014, not yet reported' (2014) 21 Maastricht Journal of European and Comparative Law 188

Van Ooik, Ronald, 'The Growing Importance of Agencies in the EU: Shifting Governance and the Institutional Balance' in D Curtin and R Wessel (eds), *Good Governance and the European Union: Reflections on Concepts, Institutions and Substance* (Intersentia 2005)

van Rijsbergen, Marloes, 'On the Enforceability of EU Agencies' Soft Law at the National Level: The Case of the European Securities and Markets Authority' (2014) 10 Utrecht Law Review 116

Vetter, Rainer, 'Die Kompetenzen der Gemeinschaft zur Gründung von unabhängigen europäischen Agenturen' (2005) 18 Zeitschrift für öffentliches Recht und Verwaltungswissenschaft 721

Vitkova, Diana, 'Level 3 of the Lamfalussy process: an effective tool for achieving pan-European regulatory consistency?' (2008) 2 Law and Financial Markets Review 158

Vogt, Matthias, *Die Entscheidung als Handlungsform des Europäischen Gemeinschaftsrechts* (Mohr Siebeck 2005)

von Bogdandy, Armin, *Gubernative Rechtsetzung. Eine Neubestimmung der Rechtsetzung und des Regierungssystems unter dem Grundgesetz in der Perspektive gemeineuropäischer Dogmatik* (Mohr Siebeck 2000)

von Danwitz, Thomas, *Europäisches Verwaltungsrecht* (Springer 2008)

Vos, Ellen, 'The Rise of Committees' (1997) 3 European Law Journal 210

Vos, Ellen, 'EU Committees: the Evolution of Unforeseen Institutional Actors in European Product Regulation' in C Joerges and E Vos (eds), *EU Committees: Social Regulation, Law and Politics* (Hart Publishing 1999)

Vos, Ellen, 'Independence, Accountability and Transparency of European Regulatory Agencies' in D Geradin, R Muñoz and N Petit (eds), *Regulation through Agencies in the EU. A New Paradigm of European Governance* (Edward Elgar 2005)

Vos, Ellen, and Frank Wendler, 'Food Safety Regulation at the EU Level' in E Vos and F Wendler (eds), *Food Safety Regulation in Europe* (Intersentia 2006)

Walker, Vern, 'The Myth of Science as a "Neutral Arbiter" for Triggering Precautions' (2003) 26 Boston College International & Comparative Law Review 197

Walla, Fabian, in R Veil (ed), *Europäisches Kapitalmarktrecht* (Mohr Siebeck 2011)

Wallace, William, and Julie Smith, 'Democracy or Technocracy? European Integration and the Problem of Popular Consent' in J Hayward (ed), *The Crisis of Representation in Europe* (Frank Cass 1995)

Wegener, Bernhard, 'Art. 19 EUV' in C Calliess and M Ruffert (eds), *EUV/AEUV. Das Verfassungsrecht der Europäischen Union mit Europäischer Grundrechtecharta* (4th edn, CH Beck 2011)

Weiler, Joseph, Ulrich Haltern and Franz Mayer, 'European Democracy and its Critique' in J Hayward (ed), *The Crisis of Representation in Europe* (Frank Cass 1995)

Weismann, Paul, 'Die neue EU-Finanzmarktaufsicht – Kann sie künftige Krisen verhindern?' (2011) 11 Bankarchiv 807

Weismann, Paul, 'The European Financial Market Supervisory Authorities and their Power to Issue Binding Decisions' (2012) 27 Journal of International Banking Law and Regulation 495

Weismann, Paul, 'Der Einheitliche Abwicklungsmechanismus (SRM)' (2014) 11 ecolex 1013

Weismann, Paul, 'Der Einheitliche Bankenaufsichtsmechanismus (SSM): ein rechtlich problematisches Konstrukt' (2014) 4 Bankarchiv 265

Weismann, Paul, 'Neues zur Delegationsproblematik: Das Urteil des EuGH in der Rs C-270/12 und seine möglichen Auswirkungen' (2014) 3 Zeitschrift für Finanzmarktrecht 123

Weismann, Paul, 'Die Bankenunion' in J Breitenlechner, M Kalteis, J Kolar, G Kristoferitsch, M Lukan, E Manolas, Y Rogatsch and K Tobisch (eds), *Sicherung von Stabilität und Nachhaltigkeit durch Recht. Tagung der Österreichischen Assistentinnen und Assistenten Öffentliches Recht*, vol V (Jan Sramek Verlag 2015)

Weiß, Wolfgang, *Der Europäische Verwaltungsverbund* (Duncker & Humblot 2010)

Witte, Andreas, 'The Application of National Banking Supervision Law by the ECB: Three Parallel Modes of Executing EU Law?' (2014) 21 Maastricht Journal 89

Wittinger, Michaela, '"Europäische Satelliten": Anmerkungen zum Europäischen Agentur(un)wesen und zur Vereinbarkeit Europäischer Agenturen mit dem Gemeinschaftsrecht' (2008) 5 Europarecht 609

Wojcik, Karl-Philipp, 'Art. 63 AEUV' in H von der Groeben, J Schwarze and A Hatje (eds), *Europäisches Unionsrecht* (7th edn, Nomos 2015)

Wolfram, Dieter, '"Underground Law"? Abgeleitete Rechtsetzung durch Komitologieverfahren in der EU: Bedeutung, Stand und Aussichten nach dem Vertrag von Lissabon' (2009) Studie Centrum für Europäische Politik 4 <www.cep.eu/ Studien/Komitologie/Studie_Komitologie.pdf> accessed 21 November 2015

Wolfers, Benedikt, and Thomas Voland, 'Level the Playing Field: The New Supervision of Credit Institutions by the European Central Bank' (2014) 51 Common Market Law Review 1463

Wymeersch, Eddy, 'The R§eforms of the European Financial Supervisory System: An Overview' (2010) 7 European Company and Financial Law Review 240

Yataganas, Xénophon, 'Delegation of regulatory authority in the European Union: The relevance of the American model of independent agencies' (2001) Jean Monnet Working Paper 3/01 <www.jeanmonnetprogram.org/archive/papers/01/010301. html> accessed 21 November 2015

Yataganas, Xénophon, 'The Treaty of Nice: The Sharing of Power and the Institutional Balance in the European Union – A Continental Perspective' (2001) 7 European Law Journal 242

Internet addresses

<http://diepresse.com/home/meinung/kommentare/leitartikel/744444/Zugelt-die-EUAgenturen-bevor-es-zu-spaet-ist> accessed 21 November 2015

<http://diepresse.com/home/politik/eu/744479/Die-verschwenderischen-EUAgenturen> accessed 21 November 2015

<http://easa.europa.eu/the-agency/easa-explained> accessed 21 November 2015

<http://ec.europa.eu/dgs/health_food-safety/dgs_consultations/regulatory_committees_en.htm> accessed 21 November 2015

<http://ec.europa.eu/dgs/home-affairs/what-we-do/policies/borders-and-visas/agency/index_en.htm> accessed 21 November 2015

<http://ec.europa.eu/enlargement/archives/ear/agency/agency.htm> accessed 21 November 2015

<http://ec.europa.eu/smart-regulation/impact/ia_carried_out/cia_2015_en.htm> accessed 21 November 2015

<http://ec.europa.eu/transparency/regcomitology/index.cfm?CLX=en> accessed 21 November 2015

<https://eiopa.europa.eu/Pages/About-EIOPA/Organisation/Committees/Committees.aspx> accessed 21 November 2015

<https://eiopa.europa.eu/Publications/Administrative/EIOPA%20Organigram%202015%2011.pdf> accessed 21 November 2015

<http://eit.europa.eu/eit-community/eit-glance/mission> accessed 21 November 2015

<http://europa.eu/agencies/regulatory_agencies_bodies/index_en.htm> accessed 4 December 2012

<http://europa.eu/legislation_summaries/institutional_affairs/treaties/treaties_ecsc_en.htm> accessed 21 November 2015

<http://osha.europa.eu/en/about> accessed 21 November 2015

<http://srb.europa.eu/> accessed 21 November 2015

<www.consilium.europa.eu/en/policies/banking-union> accessed 21 November 2015

<www.consilium.europa.eu/uedocs/cms_data/docs/pressdata/en/ec/131359.pdf> accessed 21 November 2015

<www.cpvo.europa.eu/main/en/home/about-the-cpvo/its-mission> accessed 21 November 2015

<www.eba.europa.eu/about-us/organisation/joint-board-of-appeal/members> accessed 21 November 2015

<www.eba.europa.eu/about-us/organisation/management-board/members> accessed 21 November 2015

<www.eba.europa.eu/about-us/organisation/organisation-chart> accessed 21 November 2015

<www.eba.europa.eu/documents/10180/15748/EBA-BS-2011-137-Final-EBA-work-programme-for-2012-FINAL.pdf/cbe1d67b-c5fd-400c-ab4c-23fb5279a3f9> accessed 21 November 2015

<www.eba.europa.eu/regulation-and-policy/recovery-and-resolution/guidelines-on-how-information-should-be-provided-under-the-brrd> accessed 21 November 2015

<www.eba.europa.eu/regulation-and-policy/single-rulebook> accessed 21 November 2015

<www.eba.europa.eu/supervisory-convergence/supervisory-colleges> accessed 21 November 2015

<www.ecb.europa.eu/press/pr/date/2014/html/pr140904_2.en.html> accessed 21 November 2015

<www.ema.europa.eu/ema/index.jsp?curl=pages/about_us/general/general_content_000091.jsp&murl=menus/about_us/about_us.jsp&mid=WC0b01ac0580028a42> accessed 21 November 2015

<www.emsa.europa.eu/about/what-we-do-main/mission-statements.html> accessed 21 November 2015

<www.emcdda.europa.eu/about/mission> accessed 21 November 2015

<www.enisa.europa.eu/about-enisa/activities> accessed 21 November 2015
<www.era.europa.eu/Core-Activities/Pages/home.aspx> accessed 21 November 2015
<www.esma.europa.eu/system/files/organigramme_2.pdf> accessed 21 November 2015
<www.esm.europa.eu/about/governance/board-of-directors/index.htm> accessed 21 November 2015
<www.etf.europa.eu/web.nsf/pages/Where_we_work> accessed 21 November 2015
<www.euinside.eu/en/analyses/bulgaria-banking-union-membership> accessed 21 November 2015
<www.eurojust.europa.eu/Pages/home.aspx> accessed 21 November 2015
<www.europol.europa.eu/content/page/mandate-119> accessed 21 November 2015
<www.google.at/url?sa=t&rct=j&q=&esrc=s&source=web&cd=2&ved=0CCcQFjAB
    &url=http%3A%2F%2Fwww.esm.europa.eu%2Fpdf%2FFFFA%2520Spain_Main%
    2520Agreement_Execution%2520Version.pdf&ei=6kOWVd6WJMOpyQPN14HA
    Ag&usg=AFQjCNF5pxmEhe6790xgcMRLECAuDVhy_A&bvm=bv.96952980,d.
    bGQ> accessed 21 November 2015
<www.iss.europa.eu/about-us> accessed 21 November 2015
<www.official-documents.gov.uk/document/cm83/8363/8363.pdf> accessed 21 November 2015
<www.oxforddictionaries.com/definition/english/decision> accessed 21 November 2015
<www.satcen.europa.eu> accessed 21 November 2015

Decisions, other binding and non-binding acts and documents

Austrian Verfassungsgerichtshof, collection number 18747
Basel Committee on Banking Supervision, 'Principles for effective supervisory colleges' (Bank for International Settlements) of June 2014 <www.bis.org/publ/bcbs287. pdf> accessed 21 November 2015
Board of Appeal, Decision BoA 2013-008 of 24 June 2013
Board of Appeal, Decision BoA 2013-14 of 10 January 2014
Board of Appeal, Decision BoA 2014 05 of 10 November 2014
Board of Appeal, Decision BoA 2014-C1-02 of 14 July 2014
Board of Appeal, Rules of Procedure BoA 2012-002 of 18 July 2012
CEBS and CEIOPS, 'Colleges of Supervisors – 10 Common Principles' CEBS 2008 124/CEIOPS-SEC-54/08/IWCFC 08 32 of 27 January 2009
CEBS, Annual Report 2004
CEBS, Charter of the Committee of European Banking Supervisors of July 2008 [CEBS-Charter]
CEBS, Guidelines for the Operational Functioning of Supervisory Colleges GL 34 of 15 June 2010
CEIOPS, Annual Report 2004 and Work Programme 2005
CEIOPS Charter of the Committee of European Insurance and Occupational Pensions Supervisors of November 2009 [CEIOPS-Charter]
CEIOPS, CEIOPS Annual Report 2010. EIOPA Work Programme 2011. 3L3 Annual Report 2010
CESR, Action Plan for 2005 of October 2004
CESR, Charter of the Committee of European Securities Regulators CESR/08-375d of September 2008 [CESR-Charter]

CESR, Consultation Paper 'The Role of CESR in the Regulation and Supervision of UCITS and Asset Management Activities in the EU' CESR/03-378b of October 2003 <www.esma.europa.eu/system/files/03_378b.pdf> accessed 21 November 2015

Commission Decision 2001/527/EC of 6 June 2001 establishing the Committee of European Securities Regulators [2001] OJ L191/43 [CESR-Decision]

Commission Decision 2001/528/EC of 6 June 2001 establishing the European Securities Committee [2001] OJ L191/45 [ESC-Decision]

Commission Decision 2004/10/EC of 5 November 2003 establishing the European Banking Committee [2004] OJ L3/36 [EBC-Decision]

Commission Decision 2004/5/EC of 5 November 2003 establishing the Committee of European Banking Supervisors [2004] OJ L3/28 [CEBS-Decision]

Commission Decision 2004/6/EC of 5 November 2003 establishing the Committee of European Insurance and Occupational Pensions Supervisors [2004] OJ L3/30 [CEIOPS-Decision]

Commission Decision 2004/7/EC of 5 November 2003 amending Decision 2001/527/EC establishing the Committee of European Securities Regulators [2004] OJ L3/32

Commission Decision 2004/9/EC of 5 November 2003 establishing the European Insurance and Occupational Pensions Committee [2004] OJ L/34 [EIOPC-Decision]

Commission Implementing Decision 2013/778/EU of 13 December 2013 establishing the Research Executive Agency [2013] OJ L346/54

Commission, Commission package of measures to improve regulation and supervision of banking, insurance and investment funds – frequently asked questions MEMO/03/220 of 6 November 2003

Commission, Communication 'A Roadmap towards a Banking Union' COM (2012) 510 final of 12 September 2012

Commission, Communication 'Conferment of implementing powers on the Commission' SEC (90) 2589 final of 10 January 1991

Commission, Communication 'Driving European recovery' COM (2009) 114 final of 4 March 2009

Commission, Communication 'European financial supervision' COM (2009) 252 final of 27 May 2009

Commission, Communication 'Externalisation of the management of Community programmes including presentation of a framework regulation for a new type of executive agency' COM (2000) 788 final of 13 December 2000

Commission, Communication 'Financial Services: Building a Framework for Action' COM (1998) 625 final of 28 October 1998

Commission, Communication 'Implementation of Article 290 of the Treaty on the Functioning of the European Union' COM (2009) 673 final of 9 December 2009

Commission, Communication 'On the application, from 1 August 2013, of State aid rules to support measures in favour of banks in the context of the financial crisis ("Banking Communication")' 2013/C 216/01 of 30 July 2013

Commission, Communication 'Programming of human and financial resources for decentralised agencies 2014–2020' COM (2013) 519 final of 10 July 2013

Commission, Communication 'Proposal for an Interinstitutional Agreement on Better Regulation' COM (2015) 216 final of 19 May 2015

Commission, Communication 'Review of the Lamfalussy process. Strengthening supervisory convergence' COM (2007) 727 final of 20 November 2007

Commission, Communication 'The European Agencies – The Way Forward' COM (2008) 135 final of 11 March 2008

Commission, Communication 'The operating framework for the European Regulatory Agencies' COM (2002) 718 final of 11 December 2002

Commission, Council, Parliament, Common Understanding on delegated acts (2011) [Common Understanding] <http://register.consilium.europa.eu/doc/srv?l=EN &f=ST%208640%202011%20INIT> accessed 21 November 2015

Commission, Draft Interinstitutional Agreement on the operating framework for the European regulatory agencies COM (2005) 59 final of 25 February 2005

Commission, European agencies – The way forward MEMO 08/159 of 11 March 2008

Commission, European Parliament's endorsement of the political agreement on Market Abuse Regulation MEMO/13/774 of 10 September 2013

Commission, Europeans, the European Union and the Crisis (2014) 81 Standard Eurobarometer <http://ec.europa.eu/public_opinion/archives/eb/eb81/eb81_ cri_en.pdf> accessed 21 November 2015

Commission, Guidelines on the prevention and management of conflicts of interest in EU decentralised agencies (Annex IV to the Commission progress report on the implementation of the Common Approach) of 10 December 2013 <http://europa. eu/agencies/documents/2013-12-10_guidelines_on_conflict_of_interests_en.pdf> accessed 21 November 2015

Commission, Progress report on the implementation of the Common Approach on EU decentralised agencies COM (2015) 179 final of 24 April 2015

Commission, Progress report on the implementation of the Common Approach of 10 December 2013

Commission, Proposal of 12 November 2008 for a Regulation of the European Parliament and of the Council on Credit Rating Agencies COM (2008) 704 final

Commission, Proposal of 12 September 2015 for a Council Regulation conferring specific tasks on the European Central Bank concerning policies relating to the prudential supervision of credit institutions COM (2012) 511 final

Commission, Proposal of 12 September 2015 for a Regulation of the European Parliament and of the Council amending Regulation (EU) No 1093/2010 establishing a European Supervisory Authority (European Banking Authority) COM (2012) 512 final

Commission, Proposal of 17 July 2013 on the establishment of the European Public Prosecutor's Office COM (2013) 534 final

Commission, Proposal of 23 September 2009 for a Regulation of the European Parliament and of the Council establishing a European Banking Authority COM (2009) 501 final

Commission, Proposal of 27 March 2013 for a Regulation amending Council Regulation 207/2009 on the Community trade mark COM (2013) 161 final

Commission, Report on the mission and organisation of the ESRB, COM (2014) 508 final of 8 August 2014

Commission, Report on the operation of the European Supervisory Authorities (ESAs) and the European System of Financial Supervision (ESFS) COM (2014) 509 final of 8 August 2014

Commission, Report on the working of committees during 2006 COM (2007) 842 final of 20 December 2007

Commission, Report on the working of committees during 2013 COM (2014) 572 final of 16 September 2014

Commission, Report on the working of committees during 2014 COM (2015) 418 final of 3 September 2015

Commission, Roadmap on the follow-up to the Common Approach on EU decentralised agencies 1 <http://europa.eu/agencies/documents/2012-12-18_roadmap_on_the_follow_up_to_the_common_approach_on_eu_decentralised_agencies_en.pdf> accessed 21 November 2015

Commission, Staff Working Document 'Ex-Ante Evaluation for establishing a Community programme to support specific activities in the field of financial services, financial reporting and auditing' SEC (2009) 54 of 23 January 2009

Commission, Staff Working Document 'The Application of the Lamfalussy Process to EU Securities Markets Legislation' SEC (2004) 1459 of 15 November 2004

Commission, Standard rules of procedure for committees – Rules of procedure for the [name of the committee] committee [2011] OJ 2011/C206/06 [Standard RoP for committees]

Commission, White Paper 'Completing the Internal Market' COM (85) 310 final of 14 June 1985

Commission, White Paper 'European Governance' COM (2001) 428 of 25 July 2001

Committee of Wise Men, 'Initial Report on the Regulation of European Securities Markets' of 7 November 2000

Committee of Wise Men, 'Final Report on the Regulation of European Securities Markets' of 15 February 2001 [*Lamfalussy* Report]

Council (Ecofin), Note 8515/3/08 Rev 3 of 15 May 2008

Council Decision 1999/468/EC of 28 June 1999 laying down the procedures for the exercise of implementing powers conferred on the Commission [1999] OJ L184/23 [*Comitology II*]

Council Decision 1999/8/EC of 31 December 1998 adopting the Statutes of the Economic and Financial Committee [1999] OJ L5/71

Council Decision 2002/187/JHA of 28 February 2002 setting up Eurojust with a view to reinforcing the fight against serious crime [2002] OJ L63/1

Council Decision 2005/681/JHA of 20 September 2005 establishing the European Police College (CEPOL) and repealing Decision 2000/820/JHA [2005] OJ L256/63

Council Decision 2006/512/EC of 17 July 2006 amending *Comitology II* [2006] OJ L200/11

Council Decision 2009/371/JHA of 6 April 2009 establishing the European Police Office (Europol) [2009] OJ L121/37

Council Decision 2011/411/CFSP of 12 July 2011 defining the statute, seat and operational rules of the European Defence Agency and repealing Joint Action 2004/551/CFSP [2011] OJ L183/16

Council Decision 2014/401/CFSP of 26 June 2014 on the European Union Satellite Centre and repealing Joint Action 2001/555/CFSP on the establishment of a European Union Satellite Centre [2014] L188/73

Council Decision 2014/75/CFSP of 10 February 2014 on the European Union Institute for Security Studies [2014] OJ L41/13

Council Decision 87/373/EEC of 13 July 1987 laying down the procedures for the exercise of implementing powers conferred on the Commission [1987] OJ L197/33 [*Comitology I*]

Council Decision 98/743/EC of 21 December 1998 on the detailed provisions concerning the composition of the Economic and Financial Committee [1998] OJ L358/109

Council and ECB, Memorandum of Understanding on the cooperation on procedures related to the SSM (December 2013)

Council, 'Monthly Summary of Council Acts in November 2010' 5455/11 of 18 January 2011 <http://register.consilium.europa.eu/doc/srv?l=EN&f=ST%205 455%202011%20INIT> accessed 21 November 2015

Council, Note 11450/12 of 18 June 2012

Council, Press Release 15698/07 of 4 December 2007 (provisional version) <www.consilium.europa.eu/uedocs/cms_data/docs/pressdata/en/ecofin/97420. pdf> accessed 21 November 2015

Court of Auditors, 'The European Union's Agencies: Getting Results' Special Report 5/2008

Directorate-General for Economic and Financial Affairs of the Commission, 'The Economic Adjustment Programme for Ireland' (2011) 76 European Economy Occasional Papers 1 <http://ec.europa.eu/economy_finance/publications/ occasional_paper/2011/pdf/ocp76_en.pdf> accessed 21 November 2015

EBA, 'Guidelines on Advanced Measurement Approach (AMA) – Extensions and Changes' GL 45 of 6 January 2012 <www.eba.europa.eu/documents/10180/ 105108/EBA-BS-2012-267—AOB_GL-AMA-extensions-changes-_1.pdf> accessed 21 November 2015

EBA, 'Guidelines on Internal Governance' GL 44 of 27 September 2011 (compliance table) <www.eba.europa.eu/documents/10180/103861/EBA-2011-12-16-(Confirmation-of-Compliance-table—-GL44-Internal-Governance).pdf> accessed 21 November 2015

EBA, Annual Report 2011

EBA, Annual Report 2014

EBA, Budget for 2011 <www.eba.europa.eu/documents/10180/15784/Budget-2011—-Annex.pdf/1206f411-49b0-49ca-9156-e0a56c04cfe0> accessed 21 November 2015

EBA, Budget for 2015 <www.eba.europa.eu/documents/10180/1041337/EBA+ 2015+Amending+Budget.pdf/d12c1b6c-4650-416c-8c7f-902271988a39> accessed 21 November 2015

EBA, Decision EBA DC 006 of 12 January 2011

EBA, Decision establishing the Review Panel of the European Banking Authority EBA DC 035 of 4 May 2011

EBA, Decision of the Management Board on Internal Language Arrangements EBA DC 003 of 12 January 2011

EBA, Decision of the Management Boards on access to documents EBA DC 036 of 27 May 2011

EBA, Decision on reporting by competent authorities to the EBA EBA/DC/ 2015/130 of 23 September 2015

EBA, Financial Regulation of 23 December 2013

EBA, GL 44

EBA, GL 45

EBA, Recommendation EBA/REC/2014/02 of 17 October 2014

EBA, Review panel methodology for the conduct of peer reviews EBA BoS 2012 107 of 24 May 2012

EBA, Rules of Procedure for Investigation of Breach of Union Law EBA/DC/2014/100 of 14 July 2014

EBA, Rules of Procedure for the non-binding mediation between competent authorities EBA/DC/2014/093 of 18 June 2014

EBA, Rules of Procedure for the settlement of disagreements between competent authorities EBA/DC/2014/091 of 20 February 2014

EBA, Rules of Procedure of the Board of Supervisors EBA/DC/2011/001 of 27 November 2014

EBA, Rules of Procedure of the Management Board EBA/DC/2014/095 of 7 July 2014

EBC, Rules of Procedure of 6 December 2010 [EBC-RoP]

ECB Decision 2004/257/EC of 19 February 2004 adopting the Rules of Procedure of the European Central Bank [2004] OJ L080/33 [ECB-RoP]

ECB Decision 2014/360/EU of 14 April 2014 concerning the establishment of an Administrative Board of Review and its Operating Rules [2014] OJ L175/47

ECB Decision 2014/427/EU of 6 February 2014 on the appointment of representatives of the European Central Bank to the Supervisory Board [2014] OJ L196/38

ECB Decision 2014/434/EU of 31 January 2014 on the close cooperation with the national competent authorities of participating Member States whose currency is not the euro [2014] OJ L198/7

ECB Decision 2014/723/EU of 17 September 2014 on the implementation of separation between the monetary policy and supervision functions of the European Central Bank [2014] OJ L300/57

ECB, 'Review of the Application of the Lamfalussy Framework to EU Securities Markets Legislation. Contribution to the Commission's Public Consultation' of 17 February 2005 <www.ecb.europa.eu/pub/pdf/other/lamfalussy-reviewen.pdf> accessed 21 November 2015

ECHA, General Report 2007

ECHA, General Report 2008

ECHA, General Report 2009

ECHA, General Report 2014

EIOPA, Action Plan for Colleges 2012 EIOPA-BoS-12-004 of 12 January 2012

EIOPA, Annual Report 2011

EIOPA, Annual Report 2014

EIOPA, Budget for 2011 <https://eiopa.europa.eu/Publications/Administrative/EIOPA_Budget_2011.pdf> accessed 21 November 2015

EIOPA, Budget for 2015 <https://eiopa.europa.eu/Publications/Administrative/EIOPA%20budget%202015.pdf> accessed 21 November 2015

EIOPA, Decision EIOPA-BoS-11-017 of 25 June 2014

EIOPA, Decision EIOPA-MB-11/043 of 10 February 2011

EIOPA, Decision establishing the Review Panel of the European Insurance and Occupational Pensions Authority EIOPA-RP-11/005 of May 2011

EIOPA, Decision of the Management Board on Internal Language Arrangements EIOPA-MB-11/003 of 10 January 2011

EIOPA, Decision of the Management Board on access to documents EIOPA-MB-11/051 of 31 May 2011

EIOPA, Financial Regulation of 15 March 2012

EIOPA, Rules of Procedure of the Board of Supervisors EIOPA-BoS-11/002 of 14 June 2012

EIOPA, Rules of Procedure of the Management Board EIOPA-MB-11/002 of 10 January 2011

EIOPC, Rules of Procedure of 30 June 2005 [EIOPC-RoP]

EMCDDA, 'European report on drug consumption rooms' of February 2004

EMEA, CHMP Rules of Procedure EMEA/MB/87146/2007 of 29 July 2004 [RoP of the CHMP]

EMEA, COMP Rules of Procedure EMEA/COMP/8212/00 Rev. 3 of 12 April 2007 [RoP of the COMP]

EMEA, CVMP Rules of Procedure EMEA/MB/47098/2007 of 14 July 2004 [RoP of the CVMP]

ESC, Rules of Procedure of 12 April 2004 [ESC-RoP]

ESMA Annual Report 2011

ESMA, Annual Report 2014

ESMA, Budget for 2011 <www.esma.europa.eu/system/files/Budget_2011pdf.pdf> accessed 21 November 2015

ESMA, Budget for 2015 <www.esma.europa.eu/system/files/2015-327_esma_2015_budget.pdf> accessed 21 November 2015

ESMA, Decision ESMA/2011/MB/6 of 11 January 2011

ESMA, Decision ESMA/2012/BS/87 of 19 June 2012 (as amended on 9 July 2014)

ESMA, Decision establishing its Review Panel ESMA/2001/BS/229 of 8 November 2011

ESMA, Decision of the Management Board on Internal Language Arrangements ESMA/2011/MB/3 of 11 January 2011

ESMA, Decision of the Management Board on access to documents ESMA/2011/MB/69 of 24 May 2011

ESMA, Rules of Procedure of the Board of Supervisors ESMA/2011/BS/1 of 11 January 2011

ESMA, Rules of Procedure of the Management Board ESMA/2012/MB/1 of 18 June 2012

ESMA, Work Programme 2015

ESMA, Work Programme 2016

EU Agencies Network, Implementation of the Common Approach – Final Report of February 2015

EU Presidency, Press Communiqué 'Belgian EU Presidency reaches agreement on new "Comitology" rules' of 16 December 2010

EU working group, Analytical Fiche No 1 (2010) <http://europa.eu/agencies/documents/fiche_1_sent_to_ep_cons_2010-12-15_en.pdf> accessed 21 November 2015

EU working group, Analytical Fiche No 5 (2010) <http://europa.eu/agencies/documents/fiche_5_sent_to_ep_cons_2010-12-15_en.pdf> accessed 21 November 2015

EU working group, Analytical Fiche No 6 (2010) <http://europa.eu/agencies/documents/fiche_6_sent_to_ep_cons_2010-12-15_en.pdf> accessed 21 November 2015

EU working group, Analytical Fiche No 10 (2010) <http://europa.eu/agencies/documents/fiche_10_sent_to_ep_cons_2011-03-16_en.pdf> accessed 21 November 2015

EU working group, Analytical Fiche No 11 (2010) <http://europa.eu/agencies/documents/fiche_11_sent_to_ep_cons_2011-03-16_en.pdf> accessed 21 November 2015

EU working group, Analytical Fiche No 31 (2010) <http://europa.eu/agencies/documents/fiche_31_sent_to_ep_cons_2010-10-22_en.pdf> accessed 21 November 2015

European Convention, 'Final report of Working Group V' (complementary competencies) CONV 375/1/02 of 4 November 2002

European Council, Conclusions EUCO 104/2/13 of 27–28 June 2013 (Brussels)

European Council, Presidency Conclusions of the Brussels European Council 7652/1/08 Rev 1 of 13 and 14 March 2008 <http://register.consilium.europa.eu/pdf/en/08/st07/st07652-re01.en08.pdf> accessed 21 November 2015

European Council, Presidency Conclusions of the European Council of 23 and 24 March 2001 in Stockholm <www.consilium.europa.eu/en/uedocs/cms_data/docs/pressdata/en/ec/00100-r1.%20ann-r1.en1.html> accessed 21 November 2015

European Union Committee of the House of Lords 'Delegation of powers to the Commission: reforming comitology' HL 1999-2 <www.parliament.the-stationery-office.co.uk/pa/ld199899/ldselect/ldeucom/23/2303.htm#a13> accessed 21 November 2015

European Union Committee of the House of Lords, 'The Euro area crisis' HL 2010-2012-25 <www.publications.parliament.uk/pa/ld201012/ldselect/ldeucom/260/260.pdf> accessed 21 November 2015

German Auswärtiges Amt, Denkschrift zum Vertrag von Lissabon vom 13. Dezember 2007 AS-RK 2007 of 11 December 2008 <www.europarl.europa.eu/brussels/website/media/Basis/Mitgliedstaaten/Deutschland/Pdf/AA_Denkschrift_Lissabon.pdf> accessed 21 November 2015

German Bundesrat, Drucksache 134/08 (decision of 14 March 2008)

German Bundesrat, Drucksache 228/08 (decision of 4 July 2008)

Group 3a, Report by the Working Group 'Establishing a Framework for Decision-Making Regulatory Agencies' SG/8597/01-EN of June 2001 <www.epha.org/IMG/pdf/White_paper_on_governance.pdf> accessed 21 November 2015

High Authority Decision 14/55 of 26 March 1955

High Authority Decision 22/54 of 26 March 1954

High-Level Group on Financial Supervision in the EU, Report of 25 February 2009 [*de Larosière* Report]

Intergovernmental Agreement on the transfer and mutualisation of contributions to the Single Resolution Fund [Intergovernmental Agreement]

Inter-institutional Monitory Group, 'Final Report Monitoring the Lamfalussy Process' of 15 October 2007

Joint Committee of the ESAs, Rules of Procedure JC DOC 2011 001 of 21 June 2011 [RoP of the Joint Committee 2011]

Joint Committee of the ESAs, Rules of Procedure JC DC 2014 001 of 13 November 2014 [RoP of the Joint Committee 2014]

National Research Council, Risk Assessment in the Federal Government: Managing the Process (National Academy Press 1983) <www.nap.edu/openbook.php?record_id=366&> accessed 21 November 2015

Ombudsman, case 2497/2010/FOR [2011]

Ombudsman, case 726/2012/(RA)FOR [2014]

Parliament, 'Parliamentary questions – answer given by Mr Barroso on behalf of the Commission' E-2022/2008 of 7 May 2008 <www.europarl.europa.eu/sides/getAllAnswers.do?reference=E-2008-2022&language=EN> accessed 21 November 2015

Parliament, Council, Commission, Joint Statement on decentralised agencies of 19 July 2012 (with an annexed Common Approach)

Parliament and Council, Decision 716/2009/EC of 16 September 2009 establishing a Community programme to support specific activities in the field of financial services, financial reporting and auditing [2009] OJ L253/8

Parliament, Council and Commission, Modus Vivendi concerning the implementing measures for acts adopted in accordance with the procedure laid down in Article 189b of the EC Treaty of 20 December 1994 [1994] OJ 1996 C102/01

Parliament and ECB, Interinstitutional Agreement 2013/694/EU on the practical modalities of the exercise of democratic accountability and oversight over the exercise of the tasks conferred on the ECB within the framework of the Single Supervisory Mechanism [2013] L320/1

Parliament, Report on the modification of the procedures for the exercise of implementing powers conferred on the Commission – 'commitology' [sic] of 3 August 1998 A4-0292/98 [*Aglietta* Report]

Parliament, Resolution on prudential supervision rules in the European Union 2002/2061 (INI) [2004] OJ C 25 E/394

Parliament, Review of the New European System of Financial Supervision (ESFS). Part 1: The Work of the European Supervisory Authorities (EBA, EIOPA and ESMA) (2013)

Parliament, Review of the New European System of Financial Supervision (ESFS). Part 2: The Work of the European Systemic Risk Board (ESRB) (2013)

Rambøll Management-Euréval-Matrix, Evaluation of the EU decentralised agencies in 2009. Final Report Volume I: Synthesis and prospects (2009)

Zentraler Kreditausschuss, 'Comments of Zentraler Kreditausschuss on the EU Commission's Consultation concerning the "de Larosière-Report" dated 25 February 2009 and on the Commission's Communication Paper "Driving European Recovery" dated 4 March 2009' of 9 April 2009 <www.die-deutsche-kreditwirtschaft.de/uploads/media/090409deLarosierereport.PDF> accessed 21 November 2015

Regulations and directives

Council Directive 81/851/EEC of 28 September 1981 on the approximation of the laws of the Member States relating to veterinary medicinal products [1981] OJ L317/1

Council Implementing Regulation (EU) 2015/81 of 19 December 2014 specifying uniform conditions of application of Regulation (EU) 806/2014 of the European Parliament and of the Council with regard to ex ante contributions to the Single Resolution Fund [2015] L15/1

Council Regulation (EC) 1/2003 of 16 December 2002 on the implementation of the rules on competition laid down in Articles 81 and 82 of the Treaty [2003] OJ L1/1

Council Regulation (EC) 1035/97 of 2 June 1997 establishing a European Monitoring Centre on Racism and Xenophobia [1997] OJ L151/1

Council Regulation (EC) 1408/71 of 14 June 1971 on the application of social security schemes to employed persons, to self-employed persons and to members of their families moving within the Community [1971] OJ L149/2

Council Regulation (EC) 168/2007 of 15 February 2007 establishing a European Union Agency for Fundamental Rights [2007] OJ L 53/1

Council Regulation (EC) 1756/2006 of 28 November 2006 amending Regulation (EC) 2667/2000 on the European Agency for Reconstruction [2006] OJ L332/18

Council Regulation (EC) 2007/2004 of 26 October 2004 establishing a European Agency for the Management of Operational Cooperation at the External Borders of the Member States of the European Union [2004] OJ L349/1

Council Regulation (EC) 2062/94 of 18 July 1994 establishing a European Agency for Safety and Health at Work [1994] OJ L216/1

Council Regulation (EC) 207/2009 of 26 February 2009 on the Community trade mark (codified version) [2009] OJ L78/1

Council Regulation (EC) 2062/94 of 18 July 1994 establishing a European Agency for Safety and Health at Work [1994] OJ L216/1

Council Regulation (EC) 2100/94 of 27 July 1994 on Community plant variety rights [1994] OJ L227/1

Council Regulation (EC) 2454/1999 of 15 November 1999 amending Regulation (EC) 1628/96 relating to aid for Bosnia and Herzegovina, Croatia, the Federal Republic of Yugoslavia and the former Yugoslav Republic of Macedonia, in particular by the setting up of a European Agency for Reconstruction [1999] OJ L299/1

Council Regulation (EC) 2965/94 of 28 November 1994 setting up a Translation Centre for Bodies of the European Union [1994] OJ L314/1

Council Regulation (EC) 58/2003 of 19 December 2002 laying down the statute for executive agencies to be entrusted with certain tasks in the management of Community programmes [2003] OJ L11/1

Council Regulation (EC) 768/2005 of 26 April 2005 establishing a Community Fisheries Control Agency and amending Regulation (EEC) 2847/93 applicable to the common fisheries policy [2005] OJ L128/1

Council Regulation (EC, Euratom) 1605/2002 of 25 June 2002 on the Financial Regulation applicable to the general budget of the European Communities [2002] OJ L248/1

Council Regulation (EEC) 1210/90 of 7 May 1990 on the establishment of the European Environment Agency and the European environment information and observation network [1990] OJ L120/1

Council Regulation (EEC) 1365/75 of 26 May 1975 on the creation of a European Foundation for the Improvement of Living and Working Conditions [1975] OJ L139/1

Council Regulation (EEC) 337/75 of 10 February 1975 establishing a European Centre for the Development of Vocational Training [1975] OJ L39/1

Council Regulation (EEC) 907/73 of 3 April 1973 establishing a European Monetary Cooperation Fund [1973] OJ L89/2

Council Regulation (EU) 1024/2013 of 15 October 2013 conferring specific tasks on the European Central Bank concerning policies relating to the prudential supervision of credit institutions [2013] OJ L287/63 [SSM-Regulation]

Council Regulation (EU) 1096/2010 conferring specific tasks upon the European Central Bank concerning the functioning of the European Systemic Risk Board [2010] OJ L331/162

Council Regulation 31 (EEC) laying down the Staff Regulations of Officials and the Conditions of Employment of Other Servants of the European Economic Community and the European Atomic Energy Community [1962] OJ 45/1385

Council Regulation 3245/81 of 26 October 1981 setting up a European Agency for Cooperation [1981] OJ L328/1

Council Regulation 802/68/EEC of 27 June 1968 on the common definition of the concept of the origin of goods [1968] L148/1

Directive 2002/87/EC of the European Parliament and of the Council of 16 December 2002 on the supplementary supervision of credit institutions, insurance undertakings and investment firms in a financial conglomerate and amending Council Directives 73/239/EEC, 79/267/EEC, 92/49/EEC, 92/96/EEC, 93/6/EEC and 93/22/EEC, and Directives 98/78/EC and 2000/12/EC of the European Parliament and of the Council [2003] OJ L35/1

Directive 2005/1/EC of the European Parliament and of the Council of 9 March 2005 amending Council Directives 73/239/EEC, 85/611/EEC, 91/675/EEC, 92/49/EEC and 93/6/EEC and Directives 94/19/EC, 98/78/EC, 2000/12/EC, 2001/34/EC, 2002/83/EC and 2002/87/EC in order to establish a new organisational structure for financial services committees [2005] OJ L79/9

Directive 2009/138/EC of the European Parliament and of the Council of 25 November 2009 on the taking-up and pursuit of the business of Insurance and Reinsurance [2009] OJ L335/1

Directive 2013/36/EU of the European Parliament and of the Council of 26 June 2013 on access to the activity of credit institutions and the prudential supervision of credit institutions and investment firms, amending Directive 2002/87/EC and repealing Directives 2006/48/EC and 2006/49/EC [2013] OJ L176/338

Directive 2014/17/EU of the European Parliament and of the Council of 4 February 2014 on credit agreements for consumers relating to residential immovable property and amending Directives 2008/48/EC and 2013/36/EU and Regulation (EU) 1093/2010 [2014] OJ L60/34

Directive 2014/49/EU of the European Parliament and of the Council of 16 April 2014 on deposit guarantee schemes [2014] OJ L173/149

Directive 2014/59/EU of the European Parliament and of the Council of 15 May 2014 establishing a framework for the recovery and resolution of credit institutions and investment firms and amending Council Directive 82/891/EEC, and Directives 2001/24/EC, 2002/47/EC, 2004/25/EC, 2005/56/EC, 2007/36/EC, 2011/35/EU, 2012/30/EU and 2013/36/EU, and Regulations (EU) 1093/2010 and (EU) 648/2012, of the European Parliament and of the Council [2014] OJ L173/190 [Bank Recovery and Resolution Directive – BRRD]

Directive 2014/65/EU of the European Parliament and of the Council of 15 May 2014 on markets in financial instruments and amending Directive 2002/92/EC and Directive 2011/61/EU (recast) [2014] OJ L173/349

Directive 2014/92/EU of the European Parliament and of the Council of 23 July 2014 on the comparability of fees related to payment accounts, payment account switching and access to payment accounts with basic features [2014] OJ L257/214

ECB Regulation 468/2014 of 16 April 2014 establishing the framework for cooperation within the Single Supervisory Mechanism between the European Central Bank and national competent authorities and with national designated authorities (SSM Framework Regulation) [2014] OJ L141/1

Regulation (EC) 1060/2009 of the European Parliament and of the Council of 16 September 2009 on credit rating agencies [2009] OJ L302/1

Regulation (EC) 1211/2009 of the European Parliament and of the Council of 25 November 2009 establishing the Body of European Regulators for Electronic Communications (BEREC) and the Office [2009] OJ L337/1

Regulation (EC) 1339/2008 of the European Parliament and of the Council of 16 December 2008 establishing a European Training Foundation (recast) [2008] OJ L354/82

Regulation (EC) 1406/2002 of the European Parliament and of the Council of 27 June 2002 establishing a European Maritime Safety Agency [2002] OJ L208/1

Regulation (EC) 178/2002 of the European Parliament and of the Council of 28 January 2002 laying down the general principles and requirements of food law, establishing the European Food Safety Authority and laying down procedures in matters of food safety [2002] OJ L31/1

Regulation (EC) 1907/2006 of the European Parliament and of the Council of 18 December 2006 concerning the Registration, Evaluation, Authorisation and Restriction of Chemicals (REACH), establishing a European Chemicals Agency, amending Directive 1999/45/EC and repealing Council Regulation (EEC) 793/93 and Commission Regulation (EC) 1488/94 as well as Council Directive 76/769/EEC and Commission Directives 91/155/EEC, 93/67/EEC, 93/105/EC and 2000/21/EC [2006] OJ L396/1

Regulation (EC) 1920/2006 of the European Parliament and of the Council of 12 December 2006 on the European Monitoring Centre for Drugs and Drug Addiction (recast) [2006] OJ L376/1

Regulation (EC) 1922/2006 of the European Parliament and of the Council of 20 December 2006 on establishing a European Institute for Gender Equality [2006] OJ L403/9

Regulation (EC) 216/2008 of the European Parliament and of the Council of 20 February 2008 on common rules in the field of civil aviation and establishing a European Aviation Safety Agency, and repealing Council Directive 91/670/ EEC, Regulation (EC) 1592/2002 and Directive 2004/36/EC [2008] OJ L79/1

Regulation (EC) 294/2008 of the European Parliament and of the Council of 11 March 2008 establishing the European Institute of Innovation and Technology [2008] OJ L97/1

Regulation (EC) 401/2009 of the European Parliament and of the Council of 23 April 2009 on the European Environment Agency and the European Environment Information and Observation Network (codified version) [2009] OJ L126/13

Regulation (EC) 713/2009 of the European Parliament and of the Council of 13 July 2009 establishing an Agency for the Cooperation of Energy Regulators [2009] OJ L211/1

Regulation (EC) 726/2004 of the European Parliament and of the Council of 31 March 2004 laying down Community procedures for the authorisation and supervision of medicinal products for human and veterinary use and establishing a European Medicines Agency [2004] OJ L136/1

Regulation (EC) 851/2004 of the European Parliament and of the Council of 21 April 2004 establishing a European centre for disease prevention and control [2004] OJ L142/1

Regulation (EC) 881/2004 of the European Parliament and of the Council of 29 April 2004 establishing a European Railway Agency [2004] OJ L164/1

Regulation (EU) 1077/2011 of the European Parliament and of the Council of 25 October 2011 establishing a European Agency for the operational management of large-scale IT systems in the area of freedom, security and justice [2011] OJ L286/1

Regulation (EU) 1092/2010 of the European Parliament and of the Council of 24 November 2010 on European Union macro-prudential oversight of the financial system and establishing a European Systemic Risk Board [2010] OJ L331/1 [ESRB-Regulation]

Regulation (EU) 1093/2010 of the European Parliament and of the Council of 24 November 2010 establishing a European Supervisory Authority (European Banking Authority), amending Decision 716/2009/EC and repealing Commission Decision 2009/78/EC [2010] OJ L331/12 [EBA-Regulation]

Regulation (EU) 1094/2010 of the European Parliament and of the Council of 24 November 2010 establishing a European Supervisory Authority (European Insurance and Occupational Pensions Authority), amending Decision 716/2009/EC and repealing Commission Decision 2009/79/EC [2010] OJ L331/48 [EIOPA-Regulation]

Regulation (EU) 1095/2010 of the European Parliament and of the Council of 24 November 2010 establishing a European Supervisory Authority (European Securities and Markets Authority), amending Decision 716/2009/EC and repealing Commission Decision 2009/77/EC [2010] OJ L331/48 [ESMA-Regulation]

Regulation (EU) 182/2011 of 16 February 2011 of the European Parliament and of the Council laying down the rules and general principles concerning mechanisms for control by Member States of the Commission's exercise of implementing powers [2011] OJ L55/13 [*Comitology III*]

Regulation (EU) 236/2012 of the European Parliament and of the Council of 14 March 2012 on short selling and certain aspects of credit default swaps [2012] OJ L86/1

Regulation (EU) 439/2010 of the European Parliament and of the Council of 19 May 2010 establishing a European Asylum Support Office [2010] OJ L132/11

Regulation (EU) 526/2013 of the European Parliament and of the Council of 21 May 2013 concerning the European Union Agency for Network and Information Security (ENISA) and repealing Regulation (EC) 460/2004 OJ L165/41

Regulation (EU) 575/2013 of the European Parliament and of the Council of 26 June 2013 on prudential requirements for credit institutions and investment firms and amending Regulation (EU) 648/2012 [2013] OJ L176/1

Regulation (EU) 806/2014 of the European Parliament and of the Council of 15 July 2014 establishing uniform rules and a uniform procedure for the resolution of credit institutions and certain investment firms in the framework of a Single Resolution Mechanism and a Single Resolution Fund and amending Regulation (EU) 1093/2010 [2014] OJ L225/1 [SRM-Regulation]

Regulation (EU) 912/2010 of the European Parliament and of the Council of 22 September 2010 setting up the European GNSS Agency, repealing Council Regulation (EC) 1321/2004 on the establishment of structures for the management of the European satellite radio navigation programmes and amending Regulation (EC) 683/2008 of the European Parliament and of the Council [2010] OJ L276/11

Regulation (EU, Euratom) 966/2012 of the European Parliament and of the Council of 25 October 2012 on the financial rules applicable to the general budget of the Union and repealing Council Regulation (EC, Euratom) No 1605/2002 [2012] OJ L298/1

Index